# Teaching of English

Sadhan Kumar Dey

PEARSON

Delhi • Chennai • Chandigarh

*Associate Editor–Acquisitions:* Qudsiya Ahmed
*Associate Editor–Production:* Amrita Naskar



ISBN 978-81-317-5992-9

**First Impression**

Published by Dorling Kindersley (India) Pvt. Ltd, licensees of Pearson Education in South Asia.

Head Office: 7th Floor, Knowledge Boulevard, A-8(A), Sector 62, Noida, UP 201309, India.
Registered Office: 11 Community Centre, Panchsheel Park, New Delhi 110017, India.

*Compositor:* Aptara®, Inc.
*Printer:* HT Media Ltd., Noida

# Contents

# Preface

The book *Teaching of English* is the outcome of our orchestrated efforts to bring out the best text book for the teacher trainers and teacher trainees. We have tried our best to focus on three important dimensions of English teaching in pre-independent and post-independent India. They are, namely:

- English as 'Carrier Language' (used by all professional experts irrespective of their domain of expertise),
- English as 'Content Subject' (learned by all up to a certain stage and the subject specialists in UG/PG level),
- English as a 'Professional Tool' of British hegemony as well as Indian Government (used by administrators and government officials of the legislative, executive and the judiciary).

The book provides a thorough knowledge base and fair pedagogic direction for the English teachers who often face the following questions:

- Should English be used in the classroom as the medium of instruction for teaching English?
- Should any regional language be used in the classroom as the medium of instruction for teaching English in a particular provincial state?
- What would be the medium of instruction for teaching English in a state like Andhra Pradesh where there are several regional languages like Tamil, Telegu, etc.?
- Should any specific dialect of the regional language be used in the classroom as the medium of instruction for teaching English?
- Should any other classical Indian language (like Urdu, Arabian or Persian) be used in the classroom as the medium of instruction for teaching English?
- Should Hindi as official national language be used in the classroom as the medium of instruction for teaching English in India? Again, which dialect of Hindi should the teachers use?
- Should the pedagogy of teaching English be the same as teaching foreign languages like German, French, Italian, Chinese or Japanese?

The book can also be used as a reference book for undergraduate and postgraduate students of other subjects like English, Communicative English, Linguistics, Applied Linguistics, English Language Teaching and Education of Indian and Foreign Universities. Let us draw your attention to the following features of the book:

- Syllabus outlines of 18 universities of India have been maintained,
- NCTE outlines for teaching English as method paper have been consulted,
- Authentic materials have been used for exemplification,
- English teaching methods have been discussed in detail,
- Detailed discussions of all the aspects of English language teaching,
- Techniques of classroom English teaching have been discussed in detail,
- Detailed discussion and analysis of English teaching approaches,

- English teaching skills have been emphasized in detail,
- Project work on English teaching has been exemplified in detail,
- Sufficient exercises for practice have been incorporated,
- Inclusion of chapterwise bibliographic references,
- Latest researches in the ELT field consulted in detail,
- Supportive documents compiled as appendices,
- Lucid language and diagrams used for fostering easy understanding.

## Acknowledgements

I would like to take this opportunity to extend my heartfelt thanks to my teacher par excellence, Arpita Banerjee, former Professor, Institute of English, Kolkata, and a doyen in the ELT domain in India, who instilled in me a deep passion and an urge for doing something innovative in terms of English language pedagogy during my deputation at the Institute of English, Kolkata.

I would also like to thank Paresh Chandra Biswas, Professor, Department of Education at Kalyani University, who requested me to update and redesign the syllabus of the English method paper for B.Ed. under Kalyani University. While working on the said project, I came to know about the problems of B.Ed. students, a majority of whom are postgraduates in English and many of whom are deputed teacher trainees. It is needless to mention that they are the worst sufferers of the existing gap between the standard study materials required for the syllabus outlines prescribed by NCTE and the paucity of good books in the Indian market. I started literature survey on English language teaching keeping an eye to write a comprehensive and standard text book on teaching English for B.Ed. and M.Ed. students.

I am personally grateful to K. C. Dhar, former Joint Secretary of the Department of Education under the state of Mizoram, for his inspirational guide during the budding years of my authorship. I am grateful to all the authors and the publishers, for that matter, whose works I have consulted during the preparation of the manuscript. I have mentioned the source wherever I adapted or abridged any stipulated teaching design or teaching approach, already used by others in different situations.

I would like to extend my heartfelt thanks to the team at Pearson Education for all kinds of support they have extended to me. I am personally thankful to Debjani Dutta and Qudsiya Ahmed.

I would also like to express my heartfelt thanks to Sikha Datta (Dey), my wife, and Alice Dey, my daughter, for bearing with all the domestic hassles and coping up with all types of material exigencies to allow me sufficient time to finish the work in time.

This book is the outcome of my rigorous efforts for the last two years to bring out something matchless especially for the teacher trainers and teacher trainees. I would feel amply satisfied if it serves the purpose of its target audience.

**Sadhan Kumar Dey**

# English Language Teaching in India—Past and Present 1

## CHAPTER OUTLINE



## LEARNING OBJECTIVES

This chapter will present:

- A broad overview of historical developments during the last 400 years in the field of English language teaching (ELT) in India.
- A historical insight into the never-ending key issues involving ELT in India.
- All the landmark events and main issues.
- All the historical and contemporary perspectives of English teaching in India.

## Introduction

Historically speaking, since the *Aryan* invasion in circa 3000, India has been a rich field of various linguistic experimentations for all types of invaders, who put their linguistic knowledge into the 'melting pot' of aborigines and earlier inhabitants of the country. Naturally, when the East India Company set foot in India (first in Kerala and Carnatic regions), they were well-received and their language well-adapted in India in course of time. Before the British East India Company could do anything, the background of English teaching was already made through the teaching of *Portuguese, Dutch* and *French* (all modern branches of Indo-European languages). (See Table 2.6 Cardinal Vowels in Chapter 2 for details.)

English was first introduced by the English Missionaries here in India to spread the teachings of the anglicized Bible (1611) under King James I's patronage.

**Fascinating Facts**

- Portuguese was already a *lingua franca* in Deccan when English was first introduced in India.
- British Chaplains were well-versed in Portuguese.
- Portuguese was taken as the medium of instruction for teaching English.
- European foreign policy and international relations of the respective colonial countries decided the fate of their respective positions in India.
- English language was *sine qua non* of British factories. (See Glossary for details.)

British traders were accompanied by Christian Missionaries since the 1698 inclusion of 'Missionary clause' into the charter of British East India Company.

The prime issues at the outset were:

1. What would be the contents of English?
2. What would be the extent of ELT?
3. What would be the medium of instruction?

It is noteworthy that the British East India Company was never interested in beginning an organized education system in India during the first 150 years when it was merely a trading company. It was only under the instruction of the Ministry of Religion, that the Company had to shoulder the expenses of chaplains who were mainly responsible for establishing Anglo-Indian schools for the newly converts and for the children of the Company officials. During the 19th century, English worked as the prime link language of the nation and fostered the spirit of real *Renaissance* and *patriotism* during the struggle for freedom. Britishers were afraid of 'the upsurge of English' than the country-made pipe guns and bombs.

Immediately after independence, the key issue was the status of English in India. At the same time, educational commissions have tried to settle some other key issues relating to the position of English and its importance in modern Indian education. Under the theme of *globalization* and *liberalized* economy, teaching of English language has again been a matter of serious discussion till recent times.

Thus, we see what began as a tool for colonial success of the Britishers and which later on aimed at creating 'Indians by blood, but English in culture' during imperial heyday of the Britishers, has grown to be a key language in India, making teaching of English itself an important historical perspective in modern India.

## Early Phase

### English Language Teaching in India under British East India Company (1600–1765)

British East India Company was set up on 31 December 1600. As early as 1614, a directive was issued to take steps 'for the recruitment of Indians' for the propagation of the *Gospel* among their countrymen and for imparting to these Missionaries such education at the Company's expense, as it would enable them to carry out effectively the purpose for which they were enlisted. In 1659, the Court of Directors made it clear that they earnestly desired to spread Christianity in India and permitted Christian Missionaries to embark on their journey to India. This was further confirmed by the inclusion of the famous 'Missionary clause' in the Company's charter in 1698, requiring it to maintain Ministers of Religion at their factories in India and to have a chaplain on board of every ship of 500 tons or more. The said charter also directed the Company to maintain schools in all their garrisons and bigger factories for the education of European and Anglo-Indian Christians. The chaplains were instrumental in setting up the charity schools for Anglo-Indian children, which is an important landmark in the history of ELT in India.

It is interesting to note that these Ministers of Religion had to learn Portuguese and conduct schools in that language because Portuguese was the *lingua franca* of the time among the lower employees of the Company factories. This attempt never became popular and was soon given up in favour of English as the medium of instruction. The oldest charity school to be established on this new model was St Mary's Charity School in Madras, now called Chennai, founded by Rev. W. Stevenson in 1715, followed by others in Bombay, now called Mumbai, (1719) and Calcutta, now called Kolkata, (1720). These schools were encouraged by the Company, but mostly survived on subscriptions and donations. Though these schools were not meant for the general native Indian children, the Charter of 1698 is, nevertheless, important because it laid the foundation of formalized English education in India.

Missionary enterprises that had played a key role during the period mentioned and had worked very sincerely were (i) the Danish Mission in Madras Presidency and (ii) the Serampore Trio and others in Bengal Presidency. From its days of inception, English enterprise in India was closely associated with the Danes. The reason for this was that both the English and the Danes were Protestants, and the Danes had no unseemly imperial aspiration unlike the French. Ziegenbalg and Plustchau—the pioneers of the Danish Missionary movement—arrived at Travancore in South India in 1706. They set up a printing press in Tamil (1713) and the first English teaching-training institution (1716). In the following year, two charity schools with Portuguese and Tamil as the media of instruction were opened in Madras. Other Missionaries, such as Kiernander and Swartz, followed them. Kiernander founded charity schools for Eurasians as well as Indians in Fort St David in 1742. His work became so famous that Robert Clive, the first Governor of Bengal Presidency, invited him in 1758 to open a charity school in Calcutta. Kiernander thereafter stayed on to do pioneering service in Bengal. As European educational activities in India flourished, there started to emerge the problem of choice of the medium of instruction (Indian or Western languages). The problem of content and extent also remained the key issues till 1765.

## Later Phase

### English Language Teaching in India (1765–1818)

Swartz meanwhile founded an English-medium school for European and Eurasian boys at Trichinopoly, now called Tiruchirappalli, (1772) and an English charity school at Tanjore with the help of Haider Ali, the ruler of Mysore. He was also instrumental in persuading the *Rajas* (Rulers) of Tanjore and Marwar to establish schools for teaching English to Indian children (1785). These may be said to be the earliest schools for teaching the English language to Indians. Incidentally, at this time John Sullivan was the resident at Tanjore, and he actively encouraged the establishment of English-medium schools hoping that they would help the Company and the native people to understand each other and to 'facilitate commercial dealings of all kinds between them.' Sullivan's observations are significant as this was the earliest effort of setting up of the Occidental schools for teaching English in India.

After Kiernander set up his school at Mission Church Lane in Calcutta in 1758, there was a spurt of establishment of Missionary schools in Bengal. This included the first girls' school—Hedges Girls' School

(1760). Not all of these were established by Missionaries however, and in 1791 Ramjoy Datta became the first gentleman to set up an English school at Colootola, Calcutta. It was in 1800 that the Fort William College was established, where such stalwarts as Carey, Colebrook and Gilchrist worked. Dr William Carey of the Baptist Missionary Society joined with two other Missionaries, i.e., William Ward, an expert printer, and Joshua Marshman, a famous teacher, to establish the Serampore Mission at Serampore, a Danish settlement. The Serampore Trio as they came to be known, though not particularly in favour of English education for the 'natives', have to be mentioned in any historical record of modern Indian education. They were instrumental in translating and publishing numerous books in Bengali and other Indian languages.

In 1801, William Carey translated the New Testament into Bengali and also published his book on Bengali grammar. One of his singular achievements was the preparation of an Anglo-Bengali journal—Samachar Darpan (1818). Enlisting the manifold achievements of the Serampore Trio is beyond the scope of this chapter. It would suffice to say that they contributed immensely to the growth of Bengali literature, journalism and English education through Bengali medium. No doubt they had great contribution to make to English education in Bengal. Carey and Marshman established the Calcutta Benevolent Institution in 1810 and Marshman established a boarding school in Serampore in the same year.

By 1817, there were 115 schools established by the Trio. In 1818, the Serampore College was established to instruct Christian and non-Christian Indian youth in Western arts and sciences and to train teachers. This was the first English Missionary college in Bengal. We must not forget that after 1765 when the Company became a political power in India, its educational policy changed from its professed earlier stand.

Previously, the Company had restricted its attention to the education of European and Anglo-Indian children. Now, it began to feel that it must do something for the Indian people. The native Indians were steadfast adherents of traditional religion and culture and the proselytizing efforts of the Missionaries did not find favour with them. With the object of winning over the 'natives', the Company now placed a check on the Missionaries as it became conscious of the political importance of maintaining a strict religious neutrality. The Company found it convenient under the circumstances to pose as the champion and preserver of Hindu and Muslim culture, education and traditions.

The Company's Supreme Council in India, under the leadership of Warren Hastings (Governor General of India, 1772–1785), adopted a distinctive policy to increase British influence on the people and to find access to the masses. They squarely opposed any hasty attempt to impart Western knowledge and chose, rather, to support traditional learning. Moreover, the Company wanted to educate the sons of influential Indians for their promotion to higher posts under government and, thereby, to win the confidence of the upper classes and consolidate its rule in India. Therefore, the Company decided to establish some centres of higher learning for the Hindus and Muslims and thus the Calcutta Madrasah and the Benares Sanskrit College came into existence.

Warren Hastings established the Calcutta Madrasah in 1781 with Islamic theology, law, logic, grammar, geometry and arithmetic as curricular subjects and Arabic as the language. The resident of Benares, Jonathan Duncan, emulated this example to establish Benares Sanskrit College (1791) with Hindu theology, law and grammar, medicine, etc., as curricular subjects and Sanskrit as the language. This marks the beginning of the Oriental School of Education Policy. Obviously, this school of thought was prompted more by the political rather than the educational considerations, and it made its policy decisions on politically expedient grounds. The Oriental views were readily accepted by the Court of Directors and between 1765 and 1812, the principal objective of the educational policy of the Company was to encourage traditional Oriental learning in Sanskrit and Arabic.

Between 1793 and 1813, the Company did not ordinarily issue a permit to any Missionary to work within its territories and expelled several Missionaries as soon as they became active. The Missionaries began an intensive agitation to persuade the British Parliament to legislate on the matter. The foremost among those who thus agitated was Charles Grant who is sometimes called 'the father of English education' in British India.

***Charles Grant and English Language Teaching.*** Charles Grant, who lived at Malda in Bengal Presidency from 1783 to 1790, as Commercial Resident, lamented over the 'social and intellectual decline' of India. In 1792, he wrote an important treatise titled *Observations on the State of Society among the Asiatic Subjects of Great Britain,* particularly with reference to morals and the means of improving it. He maintained a close description of the utterly immoral, depraved and wretched condition of the Indian society and then proceeded to analyze its causes and to suggest a remedy.

According to Grant, the causes of the miserable condition of the Indian people were ignorance and lack of a proper religion. He, therefore, felt that the situation could only be improved if the Indians were first educated and finally converted to Christianity. Now the question naturally arose: In what medium should this education be imparted to the Indian people? Grant suggested that the English language should be adopted as the medium of instruction. He foresaw the use of English in all administrative, judicial and educational spheres and emphasized the need for English education to foster greater understanding between the ruler and the ruled, which would ultimately lead to greater expansion of British commercial and political interest in India. He also suggested that a special emphasis be laid on the teaching of *Natural sciences* and the use of mechanical inventions in order to bring about agricultural and industrial development of the country. The most precious subject of instruction, however, according to Grant, was the Christian religion.

The veracity of Grant's opinions regarding the condition of the Indian people was never beyond doubt yet his treatise is historically very significant because of the prophetic nature of his suggestions. His proposal that English be adopted as the language of government was taken up 40 years later by Lord Bentinck and his suggestion of adopting English as a medium of instruction was made a reality by the famous 'Minute of Macaulay in 1835'. His view on the possibility of Indians becoming English teachers was also not a misplaced one as history has it.

While the Missionaries were agitating in this manner in England, the officials of the Company in India were proposing expansion in Oriental education and asked for more funds to revive and improve classical Indian learning. In his Minute dated 6 March 1811, Lord Minto (Governor-General of India, 1806–1813) extolled the worth of Oriental literature and felt that the government support should be extended to promote its study and open up its literary riches to the Western world as well.

Grant's arguments, however, carried the day and the prestige he enjoyed as one who had known India personally as an influential director of the Company and a Member of Parliament, who lent weight to his suggestions and ultimately paved the way for the English education in India through the Charter Act of 1833.

## Last Phase of Company Rule

### English Language Teaching (1818–1857)

When the charter of the Company came up for renewal in 1813 and subsequently in 1833, the British Parliament had to decide upon two controversial issues:

(a) Attitude towards the Christian Missionaries' role in English education in India.
(b) The nature and extent of the role of the Company in Indian education.

On the first issue, the Missionaries won in as much as they were permitted to preach and teach freely in India again. On the second issue, the Company directors were reluctant to reduce their dividend by increasing their expenditure on education. But the opponents of the 'Mission Clauses' also felt the need to create a rival agency in Indian education to counteract the results of Missionary enterprise. So, the 43rd clause was inserted in the Charter Act of 1813, which required the Company to provide an annual sum of Rs 1 lakh for the 'revival and improvement of literature and the encouragement of the learned natives of India and for the introduction and promotion of knowledge of the sciences among the inhabitants of the British territories in India'.

The principal implication of this clause was that the Company would create its own agency to spend this amount of Rs 1 lakh and try to educate the people of India in a secular and conservative fashion as opposed to the proselytizing and revolutionary proposals of the Missionaries. This, in fact, laid the foundation of a state educational system in India; and the Charter Act of 1813, therefore, is a turning point in the history of Indian education.

However, there was a deliberate ambiguity in this Act regarding the type of education—Oriental or Occidental—that was to be aided. There was an ambiguity in regard to the medium of instruction—English or modern Indian regional language—also. The directors themselves were in a dilemma as to how to interpret the Act. It was obviously a compromising solution, produced by the inability of the British Parliament to reach a final resolution. It took another 30 years and the intervention of a hide-bound Anglicist—T.B. Macaulay—to resolve this ambiguity.

***Macaulay's Minute.*** When Macaulay came to India in 1834 as the newly appointed Legal Adviser to the Supreme Council of India, the argument that centred around the Charter Act of 1833 between the Orientalists and the Anglicists was already in full swing. The people, who desired education and were unable to get it from the Company, quenched their thirst in the Missionary schools. As the General Committee of Public Instruction (GCPI) could not resolve the dispute, the matter was placed before the Executive Council of which Macaulay was an influential member. This was the time when he wrote his famous Minute (2 February 1835) regarding the new educational policy. Referring to Section 43 of the Charter Act of 1833, Macaulay unequivocally stated that 'Literature' could only be interpreted to mean English literature and that a 'Pundit', i.e., 'a learned native of India' could only refer to a person well-versed in Milton and Locke. Macaulay dismissed whatsoever the importance of all the wealth of Indian and Arabic literature.

Macaulay said that all the Eastern literature could not equate with that which was contained in 'a single shelf of a good European library'. Western learning alone could reawaken and regenerate the Indians morally. As regards the medium of instruction, he felt English 'stands pre-eminent even among the languages of the West' and accordingly recommended English as the language 'best worth knowing' and 'most useful to our native subjects'. At the same time, Macaulay recommended a policy of restricted education facilities.

> It is impossible for us with our limited means to attempt to educate the body of the people. We must at present do our best to form a class who may be interpreters between us and the millions whom we govern--a class of persons Indian in blood and colour, but English in tastes, in opinions, in morals and intellect to that class we may leave it to refine the vernacular dialects of the country to enrich those dialects with terms of science, borrowed from the Western nomenclature, and to render them by degrees fit vehicles for conveying knowledge to the great mass of the population.

***Revival of Missionary Enterprise and English Language Teaching.*** Missionary enterprise in education got a fresh impetus after the Charter Act of 1813. Prior to 1813, the Missionaries had worked mainly in the field of primary education through the modern Indian languages, but after 1813, although they did not withdraw from primary education, their attention was gradually shifted to secondary and higher education. English was consciously adopted as the medium. At this time, the Missionaries did extremely valuable pioneering work in the field of women's education by opening day schools for Indian girls and arranging for domestic instruction in the families of the middle and upper classes. Rev. May's Girls School at Chinsurah began this movement for women's education. William Carey founded a girls' school at Serampore the following year and others soon followed in Madras and later in Benares, Mirzapur, Allahabad and Bareilly, etc. By 1853, a strong foundation for women's education in India had already been laid.

Meanwhile, the Missionary activities in India were principally conducted by the Missions based in the United Kingdom. But the Charter Act of 1833 opened up the portals of Indian education to Missionaries of other countries as well. Prominent among them were the German and American Missionaries who did considerable Missionary work in India. The Christian Missionaries had already started school and college teaching through English as the only medium of instruction. Boys and girls from upper classes flocked to these institutions to learn English and thus the Missionaries got an excellent opportunity to preach the *Gospel* to them. A lead role in this direction was played by Alexander Duff, the Scottish Missionary who ran the General Assembly Institution in Calcutta from 1830 to 1843. The Missionaries set up colleges in Calcutta, Madras, Bombay, Agra, Nagpur, Masulipatam, etc. Thus, the quarter century from 1833 to 1857 can justly be called 'the period of Missionary schools and colleges' in India.

We should take care to note down the fact that during this period (1833–1857) the relationship between the Company officials and the Missionaries seemed to be very cordial. The Mission schools with their insistence on Bible-teaching and secular school conducted by the Company grew up competitively independent of each other. It soon became apparent that the Company-run schools and private enterprise-run schools were serious business competitors to the Mission schools. Therefore, some of the Missionaries started criticizing the former as 'godless' and the latter as 'heathen'. They were of the opinion that the sole purpose of English education was to convert the Hindus and Muslims into 'good' Christians. Thus, a conflict developed between religious Western education and secular Western education.

***Private Enterprises and English Language Teaching.*** The Missionaries were not the only non-official enterprises in education in India during this period. A pioneer British gentleman who tried to build up a new educational system for India was a retired watchmaker and jeweller from Calcutta, David Hare (1775–1842). He was no scholar, but was keenly interested in the spread of English education. Like the Missionaries, he believed that knowledge of the English language and literature was essential for the regeneration of the Hindu society; but being a secularist he could not support their views on the subject of religious instruction. Hare established a junior school at Pataldanga, which subsequently came to be known as Hare School. Meanwhile, the Calcutta School Book Society was formed in 1817 to produce and distribute textbooks.

In 1819, the Calcutta School Book Society started to establish English and Bengali schools and by 1821, the number of schools run by it was 115. In Madras also a school book society was formed. In Calcutta, a few Indian and European gentlemen joined hands together to establish the Hindu Vidyalaya (or College) in 1817. David Hare became associated with it in 1819 and thereafter worked zealously to impart secular Western collegiate education. Raja Rammohun Roy and Derozio were also associated with this prestigious institute. Later, the Vidyalaya was handed over to the Company due to financial difficulties and was renamed as the Presidency College in 1854. This college has been elevated to a state university very recently.

A mention must also be made in the context of private educational enterprise of J.E.D. Bethune (1801–1851) who was a Law-member of the Executive Council and the President of the Council of Education (1848–1851). He was keen on educating women but as the Company's official stand was contrary to it, he decided to establish a secular school for girls in his own individual capacity. In his school, English was taught as a subject and instructions were given in Bengali as well as in English.

In Bombay, the Bombay Education Society (1815) took the responsibility of running the charity schools, established earlier. It founded a number of new charity schools also. When Monstuart Elphinstone became the Governor of the Province in 1819, he supported the society's work. In 1820, the society appointed a special committee to improve existing schools, establish/aid new ones and prepare books. By 1822, the society's work had expanded so much that the committee was now formed into a separate society called the Bombay Native School Book and School Society, better known as the Bombay Native Education Society, to oversee the establishment of new schools, print textbooks and train teachers.

***Official Survey and English Language Teaching.*** By the time the Company's charter came up for renewal in 1853, it was found that a comprehensive survey of the whole field of education in India was indispensable. Many of the old controversies still needed to be resolved even as new problems, such as the need to establish a complete system of education for school and college level, accrued from the existing issues, were becoming apparent. A select Committee of the House of Commons held a thorough enquiry into educational developments in India and on the basis of this the Court of Directors sent their Educational Dispatch on 19 July 1854. This is perhaps the most important educational document under the Company and is even referred to sometimes as the Magna Charta of English education in India. The Dispatch became famous as the Wood's Dispatch of 1854 after the name of Charles Wood, President of the Company's Board of Control.

So far, as ELT is concerned the Wood's Dispatch was significant as English was to remain as the medium of instruction only for higher branches of education and particularly for the new universities as the Dispatch envisaged. For mass education purposes, the vernacular languages were preferred to English as a medium of instruction. The content of instruction, however, would still be the 'superior' European knowledge written in English. 'We look, therefore, to the English language and to the vernacular languages of India together as the media for the diffusion of European knowledge', Wood proclaimed in 1854. The Wood's Dispatch was thus responsible for creating a vertical split in the Indian society. The upper class elite were associated with English and lower classes were associated with 'vernacular' languages—a situation that has unfortunately continued till date in some other forms.

## English Language Teaching in India During the Crown Rule (1858–1947)

The period under survey was a period of consolidation not only for the British Empire in India, but also of Western education in modern India. Wood's Dispatch set the general tone for the educational policies of this period and its recommendations continued to be broadly followed until the early years of the 20th century when Lord Curzon (Viceroy of India from 1899 to 1905) initiated another new innings in Indian education. The most significant aspect of the Dispatch was that it removed the obstacles to English education and created the scope for its expansion. Indeed, the influence of university education firmly established by the Dispatch still holds sway. The mother tongue was accorded recognition in the Dispatch, but the monopoly of English in the universities created a pressure on the secondary schools to anglicize them. An apparent gulf appeared between primary education in the vermicular on the one hand and secondary education in English on the other hand, which is still a rampant issue centreing rural primary schools and urban English medium private/autonomous schools.

***Wood's Dispatch and English Language Teaching.*** In consequence of the Dispatch, Departments of Public Instruction were established in the provinces between 1855 and 1856 and a Central Committee was appointed in 1855 to plan the universities. In 1857, the first three Indian universities at Calcutta, Bombay and Madras came into existence by the Acts of Incorporation of the Central Executive Council. This was also the time when the Company Education Cell established Presidency Colleges in the provinces. In Calcutta, the senior section of the Hindu College was merged into the Presidency College, established in 1855 by Lord Dalhousie (Governor-General of India, 1848–1856). The Madras Presidency College was established in 1857. In Bombay, the Elphinstone College, which was set up in 1856, got the Company patronage as other Presidency Colleges of India.

The Sepoy Mutiny of 1857 intercepted the process of implementation of any of the recommendations of the Dispatch, and subsequently in 1858 the East India Company ceased to be a political power and as a result, the Government of India came directly under the Crown. Lord Stanley, the first Secretary of State for India, who confirmed most of the directives of the Dispatch of 1854 in his Dispatch of 1859.

***Indian Education Commission.*** Two of the important recommendations made by Charles Wood related to grants-in-aid to Missionary institutions and the spread of primary education/popular education among masses. However, the events of 1857 prompted Queen Victoria to declare in her proclamation (Queen's Proclamation) of 1858 a policy of strict neutrality in religious matters. As a result, the British Government was extremely unsympathetic to Mission schools between 1858 and 1882. This attitude on the part of the British government prompted the Missionaries to move an agitation in England about the educational system of India as it disregarded the Dispatch of 1854.

On the other hand, although the Dispatch had announced a policy of patronage to primary education, no substantial amount was released from the government Exchequer. The government resources were mostly spent on secondary education in the towns at the cost of primary, vocational, rural and indigenous education. Meanwhile, private Indian enterprises in education had increased enormously and the government had to face the growing national consciousness of the educated Indians, better known as *renaissance*. The government sensed danger and Lord Ripon, Viceroy of India (1880–1884), felt obliged to appoint the first Indian Education Commission (1882–1883) to make a thorough survey of the field of primary and secondary Indian education and to 'inquire particularly into the manner in which effect has been given to the principles of the Wood's Despatch of 1854'.

***Hunter Commission and English Language Teaching.*** The first Indian Education Commission, better known as Hunter Commission after the name of its President, Sri William Hunter, submitted its recommendations on primary and secondary education in 1883. It unanimously rejected the governmental withdrawal from education and strongly endorsed secular education in the government institutions. It recommended that priority be given to primary education and the responsibility for this would be taken up by the local self-government bodies. Moreover, it recognized the vitality and need for indigenous institutions and their languages. So far, as the Missionary representation was concerned, the opinion of the Commission went against them. It decided that the Missionary educational enterprises would have to occupy a secondary position in Indian education and the Company government would not withdraw in favour of Missionary managements. All hopes of the Missionaries for gaining ascendancy in the educational sphere in India were extinguished and thereafter the Missionaries concentrated on running efficiently a few educational institutions only. Till 1882, Missionary institutions had dominated the private educational effort in India but gradually they were overtaken by private indigenous enterprises in education.

There was also a growth in the number of universities during this period. By 1902, there were five universities in India, including three earlier ones. Punjab University (1882) and Allahabad University (1887) were established by special Acts of Incorporation. It is worthwhile to note that all the five universities were merely affiliating and examining bodies and did no direct teaching work themselves.

***Turning Point in English Language Teaching.*** The post–1854 era, which was one of rapid multiplication of secondary schools, mostly catered to the growing demand for English education. The Hunter Commission recommended that the mother tongue should be the medium of instruction at the primary stage. There was an option of either using English or the mother tongue at the middle school level, but nothing explicit was said about the secondary stage. Eventually English continued to be medium of instruction. Secondary Education was to set ready link with College Education through English language teaching. In Bombay and Bengal, there were some medical schools where instructions were given in the modern Indian languages. However, these experiments in teaching in the mother tongue were discontinued by 1880 in favour of medical degree courses, which were taught in English. Since the Hunter Commission focused mainly on primary and secondary education, English was the preferred medium at the latter stage.

Let us now consider a few implications of English teaching in India.

First, there was a definite bias in favour of English education at the secondary level, as it was geared to university education in English. At the high school stage, English was invariably used as the medium of instruction.

Second, the study of English as a language was often started when the pupil was not properly trained in his own mother tongue.

Third, English was taught as a subject (at the lower secondary level) before it was used as a medium of instruction.

Moreover, the period of its study as a subject was too short to allow the pupils enough time to master the language.

In terms of teaching English language skills, proper exposure to a foreign language is essential for its successful use as a medium of instruction.

However, the Indian Education Commission did neither favour English nor specify any modern Indian language as medium of instruction. Consequently, the dominance of English in the secondary course continued unabated. The teaching of English (and not European knowledge as such) became the prime object of the secondary course. Even a cursory examination of English Language Teaching Journals in India will reveal that the remnants of some of these problems linger even today.

***Indian Universities Commission.*** Lord Curzon might have been an arrogant imperialist, but no account of education in modern India would be complete without acknowledging his considerable contribution in this sphere. As soon as he came to India in 1899, he moved swiftly to introduce long overdue changes in the Indian education. He began by convening an educational conference at Simla (1901) where educated Indians' opinions on teaching and research were sought. It was found to be lacking greatly at the highest levels. Curzon felt the need for urgent university reformation and thus, he appointed the Indian Universities Commission in 1902.

The Commission was empowered to examine the condition and prospects of Indian universities and suggest ways of improvement. The Commission recommended a number of proposals and suggestions that aimed at achieving a qualitative improvement in university administration. It recommended the assumption of teaching functions by the universities for the first time. Curricula and standards of teaching (particularly English) were to be improved and the examination system was to be reformed accordingly. In pursuance of these recommendations, the Indian Universities Act, 1904, was passed which determined territorial jurisdictions of each university. It reformed university administration and most importantly, vested veto power to the government regarding decisions taken by the respective senate of each university. The last provision ensured tight state control over university and college administration.

***Government Education Policy 1904.*** After dealing with the universities, Lord Curzon turned his attention to secondary education. The rapid expansion of secondary education after 1882 had undoubtedly led to a quantitative progression; however, there was a qualitative regression. Curzon adopted some positive measures enunciated in the form of a Government Resolution of Educational Policy in 1904, where he clearly reiterated that the mother tongue of the pupils should be used as the medium of instruction both at the primary and middle school stages—and English should not take the place of the mother tongue. English should have no place in primary education at all, but some mastery over English at the middle stage was necessary so that the learners could cope better in the High School stage where English was the medium of instruction. He encouraged the study of the vernacular languages throughout the secondary course and the application of the Direct Method in the teaching of English. (See Chapter 3 for details.)

***Important Educational Documents.*** From the end of the 19th century, Indian enterprises in education had been developing a nationalist slant which gradually gained prominence in the final phase of education in British India. This was indeed the beginning of the nationalization of Indian education. The need to give more attention to primary education had been emphasized since the time of the Hunter Commission (1883), but it was Gopal Krishna Gokhale who first tabled his famous Bill on Compulsory Primary Education in the Central Legislative Assembly in 1910. This motion was rejected in 1912 but the government could not totally ignore the claims of primary education and passed the Government Resolution of Educational Policy in 1913 endorsing increased government responsibility for the expansion of primary education.

***National Education Movement.*** Meanwhile, the resolutions passed at the Calcutta convention of the Indian National Congress in 1906 began what is better known as the National Education Movement (1905–1938). The resolutions clearly mentioned that education through the mother tongue was all-important. As a consequence of this growing trend, the National Council of Education was established in 1906 and it gave a clear directive that education would be imparted ordinarily through the medium of the vernacular with English as a compulsory subject. The demand for Indian control over education became persistent. The conflict was the most pronounced in higher education. Several new universities, some with an indigenous bias, were set up during this period. They are:

Mysore University (1916); Benares Hindu University (1917); Patna University (1917); Osmania University (1918); Aligarh University (1920); Poona S.N.D.T. (1920); Dacca University (1920) and Lucknow University (1920).

***Sadler Commission.*** The Calcutta University Commission was instituted in 1917 to report on the situation of the implementation of the University Act, 1904. This is better known as the Sadler Commission (1917–1919) named after its President, Dr Michael E. Sadler, the then Vice-Chancellor of the University of Leeds, England. The Commission recommended that the intermediate classes should be separated from universities and a curriculum spreading over three years was prescribed for the B.A. degree. It also recommended that the mother tongue should be used as the medium of instruction in intermediate colleges and efforts should be made to promote the study of vernaculars in secondary schools, intermediate colleges and universities.

***Hartog Committee Report.*** Around this time, rapid developments were taking place on the political front. The Sadler Commission Report was followed by the Constitutional Reforms of 1919 which introduced Diarchy, and education became a transferred subject under provincial government. Indians, however, found these reforms unsatisfactory and their continued agitation precipitated the appointment of a Royal Commission presided over by Sir John Simon in 1927, to enquire into different issues, including education. The Commission appointed an Auxiliary Committee of the Indian Statutory Commission (popularly known as the Hartog Committee, after its Chairman, Sir Philip Hartog) to enquire into all aspects of the organization of education in India. The Committee submitted its report in 1929 recommending the consolidation and improvement of education rather than indiscriminate expansion and putting particular emphasis on primary education. It deplored the low standard of English at the higher education level.

***Abbot-Wood Report.*** The next educational document of this period was the Abbot-Wood Report (1936–1937), which recommended technical education as an integral part of education. It also said that if English is taught to children of middle school age it should not be allowed to result in an excessive amount of linguistic load. The mother tongue should, as far as possible, be the medium of instruction throughout the High School stage, but English should be a compulsory language for all pupils at this stage. The teaching of English should be made more realistic.

***Fate of Modern Indian Languages.*** By 1937, modern Indian languages had been adopted as media of instruction on a very large scale. Nevertheless, the use of English as a medium of instruction was not completely abandoned for reasons as mentioned below:

(a) The secondary course was still viewed as an appendage of the university course and the use of English as a medium of instruction at the university level dictated similar use at the secondary level also;
(b) Government competitive examinations were still conducted in English and proficiency in that language ensured a greater chance of success in such examinations;
(c) Lack of terminology textbooks, etc., were still shown as excuses to retain the use of English.

***Basic Education Scheme.*** The case for the mother tongue as the medium of instruction was considerably strengthened by the announcement of the Basic Education Scheme by Mahatma Gandhi in 1937. Gandhi categorically stated that the medium of instruction had to be the mother tongue. Likewise, Rabindranath Tagore also rejected the manner and content of English education at his experimental school, set up at Santiniketan in 1901. The Zakir Hussain Committee Report (1938) was prepared largely under the influence of Mahatma Gandhi who said that the proper teaching of the mother tongue is the foundation of all education.

***Sergeant Report.*** The last major educational document of the British period was the Post-War Plan of Educational Development (1944), also known as the Sergeant Report after John Sergeant, the then Educational Adviser to the Government of India. The object of this plan was to create in a span of 40 years the same standard of education as was present in England. The report focused on universal, compulsory and free basic (primary and middle) education for all children between the ages of six and fourteen. It reiterated earlier views endorsing the use of the mother tongue as the medium of instruction. It also suggested that English be not introduced as an optional subject in the basic schools. High schools, it suggested, should be of two types:

(i) Academic Schools
(ii) Technical Schools

It confirmed that in all High schools the medium of instruction should be the mother tongue. English should be a compulsory second language. The Sergeant Report also made a thorough survey of the universities—technical & vocational, adult education and teacher training—and presented a comprehensive plan for the complete educational reconstruction of India. But hardly had the first steps been taken for the implementation of this plan by the government when India got freedom on 15 August 1947.

## Post-independent Phase

### English Language Teaching in Independent India (1947–2000)

Post-independent India is characterized by the appointment of a number of commissions to survey the field of education system and thereby to consider the fate of English language in India. We would delineate here the major points concerning ELT, as envisaged by different educational commissions in India.

***University Education Commission or Radhakrishnan Commission's Recommendations on the Medium of Instruction and Role of English (1948–1949).*** The University Education Commission, better known as Radhakrishnan Commission, examined the sensitive issue of the medium of instruction in great detail and made the following recommendations:

The federal language be developed through the assimilation of words from different sources. For the medium of instruction for higher education, English be replaced as early as practicable by an Indian language which cannot be Sanskrit on account of vital difficulties. The regional language should be the medium of instruction at the higher level.

International technical and scientific terminology be adopted with appropriate Indianization of pronunciation and spelling and uniform technical and scientific terms should be used in all the Indian languages.

The Devanagari script is to be adopted for Hindi with necessary modifications.

Pupils at the lower secondary stages are to be made conversant in three languages (mother tongue, regional language and English as the second language). Pupils at the secondary and higher secondary stages are required to take any one out of the regional language or the federal language, i.e., Hindi and English as the second language, English be studied in High school and in the universities in order that we keep ourselves in touch with the living stream of ever-growing knowledge.

As far as the role of English was concerned, the report says:

'Now it is a fact that the English language has been one of the potent factors in the development of unity in the country. In fact, the concept of nationality and the sentiment of nationalism are largely the gifts of the English language and literature of India.'

English has become so much a part of our national habit that a plunge into an altogether different system seems attended with unusual risks. It appears to us, however, that the plunge is inevitable. English cannot continue to occupy the place of state language as in the past. The use of English, as such, divides the people into two nations, the few who govern and the many who are governed—the one unable to talk in the language of the other and mutually uncomprehending. This is the negation of democracy (Radhakrishnan; Page 316 as in Kachru: 1991).

Ultimately, it concludes, 'English will disappear from the scene' (Radhakrishnan: 325).

Again, when it considers what the future role of English might be, the report equally emphatically avers that English 'must continue to be studied' (Ibid) and taking our Yugadharma into account, recommends, 'that English be studied in High Schools and in the Universities' (Ibid: 326) and specially in such universities where the regional language is the same as the federal language.

As per recommendations of the Radhakrishnan Commission, the transition from English to the regional languages was to be made within a period of five years. But, by large, the universities failed to respond. In 1962, no more than four Indian universities were using languages other than English as the chief medium of instruction.

***Recommendations of the Mudaliar Commission (1952–1953).*** The Mudaliar Commission made important and extensive recommendations regarding the structural pattern and curriculum at the secondary level. The suggested curriculum would include English and the mother tongue (MT) at the lower secondary stage in addition to other compulsory subjects. At the higher secondary stage, the compulsory 'core' subjects would include (a) the MT or regional language and (b) two more elective languages including English, in addition to other subjects.

The report also made valuable recommendations on teaching methodology and the examination system, which though applicable to all subjects, has particular relevance for the study of English. On methods, the Commission insisted that the emphasis in teaching should shift from verbalism and memorizations to learning through purposeful, concrete and realistic situations and for this purpose the principles of 'Activity Method' and 'Project Method' should be assimilated in school practice.

A well-thought-out attempt should be made to adopt methods of instruction to cater to the needs of individual students as much as possible so that dull, average and bright students may all have a chance to progress at their own pace (Agarwal: 115–6).

On the matter of textbooks for languages, the Commission recommended that 'definite textbooks should be prescribed for each class to ensure proper gradation' (Agarwal: 115).

The Mudaliar Commission recommended a three-language formula for secondary education, i.e., (i) MT (or the regional language), (ii) English and (iii) Hindi. A classical language might also be taken up on an elective basis. As far as the language curriculum was concerned, the Commission mentioned that the following five distinct groups of languages had to be taken into consideration for inclusion in any curriculum:

(a) The mother tongue ($L_1$)
(b) The regional language
(c) The official language of the Centre
(d) The classical language
(e) English

For those whose mother tongue ($L_1$) was Hindi it was suggested that they should learn another language.

For the high and higher secondary stages it recommended only two languages—(i) mother tongue ($L_1$) or the regional language and (ii) one of the following options:

Hindi; Elementary English; Advanced English; a modern Indian language (other than Hindi); a modern foreign language (other than English); or a classical language.

The Commission further observed that 'in those areas where the Mother Tongue ($L_1$) and the regional language are the same, the number of languages to be taken into consideration will be limited to four and in those areas where the Mother Tongue and the regional language are the same, the number of languages to be taken into consideration will be limited to four and in those areas where the regional language, the Mother Tongue and the language of the Union are the same, the number of languages to be taken into consideration will be limited to three' (Mudaliar: 58).

This formula was in general terms applied with slight amendments in different states. In West Bengal, for example, the formula became:

(i) Mother tongue was to be taught all through the school stage;
(ii) English was to be taught as a subject from class V all through;
(iii) Hindi was introduced at the junior secondary stage only;
(iv) The teaching of Sanskrit was made compulsory in the two upper grades of junior secondary education.

The report of the Mudaliar Commission was, in the main, accepted by the Government of India and the new scheme was launched in 1956 and continued till the Kothari Commission Report (1964–1966) was implemented.

***Recommendations of the Kothari Commission (1964–1966).*** The Kothari Commission extensively examined the knotty issue of languages in education and recommended a modified version of the three-language policy. The general recommendations it made regarding languages are summed up as follows:

All modern Indian languages should be developed and used as media of instruction at the university stage and as the languages of administration in the provincial states concerned.

Hindi should be developed as the *lingua franca* for the country as a whole for purposes of internal communication and also as the official language of the Union.

English should continue to be studied as the most important library language and as a channel of international communication.

Side by side, the study of other library languages, like Russian, German, French, Chinese or Japanese, should also be encouraged.

It also recommended that the three-language formula should be adopted in a modified form.

At the lower primary stage, one language should be studied compulsorily—the mother tongue or the regional language, at the option of the pupils—and the medium of instruction should be the mother tongue.

At the higher primary stage, only two languages should be studied on a compulsory basis: (i) the mother tongue or the regional language and (ii) the official (Hindi) or the associate official (English) language of the Union.

At the lower secondary stage, a study of three languages should be obligatory; in non-Hindi areas these would be—the regional language, Hindi and English, and in Hindi areas the pupils would study Hindi, English and a modern Indian language.

At the higher secondary stage, only two of the above mentioned three languages would be compulsory. However, the students could study one or more additional languages on an optional basis.

No language would be compulsory at the university stage.

The Commission took note of the language riots in Tamil Nadu, but still recommended that both Hindi and English, which function as instruments of national and social integration, should be link languages of the country. The Commission also felt 'English will continue to enjoy a high status as long as it remains the principal medium of education at the University stage (indeed it recommended that English should be the *medium of instruction* in all major Universities), and the language of administration at the Centre and in many of the States. Even after the regional languages become media in higher education in the Universities, a working knowledge of English will be a valuable asset for all students and a reasonable proficiency in the language will be necessary for those who proceed to the University' (Kothari: 192).

The Commission made some recommendations specifically with regard to English, which are as follows:

(a) Teaching of English should begin in class V and not in class III.
(b) The use of the Structural Approach for teaching English was endorsed.
(c) Teaching English as a language skill as distinct from teaching English literature was emphasized.

The findings and recommendations of the Kothari Commission provided the basis for the formulation of the National Policy on Education in 1986.

## Present Position of English Teaching/Learning in Indian School Curriculum

### National Policy on Education and Programme of Action (1986)

The next significant landmark is the National Policy of Education and the Programme of Action (1986). However, the policy merely reiterates the 1968 national policy and says: 'The Education Policy of 1968 had examined the question of the development of English education which is as relevant today as it was before. The implementation of this part of the 1968 Policy has, however, been uneven. The Policy will be implemented more energetically and purposefully.'

The 1968 policy does not make any mention of the medium of instruction in its chapter on Higher Education but says that a major effort will be directed towards the transformation of teaching methods and that 'urgent steps will be taken to protect the system from degradation.'

One important stamp that the Programme of Action recommended was the establishment of a rural institution, with the objective of identifying and promoting excellence. The 1968 report had also proclaimed, 'concomitant with de-linking, and appropriate machinery such as a National Testing Service will be established in appropriate phases to conduct tests on a voluntary basis to determine the suitability of candidates for specified jobs and to pave the way for the emergence of norms of comparable competence across the nation.' This has been criticized, however, as it was creating another form of elitism and widening social and educational gaps.

***The Acharya Ramamurti Commission Report (1990).*** The Acharya Ramamurti Commission, appointed to review this 1986 policy, submitted its report in 1990. It observed, however, that whatever the difficulties or the unevenness in the implementation, the 'three-Language Formula' had 'stood the test of time' and that it was not 'desirable or prudent to re-open it.'

About the learning of Hindi and English, the Ramamurti Commission also made the pertinent observation, reiterating a statement made by the Education Commission Report (1964–1966) that the criteria should be not years of study but hours of study and even more importantly, levels of attainment. In view of these considerations, this Commission suggested that the KHS (Kendriya Hindi Sansthan), CIEFL (Central Institute of English and Foreign Languages, now called EFLU) and CIIL (Central Institute of Indian Languages) charged with the development of Hindi, English and modern Indian languages respectively, should come together and in consultation with CBSE (Central Board of Secondary Education) and NCERT (National Council of Educational Research and Training) and the state governments should spell out modalities of ensuring uniformity in the matter of acquisition of language competency by the students in the school system. The Ramamurti Commission also stated the need for a fresh linguistic survey of India.

***Report of the Curriculum Development Centre (CDC).*** One more report with regard to the place of English education in India is the Report of the Curriculum Development Centre (CDC) which was set up by the UGC (University Grants Commission) in 1987 and which submitted its recommendations in 1989. In 'A Note on the New Curriculum', the CDC report on English says that the new undergraduate curriculum comprises a general English course and a special English course. It adds: 'to cater to the heterogeneous tertiary level student population (the range of linguistic competence is extremely varied since students from both English Courses is conceived as comprising different units and modules suited to the different levels of learners. The Patterning of the courses is such that students depending on their linguistic competence at the time of admission would not only begin their General English programme at different levels but also reach different levels at the time of graduation'.

After talking about a learner-oriented teaching, the CDC report in English has streamed only the learners on the basis of some tests administered and not the teachers. It is well known that not all teachers can teach the gifted, the average and below average students; the 1986 report said that 'methodologies will be developed for evaluation of teacher performance through self-appraisal, through peer groups and also by students'. This was forgotten completely and it was taken for granted that all teachers of English can teach the subject to the gifted group! The concept of streaming the learners has been applied only to the teaching of English but not to the teaching of other languages or subjects. It is encouraging to note a few words from the CDC report in English: 'If Education was to be viewed as an instrument of human resource development, then, it was argued, why should we continue an MA programme in English Literature (and that too chiefly British Literature) only. It was felt that we would introduce a multiplicity of MA courses in English such as MA in Creative Writing in English, MA in Modern English Language, and MA in ELT, and so on, as several universities in Britain and America currently do. While there was a broad agreement on this view it was felt none the less that the time was not yet right for such diversification—chiefly because we do not have the human resources necessary to implement it.'

***Recommendations of the Ashok Mitra Commission.*** Keeping in tune with the reports of earlier commissions regarding the teaching of English at different academic levels, we come to the recommendations of the Ashok Mitra Commission, which says that an undercurrent of dissatisfaction persisted concerning the state government's decision to discard English at the primary stage in West Bengal. The experience of other states was not considered to be of particular relevance. The problem of West Bengal was special. It was felt that unless students learn English from the primary stage, the prospect of their being able to hold their own position in competitive examinations and in other spheres at the national level seemed to be bleak. In the circumstances, it was felt that it would be wise to return to the earlier system of teaching English from the primary stage. This, in view of the members of the Commission would be throwing out the baby along with the bath water; because a proper method and a proper set of textbooks had been found wanting (a clause of the dissatisfaction), one could not abandon a cardinal principle of educational policy, but cross over to a new method which would assure greater success. The load of learning for very young children should be light and to re-introduce English at the primary level would aggravate the burden which is already upon them, for nobody would suggest that English should be put in at the primary stage as substitute for arithmetic, history or geography. It should also be kept in mind that children entering the primary schools in the state of West Bengal came from extremely poor households where parents were often without letters and adding English to the curriculum could have an adverse effect on enrolments. One suggestion, however, before the

Commission was that the government might consider the teaching of English in government and government-aided institutions, which might commence from class V where learners would be introduced to the English alphabet and only learn the meaning of simple words and expressions. Specialists in language teaching should be appointed to reframe the text books. The method of teaching demanded reviewing and rethinking.

***Recommendations of the Pabitra Sarkar Commission (Case Study, West Bengal).*** English education in India has aroused a lot of interest, enthusiasm and controversy in different parts of India at the same time. This has resulted in the publication of several reports of different Commissions. The most current report is the Pabitra Sarkar Commission Report. Let us read the report as a Case Study.

This Commission recommends that the teaching of English in West Bengal should be started from class III with the aid of an appropriately devised text. Apart from the continuous evaluation system, which has to be implemented with rigour, no test in English need be taken, nor detention affected on its basis till the end of class IV. A public test after class IV may be in vogue.

The Commission suggested that the introduction of English from class I would be untenable in view of the situation prevailing in rural West Bengal. Most of the children there have a home language, no doubt a dialect of colloquial Bengali, which is more or less distant from the school Bengali, i.e., the Standard Written Bengali, they have to learn, to read, write and also speak to an 'optimum level'. They have, therefore, to cross a dialect-barrier in order to reach the standard language. For tribe students, it is a language wall that they have to cross. English, for many of them, is almost a third language and thus a burden definitely.

The committee also feels that the government should pay more attention to teacher-training and orientation programmes for effective teaching. In addition to this, measures should be taken to break the compartmentalization that exists between the primary and secondary levels, teachers of both these levels should interact with each other and language cum literature education might also be regarded as a single process—this will perhaps enrich the teaching-learning process.

## Let Us Sum Up

In this chapter, we have come to know how ELT has become a historical reality in India. All the decisions during British rule were taken from colonial and imperial standpoints. During the post-independent period, the Government of India had considered the question of ELT very elaborately and decided to keep it as one of the scheduled languages in India. Now, it is established that there is a constant need for ELT in India to keep pace with over-advanced countries of the world and for competing at the international level where English reigns supreme. In these 400 years, English in India has essentially become an indispensable part of its socio-political and cultural matrix. No wonder, English language has got its present status not only as 'any other Indian language' listed in the Eighth Schedule of the Indian Constitution, but also as the 'Second Language' to be taught throughout India. Hence, teaching of English has become such a big as well as a challenging issue in India.

## ◢ Glossary

missionaries: Christian missionaries
commission: a committee with a mission
Curricular: related to curriculum school
Bengali: Bengali as taught in school for written communication

*Renaissance* (Italian): rebirth of knowledge/awakening
*Lingua franca* (Italian): a link language
feasibility: practicability
heterogeneous: multiple, mixed
learner-oriented: helping the learners in autonomous learning
divergent: different
assumption: something, imagined to be true
amenable: willing to accept
matrix: environment
MT: Mother Tongue ($L_1$)

## Exercise

1. How was English language introduced in India?
2. Trace the development of ELT in India during the eighteenth century.
3. Trace the development of ELT in India during the nineteenth century?
4. Judge the role of the Missionaries in the area of ELT in India.
5. What is Macaulay's Minute? Judge its importance as one of the turning points in the history of ELT in India.
6. What were the main recommendations of the Radhakrishnan Commission regarding ELT in India?
7. How far Mudaliar Commission has led the foundation of ELT in India?
8. Trace the development of ELT in post-independent India.
9. 'English language in India has become a cultural reality.' Discuss.
10. Write a short note on any three features of English language.
11. What was the primary objective of the Christian Missionaries in Bengal?
12. Write three short notes on:
    (a) Indian Commission of Education
    (b) Hunter Commission
    (c) Ashok Mitra Commission
    (d) Acharya Ramamurti Commission
13. Trace the development of ELT in pre-independent India.
14. Trace the development of ELT in India during the nineteenth century?

## Bibliography

Agarwal, J.C. (1984), *Landmarks in the History of Modern India Education* (Delhi: Vikas).

Agnihotri, R.K. and Khanna, A.L. (1995), *English Language Teaching in India: Issues and Innovations* (New Delhi: Stage Publication).

Bagchi, K.M. and Dey, S.K. (2004), *Exploring History,* Volume I: Modern India ( Kolkata: Cambridge India).

Kachru, Braj B. (1983), *The Indianisation of English: The English Language in India* (Oxford: Oxford University Press).

Krishnaswamy, N. and Sriraman, T. (1994), English Teaching India (Madras: T. R. Publication).

# Introduction to English Language 2

## CHAPTER OUTLINE



## LEARNING OBJECTIVES

This chapter will present:

- An understanding of general features of the English language and guide the learners accordingly.
- An understanding of phonology and phonetics of the English language and apply the knowledge in classroom English language teaching.
- An understanding of contrastive phenomenon of English phonetics to apply it better in the Indian context.

## Introduction

The English language, as it is used worldwide, is known for its extraordinary receptive elasticity and highly adaptable heterogeneousness. The varied ease and readiness with which English has taken to itself materials, from almost everywhere in the world and has assimilated these outside elements, are really wonderful. When the Anglo-Saxons first conquered England in the fifth and sixth centuries, English was almost a pure or unmixed language which utilized its native resources to make new words for new ideas.

But now English has become the most mixed and cosmopolitan of all languages by receiving, throughout its history, all kinds of foreign elements with ease and assimilating them all to its own character. The richness of the English vocabulary is striking no doubt; but more striking is its variety and heterogeneousness. And, it is this general receptiveness of new elements from anywhere in the world which helps to make English a suitable and attractive vehicle in so many parts of the world.

## General Characteristics of the English Language

The first outstanding characteristic of English is its inflectional simplicity, and in the matter of inflectional simplification English has gone much further than any other European language. The manner in which English has reduced the endings it once had to a minimum is really wonderful. Inflections in the noun have been reduced to a sign of the plural and a form of the possessive case. The elaborate Teutonic inflection of the adjective has been completely eliminated except for the simple indication of the comparative and the superlative degrees. The verb has been simplified by the loss of practically all the personal endings, the almost complete abandonment of any distinction between the singular and the plural, and the gradual discard of the subjunctive mood. The relation of words in a sentence, which was once indicated by means of inflections is now expressed by prepositions for the cases of nouns and by auxiliaries for the tense of the verbs. By means of prepositions and auxiliary verbs, we are now able to express almost every shade of thought which was formerly rendered by changes in the form of the verb.

The second characteristic of English, as of other modern languages, is the use of word-order as a means of grammatical expression. Words in English do not play hide-and-seek as they often do in Latin. English shows more regularity and less caprice in the matter or word-order than most or probably all Indo-European languages. If in an English sentence, such as 'Alice broke the *pen*', we transpose the positions of the nouns, we entirely change the meaning of the sentence; the subject and the object are not denoted by any terminations to the words, as they would be in Greek or Latin or in modern German, but by their position before and after the verb. In English, an auxiliary verb does not stand far from its principal verb; an adjective almost always stands before its noun; the subject precedes the verb; the transitive verb precedes its object.

The third characteristic of English is its masculinity. English is the language of a grown-up man, and has very little childishness or femininity about it. This masculinity manifests itself most clearly in the sobriety of expression. As an Englishman does not like to use more syllables than are strictly necessary, so he does not like to say more than he can stand to. He dislikes strong or hyperbolical expressions or approval or admiration; 'that isn't half bad' or 'she is rather good looking' are often the highest praises one can draw out of him. An Englishman is always afraid of appearing ridiculous by showing strong emotions. As this sobriety is certainly found more frequently in men than in women, so this sobriety in expression of the English language is one of the signs of masculinity.

The fourth quality of English is its logic. English is, by far, the most logical of all languages with the sole exception of Chinese, which has been described as pure applied logic. In English, the difference between the past *he did*, and the present perfect *he has done* or the past perfect *he had done* is maintained with great consistency. The comparatively recent development of the expanded or progressive tenses has furnished the language with the wonderfully precise and logically valuable distinction between *I see* and *I am seeing, I saw* and *I was seeing.*

The fifth quality of English is the development of new varieties of intonation to express shades of meaning which were formerly indicated by varying the shapes of the words. In this respect, English is comparable to Chinese which greatly uses intonation as a method of expressing meaning in sentences which will otherwise seem like a series of unvarying monosyllabic roots. Thus, by varying the intonation, i.e., the pitch and intensity, the tone of the voice we make, the word 'do' yield wonderful variety of shades of meaning.

The last, but not the least, a characteristic of English is the freedom from narrow-minded pedantry which in most other languages sacrifices the logic of facts to the logic of grammar, or which makes the speakers shy of saying or writing what is not strictly grammatical.

Of all the aforesaid characteristics of English, it is the adaptable receptiveness and inflectional simplicity which have contributed the most to the general success of English. Again, it is because of its cosmopolitan vocabulary that English presents a somewhat familiar appearance to peoples of many parts of the world. Now, let us deal with its aforesaid third feature, i.e., its masculinity in detail. If ever any English teacher is asked about the predominant feature of English language, she/he might be able to tell that it is the masculinity of English. In other words, English language is positively masculine. 'It is', says Otto Jespersen, 'the language of a grown-up man, and has very little childish or feminine about it.' A great many things—things phonetic, grammatical and lexical, words and terms that are found and that are not found in the language—produce and confirm this impression.

The phonetic system of English bears out the masculine quality of English. The English consonants are clearly separated from one another in sound, and they are clearly and precisely pronounced. English has none of those indistinct or half-slurred consonants that abound in Danish. An English consonant is seldom changed by the vowels on either side of it. The vowels are, for the most part, independent of the consonants flanking them, and in this respect English has now deviated widely from the character of Old English. English has become, in all respects, clear-cut in its sounds, though this impression is blurred, to some extent, by the diphthongization of most long vowels (as in *ale, whole, eel, who* (phonetically /eil/, /ijl/, /huw/). English abounds in words ending in two or more consonant sounds as in *prompt, tempt, draught, fraught, wealth, plinth, feasts, beasts,* etc., and the pronunciation of these words requires as well as presupposes no little energy on the part of the speakers. Considered on the basis of its sounds English may be said to possess male energy.

The English language is characterized by briefness, conciseness and terseness, which are characteristics of the style of men. In grammar, it has got rid of a great many superfluities found in Old English, and in most cognate languages, reducing endings to the shortest forms possible and often doing away with endings altogether. In the expression 'all the young girls who come here' we find that *all,* the article *(the),* the adjective *(young)* and the relative pronoun *(who)* do not receive any mark of the plural number. Only the *girls* and *come* have received the sign of the plural number. The sense here is expressed with the greatest clarity imaginable.

English has certainly gained in force—though it has thereby lost something of its melodic elegance—by shortening many words of two syllables into monosyllabic ones. If there were not the great number of long foreign, especially Latin words, 'English would have approached', says Jespersen, 'the state of such monosyllabic languages as Chinese.' There are many English proverbs which possess the condensed power of the monosyllabic group of words, found in Old Chinese. Some of the examples of such monosyllabic proverbs are *first come, first served, no cure, no pay, haste makes waste, live and learn.*

A business-like shortness appears in such convenient abbreviations of sentences as are very common in English, for instance, 'While going to the college he found a snake' (while he was going); 'He did not answer when spoken to' (when he was spoken to); 'Once out of the house he gets panicky' (once he is); 'The feast over, the guests went away' (being). These expressions partake of the character of telegrams. These shortenings are in syntax what morphological shortenings are in words. Examples of morphological shortenings are *cab* for *cabriolet, bus* for *omnibus, photo* for *photograph, phone* for *telephone, rifle* for *rifle-gun.*

This business-like brevity of expression cannot be separated from a certain sobriety in expression. Just as an Englishman dislikes to use more words or more syllables than are strictly necessary for conveying his sense, so also he dislikes to say more than he can stand to. He is opposed to strong or hyperbolical expressions of approval or admiration. 'That is not half bad' or 'She is rather good looking' are often the highest praises one can draw out of him. He is always under the fear of appearing ridiculous by showing emotions. This sobriety is characteristic more of a man than of a woman, and so this feature (i.e., sobriety in expression) of the English language stamps it with a masculine trait.

The grammatical side of the English language strengthens and deepens this impression of masculinity. This masculinity appears in the fewness of the diminutives and in the rarity with which they are used. Of these diminutives—*let* is the commonest and a comparatively modern ending. The ending—*kin* and—*ling* are not very frequently employed, and they generally express the sense of contempt or hatred. The ending—*y* or—*ie* which corresponds exactly to the fondling suffixes of other languages is more or less confined to use in the nursery and is hardly used by grown-up persons except in talking to children.

Word order of the English language bears the full stamp of its businesslike, virile qualities. In English, words are not engaged in a hide-and-seek play as they are in Latin or German. In German, we find that ideas which belong together by right are widely sundered in obedience to caprice or to a rigorous grammatical rule. In English, there is a fixed word-order. In it, an auxiliary verb does not stand far from its principal verb (in the sentence 'John *has prepared* tea': '*has*' = auxiliary verb; '*prepared*' = principal verb); indeed, the distance of the auxiliary verb from its principal verb is rarely greater than in the sentence 'Alice *has* almost never *gone* through such an experience.' A negative will be found in the immediate neighbourhood of the word it negativates, generally the auxiliary verb, e.g., 'Sourav does *not read* hard' (*not* negativates *read*). An adjective nearly always stands before the noun it qualifies; notable exception to this rule occurs when there are qualifications added to it, which draw it after the noun, as in 'I have never undergone an experience so *uncanny* and *blood-curdling* as you speak of.' The subject nearly always precedes the verb, and the transitive verb precedes its object (e.g., David bit John—*subject* = David; *transitive verb* = bit; *object* = John). This word order is seen to be abandoned only for the specific purpose of emphasis as in the case of a poem—'*Him* I don't like; *her* I do.'

The logical quality of the English language bears out its masculinity. English is the most logical of the modern languages with the exception of Chinese which has been described as pure applied logic. In English, the difference between the past *he came* and the present perfect *he come* and the past perfect *he had come* is maintained with great consistency. The comparatively recent development of the expanded (or progressive) tenses has furnished the language with the wonderfully precise and logically valuable distinction between *I go* and *I am going; I went* and *I was going; I shall go* and *I shall be going.*

English is marked by freedom from the narrow-minded pedantry which in most languages sacrifices the logic of facts to the logic of grammar or which makes people shy of saying and writing what are not strictly grammatical. This freedom from pedantry appears most clearly in numbers. Thus, cabinet government, clergy, committee, family, club, etc., are grammatically singular in number, but as a matter of hard fact they connote more than one person. Most languages can treat these words only as singulars, but in English they can take a singular verb when the idea of unity is predominant, as in the sentence 'The present cabinet is better than the previous one.' On the other hand, they take a plural verb when the idea of plurality predominates, as in the sentence 'The cabinet were not unanimous in their rejection of the Party's Directive.' This freedom of choice is a great advantage, because it is conducive to clarity. In English, the speakers are also at liberty to express as a singular what is grammatically a plural, as in 'Three years is but short' (Shakespeare), or 'Ten minutes is heaps of time' (E.F. Benson).

A great many other phenomena in English show the same freedom from pedantry. The use of the passive voice, as in 'This peculiar phenomenon was taken no notice of' or of the prepositional combination or adverbs as adjectives as in 'an *almost* marriage' or 'his *out-of-the-way* humour' illustrates this freedom. Such liberties with grammar cannot be taken in French where any deviation from the grammatical rules is severely condemned. This freedom from pedantry has done much to make English such a rich and elastic language as it is now.

This freedom from pedantry marks the vocabulary. English writers have always been free to choose from anywhere the words which suited their literary purpose. In other words, the purpose of English authors has determined the choice of words and not the words the purpose, as in France and Italy. No academy as in France and Italy has been allowed to chain down the liberty of English writers. The result is that English dictionaries comprise a large number of words than those of any other nation. Since men move in wider circles of the world, they command a greater number of words than do women who move in narrower circles; and this results in a richness that is a sign of masculinity of the English language.

To sum up in the words of Prof. Jespersen, 'The English language is methodical, energetic, business-like and sober language that does not care much for finery and elegance, but does care for **logical consistency** and is opposed to any attempt to narrow-in life by *police regulations* and strict rules either of grammar or of lexicon.'

## Phonology and Phonetics of the English Language

Phonology is the branch of linguistics which investigates the ways in which speech sounds are used systematically to form words and utterances. If we wish to understand phonology, we must have a grasp of the basic concepts of phonetics, which is the study of the production of speech sounds by speakers, their perception by hearers and their acoustic properties. Most speakers of a language like English, who have not made any study of phonetics and phonology, tend to think of the sounds of speech through the medium of the ordinary alphabet. In the English language, the spelling does not suggest the accurate pronunciation of words. People who have not studied phonetics can hardly describe the spoken language except in terms of the alphabet (i.e., consonant, vowel, syllable, which are often interpreted as grapho- logical representation pertaining to the study of the written language).

Written English is often an inadequate and misleading representation of the spoken language of today. If we are to examine the essence of the English language, we must make our approach through the spoken rather than the written form. Our primary concern should be in the production, transmission and reception of the sounds of English—in other words, we have to learn the phonetics of the language. Once we abandon orthography, we will find that the analysis of the spoken form of English is by no means simple. Each of us uses an infinite number of speech sounds when we speak English. Two utterances of a particular word by the same person may show a marked difference in the quality or the sound, yet we can say that the same sound sequence has been repeated. For example, we may hear clear and considerable differences of quality in the vowel sound '**love**' as, for instance, in the London and Manchester pronunciation of the word. Or, for example, in India you can hear a clear difference of quality in the vowel of '**cot**' in the U.P. and Bengal pronunciation of the word.

**Information Box**

A language is a system of conventional signs used for communication by a human community. This pattern of conventions covers a system of significant sound units called the phonemes, the inflexion and arrangement of '**words**' and the association of meaning with the words. An utterance, which is an act of speech, is a single concerned manifestation of the system at work.

## Importance of Phonetics in Spoken Communication

In speech, we rely very heavily upon **sound** to make plain the significant distinctions of meaning which can be made by the more central operations of grammar and vocabulary. A word, when it is pronounced, must have a particular sound-shape if it is to be recognized, just as it must have a particular letter-shape when it is written.

Let's take up the word '**dot**'. When it is spoken it must have a recognizable 'd'- sound at the beginning, 'o'-sound in the middle and 't'-sound at the end, and if we use a different sound at any of these places, the word will lose the shape and cannot be recognized. If we replace the d-sound by a t-sound and we hear **tot**, which is different in meaning, or if we replace the final t-sound by a p-sound, we hear **dop**, which we do not recognize at all. Furthermore, the sounds must be in a particular order, e.g., **dot** is not meaningfully the same as *tod or *odt or *dto.

Again, in a language like English, stress very often helps to give the word its individual shape. For example, the word '**perfect**' can be distinguished by its pronunciation. When the stress or emphasis is placed on the first syllable (perfect), it is an adjective; whereas if the stress is placed on the second syllable, it becomes a verb (perfect). Similarly, stress can help to distinguish between a noun and a verb, e.g., **re**cord (N) and re**cord** (v).

It should be noticed at this point that not all the distinctions of grammar and vocabulary are reflected in sound, e.g., taut and taught or (tort) are the same where sounds are concerned. Similarly, '**by**', '**bye**' or '**buy**' is the same where sounds are concerned and not their meanings. Equally, 'a tack' and 'attack' are rarely distinguished in pronunciation. By the nature of things, most of the meaningful distinctions of the language must be capable of being given distinctive shape in sound, and it is this close dependence of sound and meaning which justifies the importance of the study of speech sound, i.e., phonetics.

To learn phonetics we have to learn first how the air is set in motion, by the movements of the speech organs and the coordination of these movements in the production of a single sound and the sequence of sounds. This whole process is known as 'articulatory phonetics'.

The next is the study of how the air vibrates between the mouth of the speaker and the ear of the listener. This study is called 'acoustic phonetics'.

The hearing process is a nerve-controlled process which is neurological in nature. Our brain is equipped with the devices which can distinguish a particular speech sound from another in terms of its length,volume, pitch and intonation. This study centres on the hearer's reaction to stimuli that is fed into his ears. This area of study is called 'auditory phonetics'.

The above three domains of phonetics are all general in scope; they may be applied impartially to the sounds of any and every language, and they may be used to describe and classify the sound feature of all known languages. Of course, phoneticians or experts in the study of phonology may not be fully satisfied with such description and classification. They would like to study further about the way in which sounds function in a particular language, how many or how few of all the sounds of language are utilized in that language and what part they play in showing the meaningful distinctions of the language.

We must know what a sound is, how it is produced, what its physical characteristics are and what effect it has on the ear. At the same time, we must know what the sound does because the same sound may have quite different tasks to perform in different languages. Study the difference in sound between **th** and **d** used in English to differentiate between one word and another, e.g., **then/d**en, la**th**er/la**dd**er, brea**the**/bree**d**, etc.

## Variation in Pitch of Voice and Change in Meaning

Variations of pitch play a part in all languages but the basic function of those variations may be different in different languages. In English, the pitch changes do not affect the shape of a word, i.e., we can pronounce a word such as '**No**' with a variety of pitch levels—rising tone, falling tone or combinations of these—so as to add overtones of doubt, certainty, apathy, interrogation, etc. Yet, the word remains the same old basic **negative**.

In a language like Chinese, however, the pitch pattern is an important part of the basic shape of the word. There are four different words in the national language of China, all of which are pronounced rather like English '**ma**', and they are distinguished by their pitch patterns. Saying '**ma**' with a high level pitch means 'mother'; with rise from medium to high pitch, the meaning changes—'**ma**' then means 'hemp'. A rise from low pitch to medium pitch gives the meaning 'scold'. So, in Chinese, pitch is an essential part of the shape of the word. In English, pitch is not a part of the word-shape but rather a part of the shape of longer bits of speech or utterances.

## Let Us Do and Learn

a) Read these words aloud. Find a word with a different vowel sound. Circle that word:

girl curl pearl shirt heard word bird third hard

b) Read these **minimal pairs** of words. If the pronunciation is the same then write [S] in the brackets given against each pair. Write [D] for different. The first one is done for you.

| | | | | | | | |
|---|---|---|---|---|---|---|---|
| (i) | hurt | heart | [D] | (ii) | curd | card | [ ] |
| (iii) | fur | far | [ ] | (iv) | son | sun | [ ] |
| (v) | Lip | leap | [ ] | (vi) | seat | sit | [ ] |
| (vii) | sew | sow | [ ] | | | | |

c) How many **speech sounds** are there in the following words:
Pronounce each word and write the number in the brackets given. The first one is done for you.

| | | | |
|---|---|---|---|
| write (2) | measure ( ) | first ( ) | scissors ( ) |
| read ( ) | lick ( ) | judge ( ) | teacher ( ) |
| mat ( ) | voice ( ) | father ( ) | through ( ) |

## Types of Sound Difference

There are a wide variety of sounds and sound features. There are perhaps 4000 languages spoken in the world today. The sound resources of each of these languages are not necessarily completely different from those of every other language, but one thing has to be kept in mind, that no two languages ever have exactly the same sound resources. Within each language, there are dialects which have their own distinctive pronunciations or accents. We can easily tell an American accent from an English accent, and so on. We can even distinguish between different accents within our own language.

However, if we notice carefully we will find that each one of us, our friends, colleagues, acquaintances, notabilities has distinctive different pronunciation. We can recognize them by the sound of their voices and the way they articulate sounds. Besides this, each one of us use a different style of pronunciation in different situations, e.g., when we talk in a relaxed way to friends or when we are addressing a big crowd at a meeting, the accent used tends to be different. We do not speak to our beloved as we would speak to a shop assistant or boss. Pronunciation is a part of the difference. So, the study of phonetics should not only include the description, classification and the use of sounds, but also the pronunciation of the language.

## Difficulties in Pronunciation

A speaker of English faces a number of difficulties where pronunciation is concerned. The difficulties are as follows:

1. He/she has to recognize readily and with certainty the various speech sounds in the language when he hears them pronounced. He must also learn to remember the acoustic qualities of these sounds.
2. He/she has to learn to produce these sounds correctly and use them in their proper places in the connected speech.
3. He/she must also learn to join each sound of a sequence on to the next and to pronounce the complete sequence rapidly without any hindrance.

The ultimate object of the language learner will be to pronounce the complete sequence properly without any hesitation. To attain this proficiency in the initial stages of his study, he must focus his attention continually on details of the speech mechanism.

Ability to speak a language or understand it when spoken, does not involve the ability to read or write in the conventional way. One can learn to speak the language perfectly without even being aware of the process of production. On the other hand, a person can learn to read and write the language without being able to pronounce it.

## Let Us Do and Learn

1. What's wrong with each of the following utterances?
   a) He was wearing a smart turban.
   b) I have ordered for a new football.
   c) I always keep my money in this box.
   d) He lives miserly in a way.
   e) People showed him respect for at the station.
2. Rewrite them in the correct sequence and read them out aloud.
3. State the kind of error and discuss with your friends.

## How to Overcome the Difficulties in Pronunciation?

The first thing that we need is a good 'ear-training'. In other words, we need to foster 'cultivation of the auditory memory'. No one can be a successful linguist unless he has a good ear. If his ear is insensitive by nature, it may be made more sensitive by training; and if his ear is good by nature, it can be made much better by practice and training, i.e., if he has a good ear, he will know whether he is pronouncing the foreign sound correctly or not. A good ear will help him to understand the language readily when spoken by native speakers, and he will be able to recognize words instantly and will not mistake one word for another.

The possession of a good ear involves:

(a) Ability to discriminate between sounds.
(b) Ability to remember the acoustic qualities of foreign sounds.
(c) Ability to recognize foreign sounds at once with certainty.

In other words, students should be able to distinguish differences between various sounds in a foreign language and foreign sounds of their mother tongue. They must be able to bring into their consciousness the memories to foreign sounds previously heard and be able to compare sounds subconsciously with the memory-images of sounds previously heard. To cultivate all this, it requires a good linguistic practice in listening for sounds.

In order to learn the form of the speech-sounds of a foreign language, the student has to learn to put his tongue, lips and other parts of the organs of speech into certain definite positions or to perform certain actions with them. In other words, the language learner should study phonetics and do, when necessary, exercises based on that theory.

Besides, the student has to learn the appropriate order in which the sounds are to be arranged, so as to make words and sentences intelligible to the listeners. A speaker, for instance, must know that if he wishes to communicate the idea expressed in French by '*armoire*' and German by '*Shrank*', he must form the English sounds /k/ /Λ/, /b/, /ɘ/, /d/, etc., one after the other in a particular order. No other English sounds will do, nor may these be placed in any other order. However well the speaker may pronounce the sounds, he will not be able to convey any meaning unless he uses this particular sequence of sounds. He must, therefore, take care to remember that this is the required sequence.

Conventional English spelling is far from being phonetic; it does not give accurate information as to the sound-order required by the speaker of English. In the first place English assigns to many of the letters of the alphabet values quite different from those which people in foreign countries are used to associate with them, as for example: the letter '**a**' in **gate**, the '**i**' in **find**, the '**u**' in **tune**. A learner may learn the phonic values of these letters without any difficulty, but as soon as the learner has learnt them, he finds so many words in which these letters have quite different values. For instance, study the sounds of the letter '**a**' in the following words:

F**a**ther, **a**ny, f**a**t, w**a**tch, f**a**ll, etc.

They are not the same.

Now, study the sounds of **/i/** in the following words:

w**i**nd (n), mach**i**ne and b**i**rd

Again, compare the sound of the letter '**u**' in **ru**le, **pu**t and **bu**t. Compare also the '**o**' in st**o**ve, m**o**ve and l**o**ve and the '**ea**' in m**ea**t, h**ea**d, gr**ea**t, b**ea**r, **ea**rn, id**ea**, etc.

What do you notice? Spelling is the same but pronunciation is different.

Again, English sounds may be spelt in a large number of ways, for instance, the words m**ee**t, m**ea**t, n**ie**ce, piq**ue**, k**ey**, qu**ay**, b**oa**rd, w**a**rn, th**ough**t, fl**oo**r, br**oa**d, etc.

You will find that there is a constant contradiction between spelling and pronunciation which leads astray not only the beginners, but also the expert. The result of such inconsistencies is that the foreign learner, who depends solely on ordinary orthography, is in innumerable cases at a loss to know what sounds should be used, and thus is continually mispronouncing the words. However, such mispronunciations may be avoided by the study and use of phonetic transcription.

We should bear in mind that phonetic transcriptions are of no value to those who have not learnt to form the sounds which the phonetic letters represent. But as soon as a learner can make the individual sounds with fair accuracy, he will be in a position to begin learning sequences of sounds. Phonetic transcriptions will tell her/him the proper sequences to learn phonetics. In order to express the ideas she/he wants to communicate, the learner should be able to pronounce each and every speech sound of all the 44 International Phonetic Alphabet (IPA) sounds with tolerable accuracy. Otherwise, she/he will not be able to pronounce the English word '**cupboard**' (**/kΛb3d/**) even if a phonetic transcription of the word is provided.

A learner will generally be able to pronounce correctly in the matter of **length**, **stress** and **pitch**, if he has been provided with such information. Sometimes, these may be applied by means of rules, and sometimes, it is better conveyed by marks in the phonetic transcriptions.

Sometimes, a learner can pronounce isolated sounds correctly, knows what sequence of sounds to use in a given word or sentence and knows the necessary details in regard to length, stress and pitch, but he stumbles over the sound sequence in longer utterances. This shows that he has not acquired the facility in passing from one sound to another, and he cannot always pronounce sequences of sounds rapidly and without stumbling. In other words, he does not '**casemate**' properly.

Besides, he may have learnt the bad habit of stopping between words. He has not realized the important principle that the only places where pauses are normally made are at the ends of certain grammatical groups called 'sense groups'.

The ability to casemate sounds, i.e., to pronounce sequences of sounds with rapidity and without stumbling, can be cultivated by continued repetition and practice.

## Types of Pronunciation

The first question that comes to the mind of a person who wants to learn an acceptable pronunciation of, let's say, English language is:

'Which of the various forms of pronunciation should I learn?'

No two persons of the same nationality pronounce their own language exactly alike. The difference may be due to the locality in which they live, social surroundings or early influences, and there may be individual peculiarities that are difficult or impossible to account for.

It is seen that the pronunciation of English among people brought up in Manchester is different from those brought up in Exeter and both differ from the pronunciation of those brought up in Edinburgh or in London.

An example of differences of English pronunciation according to locality may be found in the treatment of the letter 'r' in such words as 'part'. In Scotland, the 'r' is pronounced as a slightly rolled or flapped **r**, but in London English, the **r** is not pronounced and the pronunciation is /part/. In many parts of the north and the west of England, on the other hand, the effect of the **r** appears as a modification known as '**retroflex ion**' or '**inversion**' of the preceding vowel. In the south of England, the vowels in **boot** and **book** are different, but in Scotland, a short closed /u/ is generally used in both words.

There is also a difference in the pronunciation between the 'educated' and 'uneducated' speech. People of limited education in many parts of England omit the '**h**' sound altogether. They say **/elp/** for 'help'. In London (cockney), words like **name** are pronounced with a diphthong /ai/ or /æi/ instead of / ei/; and words like 'house', 'about' are pronounced with /æƷ/, or sometimes /ebæʊt/ or /ebæet/. In uneducated Yorkshire speech, the vowels of **put** /pʊt/ and **cut** /kʌt/ are levelled to a vowel intermediate between these two.

Individual peculiarities may be the result of habit, e.g., childish mispronunciations which have never been corrected by the parents or teachers. Such mispronunciations may also arise from some physical defect.

Because of the existence of so many differences, it becomes difficult for the foreign learner to know which type of English pronunciation to learn. It is difficult to say which type is better and which type to describe as a standard. But, certainly, the most useful type is the one based on the Southern speech which is generally used by those, who have educated at public schools and preparatory boarding schools. It is easily understood in all parts of the English-speaking countries. In fact, it is perhaps more widely understood than any other type. The term Received Pronunciation (RP) is often used to designate this type of pronunciation. However, it may be considered that there are other types of pronunciation which may be considered equally 'good'.

It is seen that all speakers use more than one style of pronunciation. A person may pronounce the same word or a sequence of words quite differently in different circumstances. For instance, consider the word 'and' which is pronounced /n/ when it is unstressed, e.g., in bread and butter which is pronounced as /bred n bte/, but when the word is stressed it is pronounced /ænd/ to rhyme with hand /hænd/.

There are several different styles of pronunciation. Notable among them are the rapid familiar style, the slower colloquial style, the natural style used while addressing an audience, the acquired style of the stage while acting and the acquired style used in singing. Of these, the slower colloquial style is perhaps the most suitable for beginners.

## Let Us Do and Learn

1. The words 'bear' and 'bare' are spelt differently but they are pronounced the same, /b>/. Make a list of five other pairs of words which are spelt differently but pronounced in the same way.
2. Read out these words and underline the **vowel sounds** in the following words. The first one is done for you:

| | | | |
|---|---|---|---|
| important | remember | alphabet | London |
| correct | English | particular | pronunciation |
| language | necessary | letter | property |

3. Find words to match the following words with a minimum difference only in the vowel sound to constitute **minimal pairs**. The first one is done for you.

| | | |
|---|---|---|
| (i) bend / **band** | (iv) broke ________ | (vii) sill ________ |
| (ii) knit ________ | (v) force ________ | (viii) win ________ |
| (iii) tale ________ | (vi) dawn ________ | (ix) ten ________ |

# ◢ English Phoneme (Contrastive Analysis with Hindi and Other Indian Languages)

The speech mechanism of a human being is capable of producing an infinite number of speech sounds. Every language makes its own selection from this vast human range of speech sounds. The selection that a particular language makes, constitutes its sound system which consists of a large number of speech sounds. But not all of these sounds are important, i.e., not all of these sounds make any meaningful difference between the words and help convey distinctions of meaning in communication between two individuals speaking that language.

Let us take for example the word **cake** /$k^h$eik/. Here, the first and the last /k/ sounds are not the same, but the phoneticians will make a distinction between the two, though they know that the two sounds are phonetically similar. The first sound /$k^h$/ in this word is aspirated (i.e., pronounced with an accompanying puff of breath) and the last /k/ sound is un-aspirated and unexploded (i.e., pronounced without an audible release of the complete closure). In the word **sky** /skai/, we have another /k/ sound which is phonetically similar to, but not the same as the two /k/ sounds in 'cake'. Now, these three /k/ sounds are neither contrastive nor distinctive, i.e., the substitution of one for another in these words will not give a different word. In other words, though these three phonetically similar sounds are different in one way or the other in English, i.e., it is not important for the purpose of communication and, therefore, these sounds can be grouped together into one sound /k/ in English.

Now, let us look at the word cake /$k^h$eIk/ and /beIk/. The difference between them consists only in one sound in the initial position. But, this difference is of a different kind from that between the /k/ sounds stated earlier. The substitution of the sound /b/ for the sound /k/ in the same position gives us a different word, i.e., it brings about the difference in meaning between cake and bake. The difference between /b/ and /k/ is thus taken to be contrastive in this position. Besides, /b/ and /k/ are phonetically more dissimilar sounds than /$k^h$/ and /k/. Sound /b/ is bilabial and /k/ is velar. So, two phonetically dissimilar sounds like /b/ and /k/, which can occur in the same position and are contrastive, are called 'phonemes'. If we substitute some other sounds for /k/ in the word /$k^h$eIk/, we will get **sake, fake, make, lake, shake, take, rake**, and **wake**. The sounds /s/, /f/, /m/, /I/, /ʃ/, /t/, /r/ and /w/ are all phonemes, because they are phonetically dissimilar and contrast with /k/ in the same position.

Similarly, if we substitute sounds which contrast with /k/ in the final position of the same word, we get **cape, case, cave, Kate, came** and **cane**, and here we get the phonemes /p/, /s/, /v/, /t/, /m/ and /n/. Again, by substituting the diphthong /ei/ in the word **cake**, which is in the medial position for other vowel sounds, e.g., kick /$k^h$ik/, cork /$k^h$ek/, Coke /$k^h$euk/, we get the phonemes /I/, /e/ and /eʊ/. In this way, we can get all the phonemes used in the English language and thus, draw up an inventory of the phonemes of any language.

Every language makes use of a limited number of phonemes, English, for example, has 44 phonemes in its sound system. We must remember that since phonemes are contrastive units of sound in the sound system of a given language, they have validity only in relation to that language.

Sounds that are phonemes of one language may be only allophones of another language, e.g., /p/, /$p^h$/ are allophones in English, but /p/ in /pal/ (moment) and /$p^h$al/ (fruit) in Hindi are two different phonemes.

## The English Allophones

In the word cake /$k^h$ eIk/ and scale /skeil/, we see that /$k^h$/, /k/ and /k/ are similar sounds, yet different from one another and the difference between them is not contrastive. The difference between them depends upon their position in the word. For example, in English, /$k^h$/ can occur only in the initial position in an accented syllable, /k/ only in the final position and /k/ in /skeIl/ only after /s/. In other words, these three sounds occur in predictable and mutually exclusive positions in English. They are in complementary distribution with one another. Such phonetically similar sounds in complementary distribution in relation to one another are called 'positional variants' or **allophones** of the same phoneme. Another example from English would be phoneme /l/ which has two positional variants in words like **loyal** and **field**. The phoneme /l/ is articulated with the tip of the tongue making a complete closure with the teeth ridge for /l/, the back of the tongue also goes up simultaneously to articulate with the soft palate. When /l/ occurs before vowels and /j/, and is called clear/l/, and when /l/ occurs before consonants (minus /j/ and word finally), and is called dark /l/. Thus, the phoneme /l/ has two **allophones**.

## The English Syllable

The **phonemes** of a language combine to form the next higher unit of an utterance. The unit at the next higher level than the phoneme is called the **syllable**. The syllable is a very significant unit in the production of speech without which we would not be able to analyze and describe **speech sounds** or utterance. It is not so difficult to identify syllables in a word as to define it. When different phonemes (e.g., consonant sounds, one or more, and one vowel sound are combined to target a specific meaning or to form a part of a meaningful word, it becomes a **syllable**). A vowel sound is enough to constitute a **syllable**. Let us study some examples mentioned below.

## Division of English Words into Syllables

A word consists of one or more than one syllable. It is easy to identify the syllables in the English words for example:

'rat' - It consists of one syllable and is known as a **monosyllabic** word.
're move' - It consists of two syllables and is known as a **disyllabic** word.
're mo val' - It consists of three syllables and is known as a **tri-syllabic** word.

'de gen er ate' - It consists of four syllables and is known as a **tetra syllabic** word.
'El ec tri ci ty' - It consists of five syllables and is known as a **quinqua syllabic** word.
'cha rac te ri za tion':- It consists of six syllables and is known as a **Hexa-syllabic** word.

Thus we see, the smallest unit of a written communication is a syllable. In other words, the syllable is a morphophonemic unit of a word which is the minimum requirement in a sentence. (See *Structuralist Approach to Teaching.*)

A syllable can be divided into three phases that coincide with its three segments. For example,

| (marginal) Releasing phase | (central) Segment | (marginal) Arresting phase | |
|---|---|---|---|
| | Oh! | | = V |
| g | o | | = CV |
| g | oa | t | = CVC |
| v | O | te | = CVC |

**Table 2.1** Displaying English Syllable Structure

## Definition of Syllable

A **syllable** is a unit of utterance containing one and only **one vowel** either alone or surrounded by consonants.

## Syllable Pattern in English

A syllable may contain as many as three consonants at the releasing phase and as many as four consonants at the arresting phase. These consonant clusters often cause problems for speakers who speak in a language that does not contain such clusters.

## Syllable Patterns—Displayed

| | | | | | |
|---|---|---|---|---|---|
| (a) Consonant clusters at the releasing phase | st | ea | | m | = CVC |
| | pr | i | nc | e | = CVCCV |
| | s | p | r | ee | = CVC |
| (b) Consonant cluster at the mid segment | s | i | mm | er | = CVCCV* |
| (c) Consonant clusters at the releasing phase | | t | ea | ch | = CVC |
| | | t | ea | ches | = CVCC |
| | | t | e | xts | = CVCCC |
| | | t | e | xts | = CVCCC |

*v = vowel; c = consonant

**Table 2.2** Displaying English Syllable Pattern

When a syllable contains no consonant sound in the arresting phase then the syllable is said to be an **open syllable.**

**Example:** /plai/ = CCV (diphthong) = open syllable.

When a syllable contains a consonant sound in the arresting phase then the syllable is said to be a **closed syllable**.

**Example:** /bout/ = CVC = closed syllable.

Different languages have different syllable patterns. Some languages have more **closed syllables** than **open syllables**, whereas some others have more **open syllables** than **closed syllables.** For example, in the **Oriya** language almost all the syllables are open. **Bengali** or **Hindi** has more open syllables than closed syllables. But English has more **closed syllables** than **open syllables.**

## Let Us Do and Learn

1. Write a set of two words for each of the following words which differ in only one sound segment. The first one is done for you.
   a) chew: **few** ________ b) waste: ________ ________
   c) bed: ________ ________ d) mew: ________ ________
   e) poor: ________ ________ f) leisure: ________ ________
   g) cattle: ________ ________ h) pin: ________ ________
2. Point out the **number of syllables** in each of the following words. Put the number in the brackets. The first one is done for you.
   ancestors = (3) monotonous = ( ) dramatists = ( )
   laboratory = ( ) remarkable = ( ) strangers = ( )
3. Write **two words** as examples for each of the following cases:
   (a) An initial consonant cluster with two consonants: ________: ________
   (b) An initial consonant cluster with three consonants: ________: ________
   (c) A final consonant cluster with three consonants: ________: ________
   (d) A final consonant cluster with four consonants: ________: ________
   (e) A syllable without any consonant: ________: ________
4. Tick off the right word and fill in the blanks in the following sentences:
   (a) There's our {bess / boss / bus} ———————— over there. We must catch it before it leaves.
   (b) Do you want this {latter / letter / later} ———————— please?
   (c) That {soap / sop / soup} ———————— smells very good and its tasty too.
   (d) The {bowl / bull / ball} ———————— we saw was black and white. Mother needs it to pour the soup.

## Function of English Phonology

Phonology studies and describes the distinctive sound units of a specific language and their relationships with one another. The phonology of a language is therefore, unique to that language and is different from that of every other language. In this unit, we are going to deal with the sounds of English language only.

A phonological approach does not attempt to establish relationship between the sounds of a specific language and the general human phonetic resources. One of its aims is to identify the contrastive units of the sound systems of a language—those units which will make the meaning of each word different from the other.

## Segmental Phonology

When we speak, we produce an infinite number of speech sounds. To identify these streams of speech sounds, we divide the streams into small bits or **segments**. For example, the word cat has three segments—/k/ a first segment, /æ/ the middle segment and /t/ the final segment. From this large number of varying phonetic segments, each language makes a selection of sounds which are functional in that language. These smallest segments of sounds are called 'phonemes'.

(See Table 2.3 to get a clear idea of the concept of phonemes.)

Two notions are important when we aim to describe a language. These are: **paradigmatic** and **syntagmatic** relations (or system and structure).

Let us clarify these notions using examples in the following table:

| | | | |
|---|---|---|---|
| p | ee | p | /pip/ |
| tr | ea | t | /trit/ |
| c | ea | se | /sis/ |

**Table 2.3** Displaying Paradigmatic and Syntagmatic Relations

The consonants in initial position (/p/, /t/, /s/) are said to be in paradigmatic relations with each other. The final (/p/, /t/, /s/) are also in paradigmatic relations with each other. The /p/, /t/, /s/ in the first set are said to be in parallel distribution with each other, i.e., they occur in the same place (initial place) in structure, whereas /p/, /t/, /s/ in the second set is said to be in complementary distribution with the first set being the same phonemes. So, all these six items will be considered as three different phonemes (and **not** six).

Items which occur at different places in a structure and which can never be contrasted can be grouped. Let us consider the items in the following paradigm:

| | | |
|---|---|---|
| k | eep | /kip/ |
| c | ap | /kæp/ |
| c | up | /kʌp/ |

**Table 2.4** Displaying Paradigmatic Relations

Here, all the /k/ sounds occur at the same place in the structure (i.e., in the initial paradigm). However, they are phonetically different because the articulation of /k/ in each case is conditioned by that of the following vowel.

These /k/ sounds cannot be contrasted because they occur in the same paradigm and the articulation of each /k/ depends on the following vowel. The three /k/ sounds are grouped into one phoneme /k/. The phonetic variants which are grouped into one phoneme are said to be **allophones** of that phoneme. So, the initial consonants in 'keep', 'cap', 'cup' are said to be allophones of /k/.

We need to remember that phonetic sounds which are phonetically dissimilar cannot be grouped into one phoneme.

***Description of English Speech Sounds.*** The description of speech sounds necessitates the provision of certain basic information:

(a) The nature of the air stream which is usually the ingressive pulmonic air stream. Though later, cases where ingressive air stream is used will be considered.
(b) The position of the vocal cords, particularly whether they are closed, wide apart of vibrating.
(c) The position of the soft palate which will decide whether or not the sound has nasal resonances.
(d) The disposition of the various movable organs of the mouth, i.e., the shape of the lips and tongue, in order to determine the nature of the related oral and upper pharyngeal cavities.

Besides this, it may be necessary to provide other information concerning the tenseness which may accompany the primary articulation, or when it is a question of a sound with no steady state to describe, an indication of the kind of movement which is taking place.

When we listen to a continuous utterance, we perceive an ever-changing pattern of sound. But, when it is a question of our own language, i.e., the mother tongue, we are not aware of the complexities of pattern which reach our ears. We consciously tend to perceive and interpret only those sound features which are relevant to the intelligibility of our language. However, despite this linguistic selection which we ultimately make, we are aware that this changing pattern consists of variations of different kinds, for example:

- Variation of **sound quality**—we hear a variety of vowels and consonants;
- Variation of **pitch**—we appreciate the melody, or intonation of the utterance;
- Variation of **loudness**—we will agree that some sounds or syllabus seem to sound louder than others; and
- Variation of **length**—some sounds are appreciably longer to our ears than others.

There are judgements made by a listener with respect to an utterance by a speaker, and if the sound stimulus from the speaker and response from the listener are made in terms of the same linguistic system, then the utterance will be meaningful for both speaker and listener alike.

It can, therefore, be assumed that there should be some constant relationship between the speaker's articulation and the listener's reception of sound variations; though an exact connection between the **production**, **transmission** and **reception** phases of speech are not always easy to establish.

Now, let us begin with the description of the consonant sounds.

***Description of Consonants.*** There are 24 distinctive consonant sounds in English. The consonants are marked by two features: functionally, they tend to be marginal in the syllable—in other words, they occur either in the syllable-initial and/or syllable-final positions, and in terms of their phonetic nature, their articulations involve obstructions or narrowings which produce a noise component.

(If you look at the above discussion, you will get a clear idea of the consonants as marginal segments in a syllable.)

The 24 consonantal phonemes are classified in two general categories:

(a) Those articulations that involve a total closure or those that involve a structure causing friction. Both groups are typically associated with a voice component. These phonemes are symbolized as:

/p/, /b/, /t/, /d/, /k/, /g/, /tʃ/, /dʒ/
/f/, /v/, /Θ/, /ð/, /s/, /z/, /ʃ/, /z/

(b) Those articulations in which there is only a partial closure or those in which the air escapes unimpeded through oral or nasal passage. Such articulations are typically voiced and frequently frictionless (without a noise component). These phonemes are symbolized as:

/m/, /n/, /ŋ/, /y/, /h/, /I/, /w/, /r/, /j/

In any classification of consonantal articulations, the essential factors which must be considered are:

1. The place of articulation.
2. The manner of articulation.
3. The presence or absence of voice.
4. The position of the soft palate.

The following chart will give you a clear picture. It is based on a vertical axis showing the **manner of articulation**; a horizontal axis showing the **place of articulation**; a pairing of consonantal types to show the **voiceless** variety on the left and the **voiced** variety on the right; and an extra column under 'manner' to include the relatively few consonantal types which require the lowered position of the soft palate. The symbols used are of the sound types of British English.

| Place<br>Manner | Bilabial | Labio-dental | Dental | Alveolar | Post-alveolar | Palato-alveolar | Palatal | Velar | Glottal |
|---|---|---|---|---|---|---|---|---|---|
| **Complete Oral closure** Plosive | p b | | | | | | | k g | |
| Affricate | | | | | | | ʧ dʒ | | |
| Nasal | m | | | n | | | | ŋ | |
| **Narrowing** Fricative | | f v | θ ð | s z | | ʃ ʒ | | | h |
| **Partial Closure** Lateral | | | | t d | | | | | |
| **Intermittent Closure** Roll | | | | (r) | | | | | |
| **Frictionless Continuant or Glide** Approximants | w | | | | r | | j | | |

**Table 2.5** Displaying Place and Manner of Articulation of Consonants

It is evident from the above table that among the English consonants:

(a) Six are plosives;
(b) Two are affricates;
(c) Three are nasals;
(d) Nine are fricatives;
(e) One is a lateral; and
(f) Three are approximates.

**A. Place of Articulation:**

The chief points of articulation (particularly the sounds of English) are as follows:

**Bilabial:** The two lips are the primary articulators (e.g., /p/, /b/, /m/).
**Labio-dental:** The lower lip articulates with the upper teeth (e.g., /f/, /v/).
**Dental:** The tongue tip and rims articulate with the upper teeth (e.g., θ, ð).
**Alveolar:** The blade, or the tip and the blade, of the tongue articulate with the alveolar ridge (e.g., /t/, /d/, /I/, /n/, /s/, /z/).
**Post-alveolar:** The tip (and rims) of the tongue articulate with the rear part of the alveolar ridge (e.g., /r/).

**Palato-alveolar:** The blade, or the tip and the blade, of the tongue articulate with the alveolar ridge, and there is, at the same time, a rising of the front of the tongue towards the hard palate (e.g., /ʃ/, /ʒ/, /tʃ/, /dʒ/).
**Palatal:** The front of the tongue articulates with the hard palate (e.g., /j/).
**Velar:** The back of the tongue articulates with the soft palate (e.g., /k/, /g/, //).
**Glottal:** An obstruction, or a narrowing causing friction but not vibration, between the vocal cords (e.g., /r/, /h/).

**B. Manner of Articulation:**

The obstruction that is made by the organs of speech may be total, intermittent, partial, or may merely constitute a narrowing that is sufficient to cause friction. The types of articulation in decreasing degrees of closure are:

(a) **Complete closure:**
(i) **Plosive:** A complete closure at some point in the vocal tract, behind which the air pressure builds up and can be released with an explosion (e.g., /p/, /b/, /t/, /d/, /k/, /g/, //).
(ii) **Affricate:** A complete closure at some point in the mouth, behind which an air pressure is built up; the release of the articulators is slow compared to that of a plosive, so that friction is a characteristic second element of the sound (e.g., /tʃ/, /d¥/).
(iii) **Nasal:** A complete closure at some point in the mouth. But the soft palate is lowered and the air escapes through the nose. These sounds are continuants and in the voiced form, having no noise component (e.g., /m/, /n/, /ŋ/).

(b) **Intermittent closure:**
**Roll:** A series of intermittent closures or tapes made by flexible organs of speech on a firmer surface (e.g., /r/) where the tongue tip taps against the alveolar ridge.

(c) **Partial closure:**
**Lateral:** A partial closure is made at some point in the mouth, the air being allowed to escape on one or both sides of the contact. These sounds may be continuant and non-fricative (e.g., /l/, /t/), or they may be sometimes accompanied by a little friction or sometimes by a considerable amount of friction.

(d) **Narrowing:** We need to narrow down our lips to a semi-closure for pronunciation of narrowing fricatives /f/,/v/ and /h/.

(e) **Fricative:** Two organs approximate to such an extent that the air passes through them with friction (e.g., /f/, /v/, /θ/, /ð/, /s/, /z/, /ʃ/, /dʒ/, /h/).

## Semi-vowels

**Semi-vowels**, such as /w/, /j/, are usually included in the consonantal category on functional grounds, but from the point of phonetic description they are more properly treated as vowel glides.

## Sounds—Made by Using Air Stream

Usually a common way of expressing surprise or pain involves the energetic inspiration of air accompanied by bilabial friction. Such sounds occur in a number of languages and in types of stammering, they are not found in normal English.

Another set of sounds, involving an ingressive air stream, is produced entirely by means of closures within the mouth cavity, normal breathing through the nose may continue quite independently if the soft palate is lowered. Thus, the sound made to show irritation or sympathy (e.g., tut-tut) is articulated by means of a double closure: the back of the tongue against the velum; and the tip, blade and sides against the alveolar ridge and side teeth. The sounds produced are known as **clicks**. These clicks are extra-linguistic in English.

## Classification and Description of English Consonants

Let us describe the English consonants in some detail.

***Plosives.*** The complete articulation of plosives, also called Stops, consists of three stages:

(a) **The closing stage:** During this stage, the articulating organs move together to form the obstruction.
(b) **The hold and compression stage:** During this stage, the two articulators remain in contact for some time.
(c) **The release or explosion stage:** During this stage, the organs rapidly form the obstruction part and allow the compressed air to escape abruptly. Vocal cords may vibrate during this stage.

***Bilabial Plosives: /p/ and /b/.*** During the articulation of /p/ and /b/ the soft palate is raised, thus shutting off the nasal passage. The lips are closed and the lung air is compressed behind this oral closure. The vocal cords are held wide apart for /p/, but in the case of articulating of /b/, the vocal cords vibrate producing voice. Therefore, /p/ is a voiceless bilabial plosive and /b/ is a voiced bilabial plosive.

***Allophonic Variations of /p/***

(i) The sound (/p/) is aspirated, i.e., released with a strong puff of breath, when it occurs initially in stressed syllables (not necessarily word-initial; it may be word-medial, but syllable-initial). In an allophonic (i.e., narrow) transcription, the symbol used to represent this allophone is /$p^h$ /.The allophone /$p^h$ / occurs in words like:

pin, paint, point, appear, appoint, please, pray, etc.

(ii) The sound /p/ is un-aspirated when it occurs in an unstressed syllable when the preceding sound is /s/, x for example:

spin, space, upper, opposite, etc.

(iii) The sound /p/ is nasally exploded (i.e., the oral closure is retained while the velum is lowered so that the air escapes through the nose instead of the mouth) immediately after articulating /m/, as in the word 'topmost'.

(iv) If /p/ occurs finally and before another plosive or affricate, it is not released audibly. Examples are:

cup, captain, ripe, apt, map, etc.

The sound /b/ is articulated exactly in the same way as /p/, except that during the articulation of /b/ the vocal cords vibrate, producing voice. Such an example can be cited in words like boy, blow, begin, banana, etc.

Compare the sound **/p/** and **/b/**:

| | |
|---|---|
| post - boast | simple - symbol |
| sopping - sobbing | cup - cub |
| pray - bray | rope - robe |

***Alveolar Plosives: /t/, /d/.*** The sound /t/—regularly spelt t, tt and sometimes th, e.g., Thames, Thomas; also -ed in verbal past tenses and participles after a voiceless consonant, other than /t/, e.g., 'jumped' and 'laughed'.

**Description.** To pronounce these two phonemes, the soft palate is raised and the nasal passage is shut off. The obstacle to the air stream is formed by a closure made between the tip and rims of the tongue and the upper alveolar ridge and side teeth. Lung air is compressed behind this closure during which stage the vocal cords are wide apart for /t/, whereas for /d/ the vocal cords may vibrate. The phoneme /t/ is, therefore, a voiceless alveolar plosive, whereas /d/ is a voiced alveolar plosive. The lip position for /t/ and /d/ is conditioned by the following vowel sound.

### *Allophonic Variants of /t/*

(i) The sound /t/ is aspirated when it occurs initially in a stressed syllable, as in the words like toy, tin, attain, time, etc.
(ii) The sound /t/ is un-aspirated when it occurs in unstressed syllables and in stressed syllables preceded by /s/, as in the words like utter, stamp, stain, daughter, etc.
(iii) The sound /t/ is exploded through the nose, if it is followed by /l/, as in the words like cattle, battle, little, etc.
(iv) The sound /t/ is released laterally when it is followed by /l/, as in the words like cattle, battle, little, etc.

### *Allophonic Variants of /d/*

(i) The sound /d/ is articulated exactly in the same way as /t/ but during its articulation the vocal words vibrate, producing voice.
(ii) The sound /d/ is partially devoiced when it occurs initially in a word like **dog**, **dear**.
(iii) The sound /d/ is exploded through the nose when it is followed by an /n/, as in the words like sudden, red nose, madness, etc.
(iv) The sound /g/ is not released audibly when it occurs in the final position followed by another plosive or affricate, for example, bagged, rugby, etc.

## Palato-alveolar Plosives: /k/ and /g/

**Compare /k/ and /g/**

| | |
|---|---|
| cap - gap | decree - degree |
| coat - goat | stacker - stagger |
| clue - glue | hackle - haggle |

***Glottal Plosive.*** In the case of the glottal plosive (stop), the obstruction to the air stream is formed by the closure of the vocal cords, thus interrupting the flow of air into the supra-glottal organs. The oral closure is affected by bringing the two vocal cords together. The air is then blocked behind the glottal closure. When the vocal cords are separated suddenly, the air pressure below the glottis is released. The glottal stop is not a distinctive sound in English. Many native speakers use the glottal stop in the speech, e.g., in expressions like 'law and order', i.e., /lɔ n ɔdə/.

### *Affricates*

**Palato-alveolar Affricates: /tʃ/ and /dʒ/**

The term **affricates** denotes any plosive whose release stage is performed in such a way that considerable friction occurs at the point where the plosive stop is made. The friction is for a short duration. The phoneme may occur in syllable-initial, syllable-final, word-medial or word-final situation.

The sound /t/ may be spelt as /tʃ/ or /t/ when /t/ is preceded by 's' or 'a', e.g., batch, nature, question, etc.

**Description:** The soft palate is raised and the nasal passage is shut off. The obstacle to the air stream is formed by a closure made between the tip, blade and the sides of the tongue and the upper alveolar ridge and the side teeth. The front of the tongue is raised towards the hard palate in readiness for the fricative release. The closure is released slowly, and the air escapes slowly over the whole central surface of the tongue. The friction occurs between the blade, front region of the tongue and the alveolar, front palatal section of the roof of the mouth. The vocal cords are wide apart during the articulation of /tʃ/, but may be vibrating for all or part of /d¥/ according to the situation in the utterance. The phoneme /tʃ/ is, therefore, a voiceless Palato-alveolar affricate. The sound /dj/ is a voiced Palato-alveolar affricate.

During the articulation of these affricates /tʃ/ and /d¥/, there is a certain amount of lip protrusion, irrespective of the lip-position required for the articulation of the immediately following vowel. The protrusion will be more if /tʃ/ and /**dj**/ are followed by back-rounded vowels, as in the words like **choose, June**.

***Bilabial Nasal: /m/***

**Description:**

During the articulation of /m/, the lips form a closure as for /p/ and /b/. They make a firm contact with each other, thereby shutting off the oral passage of air. The soft palate is lowered, allowing the air to escape freely through the nasal cavity. The vocal cords vibrate, producing voice. In fact, all the three nasal consonants are voiced. The phoneme **/m/** is thus a voiced bilabial nasal.

***Allophonic Variants***

(i) The sound /m/ is labio-dental when it is immediately followed by /f/ and /v/, as in the words like comfort, triumph, etc.

(ii) The sound /m/ is partially devoiced when preceded by /s/, e.g., smoke, smell, etc.

(iii) The sound /m/ may be syllabic in words like **rhythm, prism,** etc., that is, the second syllable may not have the neutral vowel /ə/.

**Description:**

***Alveolar Nasal /n/.*** During the articulation of /n/, the tongue forms a closure with the teeth ridge and upper side teeth as for /t/ and /d/. The soft palate is lowered and the nasal passage is open, allowing the air to pass through the nostrils and adding a nasal resonance to the sound produced.

The lip position will depend upon that of the adjacent vowels. The vocal cords vibrate, producing voice. Therefore, /n/ is described as a voiced alveolar nasal.

***Allophonic Variants***

(i) The sound /n/ is dental when it is followed by dental sounds like /θ/ and /ð/, as in the words like **tenth** and in there.

(ii) The sound /n/ is partially devoiced:

(a) when it is preceded by /s/, e.g., **'snail'**.

(b) when it is preceded by /t/, e.g., **'cotton'**.

(iii) The sound /n/ is syllabic in words like **button, cotton, sudden**, etc.

***Velar Nasal: /ŋ/***

**Description:**

During the articulation of /ŋ/, a closure is formed in the mouth between the back of the tongue and the velum or soft palate, as in /k/ and /g/. The soft palate is lowered, thereby opening the nasal cavity. The lung air escapes freely through the nostrils. The vocal cords vibrate, producing voice. Therefore, /ŋ/ is a voiced velar nasal.

***Allophonic Variants.*** There are no allophonic variants of /ŋ/ except for the lip position required for the preceding vowel, e.g., spread lip in the word 'sing' and relatively open lip, as in the word 'song'. The phoneme /ŋ/ is naturally voiced and is regularly spelt with the letters '**ng**' or '**n**', e.g., sing, tongue, sink, uncle, anxious, etc.

| **Compare:** | /m/ | /n/ | /ŋ/ |
|---|---|---|---|
| | ram | ran | rang |
| | whim | win | wing |
| | dumb | done | dung |

***Fricatives.*** Fricatives are articulated with two organs brought and held sufficiently close together, so that the air stream while escaping produces strong friction. Fricatives, therefore, like stops and affricates, are marked by a noise component. The vocal cords may or may not vibrate. Fricatives may be labio-dental, dental alveolar, Palato-alveolar or glottal according to their places of articulation.

***Labio-dental Fricatives: /f/ and /v/***

**Description:**

The soft palate is raised and the nasal cavity is shut off. The inner surface of the lower lip makes a light contact with the edge of the upper teeth, so that the air while escaping produces friction. For /f/, vocal cords are wide apart so that the air escapes freely. The vocal cords do not vibrate. Therefore, /f/ is a voiceless sound. For /v/, the vocal cords are brought together causing friction. Therefore, /f/ is a voiceless labio-dental fricative, and /v/ is a voiced labio-dental fricative. The phoneme /f/ is normally spelt with the letters: 'f' = fork; 'ff' = off; 'ph' = physics; 'gh' = enough. The phoneme /v/ is normally spelt with letters: 'v' = voice; 'f' = of; 'ph' = nephew.

***Allophonic Variants.*** No important allophonic variants of /f/ occur except those involving lip rounding. The phoneme /v/ is partially voiced when it occurs initially and finally in a word, e.g., '**vine**', '**leave**'.

| **Compare:** /f/ | **and** | /v/ | /f/ | **and** | /v/ |
|---|---|---|---|---|---|
| fine | | vine | surface | | service |
| fat | | vat | camphor | | canvas |
| few | | view | leaf | | leave |

***Dental Fricatives: /θ/ and /ð/***

**Description:**

The soft palate is raised and the nasal resonator shut off. The tip and rims of the tongue make a light contact with the edge and inner surface of the upper front teeth. The air escapes through the narrow gap between the tip of the tongue and upper front teeth causing friction. For /**ð**/, the vocal cords are wide apart and so the friction is voiceless, whereas for /**ð**/ there may be some vibration of the vocal cords producing voice. Therefore, /θ/ is a voiceless dental fricative and /ð/ is a voiced dental fricative. Both are usually spelt with the letters '**th**'.

***Allophonic Variants*** There is no allophonic variant for /θ/, so it can be said to have one allophonic /θ/ which exists in all the words in which /θ/ occurs, while /ð/, on the other hand, is partially voiced when it occurs initially and finally in a word, as in 'then', 'soothe', etc.

| **Compare:** /θ/ /ð/ | |
|---|---|
| thigh - thy | mouth (n) - mouth (v) |
| earthy - worthy | wreath - wreathe |

### *Alveolar Fricatives: /s/ and /z/*

**Description:**

During the articulation of /s/ and /z/ the soft palate is raised and the nasal passage is shut off. The tip and blade of the tongue make a light contact with the upper alveolar ridge, and the side rims of the tongue make a close contact with the upper side teeth. The air stream escapes through a narrow groove in the centre of the tongue causing an audible friction. For /s/, the vocal cords are kept wide apart. But for /z/, the vocal cords vibrate producing voice. Therefore, the sound /s/ is a voiceless alveolar fricative, and the sound /z/ is a voiced alveolar fricative.

***Allophonic Variants.*** There are no allophonic variants for /s/ except the ones that involve lip-rounding.

The sound /z/ is partially voiced when it occurs initially and finally in words like **zip** and **buzz**, etc. The sound /s/ is spelt with the letters **'s'** = so; **'ss'** = pass; **'c'** = niece; **'sc'** = science; **'x'** (=ks) = axe. The sound /z/ is spelt with the letters 's' = roses; 'ss' = scissors; 'z' = zoo; 'zz' = dizzy; 'x' = exact.

**Compare:** /s/ and /z/

| | | |
|---|---|---|
| seal - zeal | fussy - fuzzy | loose - lose |
| sink - zinc | peace - peas | pence - pens |

### *Palato-alveolar Fricatives: /ʃ/ and /ʒ/*

**Description:**

During the articulation of /ʃ/ and /ʒ/ the soft palate is raised and the nasal resonator is shut off. The tip and blade of the tongue are brought near the teeth ridge. At the same time, the front of the tongue is raised in the direction of the hard palate. The lung air is not forceful (as compared with that of /s/ and /z/), it escapes through the narrow gap with an audible friction. For /ʃ/, the vocal cords are wide apart and do not vibrate, whereas for /ʒ/ there may be some vibration producing voice.

The sound /ʃ/ is thus a voiceless Palato-alveolar fricative while the sound /dj/ is a voiced Palato-alveolar fricative.

The lips may be rounded for some speakers, for others, lip-rounding will depend on the adjacent vowel. For example, the lips may be rounded for shoe, but may be somewhat neutral or spread for 'she'. The sound /ʃ/ is spelt with the letters **'sh'** = sheep; **'ch'** = machine; **'sch'** = schedule; 's' or 'ss' before **'u'** = sure, assure; **'ti'** = nation; **'si'** = mansion; **'-sci'** = conscious; 'c' = ocean. The /ʒ/ sound is spelt with the letters **-si** = vision; **'s' 'z'** before 'u' and in French loanwords, e.g., measure, seizure, beige, etc.

### *Allophonic Variants*

There are no allophonic variants of /ʃ/ and /dj/ apart from the degree of palatalization or lip rounding that is used.

**Compare:** /ʃ/, /tʃ/ **and** /ʒ/, /**dj**/

| | |
|---|---|
| sheep - cheap | leisure - ledger |
| shore - chore | vision - pigeon |
| dish - ditch | |

### *Glottal Fricative: /h/*

**Description:**

The sound /h/ occurs only in syllabic initial positions. The air is expelled from the lungs with considerable pressure which causes some friction in the vocal tract. The upper part of the vocal tract is shaped in readiness for the articulation of the following vowel. When the vocal cords start vibrating for the vowel, the air pressure is reduced; /h/ is, therefore, a voiceless glottal fricative. It is spelt with the letter **'h'**, **'wh'**, as in **how, hat, who, when**.

The sound /h/ occurs medially in words like 'behave', 'perhaps'. The sound /h/ is not pronounced initially in words like 'hour', 'honest', 'heir', etc.

**Compare: /h/ + vowel /i/, /e/**

| | | |
|---|---|---|
| heat - eat; | hill - ill; | hedge - edge; |
| haul - all; | hate - eight; | hold - old; |

### *Laterals: /l/*

The English lateral phoneme /l/ is an alveolar lateral.

#### *Description*

The soft palate is raised shutting the nasal passage. The tip of the tongue is in contact with the upper teeth ridge, allowing the air to escape on both the sides. The position of the lips depends on the nature of the adjacent vowel. For example, for 'leap', 'feet', it is spread; for 'look', 'pool', etc., the lips are rounded.

It is usually silent after a vowel sound, e.g., talk, calm.

#### *Allophonic Variants*

(i) The sound /l/ is dental when it is followed by /θ/ as, for example, in 'health', 'wealth'.

(ii) The sound /l/ becomes voiceless when it is preceded by aspirated /p/ and /k/; e.g., 'please', 'clean', etc.

(iii) The sound /l/ is partially devoiced when it is preceded by an un-aspirated voiceless plosive, or by /s/, /f/, /θ/, e.g., 'simply' or 'slow'.

(iv) The sound /l/ is clear or palatalized when it is followed by a vowel or /j/. The /l/ thus produced has a front vowel resonance. Clear /l/ occurs in words like 'leave', 'lad', 'million', etc.

(v) The sound /l/ is dark or velarized [ɫ] when it is word-final or followed by a consonant. The /l/ produced has a back vowel resonance. The [ɫ] occurs in words like **'tall', 'pull', 'cold', 'milk'**, etc.

(vi) The sound /l/ is syllabic in words like 'kettle', 'bottle', etc. The /l/ is a voiced alveolar lateral consonant.

### *Post-alveolar Frictionless Continuant: /r/*

#### Description

The soft palate is raised and the nasal passage is closed. The tip of the tongue is held in a position near to, but not touching, the rear part of the upper teeth ridge. The back rims of the tongue touch the upper molars. The central part of the tongue is lowered with a general contraction of the tongue so that it is somewhat hollowed allowing the air to escape freely without any friction. The vocal cords vibrate, producing voice. The /r/ is thus articulated in a voiced post-alveolar.

#### *Frictionless Continuant*

The sound /r/ is usually spelt with the letters **'r'**, **'rr'**, e.g., **red, carry**. It is also spelt with **'wr'** = **'write'**; **'rh'** = **'rhythm'**.

## Allophonic Variants

(i) The sound /r/ becomes a voiceless post-alveolar fricative if it is preceded by an aspirated /p/, /t/ and /k/, as in the words like price, surprise, cry, try, etc.

(ii) The sound /j/ is partially devoiced when it is preceded by un-aspirated /p/, /t/ and /k/, e.g., 'stew', 'spatula'.

***Labio-velar Semi-vowel: /w/***

**Description**

During the articulation of /w/, there is a rapid glide from the position of articulating approximate /u/. The tongue assumes the position for this back half-close vowel and moves away immediately to the position of the following sound. The soft palate is raised so that the nasal cavity is shut off. The lips are rounded during the articulation of /w/. The vocal cords vibrate, producing voice. Therefore, /w/ is a voiced labio-velar semi-vowel.

This phoneme is spelt with the letters 'w', '**wh**' or '**u**' after q, g, as in **west**, **which**, **quick**, **language**, etc.

***Allophonic Variants***

(i) The sound /w/ is voiceless when it is preceded by aspirated /t/ and /k/, as in the words like **twig** and **quick**.

(ii) The sound /w/ is partially devoiced when it is preceded by any other voiceless sound, e.g., **sweet**, **square**, **and thwart**, etc.

Semi-vowels /j/ and /w/ occur only word-initially and word-medially, as in the words like **yard** and **wet**, **pure** and **twelve**. The /j/ and /w/ sounds never occur in the final position.

**Compare: /j/ and /w/**

yacht - what    your - war    yet - wet    yawn - warn

## Let Us Do and Learn

1. Read the following and write whether the following statements are **true** or **false**:
   a) While articulating English consonants like /p/, /t/, /k/, the vocal cords vibrate.
   b) The sounds /p/ and /b/ in English are two different phonemes.
   c) In English, /$p^h$/ and /f/ are two different phonemes.
   d) In English, /n/ and /ŋ/ are treated as allophones of the same phonemes. In English, /t/ and /d/ belong to two different phonemes.
   e) In English, /s/ and /ʃ/ both are fricative sounds and, therefore, the same phonemes.
   f) Both /v/ and /w/ are fricative sounds.
   g) Voiced plosives are never aspirated in English.
   h) English words [sun] and [son] constitute a minimal pair.
   i) The front of the tongue touches the hard palate during the articulation of a clear /l/.
2. Circle the plosive consonants in the following English words. Give a three-term label for each (i.e., place of articulation, manner of articulation and position of the glottis as well as position of the soft palate).
   (i) potato    (ii) calendar    (iii) gigantic
3. Give minimal pairs for each of the following sounds:
   /p/ and /b/; /m/ and /n/; /f/ and /v/

## Classification and Description of English Vowel Sounds

During the articulation of vowel sounds, the lung air escapes through the mouth without any friction. This is because, during the articulation of vowels there are no obstructions in the mouth, nor is there any narrowing in the mouth to allow friction. Vowels are therefore articulated with a stricture of open approximation, i.e., the active articulation is raised in the direction of the passive articulator (hard palate) in such a way that there is a sufficient gap between them to allow the air to escape freely and continuously, without any friction. Each of the vowel sounds of these words—bead, bad, booed—has a distinct quality and this is because of the different positions taken by the tongue during different vowel articulations. Therefore, it is necessary to classify vowels and describe them.

The **tongue** can assume a large number of positions during the articulation of vowel sounds, but the upper surface of the main body of the tongue is usually convex. This is because some parts of the tongue—the front, back or centre—is raised in the direction of the roof of the mouth so that the space between the highest point of the tongue and the roof of the mouth is wide enough for the air to escape without any friction. Study the following diagram:

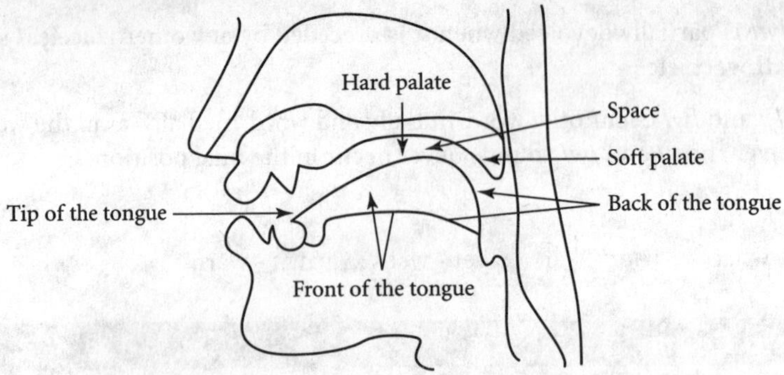


**Figure 2.1** Displaying Production of English Speech Sounds

***Front Vowels.*** Front vowels are those during the articulation of which the front of the tongue is raised in the direction of the hard palate. For example, words like **bee, bid, bed, bad,** are some front vowels.

***Back Vowels.*** Back vowels are those during the articulation of which the back of the tongue is raised in the direction of the soft palate in such a way that there is a sufficiently wide gap between them for the air to escape without friction. The vowel sound in the English words **cart, cot, caught, push** and **pool** are back vowels.

Vowels can be classified into three categories, namely **front, back** and **central**. For convenience, the tongue position is indicated in the diagrammatic table of the next page.

## Let Us Do and Learn

1. Make a list of the front vowels available in English. Use IPA symbols only.
2. Make a list of the central vowels available in English. Use IPA symbols only.
3. Make a list of the back vowels available in English. Use IPA symbols only.
4. Make a list of all the vowels available in your regional language or mother tongue. Use IPA symbols only.
5. Make a list of the semi-vowels available in English. Use IPA symbols only.
6. Make a contrastive analysis between English vowels and the vowels of your regional language/ mother tongue.

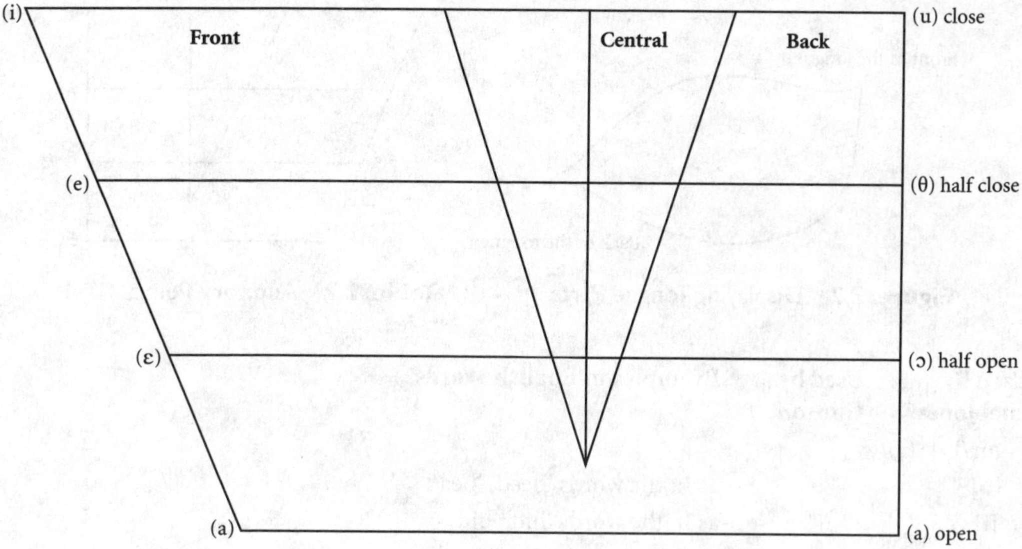


**Table: 2.6** The Vowel Diagram (Cardinal Vowels)

One of the methods of identifying vowel segments is provided by the system of Cardinal Vowels (CV). A cardinal vowel is a fixed and unchanging reference point. A number of such reference points constitute a system of CV, and any vowel sound in any language can be identified by being 'placed' within the system.

There are eight main cardinal vowels. They are arbitrarily selected, i.e., they are not based on the vowels of any existing language. The system is a general phonetic one.

There are limits in the mouth within which the highest point, whatever the vowel may be, must always lie. The space inside these limits is the vowel area of the mouth, bounded by its periphery on which lies the highest point of the tongue at its farthest extreme, in any direction, from the centre of the mouth. They provide points of reference as convenient as possible. The eight CVs selected to form Daniel Jone's system are all vowels pronounced with the highest point of the tongue lying on the periphery, as they are also called 'peripheral vowels'.

The extreme points on the periphery are /i/ and /a/. The remaining CVs hinge on these two vowels.

## Let Us Do and Learn

1. Think about the vowels of your mother tongue and make a contrastive analysis. Show your project work to your teacher.
2. Think about the consonants of your mother tongue and make a contrastive analysis. Show your project work to your teacher.

The total human range of vowel quality forms a continuous chain. Each vowel has been given a number. The eight CVs are eight equally-spaced auditory points.

***English Vowels.*** In RP (educated Southern British English), there are twenty distinctive vowel sounds, made up of twelve pure vowels (monophthongs) and eight vowel glides (diphthongs), represented by the following symbols:

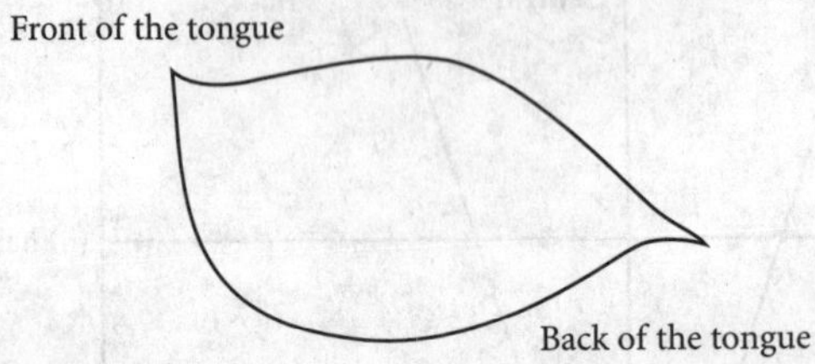


**Figure: 2.2** Displaying Tongue Parts

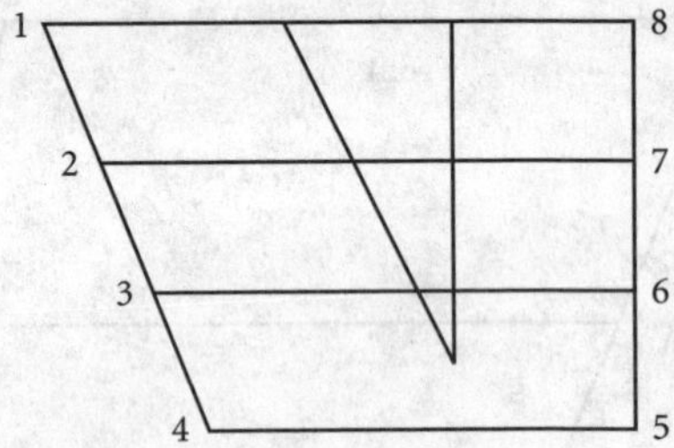


**Table: 2.7** Auditory Points

| Used by Daniel Jones | Used by Gimson | Examples in English Words |
|---|---|---|
| [e:] fur/Fe:(r)/ | | |
| [i:] | /i/ | as in the words 'heed', 'bead' |
| [i] | /I/ | as in the words 'hid', 'bid' |
| [e] | /e/ | as in the words 'head', 'bed' |
| [æ] | /æ/ | as in the words 'had', 'bad' |
| [a:] | /a/ | as in the words 'hard,' 'bard' |
| [Ɔ] | /ɔ/ | as in the words 'hot', 'bog' |
| [u:] | /u/ | as in the words 'who'd', 'booed' |
| [u] | /ʊ/ | as in the words 'hood', 'put' |
| [Λ] | /Λ/ | as in the words 'hut', 'but' |
| [e:] | /e:/ | as in the words 'heard', 'bird' |
| [e] | /e/ | as in the words '**a**bout', '**a**bove' |
| [ei] | /eI/ | as in the words 'hay," bay' |
| [ai] | /aI/ | as in the words 'hide', 'bide' |
| [ƆI] | /oI/ | as in the words 'boy," toy' |
| [eu] | /eʊ/ | as in the words 'go', 'flow' |
| /aU/ | /au/ | as in the words 'bow', 'how' |
| [iə/] | /Iə/ | as in the words 'here', 'peer' |
| [/uə/] | /ʊə/ | as in the words 'sure', 'poor' |
| [/ɛə/] | /ɛə/ | as in the words 'bare', care' |

***English Vowels.*** Five of the twelve pure vowels in English are comparatively long and the remaining seven are comparatively short. Apart from this, each vowel has a different degree of length. In accented syllables, the so-called long vowels are fully long when they are final or in a syllable closed by a voiced consonant, but they are considerably shortened when they occur in a syllable closed by a voiceless consonant. Therefore, the length of the vowel depends upon the phonetic environment in which it occurs.

For example: The sound /i/ in **beat** is only about half as long as /i/ of **bee** or **bead**.

Pure Vowels: There are twelve pure vowels in English speech sounds.

Front Vowels: Four of the twelve pure English vowels are front vowels and their tongue positions are indicated in the following chart:

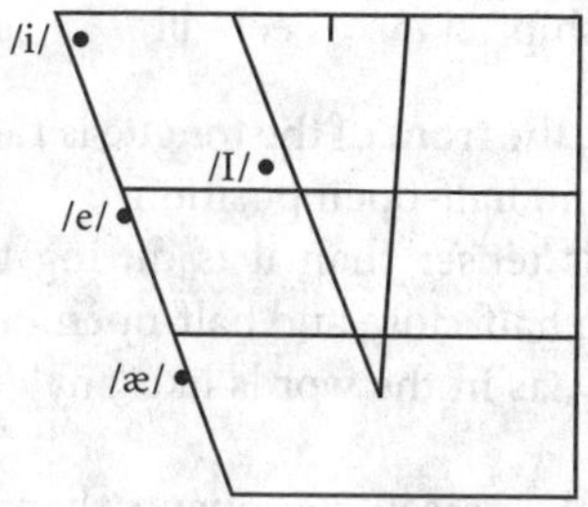


Vowel sound /i/, as in beat
Vowel sound /I/, as in bit
Vowel sound /e/, as in bet
Vowel sound s/æ/, as in bat

**Table: 2.8** Displaying Front Vowels

***English Vowels.*** Let us describe all the English vowel speech sounds in some detail.

1. **Vowel /i/**: During the articulation of this vowel, the front of the tongue is raised in the direction of the hard palate to a position almost 'near close' position.

   The tongue is tense and the lips are spread. It can be described as a front close un-rounded vowel. This vowel can occur initially medially and finally in words, as in **eat**, **beat** and **bee** respectively.

   Vowel /i/ is longer when it occurs finally in a word and before voiced consonants than it is before voiceless consonants, e.g., the /i/ in 'bee' and 'bead' is longer than the /i/ in 'beat'.

   **Spellings: Letters** 'ee', as in the words like tree, cheese and canteen
   **Letter** 'e', as in the words like complete, be, these
   **Letters** 'ea', as in the words like leaf, reason, sea
   **Letters** 'ie', as in the words like piece, field, seize
   **Letters** 'ei' & 'ey', as in the words like seize, key, receive
   **Letter** 'i', as in the words like machine, police, prestige, suite
   **Longer in:** Words like see, seed, seen, fee, feed, fees
   **Reduced in:** Words like seat, feet, piece, lease, beef, reach

2. **Vowel /I/**: During the articulation of the vowel, the rear part of the front of the tongue (that is a part of the tongue that is nearer to the centre than to the front) is raised in the direction of the hard palate, just above the half-close position.

   The tongue is comparatively lax. The lips are loosely spread.

   Vowel /I/ can be described as a centralized front un-rounded vowel just above the half-close position. The vowel can occur initially, medially and finally, as in the words like 'it', 'bit' and 'city'.

   **Spellings: Letter** 'i', as in the words like **s**it, **r**ich, **w**ith, **f**ifth
   **Letter** 'e', as in the words like pretty, needed, wicket, wicked, **e**xcept, careless, houses
   **Letter** 'y', as in the words like city, rhythm, symbol
   **Letters** 'ie', as in the words like ladies, cities
   **Letter** 'a', as in the words like private, village

   Let us use the correct pronunciation and learn:
   Sunday, bu**s**iness, women, England

**Compare: /I/ and /i/**

| | | |
|---|---|---|
| feel - fill | least - list | weak - wick |
| seen - sin | reach - rich | feet - fit |
| bead - bid | sheep - ship | eel - ill |

3. **Vowel /e/**: During the articulation of this vowel, the front of the tongue is raised in the direction of the hard palate to a height between half-close and half-open position.

The lips are loosely spread. The tongue is tenser than it is during the articulation of /I/. Therefore, /e/ is a front-founded vowel between half-close and half-open.

The vowel /e/ occurs initially and medially, as in the words like 'any', 'bed'. It does not occur finally in a word.

Vowel /e/ is slightly longer when followed by voiced consonants than it is when followed by voiceless consonants.

Thus, /e/ in 'bed' and 'led' is longer than it is in 'bet', 'let', etc.

**Spellings: Letter** 'e', as in the words like **set, bed, went**
**Letters** 'ea', as in the words like **dead, head, breath**
**Letter** 'a', as in the words like **many, Thames says**
**Letters** '**ai**', as in the word like **said**
**Letter** 'u', as in the word like **bury**
**Letters** 'eo', as in the word like **Geoffrey**
**Letters** 'ei', as in the word like **Leicester**
**Letters** 'ie', as in the word like **friend**

**Compare: /I/ and /e/**

| | | |
|---|---|---|
| sit - set | disc - desk | rid - red |
| tin - ten | knit - net | fill - fell |
| will - well | rich - wretch | hill - hell |

4. **Vowel /æ/**: During the articulation of this vowel, the front of the tongue is raised in the direction of the hard palate just below the half-open position.

The lips are neutrally open.

The vowel /æ/ is, therefore, a front un-rounded vowel just below the half-open position.

Vowel /æ/ occurs initially, as in the word 'axe' and medially, as in the word 'bat'. But, it does not occur finally in a word.

Vowel /æ/ is reduced when followed by voiceless consonants, e.g., 'bat', 'mat', but /æ/ is longer in 'bad', 'mad'.

**Spellings: Letter** 'a', as in the words **sat, hand, lamp, rash, marry**, etc.
**Letters** 'ai', as in the words **plait, plaid**

Let us use the correct pronunciation and learn:
shall, pall, mall, balcony, scalp, cap, cab, bad, bat, badge, batch, back

**Compare: /e/ and /æ/**

| | | |
|---|---|---|
| pet - pat | ten - tan | bed - bad |
| peck - pack | lend - land | beg - bag |
| said - sad | merry - marry | mess - mass |

**Back Vowels:**

Five of the twelve pure vowels of English are back vowels. Their tongue positions are indicated in the chart given below:

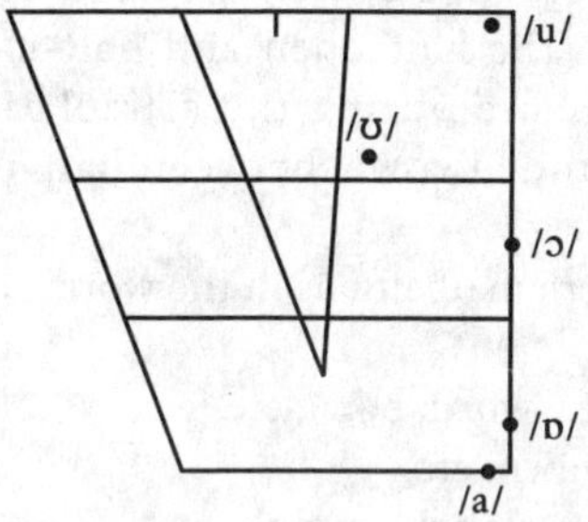


The vowel sound/u/, as in the word 'pool'
The vowel sound /ʊ/, as in the words 'pull' and 'caught'
The vowel sound /ɐ/, as in the word 'cot'
The vowel sound /a/, as in the word 'cart'

**Table: 2.9** Displaying Back Vowels

5. **Vowel /u/**: During the articulation of this pure vowel which is a long vowel /u/, the back of the tongue is raised in the direction of the soft palate to a height very near the close position. The tongue is tense. The lips are closely rounded.
The sound /u/ is, therefore, a back close rounded vowel.
The sound /u/ occurs:
initially, as in the word 'ooze';
medially, as in the word 'boot'; and
finally, as in the word 'two'.
The sound /u/ is longer before voiced sounds, e.g., in the words like 'shoe', 'rude'; rather than in the words like 'shoot', 'root'.
**Spellings: Letters** 'oo', as in the words like food, moon and spoon
**Letter** 'o', as in the words like do, who, move and lose
**Letters** 'ou', as in the words like group, soup, wounds (n) and through
**Letter** 'u', as in the words like rude, June and Susan
**Letters** 'ew', 'ue', 'ui', 'oe', as in the words like chew, blue, juice and shoe

**Compare: /u/ and /æ/**

| | | |
|---|---|---|
| pool - pal | soup - sap | whom - ham |
| root - rat | moon - man | boot - bat |

6. **Vowel /ʊ/:** During the articulation of this short vowel, the front part of the back of the tongue is raised in the direction of the soft palate to the height just above the half-close position. The tongue is lax. Lips are rounded.
Vowel /ʊ/ is, therefore, a back rounded vowel just above the half-close position.
Vowel /ʊ/ does not occur in the initial position in the words. It occurs medially in words like 'put', 'sugar' and finally in a word like 'to', only in the unaccented form.
**Spellings: Letter** 'u', as in the words like p**u**t, f**u**ll, s**u**gar, c**u**shion, b**u**tcher
**Letter** 'o', as in the words like w**o**lf, w**o**man, b**o**som
**Letters** 'oo', as in the words like g**oo**d, b**oo**k, w**oo**l, w**oo**d
**Letters** 'ou', as in the words like c**ou**ld, sh**ou**ld, w**ou**ld, c**ou**rier

**Compare: /ʊ/ and /u/**

| | |
|---|---|
| full - fool | pull - pool |
| would - wooed | hood - who'd |

7. **Vowel /ɔ/:** During the articulation of this relatively long vowel, the back of the tongue is raised in the direction of the soft palate between the half-open and half-close positions. The lips are rounded but less rounded than they are during the articulation of /ʊ/ and /u/. Therefore, /ɔ/ can be described as a back rounded vowel between half-open and half-closed position.

   Vowel /ɔ/ can occur initially, as in the word 'order'; medially, as in the word 'cord' and finally, as in the word 'law'.

**Spellings: Letters** 'or', as in the words like c**or**d, h**or**se, sw**or**d, b**or**n, etc.

**Letters** 'aw', as in the words like s**aw**, l**aw**n, j**aw**, y**aw**n, etc.

**Letters** 'ou', 'au', as in the words like b**ou**ght, **ou**ght, d**au**ghter, f**au**lt, etc.

**Letter** 'a', as in the words like **a**ll, t**a**lk, s**a**lt, w**a**ter, w**a**r, etc.

**Letters** 'ore', 'oor', 'oar', 'our', as in the words like bef**ore**, m**ore**, d**oor**, fl**oor**, **oar**, b**oar**d, c**our**t, etc.

**Compare: /ɔ/ and /e/**

| | | |
|---|---|---|
| port - pet | hoard - head | fawned - fend |
| board - bed | wart - wet | dawn - den |

8. **Vowel /ɑ/:** During the articulation of this vowel, the back of the tongue is just above the fully open position. The jaws are wide open and the lips are slightly rounded. The vowel **/ɑ/** is, therefore, a back rounded vowel just above the open position.

   Vowel /ɑ/ occurs initially in words like 'ox' and medially in words like 'box'. But it does not occur in the final position.

   Vowel /ɑ/ in 'cod' is slightly longer being followed by a voiced consonant than in the word 'cot' which is followed by a voiceless consonant.

**Spellings: Letter** 'o', as in the words like d**o**ck, d**o**g, h**o**liday, s**o**rry, g**o**ne, etc.

**Letter** 'a', as in the words like w**a**s, wh**a**t, sw**a**n, w**a**nt, w**a**tch

**Letters** 'ou' & 'ow', as in the words like c**ou**gh, tr**ou**gh, kn**ow**ledge, Gl**ou**cester

**Letters** 'au', as in the words like bec**au**se, l**au**rel, **Au**stria, **Au**stralia, c**au**liflower, etc.

**Letters** 'ach', as in the word y**ach**t

**Compare: /ɑ/ and /ɔ/**

| | |
|---|---|
| cod - cord | fond - fawned |
| cock - cork | what - wart |
| cot - court | don - dawn |

9. **Vowel /a/:** During the articulation of this long vowel, a part of the tongue that is between the centre and the back is in a fully open position. The jaws are wide open and the lips are neutrally open. The vowel /a/ is, therefore, a back open un-rounded vowel.

   There is a difference in length according to whether it occurs in a syllable ending with a voiced consonant where it is longer, whereas the effect seems to be shorter when the syllable ending is a voiceless consonant. But the difference is not as marked as for other long vowels. The vowel /a/ can occur initially in a word, as in the word 'art'; medially, as in the word 'card'; and finally, as in the word 'car'.

**Spellings: Letter** 'a', as in the words like chance, pass, **after**, **bath**, **tomato**, **father**, **branch**, etc.
**Letters** 'ar', as in the words like **part**, **car**, **march**, **bar**, **farm**, etc.
**Letters** 'ear', as in the words like **heart**, **hearth**, etc.
**Letters** 'er', as in the words like **clerk**, **sergeant**, **Derby**, etc.
**Letters** 'au', as in the words like **aunt**, **caught**, etc.

**Compare: /a/ and /ɒ/; /æ/ and /a/**

| | |
|---|---|
| cart - cute; | lack - lark |
| part - put (v); | back - bark |
| card - could; | ham - harm |

**Central Vowels:**

The following vowel chart will show the tongue positions of the three central or centralized vowels in English RP.
Vowel /Λ/, as in cup; vowel /3/, as in bird; and vowel /ə/, as in the unaccented syllables, e.g., in **submit**, **banana**.

10. **Vowel /Λ/:** During the articulation of this short centralized vowel, the centre of the tongue is raised in the direction of that part of the roof of the mouth that is between the hard and soft palates to a height just above the fully open position. No contact is made between the tongue and the upper molars. The jaws are wide and the lips are neutrally open. The sound /Λ/ can, therefore, be described as a centralized un-rounded vowel just above the fully open position.

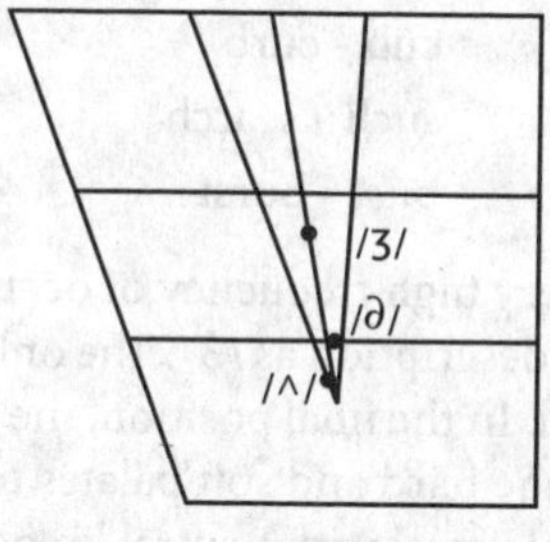


**Table: 2.10** Displaying Central Vowels

Vowel /Λ/ occurs initially, as in the word 'up' and medially, as in the word 'cup'.
But it does not occur finally in a word.
Vowel /Λ/ is slightly longer in a word before voiced consonants than before voiceless consonants.

**Spellings: Letter** 'u', as in the words like **sun**, **cut**, **dull**, etc.
**Letter** 'o', as in the words like **so**, son, **come**, **among**, **one**, **done**, **month**, **column**, **monkey**, **nothing**, **Monday**, onion, **London**, etc.
**Letters** 'ou', as in the words like **country**, **southern**, **couple**, **enough**, **young**, etc.

**Letters** 'oo', as in the words like b**loo**d, fl**oo**d, etc.
**Letters** 'oe', as in the word like d**oe**s

**Compare: /a/ and /ʌ/;** **/ɔ/ and /ʌ/**

| /a/ and /ʌ/ | /ɔ/ and /ʌ/ |
|---|---|
| cart - cut; | cot - cut |
| barn - bun; | fond - fun |
| march - much; | wander - wonder |

11. **Vowel /3/**: During the articulation of this considerably long vowel, the centre of the tongue is raised in the direction of that part of the roof of the mouth that is between the hard and soft palates to a height between half-close and half-open position. No firm contact is made between the tongue and upper molars. The lips are neutrally spread.
Vowel /3/ is, therefore, a central un-rounded vowel between half-close and half-open position.
Vowel /3/ can occur initially, as in the word 'earn'.
It can occur medially, as in the word 'learn' and finally as in the word 'err'.
Vowel /3/ in the word 'heard' (which is followed by a voiced consonant) is longer than it is in the word 'hurt'.
**Spellings: Letters 'ir', 'yr'**, as in the words like **bir**d, **fir**st, **myr**tle, etc.
**Letters 'er', 'err', 'ear'**, as in the words like h**er**, s**er**ve, **err**, **ear**th, h**ear**d, etc.
**Letters 'urr' & 'ur'**, as in the words like t**ur**n, ch**ur**ch, n**ur**se, p**urr**, etc.
**Letters 'or'**, as in the words like **wor**d, **wor**ld, **wor**k, **wor**se, etc.
**Letters 'our'**, as in the words like j**our**ney, c**our**tesy, sc**our**ge
**Letters 'ur'**, as in the words like f**ur**, b**ur**n, **ur**ge

**Compare: /ʊ/ and /3/ /ʌ/ and /3/**

| /ʊ/ and /3/ | /ʌ/ and /3/ | |
|---|---|---|
| wool - whirl; | bud - bird | fun - turn |
| pull - pearl; | cub - curb | |
| full - furl; | such - search | |
| hood - heard; | bust - burst | |

12. **Vowel /ə/**: This non-final /ə/ has a very high frequency of occurrence in unstressed (unaccented) syllables. It has the same articulatory description as /3/. The only difference between /ə/ and /3/ in the non-final position is one of length. In the final position, the centre of the tongue is raised in the direction of the mid-point between the hard and soft palates to a height just below the half-open position. Its quality is that of a central vowel with neutral lip position.
Vowel /ə/ is, therefore, a central un-rounded vowel just below the half-open position.
Vowel /ə/ is the most frequently occurring vowel in the English RP. It can occur initially in a word, as in the word 'about'. It can occur medially, as in the word 'forget' and finally, as in the word 'tailor'.
The sound /ə/ occurs commonly in the weak forms of many words, e.g., a, an, the, to, her, for, etc. The sound /ə/ does not occur in accented/stressed syllables.

**Spellings:** **Letter 'i'** - possible; **Letter 'a'** - woman;
**Letter 'e'** - gentlemen; **Letter 'o'** - oblige;
**Letters 'u'** - suppose; **Letters 'ure'** - figure;
**Letters 'er'** - mother; **Letters 'ar'** - particular;
**Letters 'ou'** - famous; **Letters 'or'** - doctor;
**Letters 'our'** - colour

## Diphthongs or Vowel Glides

There are eight vowel glides or diphthongs in the English RP. These are vowel sequences within one syllable. They may be said to have a first element (the starting point) and a second element (the point in the direction of which the glide is made). The RP diphthongs have as their first element sounds like /I/, /e/, /a/ and for their second element /I/, /ʊ/, /e/.

***Diphthongs—Gliding Towards /I/*** There are three diphthongs gliding towards /I/. The tongue positions of these diphthongs are shown in the Table: 2.11.

The dot represents the starting point and the arrow indicates the direction in which the glide moves.

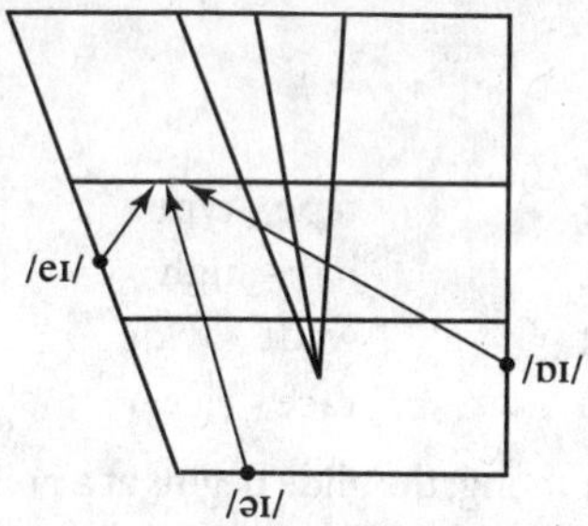


**Diphthong** /eI/, as used in the word 'they'.
**Diphthong** /aI/, as used in the word 'my'.
**Diphthong** /oI/, as used in the word 'boy'.

**Table: 2.11** Displaying Diphthongs—Gliding Towards /I/

1. **Diphthong /eI/** - During the articulation of this diphthong, the glide begins from a point slightly below the half-close front position and moves in the direction of RP /I/. The lips are spread. Therefore, the diphthong may be described as a glide from a front un-rounded vowel just below the half-close position to a centralized front un-rounded vowel just above the half-close position.

   Diphthong /eI/ can occur initially, as in the word 'aim'. It can occur medially, as in the word 'pain' and finally, as in the word 'play'.

   Diphthongs are considerably longer in case of word-final position and also when it is followed by voiced consonants. When a diphthong is long, it is the first element that is lengthened. The second element of the diphthong is very short. Such diphthongs are called 'falling diphthongs'. For example, the diphthong /eI/ in 'play' (word final) and 'plays' (which is followed by a voiced consonant) is longer than it is in the word 'place' (which is followed by a voiceless consonant).

   **Spellings:** **'a'** - **ape, late, lady, waste, base, etc.**
   **'ai', 'ay'** - **day, may, waist, rail, aim, etc.**
   **'ei', 'ey'** - **eight, veil, weigh, rein, they, etc.**
   **'ea'** - **great, break, steak, etc.**

   **Compare:** /e/ and /eI/

   | | |
   |---|---|
   | get - gate | lead - laid |
   | pen - pain | chest - chased |
   | less - lace | fell - fail |
   | red - raid | sent - saint |

2. **Diphthong /aI/** - During the articulation of this diphthong, the glide is slightly behind the front open position and moves in the direction of RP /I/. The lips are neutral and then they

become loosely spread. The jaw is wide open at the beginning and becomes narrow at the second element.

Thus, /aI/ may be described as a glide from a front open un-rounded vowel to a centralized vowel just above the half-close position.

Diphthong /aI/ can occur initially, as in the word 'ice'. It can occur medially, as in the word 'bite' and finally, as in the word 'buy'.

Diphthong /aI/ is longer in words like 'buy', 'bide' as it is followed by a voiced consonant.

**Spellings:** **'i', 'y'** - time, write, bite, climb, cry, dry, etc.
**'igh', 'eigh'** - **h**igh, **l**igh**t**, **f**igh**t**, **m**igh**t**, **h**eigh**t**, etc.
**'ie', 'ye'** - **d**ie, **l**ie, **t**ried, **d**ye, **t**ie, etc.
**'ei', 'ai'** - **ei**ther, **ei**der, **ai**sle, etc.
**'eye'** - **eyes**

**Compare:** /eI/ and /aI/

| | | |
|---|---|---|
| May - my | layer - lair | tape - type |
| mail - mile | late - light | hay - high |
| waves - wives | fate - fight | wade - wide |
| tame - time | raise - rise | race - rice |

3. **Diphthong /oI/** - During the articulation of this diphthong, the glide begins at a point between the back half-open and open positions and moves in the direction of /I/. The jaw is slightly wide in the beginning and loosely spread towards the end. The lips are open rounded for the first element, changing to neutral for the second element. Therefore, /oI/ may be described as a glide from a back rounded vowel between open and half-open to a centralized front un-rounded vowel just above the half-close position.

Diphthong /oI/ can occur initially in a word, as in the word 'oil'. It can occur medially, as in the word 'boil' and finally, as in the word 'boy'.

Diphthong /oI/ is longer in words like 'boy', 'coin', 'voice'.

**Spellings: 'oi', 'oy'** - boy, toy, noise, voice, boil, point, buoy, soil, coil, void, choice, etc.

**Compare:** /aI/ and /oI/

| | | |
|---|---|---|
| file - foil | tie - toy | line - loin |
| tile - toil | buy - boy | liar - lawyer |
| kine - coin | isle - oil | imply - employ |

### *Diphthongs—Gliding Towards /ʊ/*

There are two diphthongs gliding towards RP /ʊ/. The tongue positions of these are shown in the vowel chart Table: 2.12.

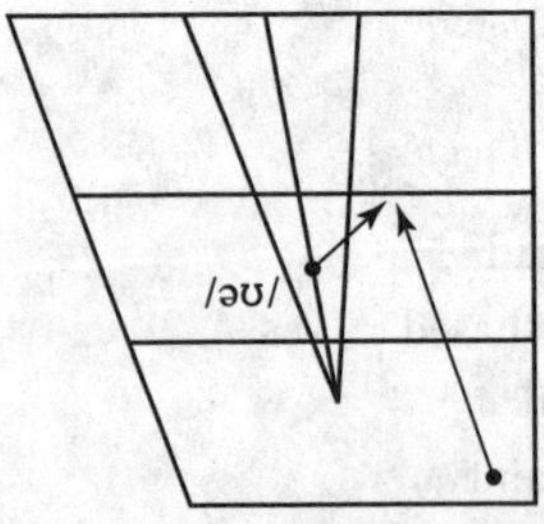


**Diphthong** /oʊ/ as used in the word 'old'.
**Diphthong** /aʊ/ as used in the word 'sound'.

**Table: 2.12** Displaying Diphthongs—Gliding Towards /ʊ/

4. **Diphthong /ɒʊ/** - Here, the glide begins at a central position, between half-close and half-open position and moves in the direction of RP /ʊ/. The lips are neutral in the beginning, and are rounded during the articulation of the second element. There is a slight closing movement of the lower jaw. The starting point may have a tongue position similar to that described for /au/. The diphthong /ɐʊ/, therefore, can be described as a glide from a central un-rounded vowel between half-close and half-open, to a centralized back rounded vowel just above the half-close position.

   Diphthong /ɒʊ/ can occur initially, as in the word 'over'. It can occur medially, as in the word 'boat' and finally, as in the word 'go'.

   It is longer in the word-final position, as in the word 'no' and in words where it is followed by a voiced consonant, as in the word 'nose'.

**Spellings:** **'o'** - so, old, home, both, folk, etc.
**'oa'** - oak, road, foal, toast, soap, etc.
**'oe'** - toe, doe, sloe, foe, hoe, etc.
**'ou', 'ow'** - soul, though, shoulder, know, blow, etc.
(Other words: mauve, broach, beau, sew, show, don't, won't, etc.)

**Compare:** /ɔ/ and /ɒʊ/

| | | |
|---|---|---|
| saw - so | born - bone | walk - woke |
| hall - hole | torn - tone | nor - no |
| call - coal | bought - boat | more - mow |
| law - low | pause - pose | raw - row |

5. **Diphthong /aʊ/** - During the articulation of this diphthong, the glide begins at a point between the back open un-rounded positions and moves in the direction of RP /ʊ/. The lips are neutral in the beginning and weakly rounded towards the end.

   Diphthong /aʊ/ occurs initially in words, as in the word 'out'. It can occur medially, as in the word 'bout' and finally in a word, as in the word 'cow'.

   Like all vowels/diphthongs, it is longer when it occurs in a word-final position and before voiced consonants, for example, in words like how, loud, town, cows, etc.

**Spellings: 'ou', 'ow'** - house, sound, out, cow, etc.

**Compare:** /ʌ/ and /aʊ/

| | | |
|---|---|---|
| fund - found | done - down | |
| bud - bowed | none - noun | |
| hull - howl | guns - gowns | buzz - bows |

The diphthongal glides of RP, namely /el/, /al/, /ol/, /ɐʊ/, and /aʊ/, are **falling** (i.e., with length and stress on the first element) and **closing** (i.e., gliding from a more open to a closer position).

### *Diphthongs—Gliding Towards /ə/:*

These are called 'centreing Diphthongs'. There are three such diphthongs in English RP. The tongue positions of these diphthongs are shown in the vowel chart Table: 2.13.

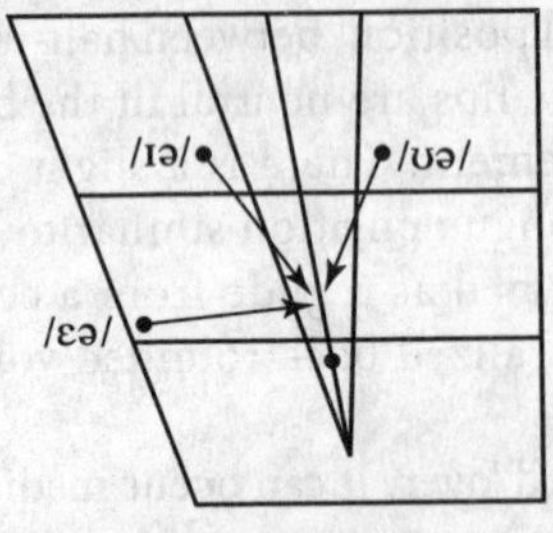


Diphthong /Iə/, as used in the word 'cheer'.
Diphthong /ɛə/, as used in the word 'chair'.
Diphthong /ʊə/, as used in the word 'poor'.

**Table: 2.13** Displaying Diphthongs—Gliding Towards /ə/

6. **Diphthong /Iə/** - During the articulation of this diphthong, the glide begins with a tongue position approximately similar to that of RP /I/ and moves in the direction of the more open variety of /ə/ when /Iə/ is final in the word. In the non-final position, e.g., **fierce**, **bread**, the glide may not be so extensive. The lips are neutral throughout, with a slight movement from spread to open. Therefore, /Iə/ may be described as a glide from the centralized front un-rounded vowel just above half-close to a central un-rounded vowel just below half-open.

   Diphthong /Iə/ can occur initially, as in the word 'ear-ring'. It can occur medially, as in the word 'fierce' and finally, as in the word 'fear'.

   Diphthong /Iə/ is longer in words like fear, fears, etc., before voiced consonants. In unaccented syllables, the first element becomes weaker, e.g., 'period', 'serious'.

   Such diphthongs with a strong second element are called 'rising diphthongs' and where the first element is stronger, they are called 'falling diphthongs'.

   **Spellings:** **'eer', 'ear', 'ere'** - deer, tear, dear, here, year
   **'eir', 'ier', 'ir'** - weird, fierce, fakir, pierce
   **'ea', 'ia', 'eu', 'eo'** - idea, Ian, museum, theological
   **'e'** - hero
   **'ea'** - real, beard
   **'eer'** - cheer

   **Compare:** /I/ and /Iə/

   | | | |
   |---|---|---|
   | rill- real | bid- beard | pin - peon |
   | quiz - queers | his - hears | is - ears |
   | lid - leered | rid - reared | |

7. **Diphthong /ɛə/** - The glide of this diphthong begins in the half-open front position and moves in the direction of the more open variety of /ə/, especially when the diphthong is final. When /ɛə/ occurs in a syllable closed by a consonant, the /ə/ element tends to be a mild /ə/ type. The lips are neutral throughout.

   **Diphthong** /ɛə/ is, therefore, a glide from a front half-open un-rounded vowel to a central un-rounded vowel between half-open and half-close, if the diphthong is non-final.

   If the diphthong /ɛə/ is final, the second element is a central un-rounded vowel just below the half-open position.

   Diphthong /ɛə/ can occur initially in a word, as in the word 'aeroplane'. It can occur medially, as in the word 'careful' and finally, as in the word 'care'.

   Diphthong /ɛə/ is longer in 'care', 'scares'.

**Spellings:** **'are'** - **care**, **rare**, **share**, **mare**, etc.
**'air'** - **air**, **fair**, **pair**, **chair**, etc.
**'ear'** - **bear**, **pear**, **tear** (v), etc.
**'eir'**- **heir**, **'ere'** - **there**, and **'ar'** - **scarce**

**Compare:** /æ/ and /ɛə/

| | | |
|---|---|---|
| marry - mare | bad - bared | callous - careless |
| rally - rarely | dad - dared | glad - glared |
| pad - paired | add - aired | fad - fared |

8. **Diphthong /ʊə/** - During the articulation of this diphthong, the glide starts from a tongue position similar to that used for /ʊ/ and moves towards the more open type of /ə/ which forms the end-point of all three centreing diphthongs with, again, more or less a closer variety of /ə/ when the diphthong occurs in a closed syllable.

   The lips are weakly rounded in the beginning and are spread towards the end. Diphthong /ʊə/ is, therefore, a glide from a centralized back rounded vowel just above half-close to a central un-rounded vowel between half-close and half-open.

   Diphthong /ʊə/ does not occur initially in a word. It can occur medially, as in the word 'during' and finally, as in the word 'cure'.

**Spellings:** **'oor'** - poor, moor
**'ure'** - pure, endure, cure, sure
**'ewer'** - sewer
**'our'** - tour, gourd, doer
(also in: jewel, fluent, truant)

**Compare:** /u/ and /ʊə/

| | |
|---|---|
| too - tour | cue - cure |
| do - doer | you - you're |
| few - fewer | sue - sewer |

## Comments on the Diphthongs Towards /ə/

Diphthongs other than those that glide in the direction of /ə/ may be followed by /ə/ within a word, either as a separable or as an inseparable part of the word. For example, **fire** /falə/, **hire** /halə/, **never** neωə/, **choir** /kwolə/, **society** /sesalti, **our** /aʊə/, **sour** /saʊə/, **towel** /taʊel/, **tower** /taʊə/; or /ə/ may appear as a suffix (morpheme) appended to the root, e.g., **greyer**, **player**, **slower**, **mower**, **higher**, **employer**, **drier** (i.e., /grelə/, /plelə/, /sleʊə/, /mouə/;/halə/; /lmplə/; /dralə/); or /ə/ may sometimes appear as a separable element internal in a composite word, e.g., 'now-a-days people are', i.e., /naʊ e delz pipl a:/.

In slow speech, the final /ə/ is heard, but in a speedy communication, in such sequences, the second elements of the diphthong (i.e., the /l/ or /ə/ is often omitted). For example, it may be noticed that often /ə/ in a word like **player** is heard as /ple ə/; as in the word **higher**, it is heard as /ha: ə/; in the word **shower**, it is heard as /sauə;.

### *Let Us Do and Learn*

1. Pronounce the following words:

   type, trial, quiet, coward, buyer, flyer, iron, ours, tower, towel, tired, powerful, bower, flower, riot, minute, showery

2. Now pronounce the following less common speech sounds:

   greyer, grower, employer, player, thrower, royal, betrayal, followers, lawyers

3. Provide IPA transcriptions of the following words:

| | | |
|---|---|---|
| grey - greyer; | high - higher; | lays - layers; |
| gay - gayer; | my - mire; | lies - lairs; |
| mow - mower; | why - wire; | boughs - bowers; |
| low - lower; | saw (N) - sour; | tied - tired; |
| sow - shower; | coy - coir; | hide - hired; |

4. Complete minimal pairs of the following words (The first one is done for you):

| /e/ - /ɛe/ | /æ/ - /ɛe/ | /ɔ/ - /eI/ | - /aI/ |
|---|---|---|---|
| very - vary; | rally -; | cork -; | hay how |
| merry -; | marry -; | walk -; | - - |
| ferry -; | pad -; | cord -; | - - |
| terror -; | bad -; | roared -; | - - |
| dead -; | dad -; | ball -; | - - |
| shed -; | callous -; | call -; | - - |
| fed -; | glad -; | fall -; | - - |

5. Fill in the appropriate vowels to complete the following words:

| | | |
|---|---|---|
| 1. r _ b (rob); | r _ b (rib); | r _ b (rub); |
| 2. p _ t° (patch); | p _ t°(pitch); | p _ t°(porch); |
| 3. f _ l (feel); | f _ l (fell); | f _ l (full); |
| 4. s _ k (sick); | s _ k (sock); | s _ k (sack); |
| 5. r _ d (read); | r _ d (red); | r _ d (reared); |
| 6. w _ v (weave); | w _ v (wove); | w _ v (wave); |
| 7. d¥ _ (jar); | d¥ _ (jaw); | d¥ _ (jew); |
| 8. b _ (buy); | b _ (boy); | b _ (bow); |
| 9. θr_ (three); | θr _ (threw); | θr _ (throw); |
| 10. ð _ (thy); | ð _ (though); | ð _ (through); |

6. Fill in the appropriate consonants to form the speech sounds of the following words:

| | |
|---|---|
| 1. (_ I _) = chick; | (_ ɔ _) = chalk; |
| 2. (_ æ _) = jam; | (_ I _) = jim; |
| 3. (_ i _) = treat; | (_ aʊ _) = trout; |
| 4. (_ aʊ _) = frowned; | (_ e _) = friend; |
| 5. (_ u _) = tooth; | (_ u _) = booth; |
| 6. (_ a _) = dart; | (_ eI _) = date; |
| 7. (_ eI _) = face; | (_ i _) = zeal; |
| 8. (_ ʊ _) = push; | (_ _) = posh; |

# Suprasegmental Features of English

Some features of phonology go beyond the study of segments and phonemic contrast alone cannot explain all the contrasts in the language. For example, the same word in English can be pronounced with the first syllable sounding stronger or the second syllable sounding stronger—e.g., **con**tent or con**tent**. The first is heard as a noun, the second as a verb. Changes in intonation can also bring about a change in the message. There are contrasts that extend beyond one segment or phoneme and are called 'suprasegmental'. The term is most commonly applied to the stress tone and pitch (i.e., intonation).

## Stress and Intonation

To describe and compare the pronunciation of different languages, we must analyze speech, i.e., we must split up into units the unbroken stream of movements resulting in an utterance. Now, let us review the syllable once again with reference to the intonation.

## Let Us Think and Learn

What would be the smallest unit of an utterance?

A syllable is the minimum unit of an utterance. Nothing less than a syllable can be uttered or pronounced, e.g., shh! hmm! ah!

Is it necessary that all the syllables be accompanied by a sound?

The answer is 'No'. It is possible to produce inaudible syllables, e.g., a rather perfunctory way of saying 'Thank you' = /θnkju/.

A syllable has three phases with which segments may coincide, i.e., a central segment (associated with phase 2), and there may or may not be marginal segments associated with phase 1 (releasing phase) or phase 3 (arresting phase).

## Definition of a Syllable

A syllable is a unit of an utterance containing one and only one vowel either alone or surrounded by consonants.

In English, the vowel of the syllable may be preceded by up to three consonants and followed by as many as four consonants. The pattern can be as follows:

| | Words | Transcriptions | Pattern |
|---|---|---|---|
| (i) The vowel may appear alone: | I | /aI/ | = v |
| (ii) It may have 1/2/3 consonants | pay | /paI/ | = cv |
| before it: | spy | /spaI/ | = ccv |
| | spree | /spri/ | = cccv |

(iii) It may have 1/2/3/4 consonants after it:

| Words | Transcriptions | Pattern |
|---|---|---|
| take | /t e k/ | = cvc |
| takes | /t e ks/ | = cvcc |
| text | /t e kst/ | = cvccc |
| texts | /t e ksts/ | = cvcccc |

## Syllable Pattern in English: We know

(a) When there is no arresting phase in a syllable, it is an open syllable.
(b) When there is an arresting phase, it is a closed syllable.

### *Let Us Do and Learn*

1. Write the number of syllables used in each word against the word in the given brackets:

| | | |
|---|---|---|
| opportunity (5) | consonants ( ) | alphabet ( ) |
| authority ( ) | laboratory ( ) | phonology ( ) |

**Note:** Sequences of two or more consonants at the beginning or the end of a syllable are called 'consonant clusters'. In other words, the sequence of consonants will have to form part of the same syllable if it has to be considered a consonant cluster.

Examples of consonant clusters:

1. The consonant cluster /pl/ in the word please
   The consonant cluster /tr/ in the word train
2. The consonant cluster /spl/ as in the word 'splendid'
   The consonant cluster /skw/ as in the word 'square'
3. The consonant cluster /ns/ as in the word 'dance'
   The consonant cluster /gz/ as in the word 'dogs'
4. The consonant cluster /kst/ as in the word 'next'
   The consonant cluster /lst/ as in the word 'whilst'
5. The consonant cluster /sksθs/ as in the word 'sixths'
   The consonant cluster /lfθs/ as in the word 'twelfths'

English is a stress-timed language, i.e., in connected speech, all important syllables are stressed.

Stress means—accent/emphasis/force/pressure. Word stress, therefore, means emphasis or force on a particular syllable in a word which stands out in an utterance carrying the meaning, particularly when the word contains more than one syllable. The degree of force on other syllables in the word is less. It is difficult to distinguish the degrees of force on each syllable.

Therefore, it is enough to consider only three degrees of force:

(i) **Primary**—(strong, main, principal) greater degree of force.
(ii) **Secondary**—(half-strong, medium) relatively lesser degree of force.
(iii) **Weak or unstressed**—no force at all in any syllable.

### *Using Stress Marks*

(a) The primary stress is marked by placing a vertical bar above the syllable, immediately before the syllable, e.g., ˋfather, ˋabove.
(b) When the word contains a number of syllables, (specially in the case of derivatives) it becomes necessary to show a secondary stress with a vertical bar just below and in front of the syllable, e.g., examine > examination; organize > organization; Europe > European.
(c) Other syllables are considered to be unstressed and show (ˋ) mark on the syllable in some dictionaries, e.g., ˋfather.
(d) In connected speech, the stress will depend on its relative importance in the sentence.

### *Possible Situations*

A word may retain its stress and tone.

A word may lose the tone but not the stress.

The stress of a word may be reduced to a subordinate one.
A word stress may disappear altogether.

## Types of Stress

(a) Lexical stress—`about.
(b) Full kinetic stress (tonic stress)—He was walking a`bout.
(c) Full static stress—It's `about what I wanted.
(d) Complete loss of stress—It's about a mile.

## Pattern of English Syllables

The fundamental patterns of English stressing are irregular and confusing because two different stress principles are in the language.

(a) The Teutonic stress pattern, i.e., stresses on the root syllable, e.g., 'love, 'lovely, 'lovable.
(b) The Romantic stress pattern, i.e., stress based on the quality- stress attracted towards end of word, e.g., e`qual, e`quality, equali`zation.

Yet, there is regularity in the irregularity. It is possible to draw up rules showing how suffixes and prefixes influence stress, subject to remarkably few exceptions.

# Stress and Its Effects on English Pronunciation

Words with more than one syllable have a stress on at least one of the syllables, and perhaps on both the syllables.

There are some rules which can often help to indicate where to put the stress, but sometimes the only way of being sure is to look up each word in the dictionary.

Now, let us find out some useful rules and see their applications. Thus, we can judge the effects of stress in English pronunciation.

Let us read the following disyllabic words and notice where the stress lies in each word.

| | |
|---|---|
| `conduct (n) | con`duct (v) |
| `convict (n) | con`vict (v) |

**Rule 1:** We can form a rule here by saying that in disyllabic words, the stress falls on the first syllable when the word is a noun or an adjective, whereas the stress falls on the second syllable when it is a verb. Examples:

| (N) | (V) |
|---|---|
| **Nouns** | **Verbs** |
| `object | ob`ject |
| `permit | per`mit |
| `progress | pro`gress |

**Exceptions**

`answer (both n/v); `echo (n/v); ce`ment (n/v);
`purchase (n/v); re`port (n/v); `promise (n/v)

Now, let us read the stress pattern in the following words:
a`broad, a`cross, a`part, con`cern, be`tween, com`pose,
be`low, re`pair, re`tire, a`mount, a`ttend, de`fend

**Rule 2:** We will find that disyllabic words with weak prefixes (such as **a-**, **be-**, **com- con-**, **de-**, **re-)** do not take any stress mark. Hence, the stress falls on the root word. Examples:

Weak Prefixes

| | |
|---|---|
| **a-** | a`cross, a`part, ad`mit, a`loud |
| **be-** | be`fore, be`tween |
| **com-** | com`pose |
| **con-** | con`cern |
| **de-** | de`fend |
| **re-** | re`pair (see Rule 11 also) |

Now, let us read the following words and see where the stress mark is given:

de`cide, dic`tate, ac`cept, ad`mit, vi`brate

**Rule 3:** All these words are verbs. So the rule could be: Verbs of two syllables are normally stressed on the second syllable. Examples:
cap`size, en`joy, ex`plain, im`prove,
su`ggest, ob`serve, per`form, pre`pare,
re`fer, af`ford, na`rrate, sel`ect, be`long

**Exceptions:** `order, `cancel, `govern, `practice, `enter, `study, `open and `suffer

**Rule 4:**

(a) In words with inflectional suffixes (such as **-es**, **-ing** and **-ed**), the stress mark falls on the root word and not on the suffix.

Examples: `match**es**, `beginn**ing**, `snatch**es**, `sing**ing**

(b) In words with some derivational suffixes, the stress mark falls on the root word and not on the suffix.
Let us study the following derivational suffixes with one example of word for each:

| | | | | |
|---|---|---|---|---|
| -en | -age | -ance | -er | -ess |
| `broad**en** | `break**age** | a`ppear**ance** | `broad**er** | `godd**ess** |
| -ful | -ify | -hood | -ice | -ish |
| `care**ful** | `class**ify** | `child**hood** | `coward**ice** | `fool**ish** |
| -ive | -less | -ly | -ment | -ness |
| a`ttract**ive** | `aim**less** | `bad**ly** | ap`point**ment** | `bitter**ness** |
| -or | -ship | -ter | -ure | -y |
| `conquer**or** | `fellow**ship** | `laugh**ter** | en`clos**ure** | 'blood**y** |
| -zen | -dom | | | |
| `citi**zen** | `free**dom** | | | |

**Rule 5:** The following endings of words cause the stress mark to fall on the last syllable:

| Word Endings | | Examples |
|---|---|---|
| -ain (verbs) | = | ascer`tain, a`ttain |
| -ee (in nouns) | = | addre`ssee, refu`gee |
| -eer | = | auction`eer, car`eer |
| -esque | = | gro`tesque, pictu`resque |
| -ique | = | ob`lique, tech`nique |
| -oon | = | ba'lloon, car`toon |
| -aire | = | million`naire, questio`naire |
| -ese | = | Assa`mese, Chi`nese |
| -ette | = | gaz`ette, cigar`ette |

**Rule 6:** The following endings normally cause the stress mark to fall on the previous syllable:

| Word Endings | Examples |
|---|---|
| -ion (-tion/-sion) | = pro`motion, in`vasion |
| -ian | = li`brarian, mu`sician |
| -ious (-eous/-uous) | = cere`monious, misce`llaneous |
| -ic | = his`toric, `magic, dram`atic |
| -ical | = dram`atical |
| -ically | = drama`tically |

Important exceptions are:

`Arabic, `Catholic, a`rithmetic, `rhetoric, `politic(s), `choleric, etc.

**Rule 7:** The following endings normally cause the stress mark to fall on the previous syllable:

| Word Endings | Examples |
|---|---|
| -it | = de`posit (exception: `deficit) |
| -ity | = cu`riosity |
| itude | = `attitude |
| -ify | = `modify, `specify |
| -ular | = par`ticular, mo`lecular |
| -iate | = im`mediate, a`lleviate |
| -cracy | = dem`ocracy, au`tocracy |
| -graphy | pho`tography |
| -grapher | = pho`tographer |
| -graphist | = pho`tographist |
| -logy | = bio`logy |
| -logist | = bio`logist |
| -sophy | = phi`losophy |
| -sopher | = phi`losopher |

| | |
|---|---|
| -sophist | = \`theosophist |
| -nomy | = a\`stronomy |
| -nomer | = a\`stronomer |
| -nomist | = e\`conomist |
| -able | = p\`alpable, w\`orkable |
| -ible | = con\`vertible |

**Rule 8:** The following endings normally cause the stress mark to fall on the third syllable from ending.

| | | |
|---|---|---|
| \`-ate | = | \`fortunate, \`cultivate, ac\`celerate |
| \`-graph | = | \`paragraph, \`autograph |
| \`-gram | = | \`telegram |

**Rule 9:** For endings such as **–ise** or **–ize**, the position of the stress mark depends on the number of syllables in the word, e.g.,

(a) If the word contains four syllables, then the stress mark normally falls on the third syllable from the ending.

**Examples:** \`au | tho | **–rize**, \`criticize, ac\`climatize

(b) If the word contains more than four syllables, then the stress mark normally falls on the fourth syllable from the ending.

**Examples: A** | m\`e | ri | ca | **nize**, re\`publicanize, le\`gitimize

**Rule 10:** In the case of endings such as **-al**, **-ant**, **-ent**, **-ous**, the position of the stress mark depends on whether the syllable preceding the ending is open or closed.

(a) If the preceding syllable is open, then the stress mark normally falls on the third syllable from the ending.

**Example:** \`ad | mi | **ral**

(b) If the preceding syllable is closed, then the stress mark normally falls on the second syllable from the ending.

**Example:** an | \`ces | **tral**

**Some More Examples:**

| | | |
|---|---|---|
| -al | = | \`medical, me\`dicinal, o\`riginal |
| | | (**Exceptions**: au\`tumnal, govern\`mental) |
| -ant | = | \`accident, \`evident, \`tolerant, \`violent |
| -ent | = | (**Exceptions**: a\`bundant, in\`cessant, tri\`umphant) |
| | | (**Exceptions:** co\`herent and ante\`cedent) |
| -ous | = | \`de co rous, \`nu mer ous, pre\`pos te rous |
| | | (**Exceptions:** de\`sirous, son\`orous, mo\`mentous, trem\`endous) |

We should remember that such a long list of words would not help if we do not consider the enormously long list of 'exceptions to the rules'. We can learn about these exceptions simply by listening to the near-native variety of English and by learning to imitate the better speakers of English.

**Rule 11: Use of 're' as Prefix:**

In pronouncing the 're' -prefix, three different vowel sounds are used, e.g., | ri |, | rl |, | re |.

The choice between these three pronunciations depends upon the stress context in a sentence where the word is used.

**Examples:** rebel: / r`ebel(n) / re`bel / (v); re`born(n) = / `ribn/

**re = | re |**

`rebel, `reci`pe, `recognize, `reconcile, `record (n), `recreate (=amuse), `reference, `refuse (n), `refuge, `relative, `relevant, `relic, `relish, `remedy, `remnant, `renovate, `replica, `reptile, `requisite, `rescue, `residence, `resolute, `restaurant, `revenue, `reverence and `reverend

**| rl- | and | ri- |**

| \| rl- \| | \| ri- \| |
|---|---|
| `react = to respond | r'e-`act = act again |
| `recall = remember | re-`call = call again |
| re`count = relate | r'e-`count = count again |
| rec`over = get back | r`e-`cover = cover again |
| re`dress (n) = remedy | r`e-`dress = dress again |
| re`form (v) = improve | r`e-`form = form again |
| re`lease (v) = free | r`e-`lease = lease again |
| re`place = substitute for | r`e-p`lace = place again |

**Rule 12: Use of 's' as /z/:**

In the following words, there is also a change in the pronunciation of 's' which is pronounced as |z|.

Example: reserve = /rlz3v/

| | |
|---|---|
| re`serve = keep back | 're-`serve = serve again |
| re`solve (v) = decide | 're-`sign = sign again |
| re`sort (v) = turn to | 're-`solve = solve again |
| re`sound = echo | 're-`sound = sound again |
| re`sign = relinquish | 're-`sort = sort again |

## Let Us Do and Learn

1. Pronounce the following words and write the number of syllables used in the brackets given. The first one is done for you.

| | | |
|---|---|---|
| opportunity (5); | consonants ( ); | alphabet ( ); |
| authority ( ); | laboratory ( ); | phonology ( ); |

2. Apply the rules and put in the stress marks on the correct syllable:

| | | | |
|---|---|---|---|
| beautiful | govern | glorify | appointment |
| monsoon | unique | childish | mountaineer |
| ending | recorded | subject (n) | scholarship |
| watches | promise | careless | wastage |
| shorten | prevent | desert (v) | contentment |

3. Put in the primary stress in the following words:

| | | | |
|---|---|---|---|
| proportionate | grammarian | economize | electricity |
| questioner | vernacular | geography | photograph |
| beautify | pension | revision | practical |

4. In each row of words, one word has stress on a different syllable. Underline that word. Insert 'Stress Mark' on all words and justify yourself by quoting rules.

| | | | |
|---|---|---|---|
| (i) college | programme | compose | authors |
| (ii) punish | July | danger | captain |
| (iii) ticket | people | final | goodbye |
| (iv) machine | canteen | luggage | select |
| (v) reserve | injure | insane | express |
| (vi) question | apply | perceive | perform |
| (vii) future | liquid | teacher | intend |
| (viii) mechanic | director | customer | election |
| (ix) cigarette | guarantee | seventeen | modify |
| (x) delightful | disbelieve | disturbance | effective |

## Compound Words

Two or more independent words are combined to form a compound. In spelling them there may or may not be any hyphen between the two elements forming the compound.

There are a number of collections. In most compound words in English, the primary stress falls on one of the elements. The most common type in English is the first of the two elements receiving the primary stress.

Here are a few examples of some very frequent collocations:

1. N + N = `kitchen garden
2. N + N –er/N-or (Nominal Agents), i.e., nouns formed from verbs
   e.g. = `house keeper
3. N + Gerund = `fault finding
4. Adjective + N = `red rose
5. -ing form + N = `eating house

As we will see, single-stressed compounds are normally stressed on the first component and are very common in English e.g., `fountain pen, whereas some compounds are double-stressed, i.e., first component takes a full stress and the second component takes a kinetic stress, e.g., `rock `salt. Most of the double-stressed compounds are adjusted according to the rhythmical variations.

The following are a few rules for using stress in the compound words, but all rules have exceptions as well.

**Rule 1: N + N** = (i) A compound word will be double stressed if it names something that is made out of or contains the first component of the compound, e.g., 'rock plant', 'dust bin' 'mutton `chop, 'olive `oil, 'milk `pudding, 'arm `chair, etc.

(ii) A compound word will be single stressed if it does not name something that is made out of or contains the first component of the compound, e.g., `rock plant, `fish market, `dust bin, `fountain pen, etc.

**Rule 2: N + N -er/N -or** = (i) When the first component names the objects of the action, the compound is invariably single stressed, i.e., `cabinet maker, `road mender, `squadron leader, `royal executor, etc.

**Exceptions**: When the first component does not name the object of action, then the compound is double stressed. There are few such examples:

e.g., `stage `manager = does not manage stage
`town `crier = does not cry town
`vacuum `cleaner = does not clean vacuum, etc.

**Rule 3: N + Gerund:** (i) When the first component has a predicative function towards the gerund, then the compound is single stressed.

The resulting compound may be a noun or an adjective, e.g., `alms giving, `blood poisoning, `sightseeing, `time serving, etc.

(ii) When the first component has an attributive function towards the gerund, then the compound is double stressed.

The resulting compound is always a noun, e.g., 'mass `meeting, `ball `bearing, `fellow `feeling, etc.

**Rule 4: Adjective + N**

The compound is single stressed in most cases, e.g., `earthenware, `flat iron, `dramatic society, `lightweight.

**Rule 5: -ing form + N (-ing form acting as an adjective)**

(i) When the second component does not do the action, mentioned in the first component, then it is single stressed, e.g., `reading lamp, `boarding house, `dressing gown.
(ii) But when the second component does the action, mentioned in the first component then the compound is double stressed, e.g., `leading `question; `floating `bridge, `working `class, `burning `bush, etc.

There may be compounds containing more than two words. Here, the stress is subject to rhythmical variation.

***Rhythmical Variations.*** Double-stressed words are subject to modification in the sentences. The first of the stressed syllable is apt to lose its stress when preceded by another stressed syllable. Similarly, the second of the stressed syllables is apt to lose its stress when closely followed by another stressed syllable.

**Examples:**

(a) **`four`teen** (double stressed) in answer to the question: How many people are there?
(b) **`Fourteen shillings** (stress on first syllable)
(c) **Just four `teen** (stress on second syllable)

**More Examples:**

'inlaid 'wood > 'all in `laid
unknown 'land > 'quite un`known
'sardine `sandwiches > a 'tin of sar`dines

## Stress of Initials and Numbers

1. Two components = (both the components are stressed) e.g., `A`D, `U`K, etc.
2. Three or four components = (first and last components are stressed)
e.g., `PM`G; `30`8; `RSV`P; `438`9

3. Five components = (the first, third and fifth components are stressed)
e.g., `AM'IC`E; `73`12`6;
4. Six components = Components are divided into two series of three,
e.g., `39,5 | `62 `1; `98,4`62`3, etc.

### Let Us Do and Learn

Put stress marks on the following words:

(a) postman, school bus, tea party, raincoat
(b) afternoon, vice-chancellor, post graduate, home-made
(c) BA, USSR, RC, PWD, USA, 235502

## Study of English Intonation

1. Connected speech is divided into intonation groups (sometimes called 'sense groups' or 'breath groups'). These groups most frequently extend over a clause but may extend over smaller or larger units. For example, the noun-phrase subject of a clause may have a group of its own; an adverbial phrase may have a group of its own; or a group may sometimes extend over a sentence made up of two clauses (as is frequently the case with short conditionals).

**Examples:**
(a) / The lorry started / and ran over him/.
(b) / The former Sheriff of Kolkata/ was waiting at the ticket counter/.
(c) / Unfortunately/ it didn't work/.
(d) / I'll do it if I can/.

2. A syllable (called the 'nucleus' or 'tonic') in each information group is selected to receive the main accent by beginning at this point one of a limited number of pitch patterns (or tones). The word in which this syllable occurs is thus made the most important syllable in the group, called the nucleus.
3. The pitch pattern from the nucleus, and including all following syllables up to the end of the group (these constitute the tail), is called the 'nuclear tone'.

One way of marking intonation is to put a short-hand mark for the particular nuclear tone before the nucleus.

**Examples:** (a) It `wasn`t very nice.
(b) `Want to g`o tomorrow?

This indicates two things. It tells us:

(a) Which syllable has been accepted for the main accent?
(b) Which syllables stand out in pitch from the unstressed syllables?

The stressed syllables are more clearly articulated than the unstressed syllables. Stress in English serves to mark the meaningful words in an utterance. Usually, the meaningful words are content words, such as nouns, adjectives, main verbs and adverbs. As we already know, word order is very important in English. Therefore, it is often possible to decode a message even if you are not able to hear the unstressed words. This knowledge is used in telegraphy. The words we pay for when sending a telegram are the stressed words or the most important words according to the need of the sender.

I. (Types of Tones)
- **static-level tones** — make no contribution to meaning
- **kinetic -level tones**
  - change in pitch
  - • add expression
  - • convey feeling
  - • express attitude friendliness, enthusiasm and boredom

II. **Change in Pitch:**
(1) {/} the rising tune (2) {\} falling tune
(3) {v} fall rise (4) rise fall {^} (5) rise-fall-rise {/\/}

III. Tunes 1 to 3 are enough for straightforward communication. Every complete utterance must have at least one kinetic stress. It usually falls on the last important word according to what the speaker wishes to express.

Let us ask a very simple question: Which word usually takes the kinetic stress?

The kinetic stress usually comes on the last stressed word of a sentence.

Let's see how we can change the whole meaning of a sentence simply by shifting the point of kinetic stress—the 'tonic stress' as it is usually called.

Examples: `John '**didn't** speak to Mary. (You've got it all wrong.)

'**John** didn't speak to Mary. (Peter did.)
'John didn't `**speak** to Mary. (He wrote a letter.)
'John `didn't 'speak to `Mary. (He spoke to Anne.)

(Notice how after the tonic stress, what's left of the sentence stays at the same pitch, with very little stress even on normally stressed syllables.)

This variation in pitch is called 'intonations'.

|| 'What did you `want to do | `that for? ||
(Pre-tonic segment) (tonic segment)

If we analyze unstressed words, we find they are usually:

(i) Pronouns = I, you, me, etc.
(ii) Auxiliary and modal verbs = shall/can, etc.
(iii) Prepositions = at/on/with/from, etc.
(iv) Articles = the/a/an
(v) Conjunctions = and/but, etc.

Sometimes, these unimportant grammatical words may be stressed for emphasis.
Let us read the following sentences:

(i) 'Come and 'meet `**me** tomorrow (i.e., special emphasis on the word 'me', which means the hearer should meet no one else).
(ii) 'Please per`mit `**me** to do that (i.e., you shouldn't allow any one else to do it).

## The Choice of a Tone

The sentence is divided into two groups and having chosen the nucleus, a speaker has to choose an appropriate tone. It is impossible to suggest particular contexts and point out that only one of the various tones should be used in these contexts. What we can do is to point out a few contexts and indicate that in these contexts a particular tone may be used.

Intonation in English serves:

(a) a grammatical function and
(b) an attitudinal function

In other words, with the help of intonation, the hearer can make out whether an utterance is a statement or a question, a command or a request.

Again with the help of intonation one can find out the attitude or mood of the speaker, i.e., whether the person is bored, annoyed, interested in the subject of conversation, or whether the person is sarcastic, etc. Here are a few examples of some tone patterns:

### *Tone Types*

**Rising Tone: ( / )**

(a) Let us read the following sentences and notice where the nucleus is:
   (i) Was it / there? (ii) Has / John come? (iii) Is / this the one?

Yes/No type of questions usually take a rising tone at the nucleus. If the nucleus shifts to the anomalous finite (i.e., was/ has /is), it suggests performance or non-performance of the action.

(b) We use the rising tone for reassuring, encouraging, e.g.,
   (i) `Cheer / up.
   (ii) It won't `last / long.
(c) Let us read the following sentences and notice the nucleus:
   (i) 'How's your / daughter? **Enquiring**
   (ii) 'When are you 'coming to / see us? **Showing interest**
   (iii) 'When did you get 'back from / holiday? **Interest**

   (Use a glide up when you wish to show as much interest in the person as in the subject.)
(d) Let us read the following sentences:
   (i) / What?
   (ii) / What did you say?
   (iii) / Where's he going?

(We usually use the glide up on the wh- words in such interrogative statements when we ask for repetition.)

(e) We use the rising tone on the nucleus in some wh- questions as the following:
   (i) When can you / come? **Polite enquiry**
   (ii) Why can't you / do it? **Threatening**
(f) We use the rising tone and the falling tone for alternate questions:
   (i) A. Will you have / this one or `that one?
   B. 'Neither', / thank you.
   (ii) A. Will you have / cake or `pastry?
   B. `Cake, / please.
(g) We use the falling tone and the rising tone in certain question tags like:
   Where the response could be either 'yes' or 'no', especially when we ask for an opinion:
   e.g.: (i) You're coming to `tea with us, / aren't you?
   (ii) He didn't look `ill, / did he?

(h) We use the rising tone at the nucleus which suggests incomplete utterance and the falling tone at the nucleus to suggest incompleteness of the utterance. For example:
   (i) 'Taken as a / whole, the res'ults aren't `bad.
   (ii) There was once a `rat named / Arthur, who 'lived in a `village.

(i) Use a glide up at the nucleus for gentle commands or requests.
   e.g.: (i) / Sit here.
   (ii) / Take this.
   (iii) 'Sit / there. **Polite invitation**
   (iv) 'Shut the / door. **Polite request**

(j) For exclamations, greetings, etc., use a rising tone:
   (i) 'Good / morning. **Cheerful greeting**
   (ii) 'Best of / luck. **Cheerful good wishes**

(k) Use the rising tone to express surprise:
   / Oh! / Really! / Well!

(l) Use the glide up for perfunctory apologies:
   / Sorry! / I'm / sorry!

(m) We use the falling tone For items in the enumeration, use a glide up and a falling tone at the last nucleus suggesting completeness:
   e.g.: She offered us / jam, / marmalade and / honey.

**The Falling Tone: (\)**

(a) (i) We use the falling tone at the nucleus for straightforward statements:
   e.g.: (a) I think you'd better 'ask the `others.
   (b) I've never 'met them.
   (ii) We use the falling tone with the stressed objects:
   (a) We prefer `coffee.
   (b) He 'wrote a 'letter to your `brother.

(b) We use the falling tone for end-position adverbials which have great semantic value, the nucleus takes a falling tone:
   (a) He's coming tomorrow.
   (b) I 'posted the letter `early.

(c) Particular wh- questions take a falling tone:
   e.g.: (i) `Why? `What for? 'How many `more?
   (ii) 'Who 'gave you the `yellow one?

(d) Normal greetings take a falling tone at the nucleus:
   e.g.: 'Good `morning. 'How d'you `do.

(e) Strong exclamations take a falling tone:
   e.g.: `Nonsense! 'Good `Heavens!

(f) Commands take a falling tone (angry commands):
   e.g.: 'Put that `down. 'Leave me a`lone.

(g) Statements with interrogative clauses:
   e.g.: (i) 'Isn't he 'like his `father. (not a question)
   (ii) 'Do that again and you're `fired. (not a command)

(h) Question tags where you wish to urge the hearer to express his agreement or approval, then the nucleus takes a falling tone:
   e.g.: (i) She'll `wait, `won't she?
   (ii) He `likes it, `doesn't he?
   (iii) He `doesn't `like it, `does he?

(i) Statements that suggest strong agreement or disagreement take a falling tone at the nucleus.
e.g.: (i) `No, I `did do it.
(ii) 'Certainly `not.

## The Falling-rising Tone: (v)

This tone normally indicates that something is implied—which is not expressed in the utterance. This can express other attitudes as well.

(i) The fall-rise can occur within the same syllable, or
(ii) The fall-rise, as we have seen, can be a divided fall-rise where the fall and the rise may occur on different syllables.

**Examples:**

1. (a) A. ι/ Do you play v tennis?
B. Sometimes. (not always, surely)
A. ι/ Now. (doubtful)
(b) A. I 'saw you at the ι/ cinema. (Reproaching—'You said you had to study for your exams.')
(c) A. 'John's here ι/ already. (so do hurry up)
(d) A. She is ι/ beautiful. (but not very clever)
(e) A. The ι/ coffee was good. (but the service was awful)
2. (a) A. `I can.(I am almost sure you can't)
(b) A. You did `quite well. (Encouraging, sympathetic)
(c) A. `That's the spirit. (Encouraging, sympathetic)
(d) A. 'When will you do it. (To know the precise time in a polite way)
(e) A. 'Mind that step. (Strong but sympathetic warning)
3. **Apologies:** Say the following utterances and see the difference in attitude.
(a) I'm 'terribly sorry.
I'm 'terribly `sorry.
I'm terribly ι/ sorry.
(b) I 'hope it's 'not going to be inconvenient for you.
4. **Thanking:** ι/ Thank you. `Thank you `very#/ much.
5. **Request to Repeat**: I beg your #/ pardon. (I haven't understood.)
6. **Hinting:** Those ι/ cakes smell nice.
7. **Warnings:** (i) You'll ι/ fall. (ii) It's #/ raining you´ know.
8. **Interrogatives:** requests
e.g., (i) Will you 'get me a 'glass of ι/ water please?
(ii) Would you mind `not ι/ smoking in this compartment?
9. **Imperatives:** 'Have a good time. Enjoy yourself.
(knock at the door) Come ι/ in. / `Come in.

## The Rising-falling Tone

In this tone, the rise reinforces the meaning conveyed by the following fall. Besides that, the initial rise may indicate warmth, anger or sarcasm.

e.g., A. The 'film was 'awful. Do you agree?
B. ^Yes. (Enthusiastic agreement)
It was ^frightful. (Enthusiastic agreement)

A. But is her ^son in the picture? (Suspicious, interest)
B. Are you ^sure he was right? (Suspicious, mocking)
A. How ^ interesting. (Sarcastic)

It is difficult to master the intonation of any foreign language. Only theoretical knowledge does not help. It is, perhaps, necessary to listen to a lot of English being spoken, for a considerable period of time, to gain mastery over this extremely complex aspect of the language.

### Let Us Do and Learn

1. Find the nucleus and mark the kinetic stress and the static stress:
   (a) A. Did you want something?
       B. Can I borrow a pen, please?
   (b) A. Where's John?
       B. He's in the bathroom.
       A. Has he got a job?
       B. No, he's on the waiting list.
   (c) A. I had a smash in the car.
       B. How did that happen?
   (d) A. It's just four o'clock.
       B. Are you sure your watch is right?
   (e) A. What's the time?
       B. Ten past two, dear.
       A. When does the train leave?
       B. Not until quarter to four.
       A. Why did you get here so early?
       B. Because you said we must allow plenty of time for traffic jams and accidents.
   (f) Mark the juncture. Find the nucleus and mark the static stress and the kinetic stress:
       When my grandmother died at the age of eighty-nine, we discovered that she had left us the contents of an unusual savings account. Throughout her life, whenever she found a coin as she cleaned the house or emptied the pockets of clothes to be washed, she deposited it in this account.

## English Pronunciation

### Weak Forms of Words

Many English Words have their two specific acceptable forms: one for Spoken' variety and the other for 'Written' variety. The first variety uses 'Weak Forms' and the second variety uses 'Strong Forms'. Therefore, the use of weak forms is an essential part of English speech. When these words are stressed or when they are pronounced in isolation, the strong forms of these words are used; when they are unstressed, the weak forms of these words are used. In the weak forms, we can see that there is reduction in the length of sounds, weakening of the vowels in them and also elision of vowels and consonants. A few common words with both strong and weak forms are given in the following chart:

| **Words** | | |
|---|---|---|
| **Articles** | **Strong Form** | **Weak Form** |
| a | \|eI\| | \|e\| |
| an | \|æn\| | \|en\| |

| | | |
|---|---|---|
| the | \|ði\| | \|ðl\| before vowel<br>\|ðe\| before consonant |
| **Auxiliary Verbs** | | |
| am | /æm/ | /em/, /m/ |
| are | /a:/ | /ə/ |
| can | /kæn/ | /ken/ |
| could | /kʊd/ | /ked/ |
| does | /d^z/ | /dez/ /z/ /s/ |
| do | /du/ | /dƷ/ /de/ /d/ |
| had | /hæd/ | /hed/ /ed/ /d/ |
| has | /hæz/ | /hez/ /ez/ /z/ /s/ |
| have | /hæv/ | /hev/ /ev/ /v/ |
| is | /lz/ | /z/ /s/ |
| must | /m^st/ | /mest/ /mes/ |
| shall | / æl/ | /'el/ /'l/ |
| was | /wz/ | /wez/ |
| were | /w ə/ | /w ə/ |
| will | /wll/ | /l/ |
| would | /wʊd/ | /ed/ /d/ |
| **Prepositions** | | |
| at | /æt/ | /et/ |
| for | /fə/ | /fa/ |
| from | /frm/ | /frem/ |
| of | /v/ | /ev/ /v/ /e/ |
| to | /tu/ | /t/ /te/ |
| **Conjunctions** | | |
| and | /ænd/ | /end/ /nd/ /en/ /n/ |
| as | /æz/ | /ez/ |
| then | /ðæn/ | /ðen/ /ðn/ |
| that | /ðæt/ | /ðet/ |
| but | /b^t/ | /bet/ |
| **Other Words** | | |
| be | /bi/ | /bI/ |
| been | /bin/ | /bIn/ |
| he | tʃ /hi/ | /hI/ /i/ /I/ |
| her | /h ə / | /h ə / / ə / |
| him | /hlm/ | /lm/ |
| she | /°i/ | /°l/ |

| | | |
|---|---|---|
| his | /hlz/ | /lz/ |
| me | /mi/ | /ml/ |
| not | /nt/ | /nt/ /n/ |
| some | /s^m/ | /sem/ |
| there | /ðεe/ | /ðe/ |

**Indefinite Adverbs**

| | | |
|---|---|---|
| us | /^s/ | /es/ /s/ |
| we | /wi/ | /wl/ |
| were | /w ə/ | /w ə/ |
| who | /hu/ | /hʊ/ /u/ |
| you | /ju/ | /U/ |

**Note:** The weak forms of prepositions are not used when they occur at the end of a sentence, e.g., /hez hl k^m **fr m**/; /landon **tu**/

An important feature of the pronunciation of English is simplification in the production of speech. We always try to make less effort in our speech without causing any hindrance to communication. Economy of effort is called 'simplification'—which is common in colloquial speech. This is done in different ways. We have already learnt the weak forms of words. The others are: (i) assimilation (ii) elision and (iii) contracted forms.

(i) Assimilation

It is defined as a process of replacing a sound by another sound under the influence of a third sound which is near to it in the word or sentence.

Sound A is replaced by sound B under the influence of sound C. For example, horse shoe > / hɔ°°u/, i.e., /s/ in horse is replaced by /°/ under the influence of /°/ in shoe.

The term may also be extended to include cases where a sequence of two sounds coalesces and gives place to a single new sound different from either of the original sounds, e.g., the sounds A and C influence each other and coalesce into the single sound B, e.g., don't you > /dontu/.

Assimilations are of two chief kinds: (i) historical and (ii) contextual.

(a) By historical assimilation we mean an assimilation which has taken place in the course of development of a language, and by which a word that was once pronounced in a certain way came to be pronounced subsequently in another way.

(b) By contextual assimilation, we mean the one which takes place when words are juxtaposed in a sentence or in the formulation of compounds, and by which a word comes to have a pronunciation different from that which it has when said by itself.

(i) **Historical Assimilation**

(a) In the thirteenth/fourteenth century—the word 'ant' was pronounced /æmete/ and written as 'amete';
later: /æmte/ and /æmt/ and
in fifteenth century: /ænt/.

(b) Some hundreds of years ago the word 'picture' was pronounced as /pIkt/. Later, the sequence of /tj/ changed to /t/.

(ii) **Contextual Assimilation**

(a) Assimilation of **voiceless to voice** and **voice to voiceless, for example:**

- /z/ is reduced to /lz/ when preceded by a voiced sound other than /z/ or /¥/.
  e.g., Who is there? = /huz ðɛ ə/
  Dinner is ready. = /dlne z redl/
  When is he coming? = /wenz (h) i k^ml/
- /lz/ is reduced to /s/ when preceded by a voiceless consonant other than /z/ /s/ or //.
  e.g., It is ready. /lt s redl/
  That is all. /ðætsɔI/
  What is the time? /wts de talm/
  The shop is open. /de ps opn/
  'has' is treated in the same way.
  e.g., Who has been here? /huz bln hle/
  Jack has been here. /djæksbinhie/

***More Examples***

(i) Assimilation affecting the position of the tongue is pronouncing consonants.

(a) Replacement of /s/ by /°/ under the influence of the following /°/,
e.g., This shop. /ð13 ʃɔp/
Of course, she does. /ev kɔ°°Id^z/

(b) Replacement of /z/ by /3/ under the influence of /ʃ/, e.g., Does she?
/d^3 ʃi/
Butcher's shop. /bʊtʃ ə3 ʃɔp/
Newspaper > /njuspelp ə/ falfpens/, etc.
Handkerchief > /hæk ətʃlf/
There are several other assimilation changes that take place in English pronunciation.

(ii) Elision

In order to maintain the characteristic rhythm of English, we often have to pronounce the unaccented syllables very fast, and in doing so, certain sounds are elided. For example, the word 'them' which is pronounced /ðem/ in isolation, may be heard as /ðm/ in connected speech, particularly when it is not stressed. Following are a few examples of elision:

(a) The sounds /t/ and /d/ at the end of a word after another consonant are elided, e.g., exac(t)ly, pas(t), ol(d), frien(d).
Read the following sentence rapidly and notice the sounds that are elided:
The postman was an old man.
The above sentence will read as follows:
/ðe pousmin wezen oulmæn/. (The sounds **/t/** and **/d/** have been elided.)
This is **contextual elision.** Here are a few more examples:
bestman = /besmæn/; soft-centered = /sfsented/
mashed potatoes = /mæ°peteltez/; brand new = /brænnju/
last time = /lastaim/; sit down = /sldaʊn/; etc.

(b) loss of /k/ in 'asked', e.g., /ast/

(c) /h/ is lost in weak forms of 'have', 'has', 'had', 'his', 'her'
'him', except when it is preceded by a pause or a vowel sound.

(d) /°/ is lost in the weak form of 'shall'.
/w/ is lost in the weak form of 'will'.

/l/ is lost after the vowel // in words like, a I ready, a II right, etc.
/r/ is elided along with an unaccented vowel /ǝ/.
When another /r/ is close, e.g., library = /lalbrl/,
literary = /lltrl/; temporary = /temprl/; February = /febrl/, etc.
These are **historical elisions.**

(e) Vowel elision is seen mainly in the unaccented syllables. This often causes loss of a syllable, e.g., loss of /ǝ/ after a consonant and before /r/, /l/, /n/ in an unaccented syllable immediately after an accented syllable, e.g., /hlstrl/, /fæmll/, /riznǝbl/, etc.
Often in words ending in—ory; -ery; -ary; -ury and -lly,
e.g., carefully = /kɛefll/
We can find elision in the second elements of a diphthong before /ǝ/,
e.g., tower = /ta/; our = /a/, etc.

There are many more examples of assimilation and elision in the English speech of native speakers of English. But it is not always necessary to have all these changes in our speech as long as it is intelligible.

(iii) The next important aspect is the use of contracted forms of verbs in English connected speech.
Some auxiliary verbs have contracted positive forms which can be used:
(a) **After a pronoun**: e.g., he's going to Mumbai; what'll you do? (b) **after a short noun**: e.g., the dog's barking or (c) **after the words:** 'here', 'there', 'now', e.g., here's something for you.

**More Examples:**

**Negative**

| | |
|---|---|
| does not = doesn't | have not = haven't |
| do not = don't | has not = hasn't |
| did not = didn't | had not = hadn't |

**Contracted Non-negative + Negative Forms:**

| | |
|---|---|
| I have = I've; | I didn't have any books. |
| He has = he's; | /al didnt hæv enl buks/ |
| She had = she'd; | |
| I am = I'm; | (a) I have never been to puri. |
| He is = he's | /al hæv nev bln t° pʊrI/ |
| She was not = She wasn't; | (b) She wasn't aware; |
| They were not = They ain't | They weren't; = /thaI wɛ ǝ nt/ |
| I cannot = I can't; | (a) I can't sing. /aI kant sIŋ/ |
| She could not = She couldn't; | / ʃI kʊdn°t/ |
| He will not = He won't; | /hl wan°t/ |
| She'll do it. = / ʃildult/ | (b) They must not = They musn't; = /ðel m^sen°t/ |

## Standards of Pronunciation: Historical Perspectives

Prof. Gimson has rightly pointed out that the English are particularly sensitive to variations in the pronunciation of their language. To quote him 'The 'wrong accent' may still be an impediment to social intercourse or to advancement in or entry to certain professions.' Such extreme sensitivity may make people claim that modern speech is becoming more slovenly, full of mumbling and mangled vowels and missing consonants. There is, however, little evidence to show that English is spoken in a more 'slovenly' manner now than it was a few centuries ago. However, what is more significant, socially as well as linguistically, is the attitude that considers a certain set of sound values as more acceptable or 'more beautiful' than another set. This factor suggests that there exists a standard for comparison although it is never explicitly imposed by any official body.

It is to be noted that no such controversy exists as far as the written form of the language is concerned. The spelling of English, the grammatical forms and structures and a greater part of vocabulary have been established, accepted and used for a long time by the majority of educated English speakers. But spoken realizations of English vary in different parts of the country and in different sections of the community. Moreover, the sounds of the language have always been subject to change, thereby giving rise to disparities between the speech sounds of younger and older generations. Two other reasons for such changes are poor communications between regions and different external influences like foreign invasions, which influenced the sound structures of the language in a particular area. These also gave rise to regional pronunciations. However, the notion that one variety of pronunciation was socially more acceptable than others has always existed in England. For reasons of politics, commerce and the presence of the (Royal) Court, the pronunciation of the south-east of England, and more particularly that of the London region became more prestigious. Public schools of the nineteenth century also helped in the dissemination of the speech of the ruling class. However, it is recognized more as the speech of a social class than of a region. With the spread of education, educated people—whether or not they belonged to the upper classes and people—who wanted to advance socially, changed their accent to sound more like the socially accepted standard.

***Standard of Pronunciation: Indian Context.*** This socially accepted standard of pronunciation still has a great prestige value and is referred to as Received Pronunciation (RP). This pronunciation gained popularity with the advent of the radio. The BBC recommended this form of pronunciation for its announcers because it was more widely understood and aroused least prejudice of the regional kind. Thus, RP became associated in the public mind with BBC English. This form of pronunciation is now most commonly described in books on the phonetics of British English and is traditionally taught to foreigners.

However, nowadays RP is not spoken exclusively by a particular section of the society. This change is due to two reasons:

The first one is the spread of education and the second one is the influence of the radio. The radio has constantly brought the RP accent to the ears of a whole range of listening public. Added to this factor is the disappearance of sharp social divisions. As a result, the notable characteristics of regional speech and that of the London region are now not as prominent as it used to be, because both are modified to sound more like RP. In a sense, RP is now considered to be the correct pronunciation.

This does not mean that regional accents have disappeared. On the other hand, some members of the younger generation reject RP because they associate it with the 'Establishment'. For them, a regional or a popular accent has a greater prestige. As a matter of fact, at present, more regional—therefore, more non-RP or non-British—accent is often heard even on BBC radio and television. The spread of pop music and culture also contributed to the tendency of especially younger generations using the regional and popular accents. Moreover, certain regional pronunciations like Scottish English accents and American English are universally accepted.

Within RP, we may distinguish three main types: the *conservative* RP form, which is mainly used by the older generation and by certain professions or social groups; the *general* RP forms, which are most commonly used and which include the pronunciation adopted by the BBC; and the *advanced* RP forms, which are mainly used by young people of mostly upper classes and in certain professional circles.

We need to remember that in addition to over 300 million people speaking English as a first language, a very large number of people from the African and the Indian continents use English as a *lingua franca* along with a large number of indigenous languages. The interference of the indigenous (i.e., local) phonological structures may affect the intelligibility of spoken English as a means of communication. Even where some reasonable degree of intelligibility is retained within any one country, serious deficiencies of a mainly phonological kind pose an acute intelligibility problem when English is used as an international means of communication (especially when we think in terms of multinational trade and commerce). It is for this reason that efforts should be made to adopt either a British or an American model when teaching English as a second language.

## Teaching Implications

All will agree that pronunciation is an important part of foreign or second language learning. For many learners, it remains an obstacle that has to be overcome.

The question arises: When should pronunciation be taught and how?

Other questions remain:

Should we begin with phonic drills before we teach grammar and vocabulary or vice versa?

Should correct pronunciation be taught at an early age or can the adult learners also pick up good pronunciation with equal ease?

Should pronunciation be taught overtly or should it be introduced gradually and unobtrusively?

Should one teach stress and intonation relatively early in the course or when the sound pattern along with vocabulary and grammar have already been mastered?

Answers to these questions vary. Opinions are still evolving with the development of modern linguistics as phonetics and phonology became associated with, and later incorporated into, this discipline.

Sociolinguistics and psycholinguistics have also made valuable contributions in evolving contemporary trends.

Before we talk about the current opinions, let us go back a little to the middle of the last century.

A systematic approach to phonology based on the concept of the phoneme was introduced into structural and audio-lingual language teaching in the 1940s and 1950s. The use of contrastive study of speech sounds across languages helped to identify the similarities and differences between the sounds of the target language and the language of origin. It was believed that the information thus gathered would systematically help learners to overcome the phonological difficulties presented by the new language.

In the 1960s, a trend was established which is still being followed. The trend is to consider discrimination as well as production of sounds. It emphasizes reaching of segmental phonemes, phonemic contrast and contrastive analysis using a variety of practical exercises. It also recognizes the importance of suprasegmental features and offers practice on stress and intonation. Most training takes place relatively early in a course and pronunciation is introduced more gradually and unobtrusively. The emphasis then shifts to global listening, speaking activities, grammar teaching, etc.

Another method advocates mimicking and imitating the teacher without offering any explanation. Specific exercises are used to deal with particular pronunciation problems as and when they arise. Phonetic or phonological explanations may be offered if none of the above procedures work. It is sometimes said that with the introduction of communicative language teaching in the 1980s, the teaching of pronunciation has been neglected. This has led other teachers to re-emphasize the need for attention to pronunciation so that the learners can communicate effectively, which is after all the goal of this approach. A number of useful techniques for pronunciation training are now available.

It is important to note the changes that the socio-linguistic view of language has brought about in the definition and objectives in reaching pronunciation. Firstly, it is now accepted that acquisition of a native-like pronunciation is no longer necessary. To decide on the kind of pronunciation you want to teach, it is more important to take into account the role of the foreign speaker in relation to the native speaker. The most important consideration is that the learner's pronunciation should be intelligible to the native speaker. Secondly, attention is paid to acceptability of pronunciation which may be called a 'social criterion'. It means that learners should avoid acquiring features of pronunciation that the native listener might consider offensive or irritating. It is, therefore, advisable that the learners are taught to articulate clearly, using a neutral pronunciation and strictly avoiding the local characteristics. Thirdly, greater attention is now paid to the teaching of rhythm, stress and intonation. It is especially important to keep in mind that the changes in pronunciation occur when we utter larger units of speech than when we utter isolated words or sentences out of context. This is the area where discourse analysis has particularly influenced the teaching of pronunciation.

Psycholinguistics has also contributed to the learning and teaching of pronunciation. For long, it was widely believed that young children are superior to adults in the acquisition of a perfect native-like pronunciation. Recent psycholinguistic studies do not sustain this belief. The other belief that psycholinguistics questions is that when a learner can perceive (i.e., understand) the difference between a native sound from the target language, he is able to produce that sound accurately. Researchers do not uphold this view. Even when he is given the feedback on the deficiencies in his production of the sounds, it does not necessarily help him to rectify his deficiency.

In the light of what has been said so far, we have realized that students need to follow a standard pronunciation, if meaningful and intelligible communication is to take place between any two sets of people. In the Indian subcontinent, mainly for historical reasons, British pronunciation is preferred and RP or a near RP model is usually selected. In Unit 3 of this module, you have had a detailed description of English phonemes and their pronunciation. Our aim is to teach the learners a model that is intelligible and acceptable to native speakers of English of any variety—British, American, Australian or any other.

In the following section, we are going to deal with the problems that each of the phonemes may pose to foreign learners. The suggestions given may help you to correct your learners' pronunciation to an accepted level.

## Difficulties with Pure Vowels/Contrastive Analysis in the Indian Context

A. **Pure Vowels /i:/and /I/**

In the production of these vowels, learners may not face any difficulty as such. However, especially in Bengali and other languages of Eastern India, e.g., Assamese or Oriya, there is a tendency to replace one phoneme with the other or produce an 'in-between' sound. This is because, though in theory these two phonemes exist in the vowel systems of these languages, (i.e., there are short and long *ee* sounds in the vowel system), in their actual production, especially in words, it is not mandatory to make this distinction to avoid misunderstanding. As a result, in pronouncing English words containing these two sounds there is a tendency to use a centralized phoneme, i.e., a sound that has an indiscriminate length between these two English phonemes. To give an example, *sheep* and *ship* may both be pronounced as / °i:p/. It is a problem serious enough to cause confusion or breakdown in communication. To overcome this problem: (i) the learners should be made aware of the difference in length between these two phonemes with suitable examples and (ii) a lot of practice with minimal pairs with these two phonemes, e.g., *heel* and *hill*, *seat* and *sit*, etc., may be given to raise their awareness. Sentences with such words should also be used to bring out the difference between words with these two phonemes.

**B. Pure Vowel /e/**

This vowel sound generally does not produce a problem serious enough to cause unintelligibility. However, some speakers may tend to equate English /e/ with a half-open variety, thereby using vowel of too open a quality which might be confused with the /æ/ sound. These learners should be taught to modify their vowels in the direction of a closer variety.

**C. Pure Vowel /æ/**

The problem with this vowel may not be acute. However, in some dialectal varieties of Eastern Indian languages this sound may not be as open as in English. In such cases, the opposition between /e/ and / æ/ sounds may be emphasized by making the sound longer in examples, such as *men, man; bed, bad.*

**D. Pure Vowels /^/ and /a:/**

The first of these two vowels is not problematic as such. However, if there is a problem, good results can be obtained in teaching by transcribing the English vowel as /a/ rather than the traditional /^/. In this way, the prejudice against the frequent orthographic spelling with *u* or *o* is avoided. The second sound may cause some problem as it is not used as a distinctive phoneme in the languages referred to. This sound is often used as a neutral sound of indiscriminate length. To avoid this tendency the retracted nature of RP /a/ should be insisted upon and to achieve this, minimal pairs, such as *cart, cot; calf, cuff*; also words like *much, march; hut, heart; bun, barn*; may be compared to underline the differences between these sounds.

**E. Pure Vowels /o/ and /a:/**

Short back open vowels in other languages often differ from English /o/ in that they are somewhat closer or more centralized, or are pronounced with stronger lip-rounding. The vowel sound which is extremely open is /a:/, and the /0/ sound may be compared with /a:/ to bring out the feature. The minimal pairs which will exemplify the sounds are *pot, part; hot, heart; dock, dark; cough, calf.*

**F. Pure Vowel /ɔ/**

Slightly longer nature of this sound should be brought out by emphasizing the slightly higher tongue position accompanied by closer lip-rounding. The [ɔ] sound that already exists in the East-Indian languages may serve as a starting point for acquiring the RP /ɔ/, the tongue and lip positions being relaxed until the correct quality is reached.

The /e/ and / ɔ/ sounds may be compared and practiced using minimal pairs, such as *pot, port; cod, cord; stock, stork*; and so on.

**G. Pure Vowels /u/ and /u:/**

The first one of these two is a short vowel and that quality has to be brought out as in the case of /I/ sound, also by pointing out that it is not just the reduced version of the /u:/ sound. Both are qualitatively and quantitatively different. The difference in quality may be heard in the pair *foot-boot* and that in both quality and quantity may be exemplified in *good-food*. Some of the minimal pairs for these sounds are *full, fool; pull, pool; wood, wooed*; etc.

**H. Pure Vowel /3:/**

This sound causes problem for almost all the speakers of the languages of eastern India and is often replaced by /a:/ sound which is of retracted nature with lips neutrally open. To have an acceptable sound, an articulation with spread lips should be insisted upon. The degree of raising of the tongue is also to be emphasized. Words, such as *father, further; bard, bird; hard, heard; cart, curt; cut, curt; bud, bird; bun, burn*; etc., may be used to bring out the differences between the various sounds.

**J. Pure Vowel /e/**

As foreign learners we should remember that this English sound has no lip-rounding and is extremely short. Standard English speakers avoid its pronunciation when it occurs before 'r'. We should also remember that this sound occurs very frequently in English and occurs in unaccented syllables, e.g., father, famous, woman, suppose, etc., /fa:ðe/, /feimes/, /'women/, /sepez /.

## Difficulties with Diphthongs

We have already learnt that diphthongs form a glide within one syllable. We may say that they have two elements within it: the first element or the starting point and the second element or the point in the direction of which the glide is made. English diphthongs have as their first elements the /I/, /e/ and /o/ sounds, and as their second elements /I/, /ʊ/ and /e/ sounds.

**A. Diphthong /eI/:** *Examples: late, day, rain, eight, great, etc.*

Indian learners should give sufficient length to the first element of this diphthong and lightly touch upon the second element which should not be fully closed as in [I]. The tendency to replace this sound with /e/ should be avoided.

**B. Diphthong /aI/:** *Examples: time, climb, high, die, either, etc.*

In this diphthong, care should be taken to avoid retracting the first element too much so that it remains within the limits of the RP vowel. To achieve this, the starting point should be in a front open position. Again, care should be taken not to glide to a too close position as for vowel [I].

**C. Diphthong /ɔI/:** *Examples: boy, noise, point, etc.*

This diphthong does not present much difficulty to foreign learners. However, care should be taken so that the quality of the first element is between the RP sounds /ɔ:/ and /I/, and the glide does not extend beyond the half-close front level /e/.

**D. Diphthong /eu/:** *Examples: old, road, foe, though, blow, etc.*

To get diphthong sound closer to the RP sound, the learners may learn /3:/ first, and then modify /3:/ by lip-rounding to the end of the vowel. Thus, *fur* may be modified to *foe, burn* to *bone*, etc. This unless when [r] link is made before a following vowel should help to keep this diphthong distinct from /ɔ:/ sound. Again, proper prominence should be given to the first element and the total length of the glide should be reduced appropriately.

**E. Diphthong /au/:** *Examples: sound, cow, mouse, etc.*

Foreign learners should be careful to get the first element correct that is a variety which is not fronted or raised. Like in other diphthongs, the first element should be prominent and the second element should be lightly touched upon, with the tongue closing to a position not higher than half-close.

**F. Diphthongs towards** /ə/, i.e., /**Iə**/, /**eə**/, /**uə**/: *Examples: dear, fierce, idea, care, air, bears, poor, pure, and curious, tour, etc.*

For the first of these three diphthongs, the first element should be nearer [I] rather than /i/. The r which occurs frequently in the spelling of this diphthong should not be pronounced finally or before a consonant. The same suggestion may be made for the second of these three diphthongs. Half-open articulation of the first element of /ee/ and to emphasize this point, it may be helpful to begin the glide from RP /æ/ as in cat. For the third diphthong in this group the first element should be a half-close kind rather than a sound resembling /u:/. The r sound in words like 'poor', 'tour' should not be pronounced.

## Difficulties with Consonants

***Plosives: /p/ /b/, /t/ /d/, /k/ /g/.*** We would like to remind you that while dealing with plosives, we should keep in mind their phonetic features, i.e., (i) their places of articulation, (ii) their force of articulation, (iii) aspiration, (iv) voicing and also (v) length of preceding sounds. To set the learners practise or to correct the production of plosive sounds, the teacher can clearly identify the area with reference to these features.

It may be pointed out to foreign learners that the phonemes /p/, /t/, /k/ are pronounced with more muscular energy and a stronger breath effort than /b/, /d/, /g/. The former set is known as *fortis* (relatively strong), and the latter as relatively weak or *lenis.*

Foreign learners are advised to pay particular attention to the aspiration of /p/, /t/, /k/ when these phonemes occur initially in an accented syllable. For example, if a word like *pin* is pronounced [pln] instead of [phin], it is likely that an English listener will interpret it as [bin], since he interprets lack of aspiration as a mark of lenis /b/. Aspiration is relatively weak in unaccented syllables, e.g., *polite, lip.* When /s/ precedes /p/, /t/, /k/, initially in a syllable, there is practically no aspiration, even when the syllable carries a strong accent, e.g., *pin* [phin] as opposed to *spin* [spin]. Care should be taken so that the release stage of aspiration is relatively inaudible.

Speakers of Indian languages, who have dental and post-alveolar or retroflex varieties, should avoid using the retroflex plosives in English (for e.g., /t/, /d/). On the other hand, they should not use their dental /t/, /d/ for English /θ/, /ð/.

***Affricates: /tʃ/, /dӡ/.*** In this group of sounds, considerable friction occurs approximately at the point where the plosive stop is made. The friction is of a shorter duration than that of fricatives proper.

The first of these affricates /tʃ/ poses no particular problem though sometimes it is replaced with the /s/ sound by some speakers. The /dӡ/ sound is also often replaced by /z/ sound by many dialect speakers. For example, the word 'jew' may be pronounced as 'zoo' causing severe intelligibility problem. Learners' attention should be drawn to the position of the tip, blade and rims of the tongue, the upper alveolar ridge and the side teeth when these affricate sounds are produced and compared with those sounds when pronouncing the fricatives /s/or /z/.

## Fricatives: /f/ /v/; /θ/ /ð/; /s/ /z/; /ʃ/ /ʒ/

Most of these sounds pose problems for Indian speakers because of misunderstanding at both perception and production levels.

The phoneme /f/ which is labio-dental is often produced bilabial as that is nearer the bilabial phoneme with aspiration in Indian languages. In some cases, the contact for /v/ is too weak, as Gimson points out. In either case, the friction is lost. Care should be taken to distinguish such pairs as *pan-fan; fan-van;* etc., to establish the distinction between plosives and fricatives on the one hand, and fortis and lenis fricatives on the other hand. A comparison between the features of the plosive sounds in Indian languages and fricatives in English may also help.

The sounds /θ/ and /ð/ also tend to be produced as plosives under the influence of the native tongue by some native speakers of Indian languages. Again, a comparison between the features of the native and target languages together with some production practice may help to get over with the problems.

The last four sounds may be taken together as in many cases both the /s/-/ʃ/ and the /z/-/ʒ/ distinction is lost. In such cases, besides getting the learners' attention to the correct places of articulation or the fortis/lenis distinction, practice with minimal pairs containing these sounds may be suggested. If a learner absolutely fails to pronounce the /dӡ/ sound, he should be allowed to make a sound nearer /°/

rather than /z/. We have already mentioned the problem with /dj/-/z/ distinction among some speakers and the steps that may be taken for rectifying the problem by the teacher.

The nasals /m/, /n/ or the lateral /l/ pose no particular problem for the speaker of Indian languages.

## Important Issues

The first issue is how much importance we should attach to phonology, sound discrimination and pronunciation teaching. Some teachers are in favour of giving a prominent place to pronunciation teaching in English as the second Language. Emphasis on correct pronunciation in early stages of learning may save hard work on remedial teaching later.

Others feel that greater importance should be given to developing spontaneity and fluency in speech. They contend that pronunciation habits are not so firmly established in the first years that they may not be rectified later.

There is no convincing evidence or argument favouring one or the other position on the merits of pronunciation teaching. However, we would like to add here that language competence also has an effective component. This suggests that learners must emotionally come to accept the target language and its challenges, whether in individual sounds, overall sound patterns or intonation patterns of the new language. Unless the learners can overcome the strangeness of the pronunciation demands of the new language, they will face difficulty in mastering almost any other aspect of the language, e.g., its grammar, vocabulary, writing system, and so on.

The general opinion is that pronunciation is never unimportant. However, at what level of teaching/learning we need to introduce pronunciation teaching and at what level of accuracy of pronunciation we need to pitch our objective, will vary for different types of courses.

## Teaching Pronunciation

When we decide to teach pronunciation, we must be clear about the objectives of such teaching. We may state our objectives in the following manner:

(i) A learner should be able to recognize and discriminate significant sound features;

(ii) He/she should be able to produce sounds in an intelligible and acceptable manner—both segmental and suprasegmental (i.e., using correct stress and intonation);

(iii) She/he should be able to interpret written language phonologically (read aloud) and recreate spoken language graphically (e.g., taking dictation, note taking). As has already been mentioned, rather than aiming to produce a native-like pronunciation, we should aim at intelligibility and acceptability using a model of clear and careful diction. Indian learners should also be able to distinguish between casual, formal or declamatory speech and identify and understand slight social or regional variants of L2. However, learners who aim at a higher level of phonological competence as language teachers or interpreters should attempt to achieve mastery over a wider range of speech varieties.

## Syllabus for Pronunciation Teaching

Teaching of pronunciation should be a continuous process within a language syllabus. It does not help if an intensive course of pronunciation teaching is followed by a period of neglect. On the other hand, the learners may not find it easy to deal with a number of sound features in a new language at a time. It has to be a gradual process and must be taken together with other language activities. A pronunciation syllabus should be taken together with a grammatical and lexical syllabus. Into this syllabus, newer and larger number of sound features should be slowly introduced keeping in mind the level of the learners.

As discourse analysis tells us, speech sounds are produced in a continuous chain. In a discourse, the individual sounds are influenced by preceding as well as following sounds. Under the circumstances, vowels and consonants are sometimes treated at a later stage in the presentation while the earlier units deal with intonation, syllable, stress and rhythm.

These days learners are exposed to varieties of speech from different speakers and varied situations. This is to make them aware of gestures, facial expressions, body postures, etc., which are part of regular speech. These activities will form the part of the course, i.e., during regular speaking and listening activities. The focus of these activities is the attention to sound features which may not be stressed upon in ordinary communication.

The assumption in the above activities is that being able to perceive a sound will make the learner produce that sound. Though it is true that we cannot produce a sound feature that we cannot perceive, it is also true that we do not automatically produce a sound feature that we are able to perceive. However, learners should be given opportunities to absorb sound features through exposure besides having opportunities to produce these features through repetition of meaningful speech in relevant situations. (See Chapter 5 for details.)

Pronunciation has to be taught so that the learners can produce a sound pattern intelligible to native speakers. Unless the learners have very specific needs for acquiring native-like pronunciation, intelligibility should be the main criteria. Whether you allow your learners to develop fluent and spontaneous speech habits before you deal with correct pronunciation will have to be decided by specific objectives and needs. We would like to emphasize here that fluency is an important criterion which cannot be neglected. Fluency practice and pronunciation teaching may be taken up simultaneously with a syllabus suitable for the purpose.

## Global Position of English as Omnivorous Language vis-à-vis Indian English: A Contrastive Analysis

In any consideration of the English language it is found to be linguistically omnivorous. The question remains: Which is its predominating characteristic?

It is natural for a language to borrow words from foreign languages in its formative stage and to cease borrowing after its standard has been evolved. But English is the language which has not stopped borrowing words from other languages even after the fixation of its standard towards the end of the Middle English period. Even now, scientific and technical terms are taken from French and Latin which have always been great feeders of English. And surprisingly enough, nowadays the English seldom naturalize their foreign borrowings and assimilate them to their customary ways of speech. Since the time of Evelyn and Dryden, their assimilative powers have fallen to the zero degree, and the French words for which they have no equivalents keep their foreign shapes and accents, and remain as 'italicized foreigners' in the midst of English words.

Words/Phrases-known

Code Switching: In Indian bilingual and multilingual scenario, code switching refers to mixing up of regional words with a little English vocabulary:

Examples: *Dil (heart) mange more;*
*dil logic; youngistan (young Hindustan)*
*taxi bhara* (taxi fare)*, etc.*

If we inquire into the causes of this linguistic omnivorousness, we shall find that the borrowing in English is never due to any inherent deficiency of the language itself. When Old English whose vocabulary was much more limited than that of Middle English or Modern English could provide natural and expressive terms for such a new world of concrete things and abstract ideas Christianity meant to the Anglo-Saxons, there is reason to believe that the borrowing in English after the Old English period has not been occasioned in most cases by real gaps in its vocabulary. 'That the borrowing is not occasioned by an inherent deficiency in the language itself', says Jespersen, 'is shown by the case with which new terms actually are framed whenever the need of them is really felt, especially by uneducated people who are not tempted to go outside their own language to express their thoughts.' Edward Morris has given interesting examples of this natural inventiveness in his *Austral English, A Dictionary of Australasian Words, Phrases and Usages.* Morris says that when the English settlers came to various parts of Australia, they found many new birds, beasts, trees, fishes, bushes and flowers for which there were no names in English. The settlers filled up these gaps in the English vocabulary 'partly by adopting words from the aboriginal languages, e,g., *Kangaroo, wombat,* partly by applying English words to objects bearing a real or fancied resemblance to the objects denoted by them in England, e,g., *magpie, oak, beech,* but partly also by new English formation' (Jespersen). Such new English formations concern the names of birds, such as *friar-bird, honey-eater, ground lark;* the names of plants, such as *sugar-grass, hedge-laurel,* etc.

The linguistic omnivorousness of English is the result of the linguistic laziness of the English—the desire of the English men of letters to keep aloof from the trouble one has to take in forming expressive and appropriate words and terms (also acceptable) out of native resources. It is the linguistic laziness which accounts for the greatest number of Latin, French and post-eighteenth century borrowings. The Anglo-Saxons could meet their need for new words by utilizing their native resources, and not by adopting words from other languages, because they were not linguistically idle. Jespersen, while pointing out the bad side of the Latin influence on the English language, has observed that it is because of their mental laziness and regard to their own momentary convenience that the English have adopted ready-made foreign words (Latin words) instead of utilizing the native resources to the utmost for the purpose. While referring to the huge influx of Latin adjectives into English he has correctly observed that 'it cannot be pretended that all these adjectives (Latin) are used on account of any real deficiency in the English language, as it has quite a number of endings by which to turn substantives into adjectives.' But instead of taking this trouble of making adjectives by adding endings to the native nouns (e.g., *fatherly*= father + -ly, *heavenly*=heaven + -ly.) they borrowed ready-made adjectives (e.g., *paternal, celestial*). Thus, in the English language we come across the unnatural phenomenon of having foreign adjectives for native nouns, e.g., mouth: *oral*; eye: *ocular*; son: *filial*; ox: *bovine*; house: *domestic*, etc.

So far, as the linguistic omnivorousness is concerned, an interesting contrast may be made between the linguistic behavior of the Dutch and the English in South Africa. When the Dutch came across in South Africa a great many natural objects which were new to them, they named them either by means of existing Dutch words or by making new compounds. Thus, *sloot* 'ditch' was applied to the peculiar dry rivers of that country and *kopje* 'a little head or cup' to the hills. Instead of following this healthy linguistic principle, the English, on the other hand, have simply taken over all these names into their own language where they now figure together with some other South African Dutch words, among which may be mentioned *trek* and *spoor* in the special significations of 'colonial migration' and 'track of wild animal' respectively.

There are certain historical movements or events such as the introduction of Christianity in England in the last decade of the sixth century, the invasion of England by the Scandinavians in the eighth, ninth and tenth centuries, the conquest of England by the Normans in the eleventh century and the Revival of Learning in the sixteenth century, which have contributed, to some extent, to the linguistic omnivorousness of the English language. The unsettled life the English lived from the eighth to the eleventh century was not congenial to the development of linguistic rigidity. Thus, many of the Norman-French words were thrust upon them and the institution like Feudalism was planted by the Normans on the soil of English civilization along with the words associated with it. The English, conquered as they were, could not make rival words out of their native resources. Many Greek and Latin words contributed by the renaissance came through literature almost imperceptibly. But the number of words forced upon the English is very small as compared with those they adopted of their own accord, and deliberately. So, it is not wise to ascribe the linguistic omnivorousness solely to the history of the English people.

The linguistic omnivorousness of English derives largely from the worldwide British Empire which caused contact with many nations. From India, the English have taken over *sahib, begum, maharajah, pundit, baboo, durbar, swaraj, sepoy, lathi, Krishnaism, Dumdum* (bullet, now a place near Calcutta i.e., Kolkata).

From Spanish, the English have adopted such military words as *armada, escapade and embargo.* To the world of games Spain has contributed such words as *quadrille, spade,* etc. The Arabic words taken over into English concern mainly mathematics, astronomy and science in general, e.g., *zero, algebra, cipher, zenith, nadir, alcohol, alchemy, elixir,* etc. *Candy* (from Arabic quand), *sugar* are also Arabic words in English. The contribution of Italy to the English vocabulary is conspicuous. The Italian words relate to fine arts and architecture, e.g., *balcony, colonnade, cornice, corridor, niche, parapet, profile,* etc. Such military words as *alarm, colonel, pistol* and *arsenal* are also taken over from Italy. Indeed, there is hardly any nation in the world which the English have not obliged from the linguistic point of view. The result is that the English vocabulary has become the richest in the world.

## Let Us Sum Up

We have seen how English language has become a truly international language. The prime features of the English language clearly focus on the fact that English has become one of the languages, recognized in the schedule of the Constitution of India. Though there is an attempt to introduce near-native pronunciation of English, standard pronunciation of Indian English has come into focus very recently. We have attempted to understand the importance of sounds in spoken English and the role it plays in an utterance for day-to-day oral communication.

We have also tried to create an awareness for the need of teaching phonetics and to draw attention to the varieties of accents used in English.

We have preferred to select one variety, used by the educated Englishmen, i.e., the RP variety of English for description.

## Glossary

omnivorousness (linguistic): capacity to eat, digest and absorb everything (in language)
heterogeneousness: intake capacity for a variety of things
near-native pronunciation: pronunciation which is very close to a native's pronunciation.
RP: received pronunciation
linguistic: related to language/linguistics
contrastive analysis: analysis related to linguistic and para linguistic contrast so that a foreign language can be learnt easily

## Exercise

1. Write down the general characteristics of English language.
2. What is phonology? What is phonetics of English language?
3. Describe bilabial plosives of the English language.
4. Describe the lil-directional diphthongs of the English language.
5. Describe /ʊ/-directional diphthongs of English language.
6. Describe the fricative consonants of the English language.
7. How would you react to the statement that Indian English has achieved a wide platform in the global market?
8. Describe the phonological features of the English language.
9. Identify at least two problem areas each in the consonant and the vowel sound features that you/your students find difficult to master. How would you correct these problems? Suggest two exercises for each of these areas.
10. Suggest ways of achieving the objectives in teaching pronunciation.
11. What are the objectives of pronunciation teaching? You may use your own experience and suggest.
12. What should you consider when you choose a standard of pronunciation to teach?
13. Write a brief note on the changing trends of pronunciation teaching from the 1940s through 1990s.
14. Discuss the contribution of sociolinguistics and psycholinguistics in pronunciation teaching.
15. What are the objectives of pronunciation teaching? Suggest objectives from your own experience and for your own needs.
16. Suggest ways of achieving the objectives you have mentioned in the answer to Question 5.
17. What would you consider a useful and workable syllabus for your students while teaching pronunciation?

## Bibliography

Abercrombie, David (1989), *Elements of General Phonetics* (Oxford: Oxford University Press).

Balasubramanian, T (2000), *A Textbook of English Phonetics: For Indian Students* (Macmillan Publishers India)

Gimson, A.C. (1962), *Introduction to Pronunciation Teaching of English* (London; Edward Arnold 4th Ed. {1989}).

Jones, D. (1998), *An Outline of English Phonetics* (Cambridge: Cambridge University Press).

Katamba, Francis (1977), *An Introduction to Phonology* (Oxford University Press).

O'Conner, J.D. (1967), *Better English Pronunciation* (CUP).

O'Connor, J.D. (1989), *Phonetics* (Pelican Publishing Company).

Stern, H.H. (1992), *Issues and Options in Language Teaching* (Oxford: Oxford University Press).

Strevens, P.D. (1977), *New Orientations in the Teaching of English* (London: Oxford University Press).

Tiffany and Corr ell (1997), *Phonetics: Theory and Application* (OUP).

# Targeting Classroom Teaching 3

## CHAPTER OUTLINE



## LEARNING OBJECTIVES

This chapter will:

- Explore basic language skills.
- Teach English language through literature.
- Teach English through authentic materials.
- Teach English through English grammar.
- Teach reference skills and study skills.
- Observe teaching skills and evaluate teaching.

## Introduction

Classroom teaching is a complex task that we teachers often take very lightly. We need to explore the various components of classroom teaching to understand how English language teaching becomes a difficult task for teachers having less teaching experience. Let us explore a classroom teaching situation by the following pedagogic cycle with which the teacher and the learner are linked up:

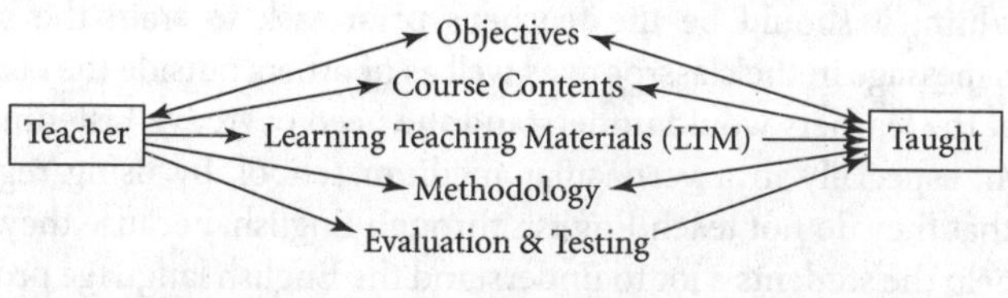


**Table 3.1** Diagram Showing Classroom Teaching

Let us now consider these components in some detail:

The starting point of English language teaching is its objective or a set of objectives. The objective should focus on why a particular language course comes into existence. Various factors like social, economic, political, educational and pragmatic needs determine the objectives.

The course contents are determined by the objectives. Sometimes, the course contents may include:

- Learning & Teaching Materials (LTM)
- Supplementary / Audio-Visual Teaching Materials
- Textbooks

The teaching methodology is selected keeping in view the objectives and course contents as well as LTM. In other words, the objectives, contents (including LTM) and methodology constitute Why, What and How of the course.

Evaluation is the process that evaluates whether the objectives have been achieved or not. Testing is a very special situation (process of evaluation).

**Fascinating Facts**

- Evaluation is no longer a tool to evaluate only the students' performance. It is used to evaluate teachers' performance and competence in classroom teaching situation.
- Evaluation may be of two types: summative evaluation & formative evaluation with reference to the students' evaluation.

## Teaching Basic Language Skills

Basic language skills are namely listening, speaking, reading and writing.

### Listening Skill

Among all the four language skills, listening skill plays an important role in learning a language. Still, we often find this to be ignored in our classroom teaching. It is rather widely overlooked. It is neglected not because we cannot identify the importance of listening in classroom teaching, but because we take it for granted that the learners should achieve this skill automatically without any special care or training. We, the teachers, believe that we are providing sufficient exposure to our students; the materials we give them for practice will suffice for developing their listening skill. But the matter is not that simple. When a teacher delivers lectures in the classroom in English, s/he is supposed to demand that the students are listening to her or him properly. A teacher always takes it for granted that students should understand what s/he explains; what instructions s/he gives, the students should carry it out; whenever s/he praises or rebukes, they should understand it. Is it really so easy? Actually, it is an important duty of a teacher to prepare them for understanding her/him; it should be the teacher's prior task to train the students especially for comprehending her/his message in the classroom as well as of others outside the classroom. Only then the teachers can expect that the learners would understand the need of Active Listening. Sometimes teachers make a wrong decision, especially in a vernacular medium school, by using regional language. Many teachers often confess that they do not teach English through English, because they believe that the use of regional language will help the students a lot to understand the English language properly. Sometimes they are forced to switch over to the mother tongue (MT) because of the growing demands of the students.

## Teacher's Role

But instead of fulfilling the demands of learners and explaining everything in the regional language or mother tongue, teachers must be conscious of making the students aware of the utility, need and importance of listening skills in English. They should set up an ideal learning environment in the classroom. It should be made in such a way that students themselves will make a serious attempt at learning English language skills in general and listening skills in particular. The students will not demand the use of regional language further. This consciousness-raising effort cannot proceed widely if it is not associated with various tasks or activities. These tasks must be interesting. They must have relevance to the students' daily lives, for that reason. But first of all, the teacher should identify the learners' needs and should make them well-equipped with specific strategies and proper motivation for their different listening needs. This is the only way to build their confidence in this skill.

## What Is Listening?

Listening is an active process. It can be depicted as follows:

Input ⟶ Processing ⟶ Output

Input here refers to the utterances by the speaker, whereas the output is the listeners' response. The listener processes the input before coming out with his/her output. Now the question arises:

What happens during the processing? Let us discuss it now.

Listening is a demanding process not only because of the complexity of the process itself, but also due to factors that characterize the listener, the speaker, the content of the message and any visual support that accompanies the message (Brown and Yule, 1983).

## Importance of Developing Listening Skill and Other Sub-Skills of Listening

At first we, as teachers, must be aware of the need and utility of teaching or developing listening skills of our learners. In a multilingual set-up like India, we have our national as well as many regional languages. For this reason, we require a language which can serve the purpose of communication well in many situations, and from that perspective English has a unanimous acceptability. There we have to listen to the English language and understand the message. For example, we can say that we should have proper listening ability while listening to radio/TV news, announcements at the out-terminus/railway stations and at the airport, instructions in an English medium school, etc. There are other real-life situations we face in banks/central government offices, while talking to an unknown person on the road or strangers on the telephone, during interviews (public/private sector), while watching movies/TV programmes, etc. In these situations, English is the only language for communication.

But listening is often said to be a passive skill while speaking is described as an active one. This is not wholly true, for listening is also an active skill as it is mainly concerned with decoding a message and understanding it. Moreover, the listener has to show that he has or has not understood the message from his response. On the other hand, it is necessary to teach/develop learners' listening skills just to improve their speaking skills. Listening to others' 'spoken English' also helps learners to improve their own 'spoken English'. At times, we need to listen to someone conversing in English. As a result, we can say that we have sheer purpose(s) for listening to somebody. For example we can say that when we listen to a political speech, it could be listening for the overall gist of what is being said or when one worker meets another in a coalmine and says, 'It's a hard work', their purpose is not an communication of information but on acknowledging each others' presence and creating a non-threatening, harmonious interaction between them so it is clear that there are two purposes—

(i) Transactional and
(ii) Interactional.

However, they are not served in mutually exclusive situations. In any situation, one can be subjected to both interactional and transactional listening. For example, a manager might use the transactional mode while discussing a project with his/her colleague(s) and later shift to a casual talk.

## How Can Listening Help the Learners Acquire English?

Current reach and theory point to the benefit of providing a silent or pre-speaking period for the beginners (Dunkel, 1991). Delaying production gives learners the opportunity to store information in their memories. It also spares them the trauma of task overload and speaking before they are ready. The silent period may be long or short. It could comprise several class periods of listening activities that foster vocabulary and build comprehension, such as Total Physical Response (TPR) approach. In this approach, the teacher gives a series of commands while demonstrating each one. Learners show their comprehension by acting out the commands as repeated by the teacher. Learners themselves begin to give commands as they feel comfortable as speakers.

## Let Us Do and Learn

1. State the purpose/purposes for which listening might be used in the following contexts.

| Context | Purpose |
|---|---|
| a. Taking down a dictation | |
| b. Listening to a joke | |
| c. Listening to a cricket commentary | |
| d. Listening to announcements at the railway station | |

2. Look at the following situations and comment on the purposes.
   (a) One student to another (in the corridor of the principal's office in a college) while waiting for their turn to meet the principal. 'It's a lovely day, isn't it?'
   (b) Colleagues greeting each other at their office. 'Hello! How are you?'
   (c) One worker to another worker in a factory/workshop. 'It's a hard work.'

**Let Us Consult an Expert**
Adrian Doff (1988; page 199) talks about two types of listening:

(a) Casual Listening: Often we listen to a person or something purposelessly. At such times we, generally, do not listen to them carefully. Unless we hear something interesting, we lack our full concentration. This type of listening is prevalent in social context when we interact with others.

(b) Focused Listening: This is 'intensive listening' for information or for transacting business. The listener, here, is attentive and pays full concentration on what the speaker is saying.

## Let Us Think About

What is the difference between listening and hearing?

## What Happens When We Listen?

It is imperative for teachers to understand that listening is an active process of selecting and interpreting information from auditory and visual cues (Richards, 1985, Rubin,1995). Most of what is known about listening stems from researches done in native language development.

The basic processes of listening have already been discussed in the previous section. It is important for us to know that these processes do not work simultaneously all the time. They may, however, work in rapid succession or backward and forward and as needed. The listener is not conscious of performing these steps. S/he usually

- determines a reason for listening,
- deposits an image of what s/he listens to, in the short-term memory,
- attempts to organize the information by identifying the type of speech event (conversation, lecture, radio advertisement) and the function of the message (to persuade, inform, request, etc.),
- predicts information expected to be included,
- recalls background information (schemata) to help interpret the message,
- assigns a meaning to the message,
- checks that the message has been understood,
- determines if the information is useful in future and helps to save the information in Long Term Memory( LTM),
- deletes the original form of the message that had been received into short-term memory (Brown, 1994, Dunkel,1999).

## Let Us Do and Learn

Read the following conversation and write down the steps that you followed to comprehend the message:

Manish: Have you used SLR?
Raj: Yes; I have.
Manish: What is the synchronizing shutter speed point?
Raj: It is 250.
Manish: Has it been taken in the morning?
Raj: Yes, at 11 o'clock. It was very sunny.
Manish: What about the aperture?
Raj: It is 11.
Manish: I think you've used zoom, haven't you?
Raj: Yes, zoom in the object.
Manish: That's why the entire row of the palm trees along with the fountain have come with the entire Victoria Memorial Hall.

## Barriers to Listening

There are some reasons which create barriers on the way to proper listening. They are:

(a) The listener may not listen to something properly.
(b) Sometimes s/he may listen to something properly but may not comprehend the message due to the usages of the difficult words or due to his/her ignorance of the sentence pattern used.
(c) Sometimes the listeners may have heard the speaker but may not have listened to him/her because of the preoccupation of their mind with something else.
(d) Very often, in spite of listening to the speaker or understanding the message, the listener cannot interpret the message successfully due to lack of his/her previous knowledge. This point should be illustrated more elaborately. Sometimes, the listeners can sense what they hear, while interpreting the spoken message with the help of their worldly or previous knowledge. But sometimes, a lack of background knowledge leads them to serious problems in comprehension.

## Case Study

This has been well-exemplified with real life experience by Anderson and Lynch (1988). One of them found it very difficult to make out a polite comment of an elderly female stranger in a street in Glasgow. She said, 'That's the University. It's going to rain tomorrow.' Though he understood every word but could not comprehend the message. When the author requested the lady to repeat, the lady repeated her comment about the university and the likelihood of rain next day. Still, he could not guess the relationship between the university and rain. In order to find out the relationship between the two, the author had to go beyond what the female stranger said by using his worldly knowledge. He said that he needed to make use of the following:

**General Factual Knowledge:**
(1) Sound is more audible downwind than upwind.
(2) Wind direction may affect the weather conditions.

**Local Factual Knowledge:**
(3) The University of Glasgow has a clock tower with a bell.

**Sociocultural Knowledge:**
(4) Strangers in Britain frequently refer to the weather to 'oil the wheels of social life'.
(5) A polite comment from a stranger usually requires a response.

**Knowledge of Context:**
(6) The conversation took place about half a mile from the University of Glasgow.
(7) The clock-tower bell was just striking the hour.

(Anderson and Lynch, 1988: 12)

Normally, the university bell is not audible. But because of the downwind it was audible on that day. Downwind also suggested that it was going to rain soon. The author actually needed that knowledge to understand what she said.

The above example shows the role of various factors in the interpretation of a message.

For another example, look at the following extract of a conversation:

A: Do you have a 286?
B: No, I've got a 486.
A: Is it Sx or Dx?
B: Dx.

A: Good ......... you don't have to wait long when you save your files.
B: I can show the PC to you.
A: Well. Does it have a single drive or a double drive?
A: Interesting! I'll come and play with the mouse.

Those who have an access to the computer world, know that A and B are talking about a computer machine. But the people who are not quite acquainted with the computer configurations will find it difficult to interpret the conversation, though the extract doesn't have any difficult words; rather some of the words like, 'save', 'mouse', 'drive', 'windows' have been used with specific meanings. And this unfamiliar use of familiar words is the cause of non-comprehension here.

## Strategies and Approaches in Teaching Listening Skill

We have already looked at the situations and purposes of listening. Now, we should concentrate on the strategies of listening. We would discuss two types of processing, namely top-down and bottom-up approaches in detail. In the former, we relate the social and situational context where we let the listeners make inferences and deductions. In the latter, we comprehend messages by understanding the phonological features, discourse markers, grammatical cohesion, lexical cohesion, etc. But we, as teachers, need to involve both the processing methods while training our students in developing listening skills. This should be our main strategy. We should even design curriculum or the tasks in such a way so that we can fulfill our Mission.

### Top-Down Processing

In this type of processing,, the responsible factor is the listener's background knowledge to make out the meaning of the message, not only the input. Listeners are supposed to guess the meaning on the basis of their worldly knowledge and are supposed to approach the input to confirm their guesses and fill out the specific details. An utterance can have many meanings depending on the context in which it is used, and usually we get the clue to the intended meaning when we see the utterance preceding or following it.

Top-down processing refers to utilizing schemata (background knowledge and global understanding) to derive meaning from and interpret the message. For example:

**There was a big traffic jam:** Alice could not reach school on time.

With the help of the above underlined utterance we can come to a point that it is offering the explanation for late-coming. But we can draw this conclusion only when we have a worldly knowledge that someone cannot reach a place on time if there is a traffic jam on the roads. It is our duty to train our learners in both kinds of processing. Learners need to be aware that both of these processes affect their listening comprehension, and they need to be given opportunities to practice using them. Sometimes, the tones of a speaker also become a factor for understanding the meaning. With the help of the tones, we can determine the attitude of the speaker.

Listeners can also know the attitude of the speaker to the preceding and subsequent propositions with the help of proposition markers, such as 'Of course', 'Really' and establish a continuity between one utterance and another with the help of discourse markers, such as 'Actually', 'Hell', 'Anyway' and 'Now'. We can also use cues, such as 'Talking about that', 'Reminds you of', 'By the way' to identify directions in topic development (Richard, 1985).

So, the following process is involved in comprehension:

1. The identification of the type of interactional act or speech event in which the listener is to be involved (e.g., conversation, lecture, discussion debate).
2. Recall of scripts relevant to the particular situations.
3. Inferring the goals of the speaker through reference to the situation, the script and the sequential position of the utterance.

4. The identification of the propositional meaning of the utterance.
5. Assigning an illocutionary meaning to the message.
6. Retaining this information and acting upon it.
7. Deleting the form in which it was originally received. (Richard,1985:193)

## Let Us Think and Learn

A senior teacher of Physics is discussing a particular topic, i.e., light, on a radio programme designed for the students of higher secondary level. Another experienced teacher and a trainee teacher of same subject are listening to the radio teacher. What processing strategies might they employ in their listening?

**Bottom-Up Processing**

In the process, the listener is solely dependent on the incoming input for the meaning of the message. After receiving the input, it is analyzed up to the initial level. First of all, sound signals are organized into words; the words into phrases; then to clauses and at last into a whole sentence. In this bottom-up process, two factors help the listeners a lot in grasping the meaning of the message: their (i) lexical and (ii) grammatical competence. Let us take an utterance from a conversation and observe the involved process through which we proceed before understanding the meaning.

**Input:** Alice could not reach school on time.
At first, the input is organized into words:
Alice/could/not/reach/school/on/time
Then, it is organized into sense groups:
Alice/could not reach/school/on time.

Our grammatical knowledge helped us in this process. With the help of our mental dictionary, we reached the propositional meaning of the utterance. It just highlighted a certain inconvenience of Alice: This is an example of applying Bottom-up Processing for comprehending a message.

Bottom-up processing refers to deriving the meaning of the message based on the incoming language data, from sounds to words to grammatical relationships, to meaning. Stress, rhythm and intonation also play a vital role in this kind of processing. It could be activated as the learner is designated to verify comprehension by the teacher asking a question using the declarative form with a rising intonation (You see that door over there?). Practice in recognizing statements and questions that differ only in intonation helps the learner develop bottom-up processing skills.

## Methods and Classroom Practice for Developing Listening Skills

To develop the learners' listening skills the teacher should stress on the teaching methods. We have already come across two types of listening—casual and focused. The teachers should be careful in giving their learners enough practice in both the learning methods.

Sometimes, we notice ignorance about the importance of listening to come in the way of Teaching and learning. A successful teacher always finds it necessary to establish the importance of listening. In this way, the learners have the right frame of mind to learn listening skills. A teacher must make the learners interested in listening activities. S/he can do that

(a) by arousing their curiosity;
(b) by appealing to their imagination and
(c) by maintaining a 'communication gap' or an 'information gap' to develop the learning attitude and aptitude.

Apart from the ignorance there are other problems too. In India, our students are hampered in their ability to listen for meaning by certain weakness. In general, they are:

(i) inadequate range of words and phrases that are understood;
(ii) inability to maintain attention;
(iii) inability to understand pronunciation other than the personal or regional pronunciation;
(iv) inability to understand fast speech;
(v) inability to understand an utterance against background noise through acoustic/electrical interference.

The main remedy for the first weakness lies in the student enriching his vocabulary through reading and by looking up unfamiliar words in dictionaries with phonetic transcriptions, such as *The Advanced Learners' Dictionary of Current English* (Latest publication in 2000; edited by Sally Wehmeier and Phonetics editor is Michael Ashby).

The second weakness is general. Many efficient listeners for short stretches lose their efficiency if they have to go on listening for an unbroken stretch of more than 20 minutes. It has been found from experience that dictation is an admirable exercise for sharpening attention. Listening to broadcasts or recordings of full-length plays, and to films, is almost certainly of great value. The dramatic situation and the variety of dialogues combine to maintain interests, and hence attention, even over long stretches.

Remedy for the third weakness is to be sought in learning the correct pronunciation of each word. This is possible with the help of a pronouncing dictionary like Daniel Jones's *English Pronouncing Dictionary (EPD)* and by listening to recordings, broadcasts and dialogues in films.

## New Phrases-Known

- Information Gap: Passing the information from simple to complex ones and maintaining a willful gap of space and time.
- Communication Gap: Maintaining a gap of knowledge in terms of communication.

The teacher can deal with the fourth weakness by adjusting his/her speech and clarity to the capacity of the class and gradually speeding up. When the context is made vivid and meaningful, it becomes easy for the students to follow even fast speech. Thus we see that right kind of 'exposure to worldly knowledge' and right kind of attention make 'fast and difficult speech' easy for understanding.

Practically, it is very important for everyone in this electronic age to listen to and understand speech against background noise. So, the fifth weakness has to be dealt with seriously and a tape-recorder and other specially prepared recordings are indispensable for this unless the whole thing is left to chance experience. A tape-recorder is even otherwise a valuable aid in much of the remedial work connected with the teaching of the four language skills.

There are many exercises which the teacher himself/herself can devise for doing remedial work. One such exercise for developing the all-round efficiency in listening skills is the answering of Multiple Choice Questions (MCQ type).

***Story-Based Method.*** A teacher can easily come up with her/his own listening activities if s/he finds the textbooks inadequate for teaching listening skills. For example, s/he can tell her/his students interesting stories, real or imaginary, and can pause frequently while narrating the story and describing the activities and ask them to guess what is going to happen next. For example,

> A few months ago, I was asleep at home as usual. At about three o'clock in the morning (**what happened?**) . . . I was suddenly awakened by a noise . . . (**What noise?**) . . . of rushing water. . . . (**What was it?**). It came from the bathroom. So I got up and went to investigate (**what was it?**). I found to my dismay that the cold water pipe

had burst and water was pouring all over the floor. . . . (**so what did I do?**) So I got a bucket and put it underneath. . . . (**What should I have done?**). Then I realized what I should have done. I went out into the hall and turned off the main tap.

**(Doff, 1988: page 205)**

Let us see another example:

Once in the evening I was relaxing in my bedroom. Suddenly my younger brother rushed to my room and he was just trembling. . . . (**What was the cause of his trembling?**). He informed me about something that scared me . . . (**What might be the information? Why did it scare me?**). He informed me that someone was shouting in one of our rooms at the back yard which was looking outside. . . . (**Who might be that person? How could he enter the room?**). Sometimes he was making peculiar sounds. . . . (**what type of sound?**). Then I opened the door. . . . (**What did I see?**). I found the sound coming out of the wardrobe. . . . (**How could it be possible?**). I opened the door. . . . (**What did I see?**). I found my small transistor radio inside and its switch was on.

Actually when we listen to an interesting story, we listen very carefully. We are always eager to know what will happen next. From that point of view, these questions are quite relevant and natural. But the teacher must notice whether each and every student is careful and is giving answers. This technique enables students to predict a sub-skill of listening.

***Task-Based Method.*** It has come into vogue in the last decade. In this method, learners have to listen to the speaker(s) and are supposed to carry out the tasks given by the speaker(s). For example, having listened to the text the learners can fill in a table, label a diagram and list the main points. Successful performance shows the full comprehension of learners. Learners get motivated to do these tasks because these resemble the natural language use.
Let us do a few tasks (listening activities) to testify the effectiveness of the method.

## Listening Task A*

C=Caller
R=Receiver

R: Good afternoon, Quest Consultancy
C: Hello, can I speak to Mr. Dey, the MD?
R: May I know, who's on the line?
C: Mr D. Gomes, Marketing Manager of G.D. Pharmaceuticals Ltd., Kolkata. Is Mr. Dey there?
R: I'm afraid, he's not available at present. Would you like to leave a message?
C: Who am I speaking to?
R: I'm his Personal Secretary, Laura Dimes.
C: O.K. Tell him I'll call him later. When will he return?
R: He should be back within an hour.
C: Thanks.
R: Welcome.

## Listening Task I

Listen to the Text-A and answer the following questions:

(a) Can you tell me what type of conversation it is?
(b) Who are the two people taking part in the conversation?
(c) What does the man in the conversation do?

---

* The above text may be pre-recorded and displayed during the class. The use of two different voices would make the text very interesting.

(d) Who is Mr. Dey?
(e) What can you say about Laura Dimes?
(f) Can you guess whether Mr. Gomes would meet Mr. Dey?

## Listening Text B*

- The Shatabdi Express will leave from platform No. 1 in a few minutes.
- Santro car No. WBM 6478, do not cross the yellow line.
- Mr. Gary Raghaban, who has arrived by IC175 from Chennai—you are requested to contact the reception please.
- Passengers travelling to London by Air India are requested to proceed for security check.
- Mr. and Mrs. Kharbanda, your daughter Sakshi is waiting for you at the police bunk near the Eastern Gate, next to stall No. 197.

## Listening Task 2

Listen to the Text-B and answer the following questions:

(i) Who is making the announcement?
(ii) Whom does he address it to?
(iii) Where is the announcement being made?
(iv) What would the person(s) addressed to on hearing each of the announcements?

## Listening Text C

1. Reema Basu, who is 29, lives in her own house in Kolkata. She is a school teacher.
2. Mr. Handa is a doctor. He works in All India Institute of Medical Sciences in New Delhi. He is 44 and lives in a flat by himself.

## Listening Task 3

Listen to the Text-C. As you listen, fill in the personal details about Reema and Mr. Handa in the table below:

| | |
|---|---|
| Name: | Name: |
| Age: | Age: |
| Occupation: | Occupation: |
| Place of Work: | Place of Work: |

## Listening Text D

Tourist: I am an American tourist. Which is the best way a visitor can see Varanasi?

Guide: I think, the best way is to take a boat ride at dawn, along the great three-mile curve of the Ganges. This curve faces east.

Tourist: What'll the view be like?

Guide: At 5.30 in the morning, a grey mist covers the river. As it clears high above the bank, you will see the splendid outlines of *Maharaja's* palaces, ashrams, temples and mosques.

Tourist: Is that all?

Guide: No, leading down to the water are wide steps and platforms. These are the famous Ghats.

* It would be more effective if pre-recorded voice is displayed.

## Listening Task 4

Listen to the Text-D and match the words in Column A with the words related to them in Column B:

| Column A | Column B |
|---|---|
| 1. Dawn | (a) River Ganges |
| 2. Mist | (b) Maharaja's palaces, ashrams, etc. |
| 3. Bank | (c) 5-30 in the morning |
| 4. Splendid | (d) wide steps and platforms |
| 5. Ghats | (e) clears |

Example: 1. Dawn > (c) 5-30 in the morning

## Listening Text E

Abacus is a device for counting. In this device, beads are strung on wires and fitted to a frame. It is used for teaching small children how to count. The Chinese use them for computing, and devices of pebbles and movable counters were known in antiquity to Egyptians, Greeks and Romans as well as the Chinese. Its great advantage in simplifying adding and subtracting Roman numerals is obvious.

## Listening Task 5

Listen to the Text-E. As you listen, draw the thing that's being described.

## Speaking Skill

We have already briefly referred to the nature of listening skill. We would like to restate the same from the point of view of teaching the art of speaking or oral communication as a skill and talk about its pedagogical implications.

(a) Oral communication is a two-way process between a speaker and a listener/listeners involving the productive skill of speaking and the receptive skill of understanding, or more precisely, listening with an understanding. It is not a static process. Both the speaker and the listener have a positive function to perform. The speaker has to encode the message to be conveyed in appropriate language. The listener has to decode or interpret the message he receives.

(b) In normal speech, the message itself contains a great deal of linguistically 'redundant' information, i.e., it conveys more information than the listener needs. So the listener does not need to follow the utterance of the speaker with utmost attention for every detail.

(c) The listener also receives help from the prosodic features, viz., the stress and intonation which accompany the spoken utterance and form part of its meaning. At the same time facial expressions, body movements like gestures also help the listener to interpret the message.

(d) Speech is characterized by incomplete utterances, sometimes ungrammatical utterances, and also by false starts and repetitions. In contrast, written language almost typically has well-structured sentences which are carefully linked together (unless it is spoken language in a written text, e.g., dialogues in a play).

## Pedagogical Implications

How does the aforementioned information influence classroom practices? Let us discuss these in detail:

**(a) Listening Comprehension:**

In classroom, the emphasis is chiefly on the ability to speak. But we saw that oral communication is not just production or speaking, but reception or listening as well. Moreover, as teachers, we cannot guarantee that as the learners are listening, they are being able to understand. Understanding of the spoken language cannot be left to take care of itself. If we do, the results are:

(i) The learners no longer have any control of what is said to them and
(ii) Poor understanding often gives rise to nervousness which in turn further inhibits the ability to speak.

Learners' ability to understand has to be more extensive than their ability to speak because they have no control on what is or will be said to them. Also, the listening models (e.g., dialogues) in the classrooms are contrived in such a way that they facilitate oral production but they do not always contain sufficiently large number of features of natural speech (as mentioned earlier). In order to cope with real life language situations, learners need regular and frequent training through a programme of listening comprehension so that they are exposed in the classroom to suitably varied models of natural speech from the earliest stages of a language course. In other words, they actually have 'to learn to listen' just as they learn to speak.

**(b) Oral Productions:**

The main goal of teaching the productive skill of speaking will be oral fluency which means ability to express oneself intelligibly, reasonably, accurately and without hesitation. This last named aspect is important because frequent hesitations may lead to breakdown in communication as the listener may lose patience and interest under such a condition.

The way to ensure fluency is (i) to guide the learners through the stages of imitation of a model (ii) to make them respond to cues to the final point (iii) to make them express their own ideas.

It requires two complementary levels of training: (a) practice in the manipulation of fixed elements of the language like grammatical patterns and lexical items, and (b) practice in the expression of personal meaning without cues from the teacher. What it implies is that, to develop oral skills, dialogues and passages may serve as a starting point; but the teacher cannot depend only on the written text if communication in an authentic situation is the goal. On the other hand, audio-visual aids provide, at all levels, a powerful way of stimulation and developing oral ability without recourse to written language.

**(c) Intelligibility—Phonology:**

Intelligibility is often defined in phonological terms (e.g., able to discriminate between /i/ and /i:/). But for the purpose of oral fluency this term needs to be extended to include a mastery of the other areas of language: grammar, vocabulary as well as phonology. The teacher has to concentrate on essential features, such as differences between weak and strong forms, key sounds, basic stress and intonation patterns, etc. More importantly, the focus should be on the reception rather than on the production of sounds. However, given the limited time that the teachers get for development of oral skills, attention should be on a balanced approach.

**(d) Intelligibility—Structure:**

The development of oral ability itself is a good motivation. A beginner derives immense satisfaction when he is able to say even a small number of sentences and this element of satisfaction must be sustained.

As opposed to free expression, practice in a controlled situation without excessive correction helps to sustain motivation. It can also be improved by: (i) placing greater emphasis on the receptive skill of listening which has the added advantage of getting the learners understand language without reference to written texts and (ii) providing opportunities for meaningful repetition of known materials.

**(e) Interdependence of Oral Skills in Communication:**

Oral communication is a two-way process involving a speaker and listener. In a normal communication, a speaker does not always initiate; s/he also responds to what s/he has heard (e.g., answers a question/makes a comment). The listener does not always remain silent; s/he is expected to give some sort of response which may not always be verbal (e.g., carries out an instruction). In the classroom, therefore, appropriate provision has to be made to see that the two oral skills are integrated through situations which permit and encourage authentic communication.

## Let Us Do and Learn

1. Consider the following task you may have set for your learners:

**Procedure:** Divide the learners into pairs.

Ask your learners to take a piece of paper and write down the following:

**A. Three Places:**

- Your favourite holiday place
- A place you would really like to visit
- A place you would rather forget

**B. Three Persons:**

- Your favourite person/relative
- A person you would like to know
- A person you find most funny

(You may choose some other categories.)

Next, each learner finds a partner and exchanges the sheets. Then the learners ask each other questions about any of the information that is of interest to them.

## Approaches for Teaching Speaking Skill

In view of the above information we would now like to see how oral skills may be developed in the classroom.

William Littlewood mentions two models of language learning:

(i) Skills learning is associated with controlled activities for pre-selected items leading to more independent form of practice in using language for communication.

(ii) Natural process or creative construction is associated with situations where language develops naturally through exposure and use.

The first model uses a set of mechanism which enables us to learn in a conscious way whereas the second set enables us to learn in a subconscious, natural way. Stephen Krashen calls the conscious process 'learning' and the subconscious process, 'acquisition'.

The question now is: Can there be an overall framework which will accommodate both kinds of learning?

The advantage of following the skill-learning model only in a classroom is that it can provide the special kind of situation needed for such learning and it also takes less time. Natural learning takes a long time in the classroom and is not very effective. So, we should try to develop the special kind of controlled learning that the classroom can support more effectively. This is the kind of approach which is used, for instance, in audio-lingual or situational language teaching methods. It helps learners avoid making errors.

However, it is argued that language learning is different from other kinds of learning and will take place more efficiently if we create contexts in the classroom where learning can take place through natural communication.

We can see that neither of the processes by itself leads to universal success and that each has its useful contribution to make in the classroom. So we should try for a broader framework integrating the two.

## Professor Littlewood's Framework

This framework consists of two components: part-skill practice for mainly skill learning and whole-task practice which combines the skills into operation fluently and correctly for meaningful communication.

## Part-Skill Practice

In the following steps, the activities are controlled in terms of grammatical structure, vocabulary and information.

- **Internalizing the language system** involves learning or mastery of the aspects of the foreign language system. In the traditional approach, it would involve learning and practicing different tenses, sentence patterns and all components of grammar and understanding and employing rules to construct sentences, etc. With the emphasis on communication as the goal, teachers today tend to reject such grammar-oriented activities. However, grammar plays an important role in communication. Therefore, active links should be maintained between grammatical choices and meanings they convey so that the linguistic system can be easily integrated into the communication system.
- **Exchanging shared knowledge** is to help learners link the language forms with their literal meanings; they are asked to focus on some area of knowledge they share and to use the new language to describe it. The information that the language carries is already familiar to everybody (e.g., describe the classroom situation where somebody is sitting, etc.). These activities may be criticized for being 'artificial' and not performing acts of communication. However, they are useful as they help learners to 'learn' to communicate.
- **Exchanging literal information** refers to the information gap when the teacher distributes the information among the learners and gives them a reason for exchanging that information (one learner develops the outlines into a story and others ask him questions to elicit more information).
- **Practicing communicative functions** using communication-oriented activities when the control is relaxed to some extent with the focus on the meaning. However, the grammatical structures used are known and controlled in terms of the functions (e.g., making suggestions, offers, requests, etc.) relating to cues or pictures given by the teacher: Would you like a cup of tea? The language use still cannot be called 'communication' as the learners are not expressing their own communicative intentions.

We should remember that there is no one-to-one link between language forms and communicative functions. The same functional meaning can be expressed by a variety of forms and the same forms can be interpreted differently in different situations. Our goal as teachers is to get the learners to choose appropriate forms to express their own meaning and communicative intentions rather than those determined by the teacher or the materials. Role-playing provides the contexts through which this progression takes place, for example, imagine that you are in a clothes shop, you greet the assistant, ask for a shirt, specify size and colour, and so on. As you can see, the communicative intentions are specified in detail and they are not the learners' own intentions.

- We can give the learners more scope by giving them a loose framework when they create their own communicative intentions (e.g., greet the assistant; ask for what you want; if the item you had asked for is sold out, ask for something else, etc.).
- By combining the principle of role-playing with the principle of information exchange we can create contexts when one learner has to find information from another who has it through an exchange of dialogue (e.g., the first person greets the assistant—the second person responds, asks what he/she wants; the first person asks for a shirt/pair of shoes/leather bag—the second person asks what size/colour/shape, etc.). The more you make the framework loose, the more choices the learners have.

## Whole-Task Practice

The progression from controlled skill-based activities to completely free communication is gradual. Along this progression, the control over the language and the meanings that are expressed vary in degrees. As we move towards the whole task, the interaction becomes less tightly controlled, and the learners themselves decide what meanings they want to express at different stages of interaction. Even at the later stages of part-skill practice, some learners may take their role-playing cues only as the starting point and exercise more freedom by creating their own interaction around them. Thus, they themselves move into the domain of whole-task practice.

The tasks suggested in the previous section consist of mainly predictable sequences of language linked to concrete facts and situations. However, real communication is unpredictable.

This dimension of unpredictability is introduced by adding an element of problem-solving. For example, instead of giving the learners a set of pictures to describe, we may give the learners the pictures in a jumbled order for them to discover the sequence themselves by working out how the pictures can be combined to tell a coherent story. The learners in a group have to negotiate the problem-solving element. This aspect depends on each learner's active contribution and cannot be predicted.

It is the 'information gap' that normally motivates the exchange of sample information, though in this case the initial information is given because the problem itself creates the communicative purpose. In case of problem-solving, the learners need to overcome the 'opinion gap' because a problem may have many solutions, and the learners will need to put forward their own opinions so that they have the scope to choose what to say. Therefore, the specific cues are replaced by more general information about the situation and the participants' roles and purposes within it. The learners now enjoy more scope to interact through personal meaning of their own and they become personally involved as communication takes place.

The concept of role-playing is useful, provided the learners are able to identify with the roles assigned to them. Role-playing provides the opportunities for them to assume the behaviour they are to produce outside the classroom and integrate these behavioural patterns with their own personalities.

The next logical step is for the learners to create the situations from the resources actually present in the classroom and use language. In other words, they develop their language skills by engaging in real experiences which require these skills.

***Task-Based Approach.*** (Gillian Brown et al. Teaching Talk: 1984) talks of a task-based approach which allows the teacher to offer the learners an opportunity to attempt a task similar to the one they have already performed though it is different in detailed content. In this case, the learner can put the lessons learnt from the first performance into practice. The tasks are graded in terms of difficulty and have information gap which is functional, i.e., the listener does not know something but which he needs to know in order to achieve a desired result.

***Strategy and Techniques for Developing Speaking Oral Skills.*** In the current scenario, when the emphasis is on using language in authentic communicative contexts, oral skills are taught using appropriate tasks where the learners negotiate the problem solving element. The tasks are graded from simple (with a lot of support knowing what it is they need to express) to complex—both in terms of form and meaning. There is a gradual progression from very controlled activities at one end to completely free communication at the other end. It is a continuum.

***The Role of English Teachers.*** The role of teachers is important in developing oral skills. Donn Byrne says the role of the teacher is to provide the best conditions for learning (Byrne,1981). However, the role differs at different stages: (i) At the presentation stage, the teacher is the informant. S/he selects new materials and presents in a way that the meaning is clear and memorable, (ii) At the practice stage, the teacher is the conductor. As the learners do most of the talking, the teacher provides the maximum amount of practice and (iii) In the production stage, the teacher is the guide. No real learning takes place until the learners use the language in a real situation. The teacher, as a guide, provides the activities for free expression.

By now, you are aware that in Communicative Language Teaching (CLT), the teacher addressing the whole class from the front does not serve any useful purpose. Now, the teacher uses pair work and group work to give the learners more autonomy so that they take the responsibility of their own learning. The learners need not sit at their own desks all the time neither does the teacher need to be at her/his table throughout the lesson. For developing oral skills, the learners need to move around the class finding new partners or groups so that they can practice and use their language skills in varied situations.

Before the learners begin to learn to speak, the teachers need to make them aware of certain rules that should be followed. According to Nolasco and Arthur, the rules are as follows:

- Only one person speaks at a time;
- The speakers change;
- The length of any contribution varies;
- There are techniques for allowing the other part or parties to speak and
- Neither the content nor the amount of what we say is specified in advance.

Teachers need to be aware of these characteristics of the native-speaker's performance and conversation if oral skills of the learners have to develop effectively. They also need to consider which of the functions of the conversations are relevant for the learners according to their levels and needs. Generally, the learners will need to give and receive information, collaborate in doing something, share personal experiences and opinions with a view to building social relationship.

***Techniques for Controlled Activities.*** Sometimes learners feel diffident to talk within a classroom situation. The Controlled Activities can only guide the learners to feel confident in their classroom interaction. As the learners develop their ability to participate in and carry on with a simple conversation using controlled activities, they gain confidence. 'Getting to know you' activities promote trust and 'articulation' activities which give the learners the opportunity to use English sounds in a safe and undemanding environment are useful in this context.

The learners also need to develop their ability to take part in sustained conversation. Activities which give them controlled practice use dialogues, by paying attention to exchange structures, short responses and grammar practice.

Here are a few examples of 'getting-to-know-you' activities:

- **Chain names** when the learners sit in a semi-circle and a learner introduces herself/himself (e.g., I'm Reena). The next one has to repeat the first name and add her/his name (e.g., Reena, I'm Sunny). The third one has to continue in the same way (e.g., Reena, Sunny, I'm . . .), and so on.

She is Reena. She's from Darjeeling. I'm Mohan. I'm from Bhubaneswar, etc.)

- **Find someone who** enables the learners to find out more about each other using task sheets like this: Find someone who can sing/type/swim/drive a car, etc. The learners go around the class and ask questions like 'Who can sing/ type/swim? Or do you swim/sing/drive a car? And so on. The activity is linguistically very simple but helps the learners to develop confidence as the structures they use are known.
- A variation is ***Guess who***? When the learners write down some information about themselves in pieces of paper and pass them anonymously to the front of the class. These are collected and redistributed. The learners go around the class asking questions like, 'Who was born in Chennai/ Singapore? Who has a pet dog called Jerry? Who is/are fond of Chinese food?' and so on.

When the learners feel more confident to handle forms (grammatical structure), the practice should be made more meaningful by building in some element of personalization or information exchange into the tasks. Here are a few ideas:

- **The Best Years of My Life**
  Aim: To give practice in simple past forms.
  Ask the learners to list five particularly personal significant dates on a piece of paper.
  Divide the class into pairs. The pairs exchange information using the following basic model (introduced by the teacher before they start):
  I remember 19 . . . . . . . . . . . . . . . . . . . when I . . . . . . . . . . . . . . . . . .
  Do you remember . . . . . . . . . . . . . . . . . . ?
  Yes, I do. It was the year when I . . . . . . . . . . . . . . . . . . ?
  . . . No, not really, etc.
- **The Old Days**
  Use old picture cards, photographs, prints of the town where the learners live.
  Group work by using '**used to**' form:

Articulation activities may take the form of practicing individual sounds of English and using in single words or short phrases like what? A big black book, A colourful cat, etc.

Then, the learners may be asked to memorize short dialogues and repeat the dialogues as best as they can. Or they may be asked to repeat a dialogue that they have heard for the first time on the tape recorder. At a later stage, they may be asked to repeat a dialogue maintaining the same rhythm, intonation, stress and pronunciation.

An important aspect of communication is to produce an appropriate response or '*gambit*' that helps to maintain the conversation. These responses may indicate agreement with the speaker (e.g., Yes, that's right/Of course, it is/Yes, I do, etc.), or may express polite disagreement (e.g., Well, not really/Er, I don't really know, etc.), or encourage confirmation or more information (e.g., Is that right?/Really?). These responses need to be built into the drills together with the right stress and intonation for authentic use.

## Techniques for Developing Awareness

The learners not only need to develop the ability to produce, but also the ability to interpret the meanings of what they hear, which leads to interaction. For this, they need to develop the awareness (i) of as to what is appropriate in conversation (ii) of strategies to further conversation to facilitate interaction in the target language. They need to learn the strategies to encourage the speaker to say more or be aware of the different uses of repetition in spoken language, how to interrupt (politely) and how to deal with interruption, and so on. They need to develop the awareness of the use of

- Weak forms: I would = I'd
- Encouraging noises like: Really? Do you? Is it? Wuhu!
- Fillers like: Well, So, er . . . , Anyway, etc.
- Gestures like: nodding/shaking head (to agree or disagree), raising/lowering eyebrows (to show annoyance/disbelief), using hands to emphasize, etc.
- Stress and intonation (e.g., I asked for a red woolen dress, not a red silk dress.).

## Techniques for Developing Fluency

The most important purposes of fluency activities are that they

- lead to **authentic response**;
- maintain and develop **social relationship**;
- help in **information exchange**;
- lead to **co-operative problem-solving** and
- lead to **expressing ideas and opinions**.

In these activities, the learners initiate and decide what they want to say. The teacher keeps a low profile to allow the learners to take the responsibility of their own learning and get involved in using the language beyond the level of producing isolated sentences.

The tasks set are relatively easy and stretches over a short period of time. To encourage, the learners are praised for their efforts. They are told that errors are not important for these tasks.

Here are some ideas for conducting fluency activities:

- I hated Moths—did you?
  Aim: To introduce learners to fluency activities.

Methodology: A task sheet with a list of school subjects on it is given to each learner. Working individually for five minutes, they choose one of the subjects they liked and list three reasons for liking the subject. Then the learners choose one of the subjects they particularly disliked and three reasons for disliking the subject.

Next, they go around the class and find out if anyone liked or disliked the same subjects as them and the reasons for their liking or disliking the subjects. They make a list under the following headings:

Reasons for liking a subject    Reasons for disliking a subject

- Exchange
  Aim: To encourage the learners to find out about each other by asking questions.

On a large sheet of paper each learner should write down the following (You may use other ideas/topics):

A. Three books
- The first book you remember reading
- The name of the last book you read
- The name of a book you will always remember

B. Three hobbies
- Something you enjoy doing
- Something you want to start doing
- A hobby you never want to start

You may add to this list.

Next, each learner finds a partner he or she does not know well and exchange sheets. They ask each other questions about any of the information that is of interest to them. They may ask questions like:

Why do you like . . . . . . . . . . . . . . . . . ?
What is . . . . . . . . . . . . . . . . . . ?
Tell me about . . . . . . . . . . . . . . . . . , etc.

. . . After five minutes they change partners. At the end of the session the learners may be asked if they found anything interesting about others in the group. These activities provide the opportunity for using English language in real time, the chance for learners to express their own opinions and ideas and using the language for a specific purpose.

## Let Us Do and Learn

Now that you have learnt some of the techniques you may use to develop your learners' oral skills, think about the following ideas and figure out in how many different ways you may use them in your class. Identify the areas of competence (e.g., grammatical/sociolinguistic/discourse, etc.). Suggest the procedure you would like to follow. Considered on the basis of level, time needed, aim, preparation, if any and procedure including steps, your plan (lesson) should have the following points:

1. Play an audio tape of a short conversation, or you may use a video tape blurring or blocking the pictures. It should not be longer than two minutes.
   Here are a few hints for your use. Ask the class or groups to build up a mental picture of the people talking.
   These prompts may help: Young/old? Male/female? Now add to the list.
   What activities can you use in groups or pairs on the basis of learners' speculations?
   How will you wind up the lesson?
2. Prepare a list of simple utterances: For example, I'm going to a party tonight; My brother is a lawyer, etc.
   Now, divide the class into small groups. Give each group a simple utterance.
   What will you ask your groups to do with these utterances? (Hint: Think in terms of meaning and intonation.)
   Which class level will your activities be good for? How long will you spend on each activity? Can each activity lead to a discussion?

## Let Us Consult an Expert

This is Donn Byrne's process model for the organization of classroom activities.

<table>
<tr><td colspan="4">Teacher Mediated</td></tr>
<tr><td rowspan="5">A<br>C<br>C<br>U<br>R<br>A<br>C<br>Y</td><td colspan="2">Whole Class</td><td rowspan="5">F<br>L<br>U<br>E<br>N<br>C<br>Y</td></tr>
<tr><td>T as 'Monitor'</td><td>T as 'Stimulator'</td></tr>
<tr><td>drills & exercises<br>language games<br>(e.g., guessing games)</td><td>informal talk<br>explanation & evaluation<br>of activities narration<br>(e.g., stories)</td></tr>
<tr><td>simulated conversation<br>questionnaires</td><td>problem-solving<br>activities role-play<br>communication games</td></tr>
<tr><td colspan="2">Pair work ⟷ Group work</td></tr>
<tr><td colspan="4">LEARNER DIRECTED</td></tr>
</table>

## Teacher-Controlled Activities in a Classroom

***Using Communicative Approach:***

- The activities are controlled in terms of both grammar and content (i.e., The message they mean to convey).
- The learners should be made aware of the appropriate use of language depending on the context.
- Such use will include, besides appropriate words and structures, appropriate stress, intonation, gestures, short expressions for encouragement, agreement, disagreement, and so on.
- The focus in the classroom should be on the use of authentic language in authentic situations.
- The teacher's role changes depending on the learners' level of competence and confidence until they can act without the teacher's intervention.

**Reading Skill:** Let us start the discussion with a very humble question:

**What is the skill of reading? Is it a process or a product?**

Perhaps, the best way of defining reading is by referring to two major elements: (1) the reader and (2) the text because reading undeniably and uncontrollably involves the two. The third element is the writer.

Reading, whether in a first or second language context, involves the reader, the text and the interaction between the reader and text (Rumelhart, 1997).

The ability to read is acknowledged to be the most stable and durable of the language modalities (Bernhart, 1991). **What** a reader reads is the product but **how** he reads is the process. And, this is true both of reading in the first and the second languages.

Several studies have been conducted to establish the process of reading as a series of sub-skills which offer us insights into **how** the reader arrived at the meaning of the text or **what** meaning exactly the reader got out of the text.

Although reading in that first language (L1) shares numerous important basic elements with reading in a second or foreign language, the processes differ greatly. Intriguing questions involve whether there are two parallel cognitive processes at work, or whether there are processing strategies that accommodate both first and second languages. Despite these interests, second language research on reading is frequently dismissed as being marginal and derivative from first language reading.

While it is true that L1 and L2 reading processes have similarities, it is also important to recognize that many factors come into play, which in turn makes second language (L2) reading a phenomenon in itself.

From time to time, different researchers have considered different variables, such as different cultural background, different motivation and different background knowledge. Some of these actually cast doubts on an attempt to describe the skill of reading exclusively as either a process or a product.

While the meaning the reader makes of the text, i.e., text as the *Product,* is important because it helps us to get different interpretations of the same text as the *Process.* The way he arrived at the interpretation, shows the way the reader understands the meaning the product.

It is, therefore, possible to say that reading can be viewed both as a process and a product. While the product gives us different levels of meaning, the process varies from reader to reader, purpose to purpose.

Reading, in the twenty-first century in most cultures, is a private activity. Several definitions have been arrived at:

Widdowson's definition, 'Reading is the process of getting linguistic information via print', is a useful one. This is a traditional view and is very often linked to other skills. Fries (1963) held the same view which implies the relationship between listening and reading, i.e., the information that can be transferred through listening could also be done through reading.

Sticht (1972) also established a strong parallel between the two skills.

Urquhart (1981) specified a number of mental operations in a particular reading situation, thereby focusing on the cognitive aspects.

Reading comprehension is a process of understanding a written text. Understanding a written text means extracting the required information from it as efficiently as possible (Francois Grellet, 1991:3).

The view that treats reading as a cognitive activity is quite old. Thorndike (1917) had argued that reading was similar to mathematical problem solving.

It follows that reading is a complex activity and that its study must be interdisciplinary. Any satisfactory definition of reading becomes all-embracing: It also implies that readers can go on becoming better readers. Mere learning of translation rules will not suffice but far more learning is required.

What is important is how to relate what is being processed to one's existing knowledge emotions, etc., and to do so with an appropriate degree of flexibility. If the ability to read involves so many aspects of language, cognition, life and learning, then no one academic view of language skills can claim to have the correct view of what is involved in the definition of reading.

Linguistics, applied linguistics, cognitive psychology, sociology, sociolinguistics, communication theory, the study of communication systems and other disciplines related to real life all have a bearing on the study of reading as a process or a product.

Review Exercise: Pick up the day's newspaper. Read a few of the headlines. Before you actually read the reports, think of the information these reports might include. Jot them down. Now, read the reports and compare your notes.

## Basic Assumptions About Reading

Let us examine how reading in the L1 is different from and similar to reading in the L2. More specifically, factors of cultural difference—content (background knowledge) scheme, formal (texture) schema, linguistic (language) schema—will be examined.

Schema theory is based on the belief that 'every act of comprehension involves one's knowledge of the world as well' (Anderson et al. in Carrell and Eisterhold 1983:73). Thus, readers develop a coherent interpretation of text through the interactive process of '*combining textual information with the information a reader brings to a text*' (Widdowson in Grabe 1988:56).

Readers' mental stores are termed 'schemata' (after Bartlett in Cook 1997:86) and are divided (following Carrell 1983) into two main types: 'content schemata' (background knowledge of the world) and 'formal schemata' (background knowledge of rhetorical structure). Theories on the contribution of schemata and culture to the reading process are discussed in this section.

## The Cultural Hypothesis and Types of Schema

If we are to consider the aspects of background and culture as contributory factors to the process of reading, it is imperative to view it from a pedagogic point of view. In this section, we will look at the processes of reading in L1 and L2 and also investigate how the culture factor influences the process and the product of reading.

Despite the similarities between reading in an L1 and reading in an L2, a number of complex variables make the process of L1 different from L2. Because the reading process is essentially 'unobservable' teachers need to make significant efforts in the classroom to understand their students' reading behaviours and be able to help students understand their own reading behaviours as well. It is, therefore, important that teachers know as much as possible about the cultural, linguistic and educational backgrounds of their readers since these factors may influence reading in an L2 context.

While examining how reading in the L1 is different from or similar to reading in the L2, the factors of cultural differences that become important are:

**Context (background knowledge) Schema**
**Formal (textural) Schema**
**Linguistic (language) Schema**

Based on such a discussion, a profile of a bi-literate reader or a reader who is proficient in reading—both in MT and a second language—is provided.

A great deal of literature is available on the research conducted in this domain. It cannot possibly be covered in its entirety here. However, the discussion that follows will provide you with an overview in this area.

## The Schema Theory

### What is Schema?

The notion of schema must be defined. Schemas, or schema as they are sometimes known, have been described as 'cognitive constructs which allow for the organization of information in long-term memory' (Widdowson, 1983).

Cook (1989) states, 'The mind, stimulated by key words or phrase in the text or by the context, activates a knowledge schema' (Cook, 1989, p.69).

Widdowson and Cook both emphasize the **cognitive** characteristics of schema which allow us to relate the incoming information to the already known information. This covers the knowledge of the world, from everyday knowledge to very specialized knowledge; knowledge of language structures and knowledge texts and forms they take in terms of genre and organization.

In addition to allowing us to organize information and knowledge economically, schemas also allow us to predict the continuation of both spoken and written discourse. The first part of a text activates a schema, that is, calls up a schema which is either confirmed or disconfirmed by what follows. For example, a text that begins with the words 'Once upon a time . . . ' almost at once suggests that a story is about to follow. At the same, there is sufficient indication that it is going to be a story for children to read. In the process of reading, 'comprehension of a message entails drawing information from both the message and the internal schemata until sets are reconciled as a single schema or message' (Anderson et al. in Hudson, 1982:187).

Although it is claimed that 'the first part of text activates a schema . . . which is either confirmed or disconfirmed by what follows' (Wallace 1922:33), the process begins much earlier than this.

According to Swales (1990:88), 'The environment sets up powerful expectations: we are already prepared for certain genres but not for others before we open a newspaper, or a scholarly journal. . . .'

The reading process, therefore, involves **identification of genre**, **formal structure** and **topic**, all of which activate schemata and allow readers to comprehend the text (Swales 1990:89).

In this way, it is assumed that readers not only possess all the relevant schemata, but also that these schemata actually are activated. Where this is not the case, then some disruption of comprehension may occur. In fact, it is likely that 'there will never be a **total coincidence of schemas** between writer and reader' (Wallace 1992:82) such that coherence is the property of individual readers. It follows then, that there will be some differences in the interpretation of a text from reader to reader.

## Problems in Reading

There are basically three problems in reading literature:

1. **The processing problem** argues that L2 learners may be proficient in the language, but they still have problems in reading. Therefore, the core of the problem is the failure to transfer reading strategies from the L1 to L2.
2. **The language problem** states that L2 reading is very different from L1 reading. It argues that the L2 reader has problems with memory span, mistakes are likely to lead to hesitation and there is a possibility of L1 interference.
3. **The short-circuit problem** aims at striking a balance between the first two problems and states that L2 readers suffer most of the time in their reading process, but it concedes that the language problem is of fundamental importance. In other words, good L1 readers are theoretically able to transfer their reading skills; but when language competence is limited, there is a short circuit. There is no conclusive evidence for this theory as yet, but the idea is intuitively appealing. Readers, who do not know enough of the language, cannot transfer skills from their L1 reading because they need to be more proficient in the L2 reading to activate the skills.

## Let Us Consult an Expert: Prof. Arpita Banerjee

Schema theory describes the process by which readers combine their own background knowledge with the information in a text in order to comprehend that text. All readers carry different **schemata** (background information) and often these are also culture-specific. This is an important concept in English as a Second Language (ESL) teaching, and pre-reading tasks are often designed to build or activate the learner's schemata.

## Applications of Schema Theory to the Teaching of ESL Reading

As described in the previous section, 'some students' apparent reading problems may be problems of insufficient background knowledge' (Carrell 1988:245). Where this is thought to be topic-related, it has been suggested that 'narrow reading' within the student's area of knowledge or interest may improve the situation (see Carrell and Eisterhold 1983:86). Similarly, where schema deficiencies are culture-specific, it could be useful to provide local texts or texts which are developed from the readers' own experience.

On the other hand, Carrell and Eisterhold (1983:89) also suggest that 'every culture-specific interference problem dealt with in the classroom presents an opportunity to build new culture-specific schemata that will be available to the EFL/ESL student outside the classroom.' Thus, rather than attempting to neutralize texts, it would seem more suitable to prepare students by 'helping them build background knowledge on the topic prior to reading, through appropriate pre-reading activities' (Carrell 1988: 245).

Carrell (1988: 245) lists numerous ways in which relevant schemata may be constructed, including **lectures, visual aids, demonstrations, real-life experience, discussion, role-play, text previewing, introduction and discussion of key vocabulary**, and **key-word/key-concept association** activities.

Examples of such contextualization include, for example, showing pictures of a city before asking the students to read a text about that city or playing a video clip from a film adaptation of the novel the class is about to study. Although helpful, these pre-reading activities are probably not sufficient alone and teachers will need to supply additional information.

Reading problems are not just caused by schema deficiencies and the 'relevant schemata must be activated' (Carrell 1988a: 105). In other words, non-activation of the schema might be a problem. This means that readers may come to a text with prior knowledge but their schemata are not necessarily activated while reading so 'pre-reading activities must accomplish both goals: building new background knowledge as well as activating existing background knowledge' (Carrell 1988: 248).

You are going to read a passage about a woman's encounter with a bear while she was hiking in an American National Park.

Before reading, answer the following questions:

(a) Do bears live in the wild in your country? What kind of bears?
(b) How would you feel if you met a bear while hiking?
(c) What do you think we should do if we encounter a bear in the wild?

Previewing the text (particularly the title, subheadings and figures) also 'helps readers predict what they are going to read' and this, hopefully, activates their schemata (Aebersold and Field 1997:73). For example:

You are going to read a passage about a man's bad experience on a camping trip in the north of England.

Before reading, do the following exercises:

(a) Write down five problems the man could have had when he was camping.
(b) Look at the title of the passage and the list of words. What do you think might have happened?

TITLE: 'Our Terrible New Year'

WORDS (in order): holiday, happy, drove, far, camped, beautiful, night, freezing, snow, morning, engine trouble, help, no phone, ran, ice, slipped, cut, disaster.

The use of MT is a very useful pedagogic device to activate schemata. Lower level students may have the schemata but not the linguistic skills to discuss them in the L2. So the first language could be used to access prior knowledge by teachers and must introduce the relevant vocabulary during the discussion, otherwise a 'schema has been activated but learning the L2 has not been facilitated' (Aebersold and Field 1997: 77).

Although pre-reading activities, such as those mentioned earlier, are potentially beneficial, there is evidence that their usefulness is limited. Let us discuss this in greater detail.

**Limitations in the Use of Schema Theory in ESL Teaching**
**Problems with Schema Theory Applications**

Despite the current popularity of pre-reading activities, their use may be limited in ESL teaching and they may not always function as intended. Carrell and Wallace (in Carrell 1988a:105-6) found that giving context did not improve recall even for advanced ESL readers suggesting that their schemata were not activated.

'Touching as few bases as necessary', they may 'apply meaning to a text regardless of the degree to which they successfully utilize syntactic, semantic or discourse constraints.'

The reading process has famously been described as a 'psycholinguistic guessing game' (Goodman in Carrell and Eisterhold 1983:74) in which 'efficient readers minimize dependence on visual detail' by utilizing background knowledge to make predication and checking these against the text (Goodman 1975:12).

Such top-down models (moving from general knowledge to specific details) have unfortunately given the misleading message to teachers that ESL reading tuition is 'mostly just a matter of providing [learners] with the right background knowledge . . . and encouraging them to make full use of that knowledge in decoding . . . texts' (Eskey 1988:97). It is now recognized that 'language is a major problem in second language reading.'

***Vocabulary and Schemata: Dr West's Theory—Revised Application.*** ESL readers need 'a massive receptive vocabulary that is rapidly, accurately and automatically accessed' (Grabe 1988:63).

Carrell (1988b:244) suggests a 'parallel' approach in which vocabulary and schemata are developed by 'pre-teaching vocabulary and background knowledge concurrently for sets of passages to be read at some later time'. Furthermore, since learners 'need to see a word many times in different contexts before it is learned' (Aebersold and Field 1997:139), they may need to read a great many more texts than is usually the case in reading courses.

This so-called 'extensive' reading (after Palmer in Bamford and Day 1997:6) is discussed next.

***Extensive Reading and Inter-Textuality: Rabindranath Tagore's Theory—Revised Application.*** Encouraging students to read for pleasure is advocated by several authors (Bamford and Day 1997; Carrell and Eisterhold 1983: 85-6; Wallace 1992: 68-9) and will hopefully lead to the kind of extensive reading learners need to do if they are to gain any 'automaticity' in their word and phrase recognition abilities (see Eskey and Grabe 1988:235).

As Bamford and Day (1997:7) state, 'Until students read in quantity, they will not become fluent readers.' Learners may be motivated to read extensively by being allowed to choose their own texts based on their own interests.

Another reason for extensive reading is related to the concept of 'inter-textuality' where 'all texts contain traces of other texts, and frequently they cannot be readily interpreted or at least fully appreciated—without reference to other texts' (Wallace 1992:47). McCarthy and Carter (1994:114) point out that 'many common, everyday texts assume that the receiver will be able to pick up . . . allusions and perceive the cultural references [to deep-rooted common cultural stores of allusions, sayings, idioms, etc.].'

### Visiting Expert Corner

- Dr Smart introduced 2,500 **essential words** in 1950s so that both receptive and productive vocabulary could be easily mastered for everyday use of English.
- Rabindranath Tagore who got Nobel Prize in 1913 for *Gitanjali* introduced the theory of 'Guessing contextual meaning' to understand topics and texts meant for extensive reading.

For example, the sentence about Princess Diana: 'The face that launched a thousand tabloids' alluding to the line about the beauty of Helen of Troy from Marlowe's 'Faust' (1588): '*Is this the face that launched a thousand ships*?' Here, it is perhaps assumed that any reader will be in a position to associate Princess Diana with Helen of Troy.

Sonclair (1990:16) claims that 'in general people forget the actual language but remember the message'. The fact remains, though, that textual memory is important because texts do carry references to other texts and, although not always crucial to the overall message, these references enhance the understanding of the text.

***Guiding Students to Use Reader's Strategies.*** We have already said that reading is a multidisciplinary skill. Most English as a First Language (EFL) teachers would agree that the overt processes involved in language—the four skills of reading, writing, listening and speaking—which have been, in the past, 'treated somewhat in isolation, in fact have so much in common with each other, that it makes much more sense to treat them holistically' (Wray & Medwell 1991:3). It has been noted that the links between reading and writing, for example, have been emphasized to such an extent that it is now normal to see them referred to as 'literacy'. Similarly, the term 'oracy' is commonly used to denote the skills of speaking and listening.

This is no doubt true, even unavoidable, in the practical classroom situation. However, it is also argued that to look at the four skills individually, in order to look for parallels between the processes, is, in theoretical terms, far more useful for those who strive to learn from these theories and use them in a constructive way. Thus, the sum of the parts may be greater, and more practically helpful, than the whole.

Each of the 'four skills' in itself composed of component sub-skills. Grabe (1992:50-3) notes six in particular in the case of **reading**. These are:

1. the perceptual automatic recognition skill;
2. linguistic skills, linguistic schema;
3. knowledge and skills of discourse structure and organization, formal schema;
4. knowledge of the world, content schema;
5. synthetic and critical evaluation skills, content schema and
6. metalinguistic knowledge and skills.

These sub-skills are, to a greater or lesser extent, also sub-skills of writing, speaking and listening. This suggests that the basic strategies used are similar, if not exactly the same, in each of the four skills mentioned earlier.

Although the four areas impose different constraints, at many different levels, they encourage a unique emphasis on particular combinations of strategies on each occasion.

In reading, the notions of 'bottom-up' and 'top-down' processing (also known as 'out-side-in' and 'inside-out' processing) are not without their problems.

### Let Us Do and Learn

*Consider the sentence (Wray & Medwell 1991:98) 'iF yuo aer a fluet reodur yuo wll hve on pRblem reodng ths sNtnce.' Write it out after making necessary correction. Now think of all that you did to get the message.*

The **bottom-up** strategy (which is essentially a code-cracking activity) cannot account for the comprehension of this sentence. **Top-down** strategies must have come into play to help you find 'meaning' in these symbols.

Reading stands parallel to Listening as receptive skill. The EFL( ENGLISH as Foreign Language) students will face difficulty in understanding Irish pronunciation if they are exposed only to RP (Received Pronunciation) English, when they find themselves listening to a speaker from inner-city Dublin would find it difficult to comprehend. Indeed, this is a difficult task for many native English speakers; however, the meaning may still be found by both groups.

Language learners often report that they do not catch every word spoken, but that they, nonetheless, manage to understand the meaning of the sentence. Conversely, it is also common that the language learners report that they 'understand' every word, but cannot grasp the meaning of the sentence.

Oakhill and Garnham (1988) assert that while good readers, and, by extension, good listeners, may indeed 'have greater contextual awareness, they do not, in fact, need to use it.'

Samuels and Kamil (1988:32) sum this up by saying that 'if a skilled reader can generate predictions, the amount of time necessary to generate a prediction may be greater than the amount of time the skilled reader needs to simply recognize the words.'

So, a total reliance on top-down processing, while initially attractive, may later lead to some practical and theoretical conclusions that are less than satisfactory; for example, it might be felt that the language learner does not need to develop much conscious knowledge of the features of written language. Therefore, the clause, or even the sentence, rather than the word, would be the most significant linguistic unit. Previous research has shown that this is not always true.

This is particularly problematic in reading theory. The L1 reading studies phonological awareness, but Goswami (1994) and others have clearly linked early ability to segment words into their constituent phonemes with letter-reading proficiency.

So, it seems that comprehension, of written and spoken discourse, relies on a symbiosis of top-down and bottom-up strategies. Thus, the perceptual-automatic recognition skill noted by Grabe (1992) above seems psychologically real and theoretically plausible, following Underwood's (1982) assertion that 'attention can only be diverted to higher-level activities, such as comprehension, when lower-level activities have become normal through skill practice.'

'However, the two modalities impose different processing constraints; they encourage the emphasis of different strategies' (Strodt-Lopez: 1996:35-36). Thus, listeners tend to rely more on top-down processing, from 'background knowledge to the particulars,' while readers tend to rely more on bottom-up strategies, from 'the particulars of the text to background knowledge' (ibid: 35-6).

## Facilitating Reading Comprehension in the Classroom

In giving the L2 students both as much input and practice as they can reasonably manage, and a strong metalinguistic awareness, the teachers give the students the tools to learn a language proficiently. It is in equipping the students with both declarative knowledge and the procedural knowledge, that they not only understand the information in the text, but also appreciate its subtle intricacies.

This is an extension of the issue of reading as a product or a process.

## Let Us Do and Learn:

**HOW DO WE READ? Match the column on the left with the definition on the right and decide which are most applicable to the categories mentioned earlier.**

| | |
|---|---|
| *Skimming* | *reading shorter texts to extract accurate detailed information* |
| *Scanning* | *quickly reading a text to get the gist of it* |
| *Extensive reading* | *quickly going through a text to find a particular piece of information* |
| *Intensive reading* | *reading longer texts, usually for pleasure* |

## Readers in a Specific Classroom Context

In this section, we will consider some practical ways of helping a particular group of students, in becoming more proficient readers. In the process, we will get an opportunity to link theory with practice. But, let us first investigate who exactly are the effective readers.

## Effective Readers

An effective reader is one who can select the correct strategy for the purpose and text. Studies have shown that most effective readers:

- discover the distinctive features in letters, words and meaning;
- try to identify meaning rather than letters or words;
- use their knowledge of the world;
- eliminate unlikely alternatives through inference and prediction;
- have a clearly defined purpose;
- locate topic sentences;
- distinguish main points from the subordinate ones, and fact from the opinion;
- are aware of cohesion and reference;
- are aware of explicit and implied relationships between sentences and paragraphs;
- are aware of the importance of argument, tone and function;
- are able to work out the meaning of unfamiliar vocabulary from context and
- have confidence in their own ability and take chances.

## Ineffective Reading

On the other hand, ineffective reading is often caused by:

- mouthing;
- word-by-word reading;
- inappropriate translation;
- inaccurate linguistic analysis;
- paying attention to unfamiliar words which are not relevant to the purpose of reading and
- panic.

Therefore, the learners who suffer from these problems do not take chances.

## What Sub-Skills Do We Need to Be Effective Readers?

**We Need the Sub-Skills of:**

- Recognizing the script of a language.
- Deducing the meaning of unfamiliar lexical items.
- Understanding the explicitly stated information.
- Understanding the communicative value of sentences and utterances.
- Understanding relations within the sentence.
- Understanding relations between sentences through grammatical and lexical cohesive devices.
- Interpreting a text by going outside it.
- Identifying the main points in a discourse.
- Extracting the salient points to summarize.
- Using the basic reference skills (contents, index and abbreviations, ordering, etc.).
- Skimming.
- Scanning.
- Trans-coding written information to tabular or diagram form and vice versa.

## Developing Attitudinal Changes Towards Reading

A general assumption about reading is that students improve their reading ability by reading a lot. Research on native speakers of English and students of ESL has shown that the amount of time spent reading is related to students' reading comprehension and vocabulary growth.

Studies have been conducted to show that students also develop more positive attitudes towards reading after the **Sustained Silent Reading** (SSR) programs. The effects are more prominent when the students are allowed to select their own reading materials, and the SSR programs are run for six months or more.

An SSR program has been implemented in schools through the Hong Kong Extensive Reading Scheme in English, which has been initiated and developed by the Hong Kong's Directorate of Education for 10 years. The aim of SSR is to help students develop a good habit of reading and improve their English proficiency in the long run.

In SSR, students read silently within a designated time period every day in school. They select their own reading material and are not asked to answer comprehension questions or write book reports. The SSR is nothing new. The term **Uninterrupted Sustained Silent Reading** was introduced as early as 1960 by McCracken (1971). Since then, it has been implemented in reading classes at all grade levels.

According to several research studies, the effects of SSR on students' reading include **improvement in reading skills** and **vocabulary acquisition**, as measured by reading test scores, developing a **positive attitude towards** reading and **cultivating a better reading habit**.

Since SSR involves substantial amounts of **natural reading**, it is probable that this practice fosters **vocabulary growth**. The researchers state that the findings indicate that reading is the most effective way to **produce large-scale vocabulary growth**. This supports the hypothesis that **incidental learning from context during free reading** is the major mode of vocabulary acquisition during the school years.

A study (Ozburn: 1995) of 60 ninth grade students in remedial classes produced similar findings. Students read a self-selected book for the first 10-15 minutes in a 55-minute class daily. They were allowed to carry home the books they had selected during their classroom activities. A reading test was administered before the study and nine months later.

Results showed that all students had improved in their reading level.

In the Project READ, which include the use of SSR, conducted in the Washington D.C. public schools, Coley (1983) reported that over the six-month period of the project, gains in reading achievement occurred in both seventh and eighth grades.

Compared with the Control Groups, students participating in the project demonstrated better reading strategies when having trouble reading a book. Coley thinks that the result of Project READ lends strong support for the inclusion of a period of non-stop reading daily.

Attitude changes/shifts towards reading have also been observed. These shifts occurred in both attitude towards reading and towards paperback books for students in Project READ.

Ozburn (1995) reported that the students checked out over 2,000 books during the SSR program. Wiesendanger and Birlem (1984) noted that nine of the eleven research studies, they analyzed, presented evidence that with SSR students develop more positive attitudes towards reading in schools.

Valeri-Gold (1995) incorporated SSR in her reading classes and found that the majority of students felt that the program had a positive influence on their attitudes towards reading. They had read a lot more since SSR was implemented into their reading classes.

In addition to **gains in achievement** and **shifts in attitude**, Grubaugh points out that the kind of wide reading that students engage in during SSR should broaden their **background of information**, thus providing them with a better knowledge base with which they could relate to their subject area textbooks and lectures.

Another study that shows significant results was conducted in India (Aranha), a school in the suburbs of Mumbai that uses English as its medium of instruction. The SSR was introduced twice a week for students in the fourth grade. Attitudes towards reading and reading achievement of the children in the experimental class were compared to that of the children in a control class which used the same language program without SSR.

The results of the study showed a high gain in **reading attitudes in the SSR** group and a loss in **attitude scores in the control group**. Girls of the experimental SSR group showed a significant improvement in **achievement scores** as compared with girls in the control group. Aranha concludes that SSR is a suitable classroom procedure for schools in Asia and Africa since it attempts to improve students' **attitudes towards reading and their achievement in reading.**

## Let Us Do and Learn

***Are you primarily a top-down or bottom-up processor?***

***Or is there a healthy mixture? Why? Why not?***

***Should we make students aware of their own reading processes? Why? Why not?***

***How can an awareness of the theories mentioned earlier help us as teachers?***

***Research in Computer-Based Reading Programmes.*** Lastly, it is absolutely imperative in the global cyber scenario today that we explore the development of **computer-based reading curricula**. As far back as late 1970s, the microcomputers led developers to consider the more practical and affordable microcomputers. The availability of such computers encouraged exclusive programs designed for a single reading skill (Reinking & Bowles, 1996).

The first major computer-based reading curriculum was the work of Richard Atkinson in 1964 at Stanford University which was supported by a grant from the US Office of Education. The project was a first-grade reading curriculum aimed to lessen the need for classroom teachers (Atkinson, 1974).

Computer-based reading curricula continued to develop but were of a commercial nature. Though some research, primarily evaluative, was conducted, most computer-based reading curricula studies have been sponsored by the companies marketing them (Reinking et al., 1996).

These research attempts were exclusively for L1 reading.

Only during the past 10 years, the use of computers in the field of teaching L2 reading has been increasing. A variety of studies have shown the importance of using computers in ESL reading (Willet, 1992).

Chun & Plass (1996) investigated how reading comprehension can be facilitated with a multimedia application for language learning. They studied the effects of a dynamic visual advance organizer on the macro level and the effects of multimedia annotations for single vocabulary items on the micro level.

Furthermore, they examined the relationship between vocabulary acquisition and reading comprehension. The results of their study indicated that the visual advance organizer does aid in overall comprehension and that annotations of vocabulary items consisting of both visual and verbal information help more than the verbal information only.

Also, a moderate correlation between vocabulary knowledge and reading comprehension was found. Chun & Plass claimed that the results (1) supported the dual coding theory and its extension to multimedia learning and (2) emphasized the significance of visual information, in addition to verbal information, to support both top-down and **bottom-up processing in reading** in a foreign language.

In another study to improve the reading speed and comprehension of ESL students using computers, Culver (1991) implemented a computer reading program to determine the exit and entrance scores of ESL college students and to find out if their reading speed and comprehension would improve. The results showed some improvements for the majority of students in the target group with an overall increase of 3-9 word grade level in the reading rate. The results showed important information about the effect of increasing reading speed on student comprehension as a result of using computers for the program.

It was concluded that the computer was a good tool for improving the students' reading rate despite the fact that the increased speed did not lead to increased levels of comprehension for some students.

Reading comprehension and text comprehension with multimedia as discussed above is enough to show: 'How L2 reading research is focusing increasingly on the cognitive processes involved in reading, that is, the interaction of lower-level, **bottom-up processes** such as vocabulary acquisition with higher level, **top-down processes** such as activating prior knowledge.' They merged this understanding with existing research on learning with technology to find out how students with different learning abilities put together 'verbal and visual information.' Their goal, in this study, was not to determine the effectiveness of multimedia on reading comprehension, but rather to determine its effectiveness on the learners who may benefit from multimedia instruction.

Whereas Chun & Plass used the underlying theory of L2 reading comprehension with multimedia, R. Preisinger et al. (1988) used the **schema theory** as a basis to evaluate the reading software programs. They developed the criteria and questions to evaluate:

(1) **interactive capabilities** of the reading software (e.g., its flexibility, response to student errors and ability to make a distinction between the major and unimportant errors),
(2) **information processing** (e.g., support of the use of prediction and problem-solving strategies, use of text-based activities in the context of reading passage and encouragement of analyzing tests),
(3) **background knowledge** (e.g., building schemata through pre-reading activities) and
(4) **general software construction and implementation**.

The goal of the study was to develop an evaluation tool, based in the light of a theory, to help teachers choose the right reading programs for their students.

In drawing conclusion about the use of computers for reading instructions, previous research clearly supported the idea that computer-based instruction facilitates **students' reading comprehension and increases their reading speed.**

This conclusion is supported by the results of the preceding studies and a series of other studies conducted by Kulik, Bangert, & Williams, 1983 who found significant increases in students' reading speed and comprehension across studies of computer-assisted reading instructions.

These results should encourage ESL reading teachers to use computers in their classrooms not because they are 'new technology' as reported by Wellington, 1995, but rather because of the positive results they bring to students' achievements.

After examining the previous research that dealt with computers and reading, it was found that computers were very useful in many aspects of literacy instruction. Using computers in teaching ESL reading, however, did not get the attention it deserved. Most studies and software in the field were conducted and designed for L1 reading instruction.

You are now ready to move on to the next unit where you will have practical suggestions on techniques to be used in the classroom to develop reading skills in the students.

## Teaching Sub-skills of Reading

We already know that an efficient reader is versed in several ways of interacting with various types of text. S/he is flexible and chooses appropriate reading strategies depending on the particular text that s/he intends to read. An efficient reader is able to 'switch' styles according to the type of text. So, a reader has to match reading skills with reading purpose. We would not, for example, read an extract from a seventeenth century novel in the same way as we would read the entertainment page in the newspaper to look for a particular TV programme. Skilled readers can scan to locate specific information in a text and skim to extract general information from the text.

The main ways of reading that the reader may adopt is as follows:

**Skimming:** This includes seeing the text quickly to get the gist of the context.
**Scanning:** This includes going through a text to find particular information.
**Intensive reading:** This includes reading shorter units of text to extract detailed information. This is more of an accuracy activity.

In real life, our reading purpose often varies and so we have to devise varied exercises for practice according to the type of text and the purpose for reading it. Efficient readers interrogate materials of different types by looking for '*clues*' in titles, sub-titles and within the passage itself. Pre-reading questions can be useful because they focus the reader's attention on the kind of information that the reader is expected to come across in the text. When working on a page of classified advertisements (ads), for example, it would be highly artificial to work on exercises requiring detailed comprehension of ads. Such activities would be boring and would only discourage the students.

## Let Us Consult an Expert

Reading involves a variety of sub-skills. The main ones are listed below. (This list is taken from John Munby's *Communicative Syllabus Design*.)

Recognizing the script of a language
Deducing the meaning and use of unfamiliar lexical items
Understanding explicitly stated information
Understanding information when not explicitly stated

Understanding conceptual meaning
Understanding the communicative value (function) of sentences and utterances
Understanding relations within the sentence
Understanding relations between parts of a text through lexical cohesive devices
Interpreting text by going outside it
Recognizing indicators in discourse
Identifying the main point or important information in a discourse
Distinguishing the main idea from supporting details
Extracting salient points to summarize the text or an idea
Selective extraction of relevant points from a text
Basic reference skills
Skimming
Scanning to locate specifically required information
Trans-coding information to diagrammatic display

## Task-Based Approach

In order to develop these skills, several types of exercises can be used. These question-types can have two different functions:

1. To clarify the organization of a piece of writing. The question can be about:
   the function of a passage.
   the general organization (e.g., argumentative).
   the rhetorical organization (e.g., contrast, comparison).
   the cohesive devices (e.g., link words).
   the intra-sentential relations (e.g., derivation, morphology, etc.).
2. To clarify the contents of the passage. The questions can be about:
   plain fact (direct reference).
   implied fact (inference).
   deduced meaning (supposition).

The above skills, question-types and question-functions are constantly related, since a given exercise uses a certain type of question, with a certain function, to develop a particular reading skill.

### Task Types

The following is a list of task types that may be used in order to develop the various sub-skills of reading. Some of the task types demand non-linguistic responses, whereas some demand linguistic responses.

(a) Task types that demand non-linguistic response:
Reading and following instructions and doing something or following instructions and showing directions using a dotted line or an arrow. Examples:
**Arranging** (sequencing) by using symbols
**Completing** a map/drawing
**Putting a tick mark** (checking)
**Making a graph**
**Underlining/circling/putting in a box**
**Labeling a diagram**

**Tracing a route on a map**
**Matching exercises**

(b) Task-types that demand linguistic responses:
Examples:
**Reading and . . .**
**Filling in columns/matrix (using short responses)**
**Labeling tree diagram/ flow charts**
**Filling in gaps (with words/sentence/parts of sentences) cloze type**
**Making free notes**
**Labeling paragraphs/functions of sentences**
**Inserting headings/logical connectors**
**Inserting missing information**
**Answering short questions (open-ended: wh/- /, closed types: multiple-choice type; true-false type questions)**

***Deducting the meaning of unfamiliar words in context (Using Rabindranath Tagore's Approach).*** Words do not exist in isolation. Their meanings are defined through their relationships with other words and it is through understanding these relationships that we arrive at our understanding of words. Some of these relationships are seen in word association tests, e.g., a word or a list of words may be given and students may be asked to provide words associated with those words by forming a list.

**Examples**

| Words (as stimulus) | Response |
|---|---|
| Accident | car, truck, |
| Alive | dead, injured, |
| Baby | mother, crawl, |
| Born | die, create, |
| House | cottage, tent, |

There can be a number of different ways in which associative links between words can be organized. An important part of reading is to be able to guess the meaning of unfamiliar words. To prove this, here is an experiment using a nonsense word.

## Let Us Do and Learn

**Activity 1:** Try to understand the general meaning:
'The children were *bleebing* all over the playground.'
(Guess what the nonsense word 'bleebing' means.)
You already know: It is a verb (from the form).

**Activity 2:** Make a list of things that you have read for last seven days. Now, fill in the category table taking help from your list.

| For general information | For specific information | For pleasure and interest |
|---|---|---|
| | | |

**Activity 3:**
Think about your own students' reading purposes in relation to the points given below. Which ones are similar/different?
to obtain information for some purpose or because we are curious about some topic.
to obtain instructions on how to perform some task in our work or daily life.
to keep in touch with friends by correspondence or to understand business letters.
to know when and where something will take place or what is available.
to know what is happening or has happened (as reported in the newspapers, magazines, reports, etc.)
for enjoyment or excitement.

## Developing Lesson Planning on Teaching

***Reading Skill: Using Proper Strategies in Classroom.*** In a reading class, motivation is the most crucial point that needs to be considered. Readers must be motivated to read. An ideal starting point for motivating would be to find out first the reader's wants, needs and interests, and then to select the reading matter and devise activities that will make her/him want to read. This may be represented in the following manner:

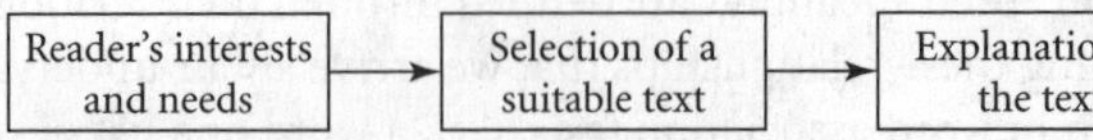


However, often it happens that the teachers find themselves obliged to use a prescribed textbook. The starting point then becomes the text rather than the reader's needs, and, therefore, exploitation of the text becomes all-important in motivation of the readers. Such a situation may be represented in the following manner:

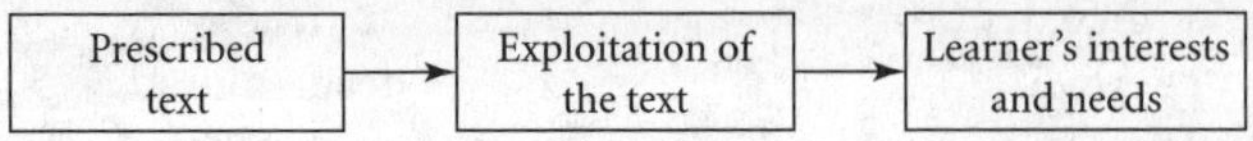


In such a case, exploitation of the text becomes most crucial. It refers to what is done in the three phases of reading, i.e., the pre-reading phase, the while-reading phase and the post-reading phase. These three phases not only help in dealing with the problem of motivation among readers, but also with other problems of language.

### *The Three Phases*

**Pre-Reading Phase:**
Pre-reading phase aims to: (i) introduce and arouse readers' interest in the topic of the text (ii) motivate readers by giving them a reason for reading (iii) provide some language preparation for the text.

Not all of these aims would be relevant for all kinds of texts. In some cases, there may not be any language problem or such, or, the language might already have been introduced. Of course, this does not mean that each and every unknown word needs to be explained, as long as the reader is able to tackle with ease the text and the tasks that go with it.

To help prepare for a pre-reading work, the following points may be kept in mind:

(i) What background knowledge the reader already has about the content of the text, and how can that knowledge be exploited?
(ii) Why should anyone want to read the text, and can the same or similar reasons be generated in the readers' psyche?

Answers to these questions will provide clues for ways of introducing the text and motivating the readers. For this, visuals, maps, diagrams or a set of questions could be used.

***While-Reading Phase.*** This phase draws the readers' focus to the text and aims to:

(i) help in understanding the writer's purpose.
(ii) help in understanding the text structure.
(iii) clarify the text content.

The following questions may be considered when preparing the while-reading tasks:

(i) What is the function of the text?
(ii) How is the text organized (e.g., a narrative, a descriptive, a reflective, argumentative, etc.)?
(iii) What information or idea needs to be exploited?
(iv) What information can be inferred or deduced?
(v) What language can be learnt from the text?
(vi) What reading styles may be practiced (e.g., skimming, scanning, intensive, etc.)?

As a rule, while-reading work should begin with a global understanding and then move on to smaller units, such as paragraphs, sentences and words. The reason is that larger units provide help to understand the smaller units—a paragraph or sentence—and thus to understand a word.

***Post-Reading Phase.*** The aim of this phase is to:

(i) consolidate or reflect upon what has been read.
(ii) relate the knowledge just acquired to the reader's own knowledge, interests or views.

The work does not refer directly to the text, but 'grows out' of it. Post-reading may also include the readers' reaction to the text. Post-reading work should, therefore, contribute, in a coherent manner, to the writing, speaking and listening skills that the programme aims to develop.

To prepare for a post-reading phase, the following questions may be kept in mind:

(i) Do the readers know of a similar situation as given in the text?
(ii) Does the text provide a situation that is good enough to be recommended?
(iii) Does the text present a situation that needs to be completed?
(iv) Does the text provide ideas or views that need to be completed?

The work that the questions lead to may be writing, interaction, drawing diagrams, etc. Motivating learners need not necessarily take place in the pre-reading phase. It may occur in the while-reading phase as well, using an interesting task. The interactive work in the post-reading phase may develop the reader's communicative skills. This may also lead on to working on projects by developing the reader's reference skills. The three-phase approach, therefore, leads to integration of the skills in a coherent manner.

## Writing Skill

Writing is one of the most difficult of language skills. It is more than putting down sign or letters or the alphabet or words and phrases in isolation. Writing requires the ability to produce language in chunks; it requires deliberate organization of ideas and their logical development with appropriate language use and meaningful expression. In a good piece of writing, we look for lexical range and syntactical correctness and further more, we look for proper format or layout development and movement in content and finally, style. These are important issues to be considered when we are talking of developing the writing skill in learners.

All writing aims at clear and efficient communication. But what goes into clear and efficient communication? Anne Raimes (1988) has diagrammatically represented this as follows:

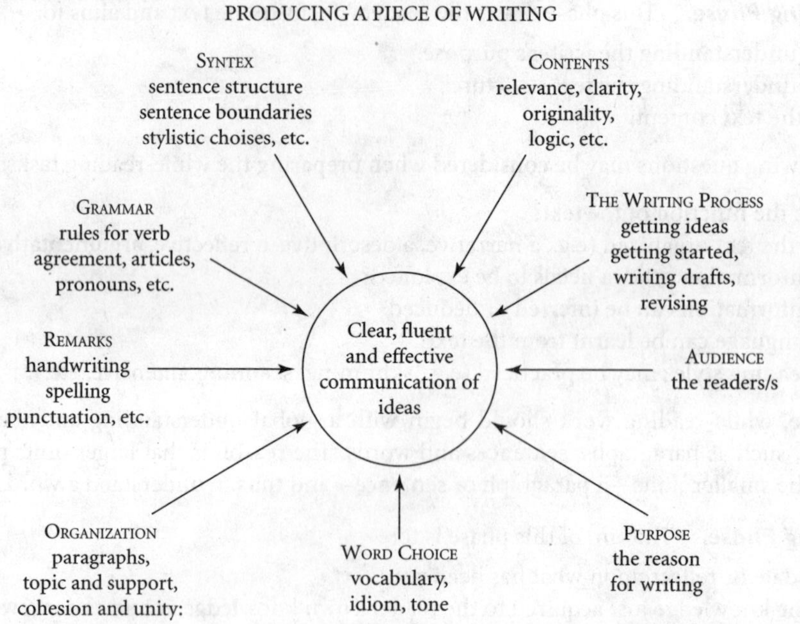


(Raimes 1983)

The diagram clearly illustrates the complex sub-skills that make a piece of writing coherent, effective and communicative.

***Teaching Writing As a Language Skill.*** To quote Tricia Hedge, 'Writing in its broad sense—as distinct from simply putting words on paper—has three steps: thinking about it, and doing it again (and again and again, as often as time will allow and patience will endure)'.

The first-step 'thinking', involves choosing a subject, exploring ways of developing it and devising strategies of organization and style. The second step, 'doing', is usually called 'drafting', and the third, 'doing again', is 'revising'.

Writing is a complex activity. As you think about a topic you are already beginning to select words and construct sentences–in other words, to draft. As you draft and as you revise, the thinking goes on: you discover new ideas, realize you've gone down a dead end, discover an implication you hadn't seen before.

It's helpful to conceive of writing as a process having, in a broad and loose sense, three steps. But remember that you don't move from step to step in smooth and steady progress. You go back and forth. As you work on a composition you will be, at any given point, concentrating on one phase of writing. But, you are always engaged with the process in its entirety.

### *Mechanics of Writing*

**Grammar, Usage and Style—Key Issues in the 'Process':**

It is not always easy to draw the line between grammar and usage or between usage and style. Broadly, grammar is what you must do as a user of English; usage, what you should do as a writer, of more or less formal (or informal) English; and style, what you select to do to work out your strategies and realize your purpose.

'Her dresses beautifully,' represents an error in grammar, and 'She dresses beautiful,' a mistake in usage. 'She dresses in a beautiful manner,' however, is a lapse in style. The sentence breaks no rule of grammar or of usage, but it is not effective (assuming that the writher wants to stress the idea of 'beauty'). The structure slurs the emphasis, which should be on the key word and which should close the statement—'She dresses beautifully.'

**The Stages of the Writing Process**

| being motivated to write | ⇄ | getting ideas together | ⇄ | Planning and outlining | ⇄ | Making notes | Making a first draft | ⇄ | revising replanning redrafting | ⇄ | editing and getting ready for publication |
|---|---|---|---|---|---|---|---|---|---|---|---|

(Hedge 1988)

The process of writing is often described as consisting of three major activities or groups of activities according to Hedge:

**(a) Pre-Writing:**

Before putting pen to paper, the skilled writer in real life considers two important questions.

**What is the purpose of this piece of writing?** This first question is to do with function. For example, is it a report which the writer hopes will be persuasive and stimulate action? Is it an explanation of how something works, which has to be careful, detailed and clear? Is it a letter of invitation to some friends or a letter applying for a job? The purpose of the writing will influence the choice of organization and language.

**Who am I writing this for?** The second question is to do with audience. The reader may be an individual, one you know well, or a group of colleagues, an institution, an examiner or a tutor. Thinking about the eventual reader(s) helps the writer to select what to say and how to present it in the most appropriate style—formal, friendly, serious or tentative.

The answers to these two questions provide the writer with a sense of purpose and a sense of audience, in other words, a writing context which significantly influences the first stage of the composition process that consists of exploring possible content and planning outlines.

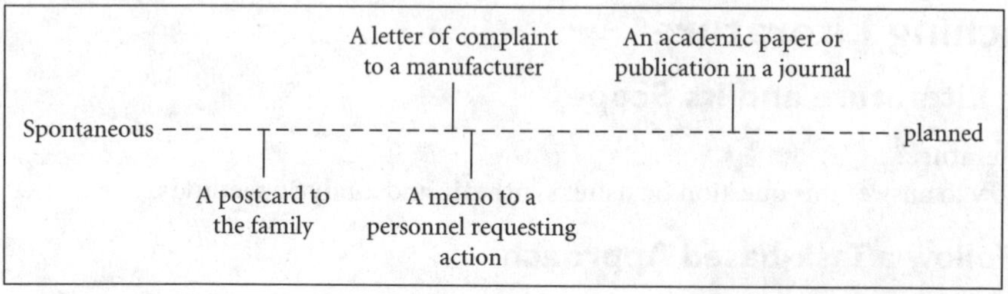


(Adapted from Hedge 1988)

The good writer generates plans for writing at this stage though, as we have seen, the amount of planning varies. We could draw a scale from comparatively spontaneous writing to very carefully planned writing and place different kinds of writing in appropriate place on the scale.

**(b) Writing and Rewriting:**

The second phase of activity is the writing itself and with good writers this consists of making a first draft. But, writing the first draft is often interrupted as the writer stops to read over and review, to get an idea of how the text is developing, to revise plans and bring in new ideas or to process the old ones. There is a good deal of recycling in the process from planning to drafting, reviewing, re-planning, revising, etc.

Good writers tend to concentrate on getting the content right first and leave details like correcting spelling, punctuation and grammar until later.

Revision involves assessing what has already been written and deciding on points like these:

Am I sharing my impressions clearly enough with my reader?
Have I missed out any important points of information?
Are there any points in the writing where my reader has to make a 'jump' because I've omitted a line of argument or I've forgotten to explain something?
Does the vocabulary need to be made stronger at any point?
Are there some sentences which don't say much or which are too repetitive and can be missed out?
Can I rearrange any sets of sentences to make the writing clearer or more interesting?
Do I need to rearrange any paragraphs?
Are the links between sections clear? Do they guide my reader through the writing?

**(c) Editing:**

The post-writing stage consists of reading through and trying to apply a reader's perspective in order to assess how clearly readers might follow the ideas. The editing process makes the final readjustments and checks accuracy so that the text is maximally accessible to the reader. Some poor writers tend not to engage in editing but assume that their writing is clear to others because it is clear to them. Alternatively, poor writers may concentrate throughout the whole writing process on accuracy in grammar, punctuation, etc., without considering whether or not the overall structure is clear.

**Let Us Do and Learn**

**Activity 1:**

ABC Private Ltd., 18, Chowringee, Kolkata-16 requires a student-counselor. The candidate must be a postgraduate having Psychology in Masters or student counseling as a method paper during B.Ed./M.Ed. Draft a suitable job application for this. Don't forget to attach your Bio-data. Sign as G. Malik.

## Developing Strategies, Methods and Techniques for Teaching Literature

### Defining Literature and Its Scope

**What Is Literature?**

Let us try to answer this question by using **synthetic** and **analytic** methods.

### Let Us Follow a Task-based Approach

***Task A.*** A group of college and university teachers all over the world were asked to write down a definition of literature.

Read through their definition and then write down your own definition of literature:

A. Literature is 'feelings' and 'thoughts' in black and white.
B. Literature is the use of language to evoke a personal response in the reader or listener.
C. Literature is a world of fantasy, horror, feelings, visions . . . put into words.
D. Literature means . . . to meet a lot of people, to know other different points of view, ideas, thoughts, minds . . . to know ourselves better.

(Adapted from Lazar, 1993)

***Task B.*** Here are a number of other quotations which 'define' literature. As you read them, think about the following questions:

(a) Are there any similarities between the definitions given here and the ones mentioned earlier?
(b) Which definition(s) do you reject? Why?
(c) Which definition confirms most closely to your idea of what literature is? Why?

- Literature could be said to be a sort of disciplined technique for arousing certain emotions. (Iris Murdoch, *The Listener*, 1978)
- Great literature is simply language charged with meaning to the utmost possible degree. (Ezra Pound, *How to Read*, Part II)
- The Formalists' technical focus led them to treat literature as a special use of language which achieves its distinctness by deviating from and distorting practical language. Practical language is used for acts of communication, while literary language has no practical function at all and simply makes us see differently. (Selden, 1989, pp. 9-10)
- [. . .] one can think of literature less as some inherent quality or set of qualities displayed by certain kinds of writing all the way from Beowulf to Virginia Woolf, than as a number of ways, in which people relate themselves to writing. It would not be easy to isolate, 'from all that has variously been called 'literature', some constant set of inherent characteristics. . . . Any bit of writing may be read 'non-pragmatically', if that is what reading a text as literature means, just as any writing may be read 'poetically'. If I pore over the railway timetable not to discover a train connection but to stimulate my general reflections on the speed and complexity of modern existence, then I might be said to be reading it as literature. (Eagleton, 1983, P.9)
- Literature is the question minus the answer. (Roland Barthes, *New York Times*, 1978)
- In the allocation of the label 'great literature' to a literary work we feel that value judgment is constituted by the social and historical conditions which determine our particular ideology. The teachers and professors who have the power to decide which books make up an English literature syllabus reflect in their choices, and in the knowledge of the literature which they survey, a fundamental structure of beliefs and interests which reflect the particular culture or section of society into which they were born and in which they grew up. (Brumfit and Carter, 1986, p.17)
- Literature and fiction, poetry, whatever it is, makes justice in the world. That's why it is almost always on the side of the underdog. (Grace Paley, Ms, 1974)

***Task C.*** Each one of the quotations in Task B has certain implications for the approach we adopt to using literature in the language classroom. These implications are examined in the following seven paragraphs. Match each paragraph with the relevant quotation in Task B.

1. One of our main aims in the classroom should be to reach out students or read literature using the appropriate literary strategies. This involves them not in reading for some practical purpose, for example to obtain information, but rather in analyzing a text; in terms of what it might mean symbolically or philosophically. Students may have already acquired this kind of literary competence in their own language, in which case we simply need to help them to transfer these skills. If not, we need to find ways of engendering the necessary competence.
2. Our main task in the classroom is to pinpoint how far literary language deviates from ordinary language. This obviously poses a problem for students—to what extent will they be confused or misled by studying deviant rather than normal language, and how far is this a useful activity for them?

3. Literary texts have a powerful function in raising moral and ethical concerns in the classroom. The tasks and activities we devise to exploit these texts should encourage our students to explore these concerns and connect 'them with the struggle for a better society'.
4. The texts traditionally prescribed for classroom use may generally be accorded high status, but often seem remote from and irrelevant to, the interests and concerns of our students. In fact, being made to read texts so alien to their own experience and background may only increase students' sense of frustration, inferiority and even powerlessness. We, therefore, need to select texts for classroom use which need not be part of the traditional literacy canon but are related to the lives and interests of our students.
5. Our main aim when using literature with our students is to help them unravel the many meanings in a text. Students often need guidance when exploring these multiple levels of meaning in a literary text—We need to devise materials and tasks which help them to do this.
6. Literature provides wonderful source material for eliciting strong emotional responses from our students. Using literature in the classroom is a fruitful way of involving the learner as a whole person, and provides excellent opportunities for the learners to express their personal opinions, reactions and feelings.
7. We should not expect to reach any definitive interpretation of a literary text with our students. Rather, we should use the text as the basis for generating discussion, controversy and critical thinking in the classroom.

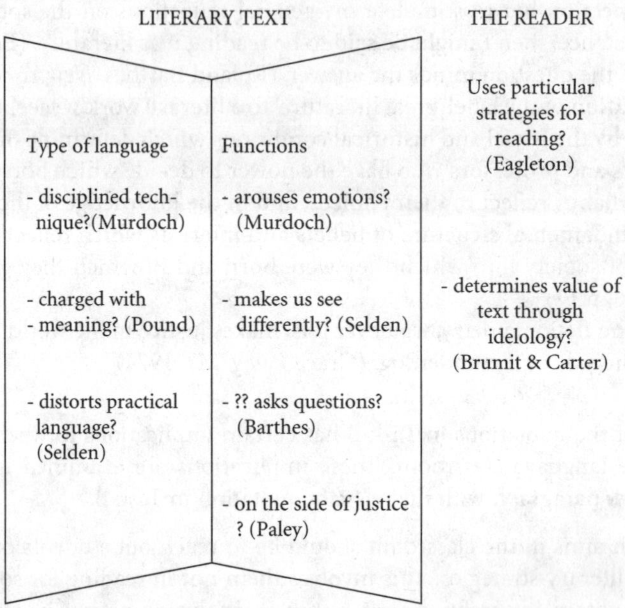


Defining Source of Literature: (Adapted from *The issue* (*Lazar, 1993*)

***Issues in the Teaching of Literature in India.*** It would be relevant for us at this stage to read what some of the eminent teachers at Undergraduate (UG) and Postgraduate (PG) levels in Indian universities have said on their experience of teaching literature. Their views and observations would help us understand not only our own problems, but also those of our colleagues and students. This is what A.K. Sinha (1993) had to say:

It has been generally observed that, with some exceptions, the teacher of English literature in India in the recent past has tended to approach his students from a certain high pedestal. This teacher has appeared to the dazed students as the 'maker', an omnipotent, omniscient entity, the reservoir of knowledge, and students of English literature have generally acted as the passive recipients of the teacher's revelations, and their experiences have often been accompanied by a mixture of interest, by 'magical' powers, lecture plan, outline and minute preparation have been generally ignored. In most cases, the teacher has just walked into the English literature classroom and harangued the students in a lecture full of sound and fury.

But who is the teacher actually talking to? After all, a teacher is an individual person speaking to other persons. He has to see if what he is saying makes sense, is communicated properly and is also received well. The personality of the teacher is vital. But it should not be so awe-inspiring that the message does not reach home clearly.

Let us raise here just three overwhelming questions which ought to be addressed to the teachers of English literature in India:

1. How many of us realize when our students have switched off and have started giving us mesomorphic stares?
2. How many of us bother to find out whether what we are saying is relevant?
3. How many of us try to make things 'apparently irrelevant' important and comprehensible?

A teacher of English literature in India should respond to these cues in various and complex ways often combining both management and instruction in her/his teaching strategies. S/he should not be overawed by her/his classroom, confused by it for being a bewildering kaleidoscope of people, behaviour, events and interactions which are only dimly understood. S/he should also not overawe her/his students with a lecture that is merely let loose with full-throated ease, being too removed from real life or the classroom situation. It is true that the rapidity, variety and complexity of classroom behaviour, often fulfilling multiple functions, are not easily comprehended. But, the teacher must immediately know whether the students are following him or not. A good teacher of English literature in India can always communicate properly and strike a neat balance between what the students think they need and what he himself thinks they should, may or would need.

This is what Prof. S. Mahalanobis has said in her article on 'Student-Teacher Interaction' in the Literature teaching:

In Kolkata University, the only indicator for the college and university teachers is the traditional canon-oriented course content (syllabus) with the humanist-artistic-stylistic emphasis. The existing English literature course is intended to help the students to simulate the best that has been thought and said in the Western tradition. For working within that constraint, the English literature teacher today directs the students from *what is* said to *how* it is said, to . . . the tone, style, figures of speech, devices of presentation and trains them in the study of texts by aiding the development of independent skills, such as:

(a) Language communication skills
(b) Descriptive analytic skills
(c) Syntactical skills

The first requirement in the framing of any course structure is the interest and involvement of students in their course work and to find in it the contemporary, the living and the relevant. Secondly, teachers need to present these courses by innovative methods, to improve the effectiveness of PG teaching and learning. The paucity of research on systematic, innovative development in PG teaching methods is most distressing. The onus is on us teachers to take time out of our own 'career-advancing' research work to find out ways and means to reinstate literary study as a meaningful activity. The canon can be challenged and replaced or (preferably) supplemented with Indian and Third World materials more relevant to our sense of anger and crisis. But apart from the inevitable danger of innovations petrifying into canons, we will be faced with an acute sense of deprivation. The Wife of Bath, Leontes and Micawber exist in non-colonial, permanently human (not necessarily universal) situations. Are they to be rolled down to oblivion in our frenzied, relentless pursuit of change?

Prof. Susan Oomen in her article 'Approaching the Classroom' has said,

Some of the problems that I seem to come across in the teaching of English literature, specifically in the environment where I work—a women's college with undergraduate, postgraduate and research programmes are:

1. A student's mentality, which causes the entire burden of the teaching process to fall on the teacher. The teacher ends up with the meaningless responsibility of seeing that a course is 'taught'. Such a self-defeating slant takes on negative implications when student-teacher personalities are not balanced or are at odds.
2. English literature is not a commonly favoured course any more—the priorities seem to be economics, commerce, mathematics and history. This leaves the teacher to deal with students who have not, very often, got the aptitude. (This however is not a comment on student intelligence or temperament.)

Given this environment, let us try to identify tasks for the PG students:

1. To read and write (to grasp and interpret, and formalize and present),
2. To organize thinking and writing,
3. To approach text analysis as a basic tool,
4. To interpret texts and look at production of meaning,
5. To be able to work in theory, whether of criticism or literary discourse,
6. To be able to work in perspectives and
7. To be able to do all the earlier mentioned tasks independently.

The teacher of English literature in India has to move towards the concept of world literature, making the students conscious of the infinite variety and representations of human nature. Literature probes deeply into life, its meanings and values and goes far beyond sociology in this respect. The teacher has to maintain a committed, constructive involvement in the classroom activities and remember that teaching is both managerial and instrumental in nature.

It is important to observe here that educational research has for a long time been employed in attempting to make reliable, systematic judgements about the effects of different types of teaching. However, its contribution in our sphere has been somewhat limited. The English teacher's instructional function in India has to be carried out in a complex environment. S/he should, therefore, try to understand how her/his own personality interacts with the context in which s/he works to mould the learning experiences of her/his students. Teaching English literature in India is not concerned only with instruction. The teacher is viewed, and should view himself/herself, as fulfilling a number of other functions.

The teacher often plays an important role in the lives of students and her/his influence undoubtedly extends far beyond formal learning. In the process of teaching English literature in India, attitudes and relationships are formed just as knowledge and skills are gained.

Therefore, the teacher of English literature in India has to remember that the content of the course that he has to deliver to his students is actually plastic material in his hands. He must plan beforehand the teaching styles that he is going to use, and yet remain flexible in the actual classroom as he cannot predict which style he is going to use when. Last minute changes or adjustments maybe, and often are, required, depending on the exact demands of the classroom situation. The personality of the teacher has to be multidimensional, and he has to keep the needs of the hour in mind.

***Let Us Do and Learn***

**Activity 1:**
Think about a group of students you are teaching now or have taught in the past. Perhaps you have used some literature with them already or perhaps you are planning to do so. Do any of the thoughts or ideas mentioned in the previous three tasks seem relevant to your teaching of these students?

Give reasons to support your answer.

**Activity 2:**
Are there any other implications arising from the various definitions of literature which you think should be considered with regard to these students?

## Using Literature in the Classroom

Once you are a student of a course leading to a PG degree in Teaching English Language and Literature the question: Why use literature in the classroom? inevitably arises. It would not be totally inappropriate here to examine the reasons for using literature not only for developing literary sensibility, but also for encouraging language and acquisition and skill development.

Let us work out a few tasks before examining the reasons for using literature. These tasks have been adapted from Lazar (1993).

**Task A:**
Following is a list of reasons for using literature with the language learner. Think about which reasons are the most important. List your reasons in order of importance.

Literature should be used with students because:

- It is very motivating—it is authentic material,
- It has general educational value,
- It is found in many syllabuses,
- It helps students to understand another culture,
- It is a stimulus for language acquisition,
- It develops students' interpretative abilities,
- It is fun and students enjoy it,
- it is highly valued and has a high status,
- It expands students' language awareness and
- It encourages students to talk about their opinions and feelings.

Are there any other reasons for using literature that you want to add to this list?

**Task B:**
In the previous task (Task A) you ranked reasons for using literature with the language learner in order of importance. The text which follows discusses some of these reasons in a little more detail. Read through the text, and then decide whether you would still rank the reasons for using literature in the way that you did.

### *Examining the Reasons for Using Literature*

**Literature-Valued Motivating Materials:**

In many countries around the world, literature is highly valued. For this reason, students of English may experience a real sense of achievement at tackling literary materials in the classroom. If students are familiar with literature in their own language, then, studying some literature in English can provide an interesting and thought-provoking point of comparison. This may apply equally well if students come from a culture with a rich oral tradition, where the body of written literature is fairly established. Ask students to retell short stories from their own culture, for example, before getting them to read an authentic story in English on a similar theme, could be highly motivating.

Literature exposes students to complex themes and fresh, unexpected uses of language. A good novel or short story may be particularly gripping in that it involves students in the suspense of unraveling the plot. This involvement may be more absorbing for students than the pseudo-narratives frequently found in the course books. A play may engage students in complicated adult dilemmas. A poem may elicit a powerful emotional response from the students. If the materials are carefully chosen, students will feel that what they do in the classroom is relevant and meaningful in their own lives.

**Literature—Getting Access to Cultural Background:**

> Literature can provide students with access to the culture or the people whose language they are studying. But this is an area of some complexity. To begin with, the relationship between a culture and its literature is not at all simple, since few novels or poems could claim to be a purely factual documentation of their society. Some novels, short stories and plays may achieve the illusion of representing reality, but they are, in the end-works of fiction. It has been argued that poetry has possibly an even more indirect link with the 'real world' since it creates its meaning by an orientation towards language itself. (Widdowson, 1985, p.149)

Secondly, if we do assume that a literary text in some way 'reflects' its culture, then the question arises exactly what aspect of that culture is being mirrored and how reliably? There is a danger that students will fall into the fallacy of assuming that a novel, for example, represents—the totality of a society, when in fact 'it is a highly atypical account of one particular milieu during a specified historical period. And if we are considering the issue' . . . how far a literary work genuinely represents its culture, then we are inevitably drawn into the question: of how culture is defined.

A further issue to consider is that English is now used globally as a first, second and foreign language. How far the language can be separated from culture is a difficult and intriguing question. Literary texts in English reflect the rich and fascinating diversities of our world. They are written by authors living in many different countries and widely divergent cultures. By exposing our students to English literature, it seems that we should be asking them to think about the range of cultures from which literature in English is produced.

***Literature—Encouraging Language Acquisition.*** In many countries around the world students have fairly limited access to spoken English, and written English often takes on primary importance for stimulating language acquisition. Literature may provide a particularly appropriate way of stimulating this acquisition, as it provides meaningful and memorable contexts for processing and interpreting new language. Obviously, at lower levels, students may be unable to cope on their own with an authentic novel or short story in English. Any extensive reading we encourage them to do—outside the classroom—would probably need to be of graded material, such as graded readers. But at higher levels, students may be so absorbed in the plot and characters of an authentic novel or short story, that they acquire a great deal of new language almost in passing. The reading of literature then becomes an important way of supplementing the inevitably restricted input of the classroom. And if recorded literary material is available, then students can acquire a great deal of new language by listening to it.

One of the debates centreing on literature teaching in the language classroom is whether literary language is somehow different from other forms of discourse in that it breaks the more usual rules of syntax, collection and even cohesion. This seems to be particularly true of poetry. Teachers often express concern that in using literature with our students, we are exposing them to 'wrong' uses of language. Let us consider these examples which seem to break, or at least bend, the usual rules and patterns we may be trying to teach:

A. 'A grief ago' (*Dylan Thomas*)

B. '. . . a fantastic farm where ashes grow like wheat into ridges and hills and grotesque gardens. . . . ' (*F.Scott FitzGerald, The Great Gatsby, Penguin, 1983*)

C. 'Though wedded we have been
These twice ten tedious years. . . . '

*(Cowper's The Diverting History of John Gilpin - quoted in Leech. 1988)*

**Analysis:**

In Example A, the abstract noun *grief* replaces what is visually a noun denoting 'a' time period, like day or month.

In Example B, ashes are described as 'growing into an unusual collection and one it is unlikely that students will find in a dictionary'.

Example C is a poetic re-ordering of syntax, since usually the past participle *wedded* would follow *we have been*.

By focusing on the 'deviant' use of literary words we can help our students not only to become aware of specific stylistic effects in this literary work, but also to make them aware of how this effect is achieved by departing from a norm. At the same time, we are involving them in the process of discovering more general features of language like collocation.

In other words, using literature with students can help them to become more sensitive to some of the overall features of English. (See Chapter 2 for details.)

**Developing Students' Interpretative Ability:**

Any learning of a new language would seem to involve the learner in the forming of hypotheses and the drawing of inference, whether these relate to when a particular idiom is used appropriately, how far a grammatical rule can be generalized or what is implied behind the literal meaning of what someone says in a conversation. Literature is particularly a good source for developing students' abilities to interpret the meaning and to make interpretations (see Rossner's interview with Widowson in ELT Journal 37/1). This is because literary texts are often rich in multiple levels . . . of meaning and demand that the reader/learner is actively involved in 'teasing out' the unstated implications and assumptions of the text. In a poem, for example, a word may take on a powerful figurative meaning beyond its fixed dictionary definition. Trying to ascertain this significance provides an excellent opportunity for students to discuss their own interpretations, based on the evidence in the text. Thus, by encouraging our students to grapple with the multiple ambiguities of the literary text, we are helping to develop their overall capacity to infer meaning. This very useful skill can then be transferred to other situations where students need to make an interpretation based on implicit or unstated evidence.

***Literature—Educating the Whole Person.*** The linguistic benefits of using literature with the language learner have been mentioned. But literature may also have a wider educational function in the classroom.

Situation in that it can help to stimulate the imagination of our students, develop their critical abilities and increase their emotional awareness. If we ask the students to respond personally to the texts we give them, they will become increasingly confident about expressing their own ideas and emotions in English. They will feel empowered by their ability to grapple with the text and its language, and to relate it to the values and traditions of their own society. (Gillian Lazar, 1993)

***Let Us Do and Learn***

**Activity 1**

Prof. Lazar's diagram is a diagram which recaps and sums up some of the questions and thoughts raised about literature in Tasks A & C mentioned earlier. Look at it and then decide if there are any more ideas you want to add. Then think back to your original definition of literature in Task A Do you still agree with it or would you like to change it in some way? Why?

**Let Us Sum Up:**

We have seen that defining literature is not an easy task, and that there is considerable controversy among literary theorists and critics as to how this can be done. For our purposes, we will take literature to mean those novels, short stories, plays and poems which are fictional and convey their message by paying considerable attention to language which is rich and multi-layered. In order for our definition of literature to be relevant to the classroom, we teachers will also go beyond the traditional literary canon to include contemporary works which recognize that the English language is no longer the preserve of a few nations, but is now used globally.

***Classroom Approaches to Teaching of Literature.*** In this section, we will discuss some of the problems faced by teachers in the literature classroom and some of the major strategies adopted to overcome them. A few other approaches which have been tried out successfully both in the Indian context and in the other countries will also be highlighted.

Let us examine the possible approaches which you could draw on when using literature with your students. Pinpointing possible approaches can help us to select and design materials for classroom use, as well as help us to assess the suitability of published materials. We begin by considering those approaches in very general terms.

**Task 1**

Following are the descriptions of three possible approaches, the methodological principles underlying each one and some notes about the selection and organization of the material that the teachers use. Go through them—are there any similarities between these approaches and your thoughts on the teaching of literature.

***Language-Based Approach (Methodological Assumption).*** Studying the language of the literary text will help to integrate the language and literature syllabus more closely. Detailed analysis of the language of the literary text will help the students to make meaningful interpretations or informed evaluations of it. At the same time, students will increase their general awareness and understanding of English. Students are encouraged to draw on their knowledge of familiar grammatical, lexical or discoursal categories to make aesthetic judgements of the text.

***Selection and Organization of Material.*** Material is chosen not only for the way it illustrates certain stylistic features of the language, but also for its literary merit.

***Literature as Content (Methodological Assumption).*** This is the most traditional approach, frequently used in tertiary education. Literature itself is the content of the course, which concentrates on areas, such as the history and characteristics of literary movements; the social, political and historical background to a text; literary genres and rhetorical devices, etc. Students acquire English language skills by relating their skills to particular contents. The MT of the students may be used to discuss the texts, or students may be asked to translate texts from one language to the other.

***Selection and Organization of Material.*** Texts are selected for their importance as part of a literary canon or tradition.

***Literature for Personal Enrichment (Methodological Assumption).*** Literature is a useful tool for encouraging students to draw on their own personal experiences, feelings and opinions. It helps students to become more actively involved both intellectually and emotionally in learning English and hence aids acquisition of the language. Excellent stimulus for group work is provided.

## Let Us Know from Experts

Vanamala Viswanatha of Bangalore University speaks of a PG level literature student, who is moving from initial response to critical interpretation.

Having suggested that the critique should be formatively used in a class, I would now like to briefly describe my experience of the next teaching unit, which, only in retrospect, I am able to see as an attempt at working out the argument in practice. This unit involved the teaching of Wordsworth's *Immortality Ode*. As a first step towards primary response, I asked the class to read the poem silently once and then got different students to read out the various stanzas. The meanings of difficult words were glossed by the joint effort of the class. As it is a long poem, I set them the task of dividing it into smaller thought units. This required them to view the poem as a whole and recognize its constituent parts. Various possibilities were discussed which were productive in themselves as well as various perceptions about the structure of the poem were taken. Indeterminate meanings and heterogeneous responses are not a luxury that only bright teachers with brighter students can handle, but they are an essential part of literature teaching. The consensus was that the first part (stanzas 1-4) described a crisis in the form of the question,

'*Whether is fled the visionary gleam?*
*Where is it now the glory and the dream?*'

While the second part (5-8) attempted to answer it with a note of despair, there was greater hope in the third part (9-11). Textual data was closely examined by students to support or reject the various proposals made about this thematic analysis.

After the learners had shared their initial perceptions of the poem, another task was discussed: 'Describe the nature of the loss that the poet is mourning'. Again different answers were tried and they could be narrowed down to three or four possibilities after some discussion. I later presented the views of different critics on the issue by reading out selected portions from each critic.

They were: (a) Geoffrey Durrant (b) C.M. Bowra (c) Lionel Trilling and (d) Cleanth Brooks. We could see that some of these views were similar to the ones the learners had already mentioned, and we compared the route of learning by which the critic and those learners had arrived at that conclusion.

This examination also revealed to us the specific orientations of different critics.'

[Ref. Provocations, Orient Longman, 1993]

## Classroom Approaches and Strategies

The more practical aspects of teaching of English literature will be discussed in the form of certain approaches and strategies of engagement which can be employed in the literature classroom.

Let us present an account of what some of the eminent teachers of literature have practiced in their classes in the name of 'Approaches'.

***1. Oblique Approach.*** The 'oblique approach' is a term coined by John Crompton, Newcastle University and it has gained wider currency in the United Kingdom at least. The phrase suggests a range of alternative strategies in negotiating, devising and setting students' assignments. The oblique approach is not asserted as a new orthodoxy replacing traditional academic models, such as essays, seminar papers, etc. But the oblique approach (sometimes misheard as 'a bleak approach!') offers both a great opportunity of student involvement and the possibility that the topic may be tailored to the needs of the individual student and her or his knowledge, level and experience.

It makes sense that the means of assessment, as well as the chosen topic, be varied according to the individual. The traditional essay question can be an ineffective blunt instrument in finding out what—to use the current jargon—the student can 'know, understand and do'. A traditional essay question on, say, *Sons and Lovers* by D.H. Lawrence might demand that students 'discuss the relationship between Paul Morel and his mother in the novel', and such an exercise would yield a variety of responses, with perhaps the majority of essays rehearsing familiar arguments and using critical material inertly. Of course, some students write excellent essays, but if we, as teachers, are interested in formative as well as summative assessment we should examine how essays can be enhanced by a variety of written tasks along with discursive answers.

So, an assignment from an oblique approach to the same topic in *Sons and Lovers* might ask students to imagine the wording of Mrs. Morel's will. A student could write,

'To my son Paul I leave this wedding photograph in a silver frame so that he can remember me as I was. . . .'

The open-ended nature of the task gives the student access to a kind of personal recognition which the inflexible essay may not offer. Each response has to be justified and located in the text and cannot be used as an excuse for any bizarre flights of fancy. The academic fear of 'personal response' is based as much on prejudice as on fact and is similar to the denial, in the teaching of drama, of any performance-related context which requires the student to say how a director or an actor would interpret the lines.

If we look at the list of 'oblique approaches' in the Open University 'manual' for the training of English teachers we find 18 possible ways of responding to literary texts, apart from 'the scholarly essay, diaries kept by characters, for example, the *Ancient Mariner* or genre transformations' which may be more immediately accessible. It is a more inviting list than a set of exam questions for the student who is more 'media literate', or who is interested in the perspective of a minor character not usually honoured with exam status. These ideas can be used in different ways—as opening up the initial response to a text, they might be discussed informally or in note form. They could also prompt longer and more polished alternative versions submitted for formal assessment.

***2. Coursework Approach.*** The 'scholarly' essay characteristic of many examination questions is only one way of responding to literary texts and demonstrating appreciation and understanding their structure, meaning and style. Responding to literature (and to non-literary texts for that matter) can be thought of as a process which involves the reader in a 'dialogue' with the text. One of the advantages of

**coursework** is that it gives students the chance to engage in many different forms of 'dialogue' with the texts and the chance to demonstrate interpretation—and understanding in a variety of ways—both through talks and writing.

Following are a number of ideas which teachers have suggested for **coursework assignments** involving responses to literature:

1. Interviews, either enacted in speech or in written scripts (e.g., between a biographer and a character or between a barrister and a 'villain').
2. Diaries kept by characters, for example, by the Ancient Mariner.
3. 'Genre transformations', turning a scene from a novel into a play, poem, etc.
4. 'Write-ons'-alternative endings or about what happened to characters 10 years later, etc.
5. Letters, for example, to or from character or from reader to character, etc.
6. Facsimile newspaper or news articles dealing with events in the text.
7. Group discussions exploring issues related to plot, motivation, style, etc.
8. Dramatic reconstructions of episodes or themes.
9. Making video films, for example 'documentaries' on issues or themes depicted in text.
10. Games, for example, board games based on a plot.
11. Comparison of book and film versions of a text.
12. Reading 'logs' or journals recording students' personal comments and evaluations of texts studied.
13. Cassette-recorded accounts, in which students, when they feel ready, record their own responses to a text, choosing aspects that interest them personally.
14. Imaginative or personal writing in response to an 'atmosphere' created in the texts.
15. Reconstructions from the perspectives of minor characters.

Milind Malshe, while presenting a taxonomy of issues, observes, 'Don Slater's admirable demonstration (which was not a prescription) of how practical drama can be used in the teaching of Shakespeare, and how an 'oblique approach' can be employed in the classroom for eliciting original responses to literary texts, must be mentioned in this context. Dramatization as a teaching strategy recommended by P. Rajani and B. Chandraka as well as V. Bharathi and A. Giricihar Rao, while emphasizing the performance aspect of Shakespeare's *A Midsummer Night's Dream*, have reported how participating in the performance of the play helped them to discover several ways of 'speaking true'.

***3. New Critical Approach.*** C.T. Indra has brought out the usefulness of the new critical method in developing the learner's literary sensibility and communication skills. Using the structuralist concept of 'literary competence', Vanamala Viswanatha demonstrated how critical interpretations can be gradually built up from the 'primary responses' of the students. Shanta Mahalanobis and Susan Oommen discussed how an interactive approach to literary texts is helpful; Prof. A.K. Sinha tried to show the importance of teaching styles and the teacher's persona.

A good teacher must possess the ability to lift a play from the page, so as to imaginatively envisage a performance when all that is available is the printed word. But unfortunately, most teachers in the country are not sufficiently acquainted with theatre, and cinema is an inadequate substitute for an authentic theatrical experience. So, considering the limitations of a teacher and also bearing in mind the restrictions imposed upon her/him by the classroom situation, the text of any play is treated as literature and a critical evaluation of it would constitute literary criticism in a very broad sense. This literary response, perforce, is bound to be different from theatrical criticism, which is based on the evaluation of a play in performance. The former becomes an academic exercise while the latter provides an account of a living experience.

But since a play is to be taught and not performed, could we not combine the literary aspect with its potential on the stage and give our students the benefit of both the experiences? Raymond Williams feels that this is possible. He observes that in much contemporary thinking, a separation between literature and theatre is constantly assumed; yet the drama is, or can be, both literature and theatre, not the one at the expense of the other, but each because of the other.

He is of the opinion that a literary text and a theatrical representation of it are not separate entities but constitute a unity. He seems to suggest that the textual analysis and the performance should have a close correspondence. The correlation may be achieved by a deliberate exercise of the imagination.

Let us provide a taxonomy of **activities** that can be slightly adopted to make them suitable for different grades of students. See the section on **Lesson Planning** also.

***Target Group: Class X + II and onwards.***
**Background: Preferably English-Medium**
**Activity 1:** Groups of students are given different sections of a dialogue from one-act play/plays which they then have to rewrite in reported speech using a range of verbs (e.g., suggest, mumble, wonder, etc.). When they are finished, they give their reported versions to members of another group to transform these versions into dialogues, which are then compared with the originals from the play. Finally, students are reminded about such points as tense changes, when the direct reported speech is changed into indirect one.

***Target Group: Class X + II and onwards.***
**Background: Preferably English-Medium**
**Activity 2:** Students are given a piece of descriptive writing from a novel or short stories from which all adverbs and adjectives are removed. They rewrite the text adding those they think will liven it up, and compare their version with the original. They may use dictionaries for help.

***Target Group: Class X + II and onwards.***
**Background: Preferably English-Medium**
**Activity 3:** After they have read it, students are given three different summaries of a short story. They have to decide which summary is the most accurate.

***Target Group: Class X + II and onwards.***
**Background: Preferably English-Medium**
**Activity 4:** Students read a dialogue from a play or a novel and then improvise their own role-play of what happens next.

***Target Group: Elementary Upwards.***
**Background: Preferably English-Medium**
**Activity 5:** Students are given three very short and simple poems in English, but without their titles. They are also given a list of six titles - three genuine and three invented. After reading the poems, they have to decide which title is the most appropriate for each poem.

***Target Group: Class X + II and onwards.***
**Background: Preferably English-Medium**
**Activity 6:** Students are given an extract from a novel or a short story in which all tenses are removed. They are provided with the actual verbs to fill in. After completion of this task, they compare their text with the original.

***Target Group: Class X + II and onwards.***
**Background: Preferably English-Medium**
**Activity 7:** Advanced students are given three different critical opinions of a play or a novel they have read. They have to decide which one among them they find the most convincing or accurate.

After you have decided what the language aims of each activity are, think about these questions:

(a) For which of the activities mentioned earlier do you think the teacher's aim could have been achieved equally well by using a non-literary text? What particular advantages might there be in using literary texts instead of non-literary texts to teach or revise a particular area of language?
(b) Are there any activities cited earlier which you think would help students to improve their competence in reading a literary text?
(c) Think about some of the activities or techniques that you commonly make use of in the classroom. For examples:
Ask students to answer True/False questions about a reading comprehension.
Ask students to provide synonyms for any new items of vocabulary you teach.
Ask students to read a text aloud to practice their pronunciation.

## Let Us Consult an Expert

**Prof. Arpita Banerjee, British Council**

The following are suggestions for teachers about how to teach literary texts in language classes:

***Choice of Text:***
Rather than selecting a text exclusively on the basis of thematic interest and linguistic simplicity, the teacher may wish to consider other criteria:

Does the text lend itself more to an efferent or an aesthetic kind of reading?
Is the narrative structure predictable or unpredictable?
Are the cultural allusions clear or unclear to foreign readers?
Are the silences in the text understandable to foreign readers?

A linear, predictable narrative structure on a familiar theme with easy-to-fill silences elicits more readily a response from foreign readers, but it can also be deceptive and tempt students into reading only on an efferent level. A linguistically easy text might present a narrative sophistication that is unfamiliar to the students, thus raising their aesthetic curiosity.

**Key Concerns:**
Before teaching a text, the teacher may wish to examine his or her own reaction as reader: What is it that s/he likes or is touched by the text? What is it that s/he does not like? Whatever the reasons (emotional resonances or personal contexts or experience, aesthetic pleasure or intellectual satisfaction), the teacher's initial reaction to the text will be her/his most valuable asset in teaching it. Ideally, a teacher should never have to teach anything to which she or he is totally indifferent; even hating a text can be the best incentive to find out something about the text and oneself as a reader.

**4. *Personal Experience Development Approach.*** It is important to develop a personal response by understanding the experience expressed through the text. Beyond the paraphrasable content, what human experience or theme is the text trying to express in words? For example, Paul's attempts to write the note to his wife rather than discuss the matter with her, and his final decision not to leave, convey a feeling of incommunicability and powerlessness. Language teachers are sometimes afraid to identify and have their students respond to such general human themes, and yet, more often than not, what a literary text puts into words are elemental experiences of life and death: love, fear, loss and alienation, wonder, motion and stillness. Once the teacher has allowed the text to make sense for her or him, he may want to find out how other readers (colleagues, friends, literary critics) have interpreted the text. It is also a good idea for the teacher to enrich her or his reading of that particular text by comparing it with other texts by the same author and by gathering information about the biography of the author, the period, and so on.

***Textual Clues:***
The teacher will want to identify the main textual features that convey the theme of the text. For example, the feeling of pettiness and confinement in San Salvador is rendered by the short static sentences describing minute details of objects on Paul's desk and by the repeated statement (*He sat there.*). This step is essential if the teacher wants to prevent the class discussion from meandering into vague generalities that have nothing to do with the text. She or he wants to elicit students' responses to the text, not loose associations with the topic.

***Focus:***
The teacher probably wants to choose no more than the main points she or he wants to make in the class that day about the text (or section or the text if read over several lessons). These points may pertain to both the story level and the level of discourse. It is wise to free oneself from any 'coverage syndrome': What has not been covered today can be dealt with in another way, another time or with another text. Furthermore, students can be trusted to discover things on their own.

***Pedagogic Format:***
The teacher will need to decide beforehand what classroom format best suits the teaching of the points she or he wishes to bring across: whole class discussion, individual student report, role-play, group work or pair work. The following are suggestions for teachers about how to teach literary texts in language classes. It is good to be ready to switch lesson plan if the class arrives unprepared, for example, giving them 10 minutes to read portions of the text silently in class or selecting a passage to read together intensively. It is less useful to try and reconstruct what happened over 10 pages if half the class has not read the text.

***Presentation of the Text:***
The teacher may want to practice the initial 'performance' of the text in front of the class, either by memorizing the poem, by practicing reciting the poem, reading the story aloud or giving paraphrase of the content of the text.

**5. *Readers' Response Approach.*** The approach comprises techniques for prompting readers' responses. They provide a contrastive backdrop of a more orate type to the more literate mode of a literary text. They respect the ornate mode of the reader and the more literate mode of the literary text, but have to interact both as the reader adds his or her voice to the voices in the text, and participates thereby in the *construction of its meaning*.

***Teaching the Narrative:***
As with any literary text, the dialogue between the reader and the text will lend itself to the two levels: that of the story and that of the discourse structure of its narration.

**Exploring the Text:**
Many excellent suggestions have been made to activate the readers' cognitive processes while reading and make the text relevant to students' lives. Let me just mention a few.

Isenberg (1990) offers information processing techniques to

**Explore:**
When? What? Why? How? of the text/storyline:
**Formulate:** questions/opinions
**Establish:** logical and analogical relationships
**Select**/reject information
Group/regroup, organize/reorganize facts and events
**Generalize:** opinions/decisions/ideas
**Rank:** in order of importance
**Explore:** consequences of actions, generate alternatives, predict outcomes
**Evaluate:** opinions/decisions/ideas

Rankin (1989) and Van Eunen (1987) suggest various ways of enlisting these different cognitive operations when teaching the German short story or fairy tale. In ESL classes, di Pietro (1987) has students rewrite storylines through strategic scenarios. Collie and Slater (1987) offer a host of communicative activities to bring the story to life when teaching novels, short stories, drama and poetry. They generally entail:

gathering the facts (linguistic and referential);
brainstorming plans and intentions and
relating both to the reader's personal experience.

Most of these activities exploit the referential aspect of texts for the language learner.

However, if reading literary texts in language classes is meant not only to reinforce students' personal experiences, but also to expand the range and the depth of those experiences, these activities are not sufficient. The following example, taken from Collie and Slater (1987) will illustrate the limits of story-based activities.

The class has finished reading William Golding's *Lord of the Flies*. An 'Inquest on Board Ship' activity is suggested. This activity has three parts:

***First Part*** (A general brainstorming session with the whole class): Imagine that on the way home the Chief Officer decides to investigate what really happened on the islands. What questions would he need to ask? What answers would be given by Ralph? Jack? Roger?

***Second Part*** (Role-play/improvisation): Roles are distributed: the presiding officer, his panel of inquiry, five boys. With the help of the recorded questions and answers, they enact the inquest scene.

***Third Part*** (The verdict): The class is divided into groups of four or five, representing the presiding officer and his panel of inquiry. They have just witnessed the questioning of the five boys, and their task is 'now to arrive at a verdict, and to write a report on the incident, which includes recommendations for the treatment of the boys when they return to England'. (Collie and Slater 1987: 161)

## Teaching Poetry

By virtue of their iconicity and their obvious formal aspects, poems are ideally suited to have learners experience early on the two main features of aesthetic experience: distance and relation. Poetry first detaches the readers from their usual frames of references by immersing them in a world of sounds, rhythms, stress and other formal features of speech. It then sensitizes them to the relationship between what linguists call the referential and the expressive aspects of language, or what a cognitive scientist calls content space—that is, ideas, facts and beliefs—and rhetorical space or mental representation of actual or intended text (Scardamalia and Bereiter 1985). This rhetorical space is based on new ways of forming sounds; new ways of shaping words, phrases, sentences; of structuring discourse; of relating to other texts and of conceptualizing experience.

I will suggest three ways of encouraging the aesthetic reading of poetic texts. One seeks to 'celebrate' poetry by giving it its full physical form; the second strives to understand poetry by exploring multiple meanings and perspectives and the third attempts to create poetry by having the students experimenting themselves with new relationships of form and meaning.

(You may follow the Appendix A for authentic syllabus/materials/prose/poetry with Model Question Types and chapters 6 & 7 for developing and testing different language skills.)

## Teaching English Through English Grammar

**The Teaching of Grammar:**

The teaching of any language involves the teaching of its grammar. The history of language teaching will show, however, that grammar is a term that has been understood and defined differently over time resulting in teaching methodologies that range from the teaching of rules as an end in itself to the opposite extreme position (held, for example, by many CLT adherents) of no grammar teaching at all. The CLT position on grammar is expressed in Newmark's (1971) comment:

'The teaching of grammar is neither necessary nor sufficient for learning a second language. That it is not necessary is proved by the first language learner's success without it. That it is not sufficient is proved by the second language learner's lack of success.'

Today, Language Awareness (LA) studies advocate the conscious awareness of and sensitivity to the grammar of language and its role in human life. The LA studies recognize the importance of the MT and its influence on the learning of a second language.

How can we define 'grammar'? According to McArthur (1883:37) '"Grammar" is not a precise term, in the way that "phonology" or "anatomy" or "sodium chloride" may be considered precise terms. . . . It behaves pretty much like the majority of words in a language; it has a core of generally agreed meaning, but is fuzzy around the edges.' This means that the term 'grammar' can have several interpretations. Think of all the meanings the term 'grammar' has.

**Let Us Do and Learn:**

What does 'grammar' mean to you? Make a list of all the meanings.

McArthur (1883; 38) cites a few sentences to show the range of meanings that the term 'grammar' can have. Define English Grammar.

1. Grammar is the rules people use when speaking or writing a language.
2. The boys went to the local grammar school.
3. That language was never written down, so it doesn't really have a grammar.
4. English is a language that doesn't have much grammar.
5. 'Grammar' and 'syntax' are really the same thing.
6. People who know a language work from grammars inside their heads.
7. The grammar of a language includes how to spell it and pronounce it.

8. Descriptive grammar is very different from prescriptive grammar.
9. Traditional grammar and modern theories like transformational generative grammar both seek to describe and explain natural language.

Vygotsky (1972), the psychologist, has posited the interesting hypothesis that learning grammar and mathematics is important for the mental growth of a child. The ancient Greeks and Romans, too, considered learning grammar as a source of disciplining the mind. Therefore, teaching grammar means an awareness of rules and their use.

## Knowing Kinds of Grammar

It is said that there are three kinds of grammar. This is a useful distinction for the teacher. The three kinds of grammar can be called G1, G2 and G3.

To quote H.N.L. Sastri (1987):

1. Grammar is the total mechanism which a language possesses and through which its users are able to communicate with each other. (To avoid confusion, let us call this Grammar 1 as G1.)

   Every native speaker of a language, literate or illiterate, knows and controls his or her G1; without this, communication is not possible.

   Each language possesses a distinctive G1, peculiar to itself—although some linguists maintain that the G1s of all languages, though superficially different from each other, are the same at some deeper level.
2. Grammar also refers to the formal analysis and description of the rules of the language. (Let us call this Grammar 2 or G2.)

   The illiterate native speaker of a language may know its G1 but its G2. However, when she/he begins to think about language consciously, to wonder what should be said in a particular situation in order to get the 'message' across, she/he is involved in G2 of the language ('Yesterday I saw two mongooses—or should that be mongeese?').

   A distinctive comparison is thus made between formal grammar (G2) which codifies and presents the 'facts about a language' and functional grammar (G1) which merely illustrates the correct use of the language.
3. Grammar also refers to the rules for the correct use of a language, which may be prescribed for its users. (Let us call this Grammar 3 or G3.)

A 'grammar' of the kind produced by Nesfield consists largely of rules which a learner is expected to master. But some modern grammars merely describe the facts of the language, instead of prescribing rules. This leads us to distinguish between descriptive and prescriptive grammar; between G2 and G3. The linguist is concerned only with G2, whereas the language teacher may be more concerned with G3.

Obviously, each language has rules, which permit even the illiterate native speaker to distinguish between acceptable and unacceptable sentences ('No, or not;* "I wants a piece of bread 'but' I want. . . .'). These rules are present in the G1 of the language, and a G2 should describe or state them. But from time to time these rules may change; there is nothing inevitable or 'natural' about them; they are merely conventions.

Thus, there may be certain changes in G1 conventions which become totally acceptable (e.g., '*It's me*'), some that are only marginally acceptable to some speakers (e.g., '*Mr. Dey wants Alice and I to see him tomorrow*') and some that remain unacceptable to everyone (e.g., '*One of my friends work in Wipro*'). A good G2 should take note of all this, but a rigid G3 (such as Nesfield's) would reject all the changes.

**Let Us Do and Learn:**
Which grammar do you think the teacher is expected to teach—G1, G2, G3?

**Grammar: Pedagogic Analysis:**
Once again, let us read what H.N.L. Sastri (1987) says:

Every learner of English language must ultimately learn its G1, since this is what enables her/him to use the language.

As for the teachers no matter what one is teaching in the English class, if she/he is using the language correctly and making her/his students use it correctly, the teacher is contributing to the learning of G1. The professor of poetry is also teaching G1, though she/he may not realize that she/he is teaching grammar.

What the 'grammar lesson' teaches is the G2 or the G3 of English. But, does the teaching of G2 or G3 helps the student in learning G1?

The Indian situation seems to provide a ready answer to that question. Many of our students know a lot of G2 or G3 (this, at least, is what their marks in the school examination indicate), but they can neither speak nor write correctly; their G1 is poor.

On the other hand, a student can certainly be made proficient in G1 without any exposure to G2 or G3—this is what happens in the case of native speakers, and could happen with a student who is able to learn in the same way as a native speaker—that is through constant 'exposure' to the language. This is what we find in the case of students of the best English medium schools in our country.

If the teaching of G2 (or G3) does not ensure the learning of G1, why is it taught?

Partly, this is a hangover from the scholarly tradition which emphasized the study of grammar (G2) as a mental discipline; it is also partially due to a failure to distinguish between G1 and G2.

It would not be true to think that all teachers are happy about this. In fact, the reaction against the teaching of G2 and G3 has gone to the other extreme; in many cases, teachers are wanted that they should 'teach the language not *about* the language.'

This new approach emphasizes, as we have already seen, the practice of language in meaningful situations: oral drilling, pattern practice, substitution exercise, etc. The student is systematically exposed to G1 (functional grammar) by the teacher, and the learner absorbs as much of it as she/he can.

At the initial stages of learning, there is no attempt to make the student think consciously about language or to provide explanations of any kind. Formal grammar (G2) is rigorously excluded, as it is believed that explanations will only confuse the young learner who does not possess the maturity to benefit from them.

Now, let us consider what Rutherford (1987) has said:

***Consciousness-Raising.*** There is a general consensus among learning theorists, educational psychologists, and language teaching professionals that the learning of anything does not occur in a vacuum. That is, successful learning of whatever kind comes about only when what is to be learned can be meaningfully related to something that is already known. Learning, in other words, must take place within some kind of familiar context or framework. The natural question to raise, then, is what such 'frameworks'—and ones familiar to the learner—we might identify for the learning of second language grammar. If we interpret 'familiar to the learner' in the broadest possible sense, then certainly we must include here what every language learner knows unconsciously—namely, the language universals.

Hitherto, some teachers have been very emphatic about one thing: Not even the best G2 can really ensure that the students learn G1. The answer is to provide more and more practice, without wasting time over formalizations.

But it is unrealistic to hope that the Indian learner can get enough practice in the use of English G1 to be able to absorb it, as a native speaker does. There isn't enough English around us for this to happen.

The teacher will have to compensate for the lack of available practice, and provide a short cut to the learning process. This is where an insightful process can help. This is called Grammatical insight.

***Grammatical Consciousness-Raising.*** To quote Rutherford, 'In what way, we are entitled to ask, would grammatical consciousness-raising (C-R) fit into this roughly drawn, very general picture of language learning?' We must first narrow the scope of inquiry a bit by asking exactly what it is that grammatical C-R is expected to accomplish. The unstated assumption of many language-teaching professionals, past and present, has long been that an essential part of language teaching is 'the teaching of grammar' (included in what we here refer to, in more general terms, as the 'grammatical consciousness-raising'). A look at what has been written over the years on the subject tells us that this assumption highlights the following:

1. Language is built up of sets of discrete entities;
2. Language learning consists of the steady accumulation of such entities by the learners and
3. The essential characteristics of the entities, e.g., the 'rules' can be directly imparted to the learner through teaching.

Grammar teaching then, for those who hold these beliefs, is looked upon as a sort of channel for direct passage to the learner's competence of discrete formal entities (and the simplified 'rules' that make up these entities) in the language he is trying to learn.

**Grammar as an Aid to Learning:**
First of all, it would be well for us to say that theories of grammar, though highly important to language pedagogy for other reasons, are not theories of language acquisition, and it is acquisition, after all, that grammatical C-R must be made to serve. Once we become accustomed to seeing grammatical theory in this light, then light is shed as well on the sensible role of grammatical C-R in pedagogy. The objects of grammatical focus and attention are there, as one well-known researcher, S.P. Corder, has put it, 'to help the learner learn whatever it is he learns, but are not necessarily *what* he learns'. Pedagogical description are *aids* to learning; not the *object* of learning; so long as we keep that firmly in our minds we shall not get confused by the ambiguity of the expression "teaching grammar". . . . ( Corder 1973)

**Rationale for Consciousness-Raising:**
Not all language-teaching professionals believe that grammatical C-R of some kind has an important place in the classroom, and some researchers hold an opinion that it has almost no place at all.

Yet the identification of crucial target-language data and the act of making the data available to the learner in a timely fashion (i.e., input) are still not enough for the design of a grammar-centred curriculum as we envisage it here. One must also be concerned with the choice of pedagogical instruments by which the data in question—already identified and appropriately available—may be absorbed by the learner (i.e., intake). These 'instruments' are really the means for raising the learner consciousness, or what we referred to in Chapter 2 as 'modes of operation'. Here and there, we have cited particular examples of such instruments (e.g., scrambled sentences, connecting lines for referential relations, propositional cluster, etc.), but we also want to take note of their broader characteristics.

The handiest frame of reference for conception of the instruments of C-R derives from what would have to be their two extremes: natural appearance of a grammatical phenomenon in 'authentic' text on the one hand and its contextless explicit formulation on the other hand. Somewhere in between these poles would occur C-R in which the grammatical phenomenon would simply be the 'highlight' or otherwise given prominence of some kind, and the learner is expected to do no more than merely '*notice*'. Much of the C-R activity however, asks that the learner not only 'notices' but also performs an operation of some kind. In other words, it is the C-R activity that is task-oriented, where the learner is actively engaged in solving problems.

In addition to selection of the appropriate C-R instrument, one must also make decisions as to the proper intensity of exposure, i.e., how much attention and for how long? There is a limit; however, to what may be specified in advance of the actual learning experience and the questions we have just raised have as much to do with methodology as with curriculum, although the distinction between the two is not always a sharp one. We will, therefore, offer a few comments here on methodology as it relates to a grammar-centred curriculum.

***Grammar Teaching Methodology.*** Though it may seem paradoxical, what is to be taught in the kind of grammar-centred approach we have been discussing is not grammar at all. If the learner is actually 'taught' anything, we would have to say that she/he is taught 'how to learn' or, better still, 'how to manage her/his own learning' (Allwright 1984). Target-language grammar enters the learner's experience not as an objectified body of alien knowledge to be mastered or as obstacles to be overcome but rather as a network of systems in which the learner is already enmeshed, the full grammatical implications of which he alone has to work out on the basis of what he comes in contact with in interaction with what he himself contributes as an already accomplished language acquirer. Methodologically speaking, grammar in this sense is not so much 'in command of learning' as it is 'in the service of learning'.

Several other methodological conclusions follow the pedagogical role we have chosen for grammar. Since no attempt is being made to force classroom learning procedures into 'lockstep' pattern, there should thus be no barrier to learners developing at a pace consistent with their own predilections for hypothesizing, projecting, generalizing and re-analyzing. One beneficial consequence of this is that if each learner is following her/his own individual learning, she/he has little chance of being competitive.

**Let Us Do and Learn:**

A. What is the distinction between rule-based teaching of grammar and consciousness-raising (C-R)?

**Underlying Principles of Teaching Grammar:**

Today, most of the principles of teaching grammar are derived from the CLT methodologies. We are teaching grammar for communication.

Let us enlist here a few general principles for an effective grammar teaching methodology:

1. Grammar teaching should be done in the context of and in relation to language skills. Grammatical forms can be developed through the use and analysis of texts, i.e., while reading, writing, listening and speaking. A variety of contexts presents a wide spectrum of meanings and structures.
2. An analysis of contextualized grammatical use can be described as an inductive form of teaching, where you move from examples or practice to rules. The extent of emphasis put on rules is of course dependent on the student's communicative needs, as well as on your perception of what language learning is. Giving labels to items should not be an end in itself, but it is useful for students to know basic terms like verb, noun, etc. The opposite method of teaching a rule first, and then following it up by examples will happen only if our objective is to learn the forms of the language first rather than communication through a particular language. This, as we have repeatedly said, is not our primary objective today but it was so when language teaching used the grammar-translation method in the teaching of classical languages (Sanskrit, Latin and Greek).

3. The focus then is on the meaning rather than on forms primarily. If meaning is 3. made interesting and continues to be so, then it is possible to start an acquisition of a grammar, similar to G1. This automatic learning could be 'unconscious' in nature.

   A corollary to this is that the conscious learning of rules, learnt contextually and with a secondary emphasis, will also take place. This is the most common kind of grammar intake that we have with the learning of the grammar of an L2 and is useful for what Krashen (1981) calls the 'monitoring' of language. Knowledge of rules does help L2 learners to correct themselves. Indeed, self-correction that is immediate (as in speaking) and not so immediate (as in writing) is perhaps the purpose of learning a G3 type of grammar.
4. What is being referred to here is the accuracy factor in language use, which is discussed in CLT. The opposite end of this dichotomy is the fluency factor. Fluency, according to CLT methodology, is to be promoted before accuracy can be demanded. If accuracy or correctness occurs in the initial stages of the development of an L2 or indeed in the development of any writing or speaking activity, then the chances are that language will not develop, and that the student might even not be motivated to use the language at all.

**Let Us Do and Learn:**

1. What are the principles of teaching grammar?
2. How can grammar be developed in a functional way through language? Give your ideas briefly for the given terms. You may consult section 3.1 for the details.

   Reading:

   Writing:

   Listening:

   Speaking:

**Discussion:**
Reading: While reading, the students can be asked to do tasks and answer questions in context. They can be asked to analyze language forms.

Writing: Writing is an activity where much time can be spent on real-life, contextualized grammar learning particularly since writing does give time for the editing of texts.

Listening: Like reading, listening, too, can be used to encourage the analysis of grammar in context. Tenses could be examined, for example, to see how meanings change. Reported speech could be used for giving and taking messages, etc.

Speaking: Like writing, speaking, too, encourages self-monitoring. However, unlike writing, the skill of speaking demands quick self-monitoring. There is very little time for thinking about the rules of grammar. That is why the notion of fluency is particularly relevant here.

3. Which skill is best for promoting the teaching and learning of grammar? Why?

**Overt and Covert Grammar Teaching and Writing:**
Editing is the last stage in the process of writing. This stage involves the checking of grammar, spelling and punctuation. This is the stage of focusing on the accuracy of language.

Focusing on the accuracy stage of reformulating texts and discourse is very important while writing. Read this extract from H.N.L. Sastri (1987). It gives us insights into practical techniques for teaching grammar.

The teacher can select passages from the text which can be analyzed to illustrate certain grammatical principles. She/he has to decide in advance which part of the grammar she/he wishes to discuss, and usually the basis for this is the known deficiencies of the students (revealed perhaps, by error-analyses). Let us suppose the teacher wishes to go over the grammar of the tense system in English, which is known to cause difficulties to the student. The problems, for example, may be:

(i) Over-use of the present continuous tense (even in places where the simple present would be more appropriate). This may be due to interference from the MT or bad teaching; sometimes the continuous tense is over-taught in school as it seems to be more useful for 'situational' teaching.
(ii.) Confusion between the simple past and the present perfect and the simple past and the past perfect.
(iii.) Confusion between different forms of expressing futurity (will/shall, 'going to', etc.).

The students do not need an exhaustive description of the tense system of English: They do need to know only the relevant facts, to help remove the confusions they might have. Grammatical explanation should be accompanied by illustrations, and these should be from a contextualized passage. So the teacher must find a passage, preferably from the text, which brings out the contrastive use of (for example) the simple present and the continuous ('I generally walk home from college but now I am driving home'), the Present Perfect, the Simple Past, etc.

Grammatical patterns should be introduced, if possible, in contrast with other patterns, rather than in isolation. It may be difficult to find a text suitable for illustrating all the uses, especially the contrastive uses, of a grammatical item, but the teacher should be able to adapt, rewrite, or even compose a suitable passage.

After this is given to the students, the teacher must make sure that it is totally comprehensible to them: He may, if necessary, use the passage for comprehension before he exploits it for grammar. The important thing is to make the student read the text carefully: in this respect the grammar lesson is no different from any other.

The teacher then draws attention to each pattern that she/he has already selected, explaining the principle(s) involved, in not too technical a language. (There is no need to fight shy of 'labels', such as noun, subject, etc. If these terms are introduced meaningfully, they are generally acceptable; and the advantage is that they permit the teacher to explain things more precisely.)

There may be some advantage; in some situations, in using the MT to explain concepts which are difficult or abstract. The MT must, however, be limited to explanations offered by the teacher. The actual practice of language items must be in English.

After the grammatical principles have been explained and illustrated, the learning must be reinforced through exercises (introduced in contextualized passages as well as in isolated sentences, for greater 'sharpness'). The students may also be invited to construct a passage, similar to the one used for explaining the grammar. Finally, the lesson should be recapitulated for the main grammatical points.

As we have seen already, the major reason for introducing grammar overtly (at the college level) is to provide remediation: There is not much 'new' grammar to be taught, and mere consolidation (by practice) of language items already learnt in school is likely to be harmful rather than beneficial.

It is not just the prose lesson and writing skills that can be used to teach grammar. We can develop grammar through role-play, language games, etc. This will be discussed in your contact programme.

## Classroom Grammar Teaching

We will depart from the customary narrative here and attempt a different kind of wrap-up for important aspects of the grammar-driven pedagogical programme outlined so far. Following, then, is the sketch of such a programme (which we again label 'organic'), whose attributes are: (1) grouped according to 'objectives', 'curriculum' and 'methodology' and (2) contrasted with an idealized sketch of the more traditionally conceived ('mechanic') grammar-centred pedagogy.

**Two Views of the Grammar-Centred Pedagogical Programme:**

| | **Mechanic** | **Organic** |
|---|---|---|
| OBJECTIVES: | Knowledge of language structure | Knowledge of language system |
| | Grammatical uniformity / / | Grammatical understanding |
| | Grammar as an end | Grammar as a means |
| CURRICULUM: | Teacher organized | Teacher/learner organized |
| | Structures | Operations |
| | Linear | Cyclic |
| | Exhaustive | Selective |
| | Uniqueness | Relationship |
| | Hierarchic | Holistic |
| | Accumulation | Metamorphosis |
| | Agglutination | Fusion |
| | Product-oriented | Process-oriented |
| | Language/learner distance | Language/learner proximity |
| | Increasing complexity | Progressive reanalysis |
| METHODOLOGY: | Teach grammar | Teach learning |
| | Transmission by teacher | Interpretation by learners & teacher |
| | Grammar is an end (necessary & sufficient) | Grammar is a means (necessary but not sufficient) |
| | Memory | Understanding |
| | Specific rules | General principles |
| | Predictable, closed | Unpredictable, open |
| | Objectification | Incorporation |
| | Competitive, divisive | Co-operative, supportive |
| | Rule articulation | Operational experience |
| | Group-focused | Individual-focused |
| | Grammar as an obstacle | Grammar as a facilitator |
| | Grammar in command | Grammar in service |
| | Speeding up (time needed for production) | Slowing down (time needed for reflection) |
| | Accentual (lockstep learning) | Chaotic (differential learning) |

## Methodology and Teacher–Learner Role Relationship in Grammar-Teaching Classroom

### TEACHING METHODS AND TEACHER & LEARNER ROLES

| **Method** | **Teacher Roles** | **Learner Roles** |
|---|---|---|
| Situational Language Teaching | Context Setter<br>Error Corrector | Imitator<br>Memorizer |
| Audio-Lingual | Language Modeller<br>Drill Leader | Pattern Practitioner<br>Accuracy seeker<br>Enthusiast |

| | | |
|---|---|---|
| Communicative Language Teaching | Needs Analyst<br>Task Designer | Improviser<br>Negotiator |
| Total Physical Response | Commander<br>Actions Monitor | Order Taker<br>Performer |
| Community Language Learning | Counselor<br>Paraphrase Maker | Collaborator<br>Whole Person |
| The Natural Approach | Dynamic Actor<br>Props User | Guesser<br>Immersed |
| Suggestopedia | Autohypnotist<br>Authority Figure | Relaxer<br>True Believer |

(You may consult Chapter 2 for details.)

## Teaching Study Skills and Reference Skills

Learning to learn well has become a watch phrase in today's world where we get a number of reading materials. Some of these we read consciously—we even look forward to reading them, like reading the newspaper early in the morning. Some we read without paying conscious attention, like reading the publicity hoardings of shops as we drive past them—unless we are particularly interested in the message on the hoarding, or we are looking for a particular shop.

The fact is that we read for different reasons—we read for information or for meaning, or we read for pleasure. Accordingly, we read different kinds of materials, e.g., textbooks, instructions, advertisements, storybooks, magazines—the list is endless. Depending on the purpose, we read fast (just to have an overall impression of the text or to spot specific information) or more slowly (to understand and/or enjoy). We will deal with all these at length in the following section:

### Study Skill—Reading with a Purpose

Before we start reading a text (a book, an article, a poem, etc.), we ask *why* we are reading it and *what* we hope to learn from it. If we do not start with clear answers to such questions in mind we may fail to understand the text, misinterpret it, lose interest and in short, waste our time. Accordingly, when we have finished reading we should ask what have we learnt? Have my purposes in reading been served?

Michael Wallace (Study Skills, 2001) suggests that we read actively which is reading with a clear purpose in the mind. Active reading also involves selective reading because part performance ensures whole performance. Other parts which are highly relevant will need to be studied in detail. Sometimes, the information that we are looking for may not be there in the text at all. In such a case, we need not waste our time reading it. When we read selectively, we concentrate only on what is relevant to the purpose.

### Knowing Efficient Reading Process

The next question that we are going to deal with is: What is an efficient reading process?

What actually happens when we read? We may think so, but our eyes do not glide smoothly from one word to the next, and then from one line to the next. Our eyes progress by little 'jumps'. They move, stop, move again. At every pause, our eyes focus on a short or long phrase, even a sentence. How many words our eyes take in at a time, constitutes our 'eye span'. The bigger our eye span, the faster we read. This habit is what you have to inculcate in your learners.

How will you achieve this? For a start, see that your learners do not move their lips, follow the lines with their fingers or with a pen or pencil while reading. These habits slow down the reading process. To increase the learners' eye span, you may show them a card with a short phrase on it for a very short time (two or three seconds) and ask them to repeat it. Gradually use longer phrases, as you reduce the time span. The idea is that they learn to take in a long phrase or a short sentence at a glance. Remember, slow readers are not necessarily better readers.

At the same time, remember that the reading speed will depend on the learner's familiarity with the language and the topic of the text or the difficulty of the topic and the language used. It also depends on our purpose of reading: Sometimes we need to read slowly to understand the material (e.g., a textbook).

## Skimming or Surveying a Text

So you should read actively, i.e., with a purpose, so that you do not waste your time reading something not relevant to your purpose. You should read at a speed suitable to your purpose. Therefore, you should know where to look for the information you want. For that you should know and practice various surveying techniques.

Surveying is a form of skimming which means you do not read every word in a text. You survey to get an overall impression of or the general information in the text.

**Learning the Art of Book Survey:**
Now let us see how to survey a book to find out whether the book is relevant to the topic you are interested in, whether it is relevant only in part/s, and if so, which part/s, whether the author is a reliable authority on the subject, and so on.

Following are the parts of a book that help us in this matter:

(a) The blurb which is usually printed on the cover of the book, e.g., *this book contains a useful general introduction on reading and outlines the ideas behind the content and organization of. . . .*

(b) The reviewer's comments: These comments are also often quoted on the back cover or book jacket. For example, *A first-class book, attractively produced, it is full of clear and step-by-step, practical and varied exercises, with some interesting ideas. . . .* But remember only the good reviews are generally quoted.

(c) The foreword or the preface: *It is often hard to imagine when reading this collection of papers, that it is only some ten years ago . . . that those engaged in the applications of linguistics to language teaching and learning announced a concern with the promotion and development of learners' communicative competence as a key concept in their new thinking. . . . It is in this. . . . Atmosphere that there is a special need for a coherent collection of specially written papers. . . .* The preface tells you what the book is about and, perhaps, what its strong points are.

(d) Contents page: A typical contents page looks like this:

**CONTENTS**

The contents page tells us about what topics have been covered in the book and at what length and also on which pages you will find the topic you want to know about.

(e) Index: Here is a part of a typical index that we will find at the end of a book.

INDEX



An index helps us to find a topic easily. It also tells us which topics have been dealt with at a greater length (e.g., compare the coverage of 'address forms' and 'apologies' in the cited index).

(f) Bibliography: It is a comprehensive list of books that have been referred to in the book or those recommended for further reading. It is also alphabetically arranged, beginning with the author and sometimes indicating multiple references to the works of the same author. It not only names the publisher, but also the year of publication, the name of the source book or journal if the article is not an original one or the author has referred to a previous article by himself or someone else.

Here is part of a typical page from a bibliography:
Jefferson, G. (1972). 'Side sequence',
Sudnow, D. (1972), 294–338.

Argumentative text is likely to have the following organization:

Problems/argument for/against—author's opinion—justification –conclusion

If we come to know how a text has been organized, we will have a better idea about where to look for the information we need. It also helps us to write a summary of the text.

## Graphic Presentation

Some common methods of graphic presentation are:

diagrams,
tables,
charts,
flow charts and
graphs of different types.

In academic writing, writers often present their data using these graphics. For the presentation of statistical data, graphic presentations are almost obligatory. For describing a process in scientific writing flow charts are often used.

***Fascinating Facts***

- 'Learning to learn well' is very important for primary students.
- 'Study skills' can also be taught like all other skills.
- Advanced students use proper 'study skills'.

***Learning the Art of Notes Taking.*** While taking notes we should remember not to copy every word.

Why do we take notes?

We take notes:

- to record the writer's main ideas;
- to help us remember when revising the text and
- to make what the writer says part of our own knowledge.

**Let Us Follow These Steps to Take Notes:**
The first thing we need to do is to survey the text to get acquainted with it, so that we can quickly find out what the writer's main points are.

The next step is to read the text again quickly making a note of the main points as they are related to each other. We may do it mentally (if the text is short) or may underline the points in the text itself or write the points in our notebook.

If we make notes in a notebook, we need to put them down in a way as they occur in the text. We may use a diagram (one of the graphic presentations) which is the most convenient method.

**Listing Systems:**
There are various listing systems that we may use. Choose a system and follow it throughout. Following are examples of some of the listing systems:

Arabic Numerals: 1, 2, 3, . . . .
Decimal System: 1.1, 1.2, 1.3, . . . 2.0, 2.1, 2.2, . . . .
Large Roman Numbers: I, II, III, . . . .
Small Roman Numbers: (i), (ii), (iii), . . . .
Capital Letters: A, B, C, . . . .
Small Letters: (a), (b), (c), . . . .

Jespersen, O. (1951): *The Philosophy of language,* London, Allen and Unwin Johnson, K. and Morow, K. (1979), *Communicate: The English of Social Interaction,* Cambridge University Press.

(g) The printing history: A book is usually printed on one of the early pages and tells you when it was first published, reprinted, new edition/s issued. The information helps you to look for the current or latest development in the field.

**Learning the Art of Chapter Survey:**
It is a good idea to survey a chapter as it is surveying a book. It is especially important when the topic is unfamiliar. By quickly surveying the chapter, we can make ourselves familiar with its general drift. This helps us to read it more efficiently.

Following are some useful hints for surveying a chapter:

- Read only the first sentence of each paragraph. Generally, the first sentence gives the main idea of that paragraph. By reading only the first sentence of each paragraph in a chapter, you may have a summary of the whole text.
- Often, the first and the last paragraphs are important because the writer may state what he intends to write about in the first paragraph, or he may summarize what he has been saying in the last paragraph.

However, these are specific to a field and may not be widely understood.

(i) We will talk about the most commonly used abbreviations next. Study this list.

cf. = *confer,* compare; e.g. = *exempli gratia,* for example; etc. = *et cetera,* and so on; i.e. = *id est,* that is; NB = *nota bene,* note well (something important); viz. = *videlicet,* namely. . . .

(ii) Then there are symbols.

➤ > = greater than; < = less than; = equal to; % = per cent; then there are common symbols like -

➔ from . . . to, leads to results in. . . .

In addition, we also make our own abbreviations for names or some commonly used words.

We can also take branching notes by using diagrammatic symbols. Here is an example.

Specialized symbols < ————––Symbols––———––——>Common symbols

**Scanning for Specified Information:**

When we want some specific information from a book or text, we scan it. In this case, we may get help from the index or the list of contents.

Here is an example of how we do the scanning.

**Let Us Do and Learn:**

In each line of the following word list, one word is printed on the left-hand side, and the same word is repeated on the right-hand side. Do this task. Scan for that word & encircle it.

- mane: name/ man/ main/ mane/ maim
- glacier: glacier/ glazier/ Glamour/ glance/ glassy
- humour: humble/ humph/ bumble/ Humber/ humour

How long did you take to do it? Did you read every word? You did not, right?
You scanned the list and stopped the moment you came across the required word, right?

**Organization of the Text:**

When we read, especially when we scan, it helps if we know how the text has been organized. For example, a scientific text often has this type of organization:

Problem- hypothesis -Experiment- conclusion;
And these systems can be and are often used in combination.

**Knowing Semantic Markers:**

These words or phrases serve as signals for the meaning and the structure of the text. They tell us how the text has been organized. So look for them while surveying or reading. The following are some of the semantic markers along with their meanings:

1. **Listing steps:** Firstly, secondly, in the first place, finally, lastly, etc.
2. **Showing cause and effect relationship between different ideas:** so, therefore, because, since, etc.
3. **Illustrating:** for instance, for example. . . .
4. **Showing opposition/contrast:** but, nevertheless, yet, on the other hand. . . .
5. **Summarizing:** to summarize, in other words, to sum up. . . .
6. **Showing time relationship:** then, next after that. . . .

There are only a few examples of the semantic markers.

**Using Abbreviations for Notes Taking**

As has already been mentioned, we do not copy every word from a text while making/taking notes. If you use symbols and abbreviations, it saves you time and effort. Students specializing in certain fields (e.g., chemistry, physics) employ widely used symbols (O for Oxygen, C for Carbon, etc.)

**Let Us Do and Learn:**

1. Here are some notes taken by a student from an article on Pyramids. Rewrite his notes briefly by using abbreviations, symbols, and strike out the unnecessary words.

   *By the word 'pyramid' we usually mean the grave of an Egyptian king of the Old and Middle kingdoms (that is, from 2680 to 1567 BC).*

   *The earliest pyramid was build for King Zoster and is called the 'Step Pyramid' because the sides go up in large steps. It is 197-feet high.*

   *The largest pyramid ever made is one of a group of three built at Giza, south of Cairo, by the kings of the Fourth Dynasty, which lasted from 2680 to 2565 BC.*

   *This pyramid is called the 'Great Pyramid', and was built by King Khufu (his Greek name is Cheops). The outside of this pyramid consists of more than two million blocks of stone. The average weight of each of these blocks is two-and-a-half tons.*

2. Look at the information on 'Listing Numbers' above. Try to organize the information by using the 'Branching' format.

***Learning Reference Skill.*** There is another area where we need to scan to get the information we want.

When we look up some words or information in a dictionary or encyclopaedia or thesaurus or newspaper ads for jobs or information on films, houses and accommodation, we need to scan such information.

**Using a Dictionary:**

We use a dictionary for specific information, and do not read it for pleasure. We scan the dictionary quickly until we come across the word and the entries under it and as we locate the specific information we stop.

What can we learn from a dictionary? It serves a lot of useful purposes, besides giving us the meaning of a word.

As teachers you should suggest that your learners use a monolingual dictionary. One reason for this is that there is hardly ever a total correspondence between words in two languages. Following are some of the reasons for using a monolingual dictionary.

1. To find out the meanings of the words (perhaps the most common reason), or whether there is more than one meaning for a particular word, by using the definitions and the examples;
2. To check out the spellings of the words;
3. To find the pronunciation of the words;
4. To see if there is any important grammar points associated with a word;
5. To find out the different forms of a word (e.g., adjective, adverb, verb, etc.);
6. To discover idioms (e.g., make a face), phrasal verbs;
7. To find out whether the word is used in American or British English, whether it is pronounced differently in either usage;
8. To find out information about written and spoken forms of words and
9. To see how words go together (collocation).

There are many more uses of a dictionary. Think about them.

**Using a Thesaurus:**

The thesaurus is a different kind of reference book. It has only the synonyms and antonyms of words. These synonyms and antonyms cover widest possible range of meanings and situations. Of course, there are thesauruses for young learners which give a limited range of meanings and opposites. Here is a typical entry from a thesaurus:

(We have quoted a few of the meanings)
*band* 1n. bandage, bandeau, belt, binding, bond, chain, cord. . . .
*band* 2n. association, body, club, combo, company, coterie, ensemble, flock, gang, group, herd. . . .
*v.* affiliate, ally, amalgamate, collaborate, consolidate, gather, group, join, merge. . . .
*antonym* disband, disburse

As you can see, the word 'band' as a noun has two different connotations. In the first meaning, it has a set of synonyms which is very different from the second one. So, you need to decide first which of these connotations you have in mind. Then from the list of synonyms you select the one you need for your purpose. Next, there is the verb 'band' which also has a range of synonyms. The antonyms are for the verb form only as their placement shows.

Notice that the synonyms range from literary to colloquial uses.

**Using an Encyclopaedia:**
An encyclopaedia has a lot of information on a given topic. The large ones like Encyclopaedia Britannica come in volumes. The entries are arranged alphabetically like in a dictionary or a thesaurus. Under each entry, all possible information about it is given. So, if it is a country, you may learn about its geographical location and features—its flora and fauna, rivers and mountains, political and economic situations, its trade and commerce, etc. There are graphic presentations and illustrations so that the information is easy to understand and remember.

**Looking Up Advertisements, Radio/TV Programmes in Newspapers/Magazines, etc.:**
When we are trying to locate the specific information we require, we usually do not need to read the whole text carefully. We try to find which paragraph has the information we are looking for; and then read this paragraph with more attention. So, we run our eyes quickly over a text in order to locate where the information might be.

For example, in 'houses and accommodation' column you get a lot of information about the different kinds of houses, flats, bungalows, etc., in different locations. If you are looking for a small flat at or near the city centre, you do not waste time on reading about big houses or bungalows in the suburbs or countryside. You may also need to consider the price of the flat and facilities, etc., available in or near the flat (e.g., number of rooms, security arrangements in the flat, or transport facilities, markets, educational institutions nearby). You will scan the text for a likely location and flat/s and then choose to read carefully the ones that meet your requirements.

**Let Us Do and Learn:**

- In addition to the reasons given for using a dictionary, add five more reasons to the list. (For help, you may scrutinize carefully any page of a dictionary.)

**Thinking As a Skill:**
So far, in this unit we have been discussing what we do when we are reading for information. But we do not always read for information only. As we gather information, we also try to understand the content. In other words, we may want to understand why the writer wrote the piece (writer's intention), how she/he made the point she/he wanted to make (function of the language): we differentiate between the facts she/he stated and the opinions she/he expressed. In short, as we are now reading for pleasure, we try to appreciate the text.

**Reading for Pleasure:**
When we read for pleasure, our focus is on the text and mode, i.e., how a fact or information has been presented. If we want to enjoy reading, we should read actively and try to interpret the text. In the process,

we draw inferences, predict a possible outcome and distinguish between facts and opinions. This heightens our enjoyment of reading.

A writer writes with a purpose which may be to argue a case, to persuade, to humour, to reach. If we understand the writer's purpose, we comprehend the text more fully. In other words, the reader has to be aware of the writer's intention, her/his point of view and her/his possible bias. To understand all this, we need to develop the ability to assess and evaluate the text.

**Drawing Inferences and Predicting a Possible Outcome:**
Now, we will discuss how we can infer or predict. We draw inferences on the basis of the information we already have.

Read the following text and then decide which information suggests that the boy in the paragraph was poor.

It was barely light when a small sturdy boy trotted down the street towards the Cotton factory; he was only 10 years old, and he had to be at work by six o' clock.

The likely answers are:

- the boy had to start very early.
- he was barely 10 years old, and he had to work.
- he worked in a factory.
- he had to walk to his workplace.

You may find some other answers. In all these cases, you are inferring or guessing the answer on the basis of the information given in the text.

Inference is when you draw conclusions on the basis of the information you have.

We may also predict the possible outcome, i.e., we try to guess what might happen next. However, our prediction may turn out to be wrong! For instance, while reading a crime thriller, we try to guess who committed the crime. It is not that we are always right in our prediction. We try to predict on the basis of some information implied in the situation, but not explicitly stated.

For example, what do you think are the occupations of the following persons whose names have been italicized?

(i) *Ms. Lucas* looked over the hastily scribbled notes on Mr. Narayan and sat down at her typewriter.
(ii) *Mr. Rabin* came out of his van and lifted his ladder, sponges and cloths.
(iii) We may predict Miss Lucas is a typist, but she may as well be the receptionist or a junior colleague, or even a friend.
(iv) *Mr. Rabin* may be a glazier (person who cleans the windows) or even a thief pretending to be a cleaner!
(v) Is he going out to work or coming home after work?

We do not have enough data to come to a definite conclusion.

**Separating Facts from Opinions:**
A fact is something that is actually true. An opinion is what a person or persons think about something.

**Let Us Do and Learn:**
Read the following passage. Then decide whether each sentence is a statement of fact or of opinion.

The train sped by at a speed of 100 km per hour. It was indeed a beautiful train. Surely, the passengers would consider it the best train they had ever travelled in. For 20 years the engine had stood idle in the transport museum. Now, it has been restored and brought back into service.

**Answer Hints:**
Sentences 1, 4 and 5 are **statements** of fact. Sentences 2 and 3 are **opinions.** How do you know? Consider the words that made you think these are words like indeed (beautiful), surely, and ever.

***Knowing Different Language Functions.*** As you can see, to differentiate between facts and opinions, it is important that we know the different functions of language.

While giving factual information, we may make a request or offer, apologize or warn, give instruction or direction, and so on. While expressing opinions, we may express our likes and dislikes, agreement or disagreement, and so on. To achieve our aim, we may repeat, exaggerate, and use words which have favourable/unfavourable connotations, words which alliterate.

***Let Us Do and Learn***

1. **Read the text and then do the following tasks:**

Helen Keller was only 18 months old when she was stricken with an illness which left her blind and deaf. You can imagine the awful shock for the parents when all this happened to their happy and intelligent child who was normal and healthy until her illness. The worry and sadness was almost incurable.

When Helen was six years old, her parents sought the help of the inventor Alexander Graham Bell, who had done work on behalf of the deaf. He recommended that Anne Sullivan should become Helen's teacher.

Anne had been almost blind herself as a child but afterwards her sight had been partially restored. From her own experience, Anne knew about the special needs of the blind. She had also done a careful study in teaching the blind-deaf. She also knew how a blind-deaf girl Laura Bridgman was taught to read, write and learn algebra, history and geography.

But, would Anne be able to help Helen who was blind and deaf and often violent as well?

**Making Inferences:**
(i) Do you think (a) Helen was physically healthy or weak? (b) Anne Sullivan was clever? Why do you think so?

**Predicting Outcomes:**
Do you think Anne Sullivan would have been appointed Helen's teacher? Why do you think so?
(ii) What do you think might have happened later on?

## Let Us Sum Up

This chapter has given us a wide coverage regarding the importance of teaching English as a combination of four primary language skills, namely listening, speaking, reading and writing with their sub-skills.

This chapter has also highlighted the need for target-oriented classroom teaching. This chapter has also analyzed the implication of using grammar for C-R and teaching study skill as well as reference skill from early years of learning. This chapter has also provided insights into the following issues:

**The definition of reading as a skill, as a process and as a product**
You must have understood that reading is a symbiosis of all these study skills.

## Process of Reading and the Schema Theory

The schema theory says that comprehension depends on the activation of schemata. These are pictures or frameworks of a situation which helps us to understand the situation.

In other words, as soon as we begin to read, we form a schema triggered by the title, format, first sentence, etc., and based upon our previous knowledge. This schema will be reinforced, adapted or discarded as we continue to read. This model has profound implications for the process of reading.

**Bottom-Up Processing:**
This process reflects the old models of reading as a simple process of decoding words into thoughts. However, it accepts that words must first be recognized and, having been decoded, the thoughts must then be remembered. It is an approach which works from parts to the whole, building up gradually in a process of growth.

**Top-Down Processing:**
This model states that readers begin with expectations and ideas about a text, based on its title, format and style, before they begin to look for words that will substantiate or refute these expectations. It is an approach which begins with a picture of the whole and deals with the parts in terms of this approach.

**Effective and Ineffective Readers:**
A familiarity with effective and ineffective reading strategies can help the teacher look for effective reading behaviours in learners, encourage wider use of these strategies, and to be on the lookout for learners using less effective strategies.

## Research Studies in Readers' Strategies and Attitudes

Several projects undertaken in different countries have been referred to attitudinal changes in readers at different levels.

**Computers and Reading:**
Several theories of reading have been effective in establishing the fact that computer-based instructions facilitates students' reading comprehension and increases their reading speed.

We realize that oral skills are neither learning the grammar rules of the language nor is it ignoring grammar altogether.

This chapter summarizes some of the researches into schema theory and its applications to ESL reading. Some of the limitations of the use of the schema-theoretic approach are also discussed. The importance both of developing the learner's vocabulary and encouraging extensive reading are also highlighted.

Carrell, Devine and Eskey (1988:4) claim that schema theory has provided numerous benefits to ESL teaching and, indeed, most current ESL textbooks attempt schema activation through pre-reading activities.

For example, students might be asked to look at a visual, listen to a song or watch the opening scene of a film/theatre/play and try to guess what they are going to read in the following session.

Schema Research highlights different kinds of reader problems. These relate to absent or alternate (often culture-specific) schemata, as well as non-activation of schemata, and even overuse of background knowledge.

However, there may be limits to the effectiveness of such activities, and there may even have been some over-emphasis of the schema perspective and neglect of other areas (Eskey 1988:93; McCarthy 1991: 168).

## Glossary

acquisition: the process of picking up a language without formal instruction and without conscious effort to learn the language

decode: the process of trying to understand the meaning of a message

cognitive process: mental processes as opposed to mechanical repetition and drills

interdisciplinary skills: skills involving different disciplines like sociology, psychology and education

schemata: mental stores which the reader brings into play as she/he processes information in a text—first suggested by Barlett in the 1930s

reading behaviour: the way one reads and processes information on the basis of her/his educational and sociocultural backgrounds
bi-literate reader: a reader who is proficient in reading text written both in MT and in L2
genre: a literary or non-literary form of spoken or written discourse
schema interference: a situation where overuse of background knowledge tends to interfere with the process of understanding of a text
schema-theoretic approach: an approach in which the notion of schema and studies leading to various hypotheses forms the basis of classroom instruction
pre-reading activity: any activity that can stimulate the reader's mind to the text before the process of reading begins
narrow reading: Reading that does not demand going beyond the knowledge of the reader
top-down mode: a process of reading that moves from general understanding to specific details included in the text.
bottom-up processing: *process of* building up meaning from the smallest textual units at the bottom (letters, words) to the larger units at the top
receptive vocabulary: items of vocabulary that are not in active use but are within the knowledge of the reader
Automaticity: independent recognition and understanding of a text
inter-textuality: where 'all texts contain traces of other texts, and frequently they cannot be readily interpreted—or at least fully appreciated—without reference to other texts'
reader strategies: skills and processes the reader uses in order to understand what she/he is reading
metalinguistic knowledge: knowledge of the codes used to refer to certain language operations, knowledge of the language used to describe language
code-cracking activity: activity designed to stimulate comprehension of the language of the reading text through a decoding process
declarative knowledge: knowledge of the code and rules of language operations (What?)
procedural knowledge: knowledge of the process of understanding (How?)
skimming: fast reading to extract the main idea of a text
scanning: reading in detail to get the specific details of a text
reciprocal teaching: A process of teaching that has been in the communicative classroom for many years, and has proven itself to be an extremely effective way of fostering the strategies of questioning, clarifying, summarizing and predicting; this is both comprehensions fostering and monitoring. Here the students take turns being the 'teacher' who is interactive with his or her students. For example, a number of students read some short passages aloud, and then the 'teacher' asks questions, and leads a discussion, on the text. All the students are expected to 'clip-in' whenever they can.
passive inattention: no active involvement of the reader resulting in lack of attention to the text and, therefore, leading to poor understanding
scaffolding: support from the teacher in providing active involvement, and not encouraging passive inattention, and feedback
learner autonomy: In declarative and procedural terms, the learners in our imaginary group may become acquainted with these ideas, consciously and sub-consciously. With these skills, they may recreate this experience, even when reading alone. It is only by doing this that they may develop their proficiency in the skill of reading.
speed reading: Skimming to get the gist or main idea of the text. Reading speed can be calculated on the basis of the number of words read per minute. Speed reading is dependent on the number of eye

fixations made per second. There is research evidence to prove that speed readers can read up to more than 1,000 words per minute.

discourse: a general term for examples of language use, language which has been produced as the result of an act of communication.

encode: the process of turning messages into a set of symbols, as part of the process of communication.

fluency: the features which give speech the qualities of being natural and normal, including the use of pausing, rhythm, intonation, stress, rate of speaking, and so on.

information gap: (In communication between two or more people) a situation where information is known only by some of those present. Without such a gap, the communication activities and exercises will be mechanical and artificial.

pedagogy: the study of teaching practices.

problem-solving: a learning strategy which involves selecting from several alternatives in order to reach a desired goal.

role-play: imitating real-life situation which consists of activities in which the learners play parts and practice language appropriate for situations they are placed in. It does not include group discussion.

simulation: classroom activities which reproduce or simulate real situations and which often involve dramatization and group discussion. In simulation activities, learners are given roles in a situation—a task or a problem to be solved—and are given instructions to follow. They later discuss their actions, feeling and what happened.

semantic: relating to the systematic study of meaning in a language

lexical: of the words of a language

cues: something (e.g., a few words or an action) that gives the signal to say or do something

behavioural psychology: A theory of psychology which states that human and animal behaviour can and should be studied in terms of physical processes only. It led to theories of learning which explained how an external event (a stimulus) caused a change in the behaviour of an individual (a response) without using concepts like 'mind' or 'ideas' or any kind of mental behaviour.

structural linguistics: an approach to linguistics which stress the importance of language as a system and which investigates the place those linguistic units (such as sounds, words, sentences) have within this system.

## Exercise

1. Listen to an incomplete story and guess the remaining part; then listen to the story and see how much of it accords with the person's guess.
2. Listen to the lecture on a topic and then read about it in a book, and checkhow much of the latter matches with the experts' lecture.
3. Listen to one side of a telephone conversation and guess what the other person responses could be; then listen to the actual conversation and compare both.
4. Go through a list of jumbled key points to be covered in a talk and then listen to the talk and number the key points in sequence while listening to the talk.
5. Listen to a conversation and say at what point the purpose of the conversation was interactional and at what point it was transactional.
6. Look at some pictures & listen to some descriptions: Identify the pictures from their descriptions and arrange them in the order in which they are described.

7. Look at the diagram of an object (e.g., a flower, a small machine) given to a person; listen to an oral description of the object and label the part of the object.
8. Listen to an advertisement for a job on the radio and more the eligibility requirements.
9. Draw a diagram with the help of an aural description.
10. Assemble an item with the help of oral instructions.
11. What do you understand by the term 'reading'?
12. Mention some of the ways in which researchers have defined reading.
13. Why is reading referred to as an interdisciplinary skill? Which other disciplines are associated with reading?
14. What do you understand by a reader's schemata?
15. What are the different views on:
    (i) The culture factor in the process of reading
    (ii) The bi-literate reader
16. Mention some of the sub-skills of reading that have been identified by researchers. Do they have anything in common with the other skills of language learning?
17. 'The text has no meaning in it as its intrinsic property. It is only the readerwho breathes meaning into it.' Do you agree? What are the views of researchers?
18. Explain with suitable examples what you understand by top-down and bottom-up approaches.
19. What is SSR? How have researchers benefited from SSR?
    Write short notes on (a) Readers' Strategies and Problems
    (b) Inter-textuality
    (c) Computer-based Reading
    (d) Effective and Ineffective Readers
    (e) Reader Attitudes
20. Why do you think the Grammar-Translation Method is one that has been derived from the teaching of the classical languages, Latin and Greek?
21. What do you think are the limitations of the Grammar-Translation Method?
22. What are some of the characteristics of the Direct Method that make it so distinctive from the Grammar-Translation Method?
23. 'In the Grammar-Translation Method, grammar is treated deductively and in the Direct Method, grammar is treated inductively.' In this context, explain the difference between deductive and inductive treatments of grammar.
24. Discuss the characteristics of teaching/learning process in the Oral Approach & Situational English Language Teaching Approach.
25. What is the role of the teacher in audio-lingual method?
26. What areas of language are emphasized in the audio-lingual method?

## Project Work/Course Work

1. Choose a reading passage from a literary work or a textbook, or write one yourself. Plan a vocabulary exercise you would use to help your students to associate the new words with their native language equivalents.
2. Choose a particular situation (such as at the bank, at the railroad station or at the doctor's office) and write a short passage or a dialogue on the theme you have chosen. Now think about how you will convey its meaning to a class.
3. Select a grammar point from a passage. Plan how you will make your students practice the grammar point. What examples can you provide them so that they can include the rules themselves?

## Bibliography

Anderson, A., Brown, G., Shillcock, R. and Yule, G. (1984), *Teaching Talk*, Cambridge University Press.

Brightr and Mc Gregor (1970), *Teaching English as a Second Language.*

Brumfit, C., Carter, R. and Walker, R. (1989), 'Literature and the Learners' *Methodological Approaches.*

Brumfit, C. (ed, 1983), 'Teaching Literature Overseas: Language-based Approaches', *ELT* Documents, 115.

Brumfit, C. J. and Carter, R. A. (eds.) (1986), *Literature and Language Teaching.*

Byrne, D. (1981), *Teaching Oral English: Longman Handbook for Language Teachers*, Longman Group Ltd.

Byrne, D. (1984), 'Oral Ability', *From Focus on the Learner* (ed.) Holden S., Modern English Publications.

Canale, M. (1984), 'From communicative competence to communicative language pedagogy' in Richards, Jack C and Schmidt, Richard W. (Ed), *Language and Communication*, Longman.

Carter, R. and Long, M. (1987), *The Web of Words.*

Carter, R. and Long, M. (1991), *Teaching Literature*, Chapter 4.

Carter, R. (ed) (1982), *Literary Text and Language Study.*

Gilliec (1972), *Longman Companion to English Literature.*

Gower, R. (1990), *Past into Present.*

Gower, R. and Pearson, M. (1986), *Reading Literature.*

Grellet F. (1981), *Developing Reading Skills.*

Horiden, S. (ed) (1988), *Literature and Language.*

Kramsch, C. (1993), *Context and Culture in Language Teaching.*

Lazar, G. (1993), *Literature and Language Teaching.*

Littlewood, W. (1992), *Teaching Oral Communication: A Methodological Framework*, Blackwell, London.

Lott, B. (1986), *A Course in English Language and Literature.*

Margthe, Ramanan Bellarmine (1993), *Provocations – The Teaching of English Literature in India.*

McRae, J. and Boardman, R. (1984), *Reading between the Lines.*

Nolasco, R. and Arthur, L., (1991), *Conversation*, ELBS Edition, Oxford University Press.

Quirk, R. and Widdowson H. G. (1985), *English in the World.*

Stephen D. Krashen (1981), *Second Language Acquisition and Second Language Learning*, Pergamon Press Inc., California / Internet Edition 2002.

Swartridge, C. (1978), *British Fiction: A Student's A-Z.*

Walker R. (1983), *Language for Literature.*

Widdowson, H.C. (1975), *Stylistics and the Teaching of Literature.*

Widdowson, H. G. (1974), Stylistics' in Corder, S.P. and Alien, P. B., *The Edinburgh Course in Applied Linguistics,* 3.

Wynne Davies, Marion (ed.) (1989), *Bloomsbury Guide to English Literature.*

# Approaches and Methods of Teaching English 4

## CHAPTER OUTLINE



## LEARNING OBJECTIVES

This chapter will:

- Distinguish between different methods and approaches of teaching English.
- Use suitable methods and approaches for teaching English language.
- Motivate the learners in accordance with the change in methods and approaches.
- Motivate you as a teacher and enact different roles for making your teaching perfect.

## Introduction

The propagation of various methods and approaches is a prominent feature of contemporary second and foreign language teaching. The classroom teacher and the programme co-coordinator have a wide variety of methodological options to choose from than even preferences of teachers and the constraints of the school of educational setting. Invention of new classroom practices and approaches to designing language programmes and materials reflects a commitment to finding more efficient and more effective ways of teaching languages. This chapter is designed to provide a detailed account of major twentieth-century trends in language teaching. To highlight the similarities and differences between approaches and methods, the same descriptive framework is used throughout.

This chapter presents and discusses all well-known language teaching methods. Some of these methods have been around for a very long time. By reading this chapter, we will gain an understanding of the principles on which these methods are based and an understanding of the techniques associated with each method. We should not equate the inclusion of a method to the endorsement of that method. Let us be informed about the existing choices and investigate each method in the light of your own beliefs and experiences. We do not expect that you will abandon the way you teach now or plan to teach in future in order to adopt one of these methods. We do believe, however, that there will be some new techniques worthy of your attention. As you read this chapter, try to imagine how you can adopt these techniques creatively in your own situation.

## Lexical Grammatical Approach

The oldest approach of teaching available is based on learning *lexis* and *grammar* of a foreign language. Let us explore the method under this approach.

### Grammar-translation Method

The Grammar-translation Method was the offspring of German scholarship as the names of some of its leading exponents like Johann Seidenstiicker, Karl Plotz, H.S. Ollendorf and Johann Meidinger suggest.

**The Grammar-translation Method was first known in the United States as the Prussian Method.**

#### *Objectives*

- The goal of this method was to help the students read and appreciate foreign language literature.
- It was thought that students would benefit from the mental discipline and intellectual development that result from foreign language study.
- Development of reading and writing skills should be the major focus.
- The sentence is to be taken as the basic unit of teaching and language practice. Much of the lesson is devoted to translating sentences in and out of the targetlanguage.
- Grammar should be taught deductively that is grammar should be at first presented and studied and then practiced through a translation exercise.
- Vocabulary selection is based solely on the reading texts used and words taught through bilingual word lists, dictionary study and memorization.
- There should be much emphasis on accuracy. Students are expected to attain high standards in translation.
- The students' native language is the medium of instruction. It is used to explain new items and to enable comprehension.

#### *Some Characteristics of the Teaching/Learning Process: Let Us See Some Notable Characteristics*

(i) Students study grammar deductively that is they are given the grammar rules and examples. They are told to memorize the rules and are then asked to apply them to other examples.
(ii) Students also learn grammatical paradigms like verb conjugations.
(iii) Students are taught to translate from one language to another. Often what they translate are materials in the target language about some aspect of the culture of the foreign language community.
(iv) They memorize native language equivalents for words from the target language.

**Did you know?**

**Lexical:** related to words

**Grammatical:** based on Grammar

### *The Areas of Language and Language Skills Which are Emphasized*

There is much emphasis on vocabulary and grammar. Reading and writing are given primary importance. Speaking and listening receives much less attention. Pronunciation receives little, if any, attention.

### *Nature of Student–teacher and Student–student Interaction*

The lessons are mostly teacher-directed. Most of the initiation of interaction is from the teacher to students. There is little student initiation and little student to student interaction.

### *Teacher's Response to Students' Errors*

Accuracy in grammar and translation is considered to be very important. If the students make errors or don't know an answer, the teacher supplies them with the correct answer.

### *Nature of Evaluation*

Written tests in which students are asked to translate from their native language to the target language or vice versa are often used to evaluate students. Questions about the foreign culture or questions that ask students to apply grammar rules are also common.

### *Role of Instructional Materials*

The instructional materials mainly consist of the textbooks containing passages for **reading** and **translation.**

These materials also consist of a number of **grammar rules** with **exercises.**

### *Role of the Students' Native Language*

The native language is the medium of instruction in the classroom. The meaning of the target language is made clear by translating it into the students' native language.

The Grammar-translation Method dominated European and foreign teaching from the 1840s to the 1940s and continued to be used in modified form in some parts of the world. In the mid and late nineteenth century, opposition to the Grammar-translation Method gradually developed in several European countries. The Reform Movement laid foundations for the development of new ways of teaching languages. You had an opportunity to examine the principles of the Grammar-translation Method.

## ◢ The Oral Approach and Situational Language Teaching

The Oral Approach and Situational Language Teaching refer to an approach to language teaching developed by British applied linguists from the 1930s to the 1960s. Prof. Harold Palmer and A.S. Hornby were two of the most prominent figures in twentieth-century Britain who attempted to develop a more scientific foundation for an Oral Approach to teaching English. This led to the foundation of the Direct Method. The result of their effort was a systematic study of the principles and procedures that could be applied to the selection and organization of the content of a language course.

## Functional/Notional Functional Method

The term, 'notional' means 'related to notion or idea'. Hence, Functional/Notional Approach did its best by focusing on the development of linguistic idea for functional use of the English language.

### *Objectives: Let Us Judge the Following Objectives*

- The method aims at the automatic control of basic structures and sentence patterns which is fundamental to reading and writing skills through speech work. The course content is taught orally before it aims at the development of **reading** and **writing skills.**
- Accuracy in both **pronunciation** and **grammar** is regarded as crucial, and errors are to be avoided at all costs.
- The method aims at the development of **four basic skills** of English language.
- The skills are approached through **random practice** of language structures.

### *Characteristics of Teaching/Learning Process*

The main characteristics of the approach are as follows:

- The **target language** is the language of the classroom.
- New language points or structures are taught orally before they are presented in a written form.
- New language points are introduced and practiced in different simulated situations.
- Vocabulary selection procedures are followed to ensure that **Essential General Service Vocabulary of Dr Smart** is covered.
- Items of grammar are graded following the principle that simple form should be taught before the complex ones.
- **Reading** and **writing** are introduced once a sufficient lexical and grammatical basis is established.

Situational language teaching uses a situational approach in presenting new sentence patterns and a drill-based manner of practicing them. Situation means the use of concrete objects, pictures which together with actions and gestures can be used to demonstrate the meanings of new language items. The practice techniques generally consist of guided repetition and substitution activities, including chorus repetition, dictation, drills and controlled oral-based reading and writing tasks. Other oral-practice techniques are sometimes used, including pair practice and group work. Pittman illustrates oral drilling on a pattern, using a box full of objects to create the situation. The pattern being practiced is:

There is NOUN + 'of (noun) in the box'; e.g., The teacher takes objects out of the box and the class repeats:

*There's a bottle of ink in the box.*
*There's a packet of pins in the box.*
*There's a jar of rice in the box.*
*There's a reel of cotton in the box.*

Pittman says that a typical lesson plan would consist of the following parts:

1. Pronunciation
2. Revision (to prepare for new work if necessary)
3. Presentation of new structure of vocabulary
4. Oral practice (drilling)
5. Reading of material on the new structure or written exercises

### *The Major Areas of Language and Language Skills Which Are Emphasized*

Speech is regarded as the basis of language and structure is viewed as being at the heart of speaking ability. Vocabulary is regarded as one of the most important aspects of foreign language teaching. Michael West's *A General Service List of English Words*, published in 1953, became a standard reference in developing teaching materials. Major grammatical structures are classified into sentence patterns (later on called 'substitution tables') to help internalize the rules of English sentence structure. The method attempts to make the students gain a practical command of the four basic skills of language but speech work precedes reading and writing.

### *Nature of Student–teacher Interaction and Student–student Interaction*

Lessons are teacher-directed. The teacher, at first, serves as a model setting up situations in which the need for the target structure is created and then more like the skillful conductor of an orchestra the teacher uses questions, comments and other cues to elicit correct sentences from the learners. In the initial stages of learning, the learner is simply required to listen and repeat what the teacher says and respond to questions and commands. Later, more active participation is encouraged which may include initiating responses and asking each other questions.

### *Teacher's Response to Students' Errors*

Errors are to be avoided as **accuracy** is considered to be absolutely necessary. The teacher is ever on the lookout for grammatical and structural errors that can form the basis of subsequent lessons.

### *Nature of Evaluation*

Evaluation may take place informally during question-answer sessions and other activities. The teacher may also take a formal test.

### *Role of Instructional Materials*

Situational language teaching is dependent upon a textbook and visual aids. The textbook contains lessons tightly planned around different grammatical structures. Visual aids may consist of charts, flashcards, stick figures, and so on. The textbook should, however, be used as a guide to the learning process. The teacher is expected to be the master of her/his textbook.

### *Role of the Students' Native Language*

The target language is the language of the classroom as the habits of the student's native language are thought to interfere with the students' attempts to master the target language.

## The Direct Method

Since the Grammar-translation Method was not very effective in preparing students to use the target language communicatively, the Direct Method gained popularity. Towards the end of the nineteenth century, researchers turned their attention to naturalistic principles of language learning which provided the foundation for what came to be known as the Direct Method. Thus, this method is most widely known as one of the natural methods of pedagogy.

The Direct Method has one very basic rule: no translation is allowed. In fact, the Direct Method receives its name from the fact that meaning is to be connected directly with the target language without going through the process of translating into the students' native language.

### *Objectives: Let Us See the Prime Objectives of This Method*

- Classroom instruction should be conducted exclusively in the target language.
- The method aims at intense oral interaction in the classroom, so as to develop oral communication skills of the students.
- Only everyday vocabulary and sentences should be taught.
- New teaching points must be introduced orally.
- There must be an emphasis on correct pronunciation and grammar.
- Grammar must be taught inductively.

**Information Box**

- We need to check our own objectives very well before considering any method for application.

### *Characteristics of Teaching/Learning Process: Let Us See Some Important Features*

1. Students speak in the target language a great deal.
2. The syllabus used in the Direct Method is based upon situations (for example, situation in a shop, in the post office). Students communicate with each other as if they were in real situations.
3. The Direct Method believes that students need to associate meaning and the target language directly. Thus, when the teacher introduces a new word or phrase from the target language, she/he demonstrates its meaning through the use of realia, pictures or pantomime instead of translating it into the students' native language.
4. Students practice vocabulary by using words in complete sentences.
5. Grammar is taught inductively that is, the students are presented with examples, and they figure out the rule or generalization from the examples. An explicit grammar rule may never be provided.

### *The Areas of Language and Language Skills Which Are Emphasized*

The method aims at development of all **four basic skills of English** but oral communication is given primary importance.

**Reading** and **writing exercises** are based upon what the students practice orally at first.

Development of **vocabulary** is emphasized over development of grammar. **Pronunciation** also receives attention right from the very beginning.

### *Nature of Student–teacher and Student–student Interaction*

Lessons are often teacher-directed but unlike the Grammar-translation Method the role of the students is less passive. The initiation of interaction may go from the teacher to the students as well as from the students to the teacher. Students also converse with one another.

### *Teacher's Response to Students' Errors*

There is an emphasis on accurate pronunciation and grammar. The teacher tries to get the students to self-correct whenever possible.

### *Nature of Evaluation*

In the Direct Method, students are asked to use the language, not to demonstrate their knowledge about the language. They are asked to do so using both oral and written skills. For example, the students might be interviewed orally by the teacher and might be asked to write a paragraph about something they have studied.

#### *Role of Instructional Materials*

Objects (e.g., maps or pictures) present in the immediate classroom environment are used to help the students understand the meaning.

#### *Role of the Students' Native Language*

The native language of the students should not be used in the classroom. The target language is the language of the classroom.

Although the Direct Method enjoyed popularity in Europe and was successful in private language schools, such as those of the Berlitz Chain, its use had declined. British applied linguist Henry Sweet had recognized its limitations. It was perceived to have several drawbacks. They are:

- It offered innovations at the level of teaching procedure but lacked a thorough methodological basis.
- It required teachers who were fluent in the target language. It was largely dependent on the teacher's skill rather than on a textbook. However, teachers were not proficient enough to adhere to the principles of the method.
- Strict adherence to the Direct Method principles were often counterproductive since teachers were required to go great lengths to avoid using the native tongue when sometimes a brief explanation in the students' native tongue would have been a more efficient route to comprehension.
- Prof. Sweet and other applied linguists argued for the development of sound methodological principles that could serve as the basis for teaching techniques. Subsequent developments led to the foundation of Audio- Lingual Method in the United States and Oral Approach or Situational Language Teaching in Britain.

## Structural Approach

Structural Approach tried to keep close attachment with grammatical structures and pointed out the importance of 'drill' and 'practice' for making language.

### Activity Time

While reading the Audio-Lingual Method try to find out the names of the experts and their theories and complete the following table:

| | Experts Associated with Structuralism | Theory of Structuralism |
|---|---|---|
| 1. | | |
| 2. | | |
| 3. | | |

## The Audio-lingual Method

The Audio-Lingual Method was developed in the United States during World War II when there was a need for people to learn foreign languages rapidly for military purposes. The main objective of the army programmes was to make the students attain conversational proficiency in a variety of foreign languages. At that time there were exciting new ideas about language and learning emanating from the disciplines of descriptive linguistics and behavioural psychology. These ideas led to the development of the Audio-Lingual Method. The term 'Audio Lingual' was coined by professor Nelson Brooks in 1964. He claimed that it would enable learners to achieve mastery of a foreign language effectively. The method was widely adopted for teaching foreign languages in North American colleges and universities.

Let us now consider the Audio-Lingual Method under the following heads:

### *Objectives: Let Us Take a Note On the Prime Objectives*

Prof. Brooks distinguishes between short-range and long-range objectives in the audio-lingual programme.

#### *Short-range objectives include*

- Training in listening comprehension and
- Development of reading and writing dependent upon prior oral skills.

#### *Long-range objectives include*

- Oral proficiency which is equated with:
  (a) accurate pronunciation and grammar and
  (b) the ability to respond quickly and accurately in speech situations.

### *Characteristics of Teaching/Learning Process*

The theory of language underlying the Audio-Lingual Method was derived from a view proposed by American linguists in the 1950s—a view that came to be known as structural linguistics. Some important tenets of structural linguistics are:

- Language is primarily **spoken** and only secondarily what is **written.**
- Language is a set of **habits.**

Thus, in a typical audio-lingual classroom you may note the following:

- New **vocabulary** and **grammatical structures** are presented through dialogues.
- The dialogues are learnt through imitation and repetition.
- Drills are conducted based upon the patterns present in the **dialogues.**
- Students' **reading** and **writing** activities are based upon the **oral** work they did earlier.
- Grammar is presented through examples. **Explicit grammar rules** are not provided.
- The method believes that language cannot be separated from **culture**. Culture is not only literature and the arts, but also the everyday behavior of the people who use the target language.
- **Cultural information** is contextualized in the dialogues presented by the teacher.

**Information Box**

- **Audio:** related to auditory organ or hearing
- **Lingual:** based on language
- Audio-Lingual Method is still used in India with some kind of improved computer mobile, network for teaching English.

### Main Objectives

- Developing awareness as good as of the native speakers and
- Developing the ability to use the language as the native speaker uses it.

### The Areas of Language and Language Skills Which are Emphasized

The syllabus is typically a structural one. The structures of the language are emphasized over all the other areas. The structures for any particular unit are included in the new dialogue. Vocabulary is also contextualized within the dialogue.

The oral/aural skills receive most of the attention.

Pronunciation is taught from the beginning.

### Nature of Student–teacher Interaction and Student–student Interaction

Most of the interaction is between the teacher and students and is initiated by the teacher. There is student to student interaction in chain drills or when students take different roles in dialogues but this interaction is teacher-directed.

### Teacher's Response to Students' Errors

Student errors are to be avoided through the teacher's awareness of where the students will have difficulty and restriction of what they are taught to say.

### Nature of Evaluation

Each question in the test would focus on only one point of the language at a time. Students might be asked to distinguish between words in minimal pair or to supply an appropriate verb form in a sentence.

### The Role of Instructional Materials

Instructional materials are primarily teacher-oriented. A textbook is often not used in the elementary phases of a course because it distracts attention from the aural input.

When textbooks and printed materials are introduced to the students, they provide the **texts** of dialogues and **cues** needed for drills and exercises.

Tape recorders and audio-visual equipment often have central roles in an audio-lingual course. If the learner is not a native speaker of the target language, the tape recorder provides accurate models for **dialogues** and **drills**.

A taped lesson may first present a dialogue for **listening practice**, allow the students to repeat the sentences in the dialogues line by line and provide follow-up **fluency drills** on grammar and pronunciation.

### Role of the Students' Native Language

The habits of the students' native language are thought to interfere with the students' attempts to master the target language. Therefore, the target language is used in the classroom, not the students' native language.

Audio-Lingual Method reached its peak in the 1960s and was applied to the teaching of foreign languages and English as second or foreign language. However, the theoretical foundations of the **Audio-Lingual Method** were regarded to be unsound, both, in terms of language theory and learning theory.

On the other hand, practitioners found that the practical results fell short of expectations. Students were often found to be unable to transfer skills acquired through audio-lingual practice to real communication outside the classroom, and many found the experience of studying through audio-lingual procedures boring and unsatisfying.

The MIT linguist Prof. Noam Chomsky rejected the **Structural Approach** to language description as well as the **Behaviourist Theory** of language learning. According to Prof. Chomsky, sentences are not learnt by imitation and repetition but **generated** from the learner's underlying common sense. Suddenly, the whole audio-lingual paradigm was called into question.

It was realized that practice activities should involve meaningful learning and language use. This led to a period of adaptation, innovation, experimentation which resulted in the emergence of new methods like **Total Physical Response, Silent Way** and **approaches** like the **Natural Approach** and **Communicative Language Teaching**. These developments will be considered in the succeeding pages.

***Let Us Do and Learn***

Note down the major differences between Functional/Notional Functional Approach and Structural Approach in English Language Teaching.

| | Functional/Notional Functional Approach | Structural Approach |
|---|---|---|
| 1. | | |
| 2. | | |
| 3. | | |
| 4. | | |
| 5. | | |

## Communicative (Learner-centred) Language Teaching Approach

The Communicative Language Teaching (CLT) originated from the changes in the British language teaching tradition that took place in the late 1960s.

By the end of the sixties it was clear that the situational approach which taught the language by the practice of basic structures in meaningful situation-based activities had run its course.

It was realized that it is insufficient for students to simply have knowledge of the target language forms, meanings and functions. Students must be able to apply this knowledge to negotiation of the meaning.

British applied linguists saw the need to focus in language teaching on communicative proficiency rather than on mere mastery of structures. This led to the development of Communicative Language Teaching.

## Communicative English Teaching or Method

## Communicative English Learning or Method

### *Objectives*

- **Communicative competence** (i.e., the ability to use the linguistic system effectively and appropriately should be the goal of language teaching/learing.)
- There should be a development of **four basic language skills** (listening, speaking, reading and writing)
- The **target language** should be the vehicle for classroom communication, not just the object of study.
- Attempts to communicate in the target language may be encouraged from the very beginning so that the **target linguistic system** will be learnt best through the process of struggling to communicate.
- **Fluency** in an acceptable variety of the target language is the primary goal.
- **Accuracy** is judged not in the abstract but in the context.
- Teachers should help learners in any way that **motivates** them to work with the language.
- One of the teachers' major responsibilities is to establish **situations** likely to promote communication. Whenever possible 'authentic language', i.e., language as it is used in a real context should be introduced.
- Students are expected to interact with others through **pair work, group work and role-play**.

### Information Box

**Communicative English Language Teaching**

***CETM: Communicative English Teaching Method.***

- The need of business world and the emergence of business communication are responsible for CETM/CELM methods.

***CELM: Communicative English Learning Method***

- The need of business world and the emergence of business communication are responsible for the innovative teaching approaches and methods.

### *Characteristics of the Teaching-Learning Process*

- **Authentic materials** are used as much as possible. Students should get an opportunity to develop strategies for understanding the language as it is actually used by the native speakers.
- Activities in the Communicative Approach are often carried out by students in small groups. Small groups of students interacting are favoured in order to maximize the time allotted to each student for **learning to negotiate the meaning**.
- The most obvious characteristic of this approach is that almost everything is done with **the aim to communicate**. Students use the language a great deal through communicative activities, such as **guessing games, role-plays** and **problem-solving tasks**.
- Activities that are truly communicative, according to Morrow have three features namely, **information gap, choice** and **feedback**.
- The range of exercise types and activities is unlimited, provided that such exercise requires the use of communicative processes like **information sharing, negotiation of the meaning** and **interaction**.

### The Areas of Language and Language Skills Which are Emphasized

Language functions are emphasized over language forms. A variety of forms are presented for each function. Only the simpler forms would be presented at first but as students get more proficient in the target language, more complex forms are learnt.

Students work on all the four skills from the beginning. They learn about **cohesion** and **coherence**.

### Nature of Student–teacher and Student–student Interaction

The Communicative Language Teaching Method's emphasis on the process of communication leads to different roles for learners. The teacher is the initiator of the activities. The teacher's primary role is to facilitate communication among all the participants in the classroom and between these participants and the various activities and texts. Sometimes the teacher is a co-communicator but more often the teacher establishes situations that prompt communication among the students. Students interact a great deal with one another. They may interact in pairs, triads, small groups and even as a whole group.

The CLT teacher assumes a responsibility for determining and responding to the learners' language needs. On the basis of such **needs analysis**, (See Chapter 5 for details.) teachers are expected to plan group and individual instruction that responds to the learners' needs. Another role assumed by CLT teachers is that of a counsellor. The CLT procedures often required teachers to acquire less teacher-centred classroom management skills. It is the teacher's responsibility to organize the classroom as a **setting** for communicative activities.

### Teacher's Response to Students' Errors

Errors of form are tolerated and seen as a natural outcome of the development of communication skills.

It is believed that students might have limited linguistic knowledge but they can be successful **communicators.**

### Nature of Evaluation

A teacher must find out whether a student can communicate in the target language in a given situation. During evaluation, fluency is given more attention than accuracy. The student who has the most control over the structures and vocabulary is not always the best communicator.

A teacher can informally evaluate her/his student's performance in her/his role as an advisor or a co-communicator. For more formal evaluation, a teacher may use a communicative test.

### Role of Instructional Materials

Instructional materials have the primary role of promoting communicative language use. There are numerous textbooks designed to direct and support CLT. A variety of **games, role-plays, stimulations** and **task-based communication activities** are used in CLT classes. Cue cards, activity cards and exercise handbooks are often used. **Realia** around which communicative activities can be built like advertisements, newspapers, maps, pictures, charts are often used.

### Role of the Students' Language

The students should realize that the target language is a vehicle for communication, not just a subject to be studied. However, native language may be used to make meanings clear especially, in the initial stages of language learning.

## Let Us Do and Learn

1. Write down any four features of Community Language Teaching/Learning Method.
2. Write any four limitations that you find in the Communicative Language Teaching Method? How do you like to overcome these limitations?

# Eclectic English Language Teaching Approach/Business English Teaching Approach

A group of linguists headed by Dr Pravu (the co-ordinator of the famous Bangalore Project) arrived at a common conclusion that no method can be foolproof for teaching English to non-native speakers. Therefore, they prescribed the Eclectic Approach of teaching English. This method is better known as Business English Teaching Approach. Let us discuss the major methods that the group of linguists prescribed.

## Total Physical Response Method

Total Physical Response (TPR) is a language teaching method which attempts to teach language through physical (motor) activity. It was developed by James Asher, a professor of psychology at San Jose State University, California. Prof. Asher claims that speech directed to young children consists primarily of commands which children respond to physically before they begin to produce verbal responses. He also emphasizes on the need of developing comprehension before the learner is taught to speak. He emphasizes on comprehension and the use of physical actions to teach a foreign language at an introductory level as it has a long tradition in language teaching. In the nineteenth century, Gouin advocated a situation-based teaching strategy in which a chain of action verbs served as the basis for introducing and practicing new language items. Prof. Palmer experimented with an action-based teaching strategy which claimed that 'no method of teaching foreign speech is likely to be economical or successful which does not include in the first period a very considerable proportion of that type of classroom work which consists of the carrying out by the pupil of orders issued by the teacher'.

### *Objectives: Let Us Focus On the Prime Objectives of the Method*

- The target language should be presented in chunks, not just word by word.
- The students' understanding of the target language should be developed before speaking.
- The teacher should aim to direct the student behavior through the use of imperatives.
- Students can learn through observing actions as well as by performing the actions themselves.
- Spoken language should be emphasized over written language.
- Learning should take place in a stress-free environment.
- Students are expected to make errors when they first begin speaking but teachers should be tolerant of them. Work on the fine details of the language should be postponed until students have become somewhat proficient.

### *Characteristics of Teaching-Learning Process*

We would find the following features:

- The students first listen to some **oral commands**. The teacher issues commands to a few students, then performs the actions with them.
- After responding to the oral commands, the students **demonstrate** that they can understand the commands by performing them alone.
- The observers also have an opportunity to **demonstrate** their understanding.
- Then, the students learn to read and write the **commands.**

Finnochiaro and Brumfit (1983) illustrate through the following stages how the procedural phases of instruction are handled in what they call 'Notional Approach'.

- Presentation of a brief dialogue or several mini-dialogues
- Oral practice of each utterance in the dialogue

- Questions and answers based on the **topic and situations** in the dialogue
- Questions and answers related to the student's personal experience but centred on the **theme** of the dialogue
- Study of the basic **communicative expressions** used in the dialogue of one of the structures that exemplify this approach's function
- Learners' discovery of **generalizations of rules** underlying the functional expression of structure
- Oral recognition, interpretative procedures
- Oral production activities, proceeding **from guided to freer communication**

### *The Areas of Language and Language Skills Which are Emphasized*

Grammatical structures and vocabulary are emphasized over other language areas. The grammatical structures and vocabulary are presented through the **imperatives.**

The imperatives are used because of their **frequency of occurrence** in the speech directed at young children learning their mother tongue (MT).

The **spoken language** is emphasized over written language.

Understanding the spoken word **should precede** its production.

### *Nature of Student–teacher and Student–student Interaction*

The teacher plays an active and direct role in this method. 'The instructor is the director of a stage play in which the students are the actors.' The teacher decides what to teach, models and presents the new materials and selects supporting materials for classroom use. The teacher is encouraged to be well-prepared and well-organized so that the lesson flows smoothly and predictably.

The teacher's role, however, is not so much to teach as **to provide opportunities for learning**. The teacher has the responsibility of providing the best kind of exposure to language so that the learners can **internalize** the basic rules of the target language. Initially, the interaction is characterized by the teacher speaking and the students responding non-verbally. Later, the students become more verbal and the teacher responds non-verbally. Students perform the actions together. They can learn by watching each other. As the students begin to speak, they issue commands to one another as well as to the teacher.

### *Teacher's Response to Students' Errors*

It is expected that the students will make errors when they first begin speaking. Teachers should refrain from too much correction in the early stages and should not interrupt to correct errors since this will inhibit the learners. As time goes on, however, more teacher intervention is expected. As the students get more advanced, teachers can 'fine tune', i.e., correct more minor errors.

### *Nature of Evaluation*

Teachers will know immediately whether the students understand or not by observing the students' actions. Formal evaluation can be conducted simply by commanding individual students to perform a series of actions. As students become more advanced, their performance of the skills they have mastered can become the basis for evaluation. (See Chapter 6 for details.)

### *Role of Instructional Materials*

There is generally no basic text in a TPR course. Initially, the teacher's voice, actions and gestures may be a sufficient basis for classroom activities. Later, the teacher may use common classroom objects, such as books, pen, furniture to support the teaching points. **Realia** plays an increasing role in succeeding learning stages.

***Role of the Students' Native Language***

The method allows limited use of **MT** for the **beginners**.

However, once the topic is introduced, the **MT** is hardly used in an advanced classroom.

The meaning is made clear through **body movements**.

The **target language** is the language of the classroom.

## Consultation Time

- Make a group of four and discuss how you would use Total Physical Response (TPR) Method in a classroom of Class X while teaching a prose or poem.
- Consult with your teacher and make a lesson plan to this effect. You may take help from Chapter 3 also.

## Community Language Learning

Community Language Learning (CLL) is the name of a method, developed by Prof. C.A. Curran and his followers. The CLL method represents the use of Counselling-Learning Theory to teach English language. Prof. Curran realized that adults often feel threatened by a new learning situation. Prof. Curran believed that a way to deal with **the fears of students** is to become 'language counsellors'. By understanding the students' fears and being sensitive to them, a teacher can help students overcome their negative feelings and turn them into positive energy to further their learning.

***Objectives: This Method Aims at the Following Objectives***

- A set of foreign language teaching practices sometimes described as 'humanistic techniques' should be used for teaching and learning.
- **Humanistic techniques** are those that help the students to be themselves, to accept themselves and to be proud of themselves.
- These techniques help to foster a climate of **caring and sharing between the teacher and the taught** in the English language classroom.

## Activity Time

Formulate a group of three people and make a lesson plan for teaching from authentic materials. Try to implement your plan in the course of Practice Teaching. You may take help from Chapter 3 also.

- Students should work together in groups and this will give them a sense of community. In this way, they can learn from each other as well as from the teacher. **Co-operation not competition** is encouraged.
- In the initial stages, the 'syllabus' is to be designed primarily by the students. Students are more willing to learn when they have created the material themselves.
- Teachers should work in a **non-threatening** way with what the learner has produced.
- Students should be able **to take up more responsibility** for their own learning.
- Students should be allowed to reflect on what they have learnt.
- In addition to reflecting on the language, students should reflect on what they have experienced.

### Information Box

- **CLL:** Community Language Learning
- **CLT:** Community Language Teaching
- Professional Training has taken the concept of CLL and CLT to conduct in- service or pre-service training of the professionals.

#### *Characteristics of Teaching-Learning Process*

Professor Curran is of the opinion that there are six elements necessary for 'no defensive learning'. The first element is **security**. The second element is **aggression** which means that the students should be given an opportunity to assert themselves and be actively involved in the learning experience. The students may be asked to conduct their own conversation. The third element is **attention**. At the initial stages, students must directly focus on or attend to one task at a time. The fourth element is **reflection**. Students may be asked to reflect on what they have experienced during the course of the lesson. **Retention** is the fifth element involving the integration of the new material that takes place within the student. The last element is **discrimination** which involves sorting out differences in target language forms by the student.

The CLL includes the following learning tasks:

- **Translation:** Learners form a small circle. A learner whispers a message he/she wants to express, the teacher translates it into (and may interpret it in) the target language and the learner repeats the teacher's translation.
- **Group work:** Learners may engage in various group tasks, such as small group discussion of a topic, preparing a conversation, preparing a summary of a topic for presentation to another group, preparing a story that will be presented to the teacher and the rest of the class.
- **Recording:** Students record conversations in the target language.
- **Transcription:** Students transcribe utterances they have recorded for practice and analysis of linguistic forms.
- **Analysis:** Students analyze and study transcriptions of target language sentences in order to focus on particular lexical usage or on the application of particular grammar rules.
- **Reflection and Observation:** Learners reflect and report on their experience of the class, as a class or in groups.
- **Listening:** Students listen to a monologue by the teacher involving elements they might have elicited or overheard during the class interactions.
- **Free conversation:** Students engage in free conversation with the teacher of other learners. They might include a discussion of what they learnt as well as the feelings they had about how they learnt.

### Information Box

- **Task:** Task is used during the phase when the teacher wants to get a particular language skill developed.

## Community Language Teaching

This method is just the same as CLL. Only the teaching aspect is emphasized.

### *Nature of Student–teacher Interaction and Student–student Interaction*

As Cardin observed, 'CLL is neither student-centered nor teacher-centered but rather teacher-student centered', with both being decision-makers in the class. In CLL, one continuing role of the teacher is to provide a safe environment for learning. Building a relationship with and among the students is very important. In a secure atmosphere, students can continue their interaction with each other as well as their interaction with the teacher.

The teacher's initial role is that of a counsellor. Initially, the learner is very dependent upon the teacher. However, as the learners continue to interact, they become increasingly independent.

The CLL methodologists have identified five stages in the gradual progress of the learner from dependency to independency. In the advanced stages, the student functions independently. The students may become counsellors to less advanced students while profiting from contact with their original source.

### *Teacher's Response to Students' Errors*

The teacher should work with what the learner has produced in a non-threatening way. One way of doing this is for the teacher to repeat correctly what the student may have said incorrectly allowing the students to match their pronunciation with that of the teacher and self-correct. The teacher may act as the human computer during the pronunciation practice. A student may choose some part of a transcript to practice pronunciation. She/he is 'in control' of the teacher. When the student tries to say the word or phrase, the teacher following the student's lead, repeats the word or phrase as often as the student wants to practice it.

The teacher does not correct the student's mispronunciation in way. It is through the teacher's consistent manner of repeating the word or phrase clearly that the student self-corrects as she/he tries to initiate the teacher's model.

### *Nature of Evaluation*

Evaluation is conducted in keeping with the principles of the method. No particular mode of evaluation is prescribed in this method. If a test is required to be taken at the end of the course, then the teacher would see to it that the students are adequately prepared for taking it. A teacher-made classroom test would likely be more of an integrative test than a discrete-point one. Students may be asked to write a paragraph, rather than being asked to answer a question which deals with only one point of the language at a time. Teachers would encourage their students to self-evaluate to look at their own learning and to become aware of their progress.

### *Role of the Students' Native Language*

Initially, the security of the learners is enhanced by using their native language. Native language equivalents of target language are given to make the meaning clear. Directions are also given in the native language. In later stages, more and more of the target language can be used. As for example, conversations in the **target language** can replace native language conversations.

### *Objectives: Community Language Teaching Aims at*

(i) Honing learners' skill using **community schema** (knowledge base)
(ii) Fostering activity and task-oriented learning

## Computer Aided Language Learning (CALL)

This method is more or less the same as CLL in its basic principles and practice. (See 4.5.2 for details.) Only a computer or a number of computers in LAN mode are used for this purpose.

### Computer Aided Language Teaching

The principles and practice of this method follow the principles and practice of Community Language Teaching. Only this method uses computer programming and set programs to hone the language skills of the learners. (See 4.5.3 for details.)

## Latest Approaches and Methods in English Language Teaching

### The Natural Approach

The Natural Approach was developed by Tracy Terrell, a teacher of Spanish in California in 1977. This was an attempt to develop a language teaching proposal that conforms to the naturalistic principles found in successful second language acquisition. The Natural Approach grew out of Terrell's experiences of teaching Spanish language. Terrell had collaborated with Krashen, an applied linguist at the University of Southern California to publish their book, *The Natural Approach* in 1983. **The Natural Approach** has many things in common with the Direct Method. Unlike the Direct Method, however, it places less emphasis on teacher monologues and answers and less focus on accurate production of target language sentences.

#### *Objectives*

- The Natural Approach focuses on teaching communicative abilities. Language is viewed as a vehicle for communicating meanings and messages. Krashen and Terrell state, 'Acquisition can take place only when people understand messages in the target language.' They also state that the Natural Approach is primarily 'designed to develop communication skills—both oral and written.'
- Krashen and Terrell observe that communication goals 'may be expressed in terms of situations, functions and topics' which are likely to be most useful to the students. The functions are not specified or suggested but are felt to derive naturally from the topics and situations.
- There should be a wide exposure to vocabulary that may be useful to basic personal communication.
- There should not be any focus on grammatical structures since the necessary grammatical structures are automatically provided in the input.
- There should be an emphasis on exposure or input rather than on practice.
- There should be a prolonged period of attention to what the language learners hear before they try to produce language.
- There should be an emphasis on the central role of comprehension-based approaches in language teaching.
- A friendly, relaxed atmosphere should be provided for learning.

#### *Characteristics of Teaching/Learning Process*

In a class taught according to the Natural Approach, the emphasis is on presenting comprehensible unit in the target language. The teacher's talk focuses on objects in the classroom and on the content of pictures, as with the Direct Method. The teacher talks slowly and distinctly. To minimize stress, learners are not required to say anything until they feel ready. Students are not expected to use a word actively until they have heard it many times. There is a gradual progression from yes/no questions, through either/or questions to questions that students can answer using words they have heard being used by the teacher. Charts, pictures, advertisements and other realia serve as the focal point for questions and the talk may even move to class members.

Pair or group work may be employed followed by whole-class discussion led by the teacher.

The Natural Approach adopts techniques and activities freely from other methods. These include command-based activities from TPR, Direct Method activities like mime, gestures used to elicit questions and answers and even situation-based practice of structures and patterns. Group-work activities are often identical to those used in CLT. What characterizes the Natural Approach is the use of familiar techniques within a method that focuses on providing comprehensible input and a classroom environment that minimize the learners' anxiety and maximize the learners' self-confidence.

### *The Areas of Language and Language Skills Which are Emphasized*

The Natural Approach is primarily designed to develop the basic communication skills both oral and written. Importance is given to providing a wide exposure to vocabulary through a wide variety of topics.

### *Nature of Student–teacher Interaction and Student–student Interaction*

The Natural Approach teacher has three central roles.

(i) The teacher should create an interesting and friendly atmosphere for the learners.
(ii) The teacher is the primary source of comprehensible input in the target language.
(iii) The teacher must organize a rich mix or classroom activities, involving a variety of group's sizes, content and contexts.

Learners' roles are seen to change according to their stage of **linguistic development**. In the pre-production stage, students participate in the language activity without having to respond in the target language. For example, they can act out physical commands, point to pictures, and so on.

In the early-production stage, students respond to either/or questions, use fixed conversational patterns (e.g., How are you? What's your name?).

In the speech-emergent phase, students involve themselves in role-play and game, give opinions and participate in group problem solving.

Learners participate in communication activities with the teacher and other learners.

### *Teacher's Response to Students' Errors*

The teacher does not force the students to speak before they are ready for it. The teacher tolerates the students' errors.

### *Nature of Evaluation*

A teacher may informally evaluate a student's performance during the course of the lessons or the teacher may take a formal test.

### *The Role of Instructional Materials*

The primary aim of materials in the Natural Approach is to promote comprehension and communication. Materials include pictures, maps, brochures, advertisements and other realia. Games are seen as a useful classroom activity.

### *Role of the Students' Native Language*

The basic aim of this approach is to make the students communicate in the target language. The learners may use speech only when they are ready. However, the use of native language is not encouraged.

## The Silent Way Method

The Silent Way is a method of language teaching, devised by Caleb Gattegno. The method is based on the premise that the teacher should be silent as much as possible in the classroom, and the learner should be encouraged to produce as much language as possible. Prof. Gattegno is well-known reviving of interest in the use of coloured wooden sticks called 'cuisenaire rods' and for his series of words in colour. It is an approach to teaching of initial reading in which sounds are coded by specific colours.

Broadly speaking, the learning hypothesis of Prof. Gattegno can be stated as follows:

(i) Learning is facilitated if the learner **discovers** or **creates** rather than remembers and repeats what is to be learnt.
(ii) Learning is facilitated by accompanying physical objects.
(iii) Learning is facilitated by **problem solving** involving the **materials** to be learnt.

Let us now consider the Silent Way Method under the following heads:

### *Objectives: Let Us Focus On the Prime Objectives of the Approach*

- Teaching of **aural/oral proficiency** as basic elements of the target language;
- Teaching of **near-native fluency** in the target language;
- Correct pronunciation of the target language *and*
- Teaching the prosodic elements of the target language.

### Activity Time

**Pair work:** Make a list of teaching situations where you can apply the Natural Approach and the Silent Way Method.

### Information Box

- Psycholinguistics has come to great help today for development of the **cognitive capacity** and language skill of the learners.

### *Characteristics of Teaching/Learning Process*

Students begin their study of the language through its basic building blocks, its sounds. These are introduced through a language specific **sound-colour chart**. Relying on what sounds students already know from their knowledge of their native language, the teachers lead the students to associate the sounds of the target language with particular colours. Colours help the students to learn the spellings as well as to read and pronounce words properly. The following is an excerpt from instructions based on the Silent Way Method intended for American Peace Corps Volunteers being trained to teach in Thailand. A word that is italicized can be substituted for by another word having the same function.

| | **Lesson** | **Vocabulary/Grammar, etc.** |
|---|---|---|
| (i) | Wood colour 'red' | Wood, red, green, yellow, brown, pink, white, orange, black colour |
| (ii) | Using the numbers 1–10 | one ...........ten |
| (iii) | Wood colour 'red' 'long'<br>Wood colour 'green' 'longer'<br>Wood colour 'orange' 'longest' | adjectives of comparison |

(iv) Reviewing Students' uses/ structures, taught in new situations, such as comparing the heights of students in the class.

(John Wilkins: Personal Communication)

The students receive a great deal of practice with a given target language structure. They gain autonomy in the language by exploring it and making choices. The teacher asks the students to describe their reactions to the lesson or what they have learnt. This provides valuable information for the teacher and encourages students to take responsibility for their own learning.

### *The Areas of Language and Language Skills Which are Emphasized*

There is focus on the structures of the language. There is, however, no fixed, linear, structural syllabus. The teacher starts with what the students know and builds from one structure to the next. The syllabus develops according to the learning needs. Explicit grammar rules may never be supplied. Vocabulary is somewhat restricted at first. Pronunciation is worked on from the beginning. All four skills are worked on from the beginning of the course. However, students learn to read and write what they have already produced orally.

### *Nature of Student-Teacher Interaction and Student–student Interaction*

Most of the time, the teacher is silent. Teacher is a unique and perhaps the most demanding aspect of the Silent Way Method. Gattegno talks of subordinating 'teaching to learning'. However, the teacher is very active—setting up situations to force awareness, listening attentively to students' speech, observing them constantly and silently working with them on their production. When the teacher does speak, it is to give clues, not to model the language.

Verbal interaction among students is desirable (students can learn from one another) and it is, therefore, encouraged. Students have an opportunity to express how they feel during the feedback sessions.

### *Teacher's Response to Students' Errors*

Student errors are seen as a natural and indispensable part of the learning process. The teacher uses students' errors as a basis for deciding where further work is necessary. Self-correction and peer correction is encouraged.

### *Nature of Evaluation*

Although the teacher may never give a formal test, she/he assesses student learning all the time. The teacher does not praise or criticize the student's behaviour since this would interfere with students' developing their own inner criteria. She/he expects students to learn at different rates. The teacher looks for steady progress, not perfection.

### *Role of Instructional Materials*

The materials mainly consist of a set of coloured rods used to directly link words and structures with their meanings in the target language thereby avoiding translation into the native language. Colour-coded pronunciation charts called 'Fields', vocabulary wall charts, a pointer and reading/writing exercises are used to illustrate the relationship between sound and meaning in the target language. The materials are to be used by the teacher independently and co-operatively in promoting language learning by direct association.

### *Role of the Students' Native Language*

Meaning is made clear by focusing on the students' perceptions, bot by translation. However, the students' native language may be used when necessary to give instructions during the feedback sessions. The students' existing knowledge of the native language may even be used to introduce new sounds in the target language.

## Did You Know?

**T.G. Grammar:** Transformational Generative Grammar

### *Let Us Do and Learn*

- Do you believe teaching should be subordinate to learning?
- Should a teacher remain silent as much as possible?
- Would you like to use the Silent Way Method's materials in your classroom?
- Which technique (s) would you like to adapt to your own approach to language teaching? Why?

## Consultation Time

Make a group of four people and make a lesson plan on the basis of the Natural Approach for teaching T.G. Grammar. You may take help from Chapter 3 of this book.

## Suggestopedia and O-zone Whole Language Teaching Method

- Suggestopedia is a method developed by the Bulgarian psychiatrist-educator George Lozanov who believes that language learning can occur at a much faster rate than what ordinarily occurs. According to Lozanov, the reason for 'our inefficiency' is that we often set up **psychological barriers** to learning. We often do not use the full mental powers that we have. In order to make better use of our mental reserves, the limitations we think of, have to be 'de-suggested'. Suggestopedia is the application of the study of suggestions to pedagogy. It has been developed to help students eliminate the feeling that they cannot be successful and help them to overcome the barriers to learning. According to Lozanov, 'The main aim of teaching is not memorization, but the understanding and creative solution of problems.'

### *Objectives: Let Us Have a Look on the Prime Objectives*

- Suggestopedia aims to deliver advanced **conversational proficiency** quickly.
- It is necessary for the students to **set goals** for themselves.
- High value is placed on **vocabulary recall**. Memorization of vocabulary is an important goal of the Suggestopedia Method.
- Learning should take place in a **relaxed, comfortable environment** in which the psychological barriers to learning are 'de-suggested'.
- The emphasis **should not be on teaching linguistic forms** but should be on using the language.

### *Characteristics of Teaching/Learning Process*

Suggestopedia course is conducted in a classroom in which the students are as comfortable as possible. There are listening activities which concern the text vocabulary of each unit. These activities are typically part of the 'pre-session phase' which takes place on the first day of a new unit. The students first look at and discuss a new text with the teacher. In the second reading, students relax comfortably in reclining chairs and listen to the teacher read the text in a certain way.

The material may be presented with varying intonations co-ordinated with sounds or illustrations. During the third reading, the material is acted out by the instructor in a dramatic manner over a background of special music. During this phase, students **lean back** in their chairs and **breathe deeply** and regularly as instructed by the teacher. This is the point at which Lozanov believes **unconscious learning system** takes over. The student may engage in various other activities and tasks like games, song role-plays and question-and-answer exercises.

### *The Areas of Language and Language Skills Which are Emphasized*

Much emphasis is given on vocabulary. Claims about the success of the method often focus on the large number of words that can be acquired. Grammar is dealt with; however, the focus is not on language forms but on using the language.

Learners should be able to speak for communication. Students should read the target language (for example, dialogues) and write (for example, imaginative composition).

### *Nature of Student–teacher Interaction and Student–student Interaction*

The primary role of the teacher is to create situations and present linguistic material in a way most likely to encourage positive reception and retention by the learner. A teacher should show absolute confidence in the method and maintain a modest enthusiasm towards the session. A teacher is also expected to be skilled in acting, singing and psychotherapeutic techniques.

The mental state of the learners is critical to success and so the learners must try to keep away from distractions and immerse themselves in the procedures of the method. Students should accept their own 'infantilisation', and they should accept the absolute authority of the teacher and give themselves over to activities and techniques like games, songs, role-playing designed to help them regain their self-confidence, spontaneity and receptivity. To assist them in role-plays and to help them detach themselves from their past learning experiences, students are given a new name and personal history within the target culture.

The teacher initiates interactions in the classroom. Initially, the students can only respond non-verbally or with a few target language words they have practiced. Later, when the students have more control of the target language, they can respond more appropriately and even initiate interaction themselves. Students interact with each other in various activities directed by the teacher.

### *Teacher's Response to Students' Errors*

In the initial stages of learning, errors are not corrected immediately since the emphasis is on students communicating their intended meaning. When errors of form do occur, the teacher uses the form correctly later on in the class.

### *Nature of Evaluation*

Evaluation is usually conducted on a student's performance during the lessons. Formal tests are believed to threaten the relaxed atmosphere considered essential for learning.

### *Role of Instructional Materials*

An instructional material consists of text, classroom fixtures like posters, soft lighting and music. The textbook should have emotional force, literary quality and interesting characters. The learning environment plays a central role in Suggestopedia. The classroom should be bright and cheery and have reeling chairs arranged in a circle for the learners to sit on.

***Role of the Students' Native Language***

The dialogue in the target language presented in the class is often translated in the native language to make the meaning clear. The teacher uses the MT in the class whenever necessary. However, as the course proceeds, the teacher uses the native language less and less.

## Let Us Sum Up

We have discussed how the proliferation of several methods and approaches has been the *sine qua non* of the twentieth century. No doubt, there are several lapses in almost all the methods and all the successive methods have tried to rectify the lapses. These experimentations with several **methods and approaches** would undoubtedly highlight some vital means that have long been in use in pedagogical situation in India.

## Glossary

foreign language literature: literature written in a foreign language
method: way or a set of ways used in teaching
approach: broad outline of the ways used in teaching
native language: mother tongue
successive: following one after another
LTM: learning and teaching materials
initiate: begin

## Exercise

(i) Explain the difference between deductive and inductive treatment of grammar with special reference to the Grammar-translation Method and the Direct Method.
(ii) Discuss the prime features of teaching and learning process in the Oral Approach.
(iii) Would you prefer 'Situational English Teaching' to teaching Rote Learning? Give reasons for your answer.
(iv) Choose a reading passage and plan vocabulary and other exercises that would help you to teach the passage.
(v) What role do the materials play in teaching? What type of materials do you prefer?
(vi) What areas of language teaching are emphasized in the Natural Approach?
(vii) What is Suggestopedia? Do you think it is a psycho-therapeutic measure?
(viii) Make a list of some points about the target language that you would want to display on posters to encourage your students' **peripheral learning**.

## Bibliography

Cohen, A., *Language Learning* (Herper Collins, 1990).
Howatt, A.P. R., *A history of English Language Teaching* (OUP, 1987).
Larsen, Freeman Diane, *Techniques and principles in Language Teaching* (OUP, 1986).
Lewis, M., *Implementing the Lexical Approach.*
Richards, J. C. and Rodgers, T. S., *Approaches Methods in Language Teaching* (OUP, 1987).

# Designing Syllabus and Curriculum 5

## CHAPTER OUTLINE



## LEARNING OBJECTIVES

**After reading this chapter, students will be able to:**

- **Understand the different types of syllabus used for English language teaching.**
- **Perform needs analysis and design effective English as a second language (ESL) syllabus and curriculum for schools.**
- **Evaluate syllabus and curriculum.**
- **Evaluate coursebook/study materials and find their efficacy in the syllabus.**

## Introduction

With the change in teaching methods, with the change in the rationale behind different teaching models, we have seen great changes in the foci of the syllabus also. We are aware of the fact that the structural syllabus of the 1960s and 1970s, the communicative syllabus of the 1980s and the task-based syllabus of the 1990s, have all made their contribution to course design. Many current communicative textbooks demonstrate all of these strands in the multidimensions in the tasks suggested. As the unit titles suggest, it is the functional list which forms the organizing principle as might be seen in lists like 'Greeting', 'Reporting', 'Narrating', etc.

Teachers wishing to design multidimensional courses of their own will be faced with the same issues as any textbook designer: Which aspect of language or of skills work or of content should be the primary organizing criterion for the course? What implications do this hold for the design and format of a course unit?

Teachers, who want to combine formal class work with less formal activities, such as projects, will be faced with further issues: What is the appropriate balance of time to spend on each activity and what are the effective ways of integrating the two?

In this chapter, we will look first at a few syllabus models and then explore the decisions confronting teachers and syllabus designers in planning and organizing learning experiences and syllabus documents.

**Let Us Do and Learn**

(i) What is a syllabus? Is it necessary at all?

(ii) What is the difference between a syllabus and a course?

(iii) Are you satisfied with the syllabus you are following? If not, why? If yes, why?

## Different Types of English Teaching Syllabus

We are already aware that a syllabus can be either product- or process-oriented.

With regard to general English language education, particularly in the early stages, many teachers take the view that a product syllabus, which presents and practices a formal set of linguistic items, is desirable. If we accept that learners also need a 'process' element of unfocused tasks, the question is how this element can be introduced and integrated into a course.

Brumfit (1980) has suggested a spiral syllabus, as shown in the Figure 5.1 on the next page in which a series of unfocused tasks will enable students to use the language they have acquired while following a basic product syllabus. This type of syllabus can be seen in textbooks where 'extension' units engage learners in less formally focused tasks.

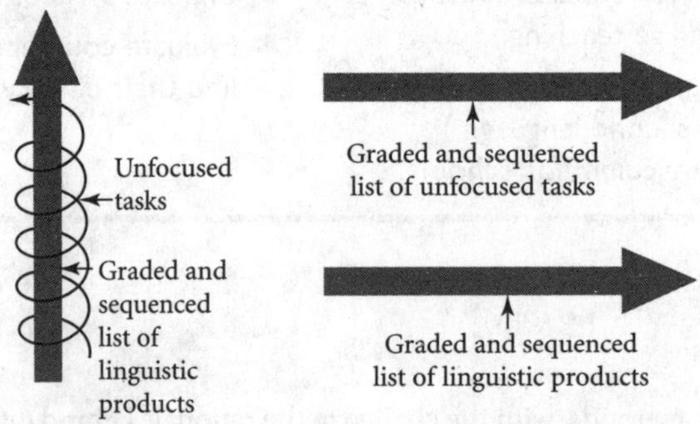


**(a) Spiral syllabus** **(b) Parallel syllabus**

**Figure 5.1** Spiral and parallel syllabuses (Adapted from Ellis 1987; 188)

Ellis (1987) suggests a parallel syllabus with separate stands, as shown on the right in the same Figure. This might well be seen in a weekly timetable of four sessions where two sessions follow a product syllabus based, say, on structures, with focused tasks, a third session is given to literature with a series of role-play, discussion, and writing tasks, and the fourth session uses project work.

Issues of grading and sequencing will still be important to a teacher following separate stands in a course. In the literature sessions, for example, a thought will need to be given to how tasks can be graded according to such factors as length of reading extract, difficulty of cultural background in the text, complexity of textual organization, number of steps in the task, number of students involved in performing the task and length of time to complete the task.

## Surveying Syllabus Types

### The Traditional Syllabus

In traditional syllabuses and materials, the linguistic content is primary. The situational and thematic choices are made once the linguistic content has been established. The selection of the linguistic content itself is based on a particular theoretical view of the nature of language and the way in which we acquire it.

The Audio-Lingual Method, for example, emphasized a careful sequencing of grammatical structures, which were presented and then repeated, with gradual memorization of the dialogue. This approach was developed following research by behaviourists, psychologists, who saw language as a system of building blocks, and language acquisition as a process of habit formation, through imitation and repetition. Such an approach tends to ignore the thematic content, and grammar and vocabulary are presented in isolated sentences without any thematic thread.

#### *Advantages*

Traditional syllabuses are suited to some types of learners. Breaking the language down into bits and pieces can help the students focus on a particular aspect of the language and avoid the focus being blurred by other problems of a lexical or phonological nature.

#### *Arguments for a More Holistic Syllabus*

Those who criticize the traditional syllabus argue that it isn't logical to break language into bits and pieces when it is always experienced comprehensively, as a whole. Language consists of more than a stock of objective facts. This means that a holistic approach uses texts, i.e., whole pieces of language, rather than individual sentences, to prepare the learners for the language they will encounter outside the classroom. Widdowson claims that we must progress from learning about the language (language usage) to considering how language works in a communicative sense (language use), which 'requires us to go beyond the sentence and look at longer stretches of language'.

This holistic view has gained prominence in recent years. A holistic syllabus will front texts, topics and tasks, placing great emphasis on meaningful communication from the learner's point of view. Texts should be authentic, tasks should be communicative, and learners will be encouraged to respond to the topics and texts rather than to isolated phonemes and morphemes.

#### *How Does This Work?*

Whereas traditional syllabuses select language items solely on the basis of linguistic criteria, a holistic syllabus will select the items the learner needs to know in order to get things done, i.e., to complete the task.

Language errors are rectified by the teacher or the class while the students are on the task. Thus, grammar is taught inductively rather than deductively. Such approaches of the course throw up their own problems, such as of how to order the tasks and how to choose the task which learners need. However, adherents of this approach would argue that a focus on function, fluency and use is still more like how learners experience the language outside the classroom than a focus on form, accuracy and analysis

**Table 5.1** Traditional and Holistic Approaches—Compared

| Traditional | Holistic |
|---|---|
| Focus on language as a sequence of grammatical patterns | Focus is on communication |
| Selects language items on the basis of complexity of linguistic criteria | Selects on the basis of what language items the learner needs to know |
| Language used tends to be more formal and bookish | Genuine everyday language is emphasized |
| Aim is to have students produce formally correct sentences. | Aim is to have students communicate effectively in order to complete the task |
| Reading and writing are emphasized | Speaking is given at least as much time as reading and writing |
| Tends to be teacher-centred | Tends to be student-centred |
| Focus is on the form of expression rather than the content. | Resembles the natural language learning process by concentrating on the content/meaning of the expression rather than the form. |

## Let Us Consult an Expert

**Vanessa Steele**

Traditional and holistic syllabuses reflect different views of language and language learning and teaching. Both viewpoints are quite valid, and most courses nowadays will reflect elements of both. It is the relative emphasis given to language as a body of knowledge to be mastered, or language as a communicative process to be developed, which will determine which of the labels '*traditional*' or '*holistic*' I would apply to a given syllabus.

## Let Us Do and Learn

Survey the English syllabus of Secondary Examination of your state and judge its type. Discuss with your friends and seek your teacher's opinion.

Survey the English syllabus of the Higher Secondary Examination (Intermediate) of your state and judge its type.

## Wilkins' View on Syllabus Types

Syllabus types can be divided into two super-ordinate classes, *synthetic* and *analytic* (Wilkins, 1974, 1976), although it may be more accurate to view synthetic and analytic as two points on a continuum rather than as a strict dichotomy (Wilkins, 1976). *Synthetic* syllabuses segment the target language into discrete linguistic items for one-at-a-time presentation: Different parts of language are taught separately and step by step so that acquisition is a process of gradual accumulation of parts until the whole structure of language has been built up. . . . At any one time the learner is being exposed to a deliberately limited sample of language. (Wilkins, 1976, p. 2)

### *Synthetic Syllabuses Refer to the Learner's Role*

The learner's task is to re-synthesize the language that has been broken down into a large number of small pieces with the aim of making his [sic] learning task easier. (Wilkins, 1976, p. 2)

The synthetic syllabus relies on the learners' assumed ability to learn a language in parts (e.g., structures and functions) which are independent of one another, and also to integrate, or synthesize, the pieces when the time comes to use them for communicative purposes. *Lexical, structural, notional* and *functional* syllabuses are synthetic. Although they need not be, so also are most so-called topical and situational syllabuses, for examination of teaching materials shows that topics and situations have traditionally been used as vehicles for structural syllabuses—a tendency which has also begun to occur with some commercially published materials that purport to be task-based, but are not.

*Analytic* syllabuses offer the learner target language samples which, while they may have been modified in other ways, have not been controlled for structure or lexis in the traditional manner. Users maintain that a prior analysis of the total language system leads into a set of discrete pieces of language. It is a necessary precondition for the adoption of a synthetic approach which is largely superfluous. Analytic approaches are organized in terms of the purposes for which people are learning a language and the kinds of language performance that are necessary to meet those purposes. (Wilkins, 1976, p. 13)

*Analytic* syllabus again refers not to what the syllabus designer does, but to the operations required of the learner. Wilkins (1976) writes:

'Since we are inviting the learner, directly or indirectly, to recognize the linguistic components of the language behavior he is acquiring, we are in effect basing our approach on the learner's analytic capabilities.' (p. 14)

Updating Wilkins' definition a little, we may add that analytic syllabuses are those which present the target language whole chunks at a time, without linguistic interference or control. They rely on (a) the learners' assumed ability to perceive regularities in the input and to induce rules (or to form new neutral networks underlying what looks like rule-governed behaviour) and/or (b) the continued availability to learners of innate knowledge of linguistic universals and the ways language can vary, knowledge can be reactivated by exposure to natural samples of the second language (L2). *Procedural, process and task syllabuses* are all examples of the analytic syllabus type. Wilkins (1976) classifies *situational, notional* and *functional* syllabuses as analytic. Notions and functions are clearly linguistic units, however, isolation of which in practice always results in a synthetic syllabus, such that exercises practicing requests or apologies replace exercises on relative clauses or the present perfect.

The analytic/synthetic distinction is partially reflected in secondary classification (Type A and Type B syllabuses), R.V. White's (1988) Type A and Type B syllabuses. However, Wilkins' categories point out differences in the way input and learner interact; White's conceptualization is broader, capturing differences in two general approaches to course design, instruction, language learning and evaluation.

### Let Us Do and Learn

Let us rename Synthetic Syllabus as Type A and Analytic Syllabus as Type B. Which type do you prefer? Give reasons for your answer. You may take help of the expert opinion.

Prof. A. Banerjee, ELT (English Language Teaching) expert, British Council, Calcutta

Type A syllabuses focus on what is to be learnt: the L2. They are interventionist. Someone preselects and predigests the language to be taught, dividing it up into small pieces, and determining learning objectives in advance of any consideration of who the learners may be or how languages are learnt. Type A syllabuses, White points out, are the external matter to the learner, other subject matters and modes of instruction are important and assess success and failure in terms of achievement or mastery.

Type B syllabuses, on the other hand, focus on how the language is to be learnt. They are non-interventionist. They involve no artificial preselection or arrangement of items and allow objectives to be determined by a process of negotiation between the teacher and the learners after they meet, as a course evolves. They are thus internal to the learner, negotiated between the learners and the teacher as joint decision-makers emphasize the process of learning rather than the subject matter, and assess accomplishment in relationship to learners' criteria for success. As will become clear, in addition to being analytic, all three task-based syllabus types focused on in this section are primarily Type B in nature: Each allows both language and task to be negotiated in the classroom. Procedural and task syllabuses do have one Type A characteristic, however, for (via different procedures) each makes an initial specification in substantive terms of the kinds of tasks learners will work on before teachers and students ever meet. That is to say, they specify the target tasks learners ultimately need to be able to handle, and then allow the task teachers and learners to work on in the classroom, that is, the pedagogic tasks, to be negotiated. Process syllabuses, conversely, are Type B thoroughbreds: They allow negotiation of language and task and, in theory at least, place no constraints on the tasks chosen.

## Needs Analysis and Designing Effective Syllabus/Curriculum

A close survey of different types of syllabus will pose a serious question:

What is more important factor behind an effective syllabus?

The answer to this question is simple enough, i.e., needs analysis, which means analysis of learners' needs—in which context the learners are going to use the language.

Language teaching has not profited much from more general views of educational design. The curriculum perspective comes from general education and views successful instruction as an interweaving of knowledge, instructional, learner and administrative considerations. From this perspective, methodology is viewed as only one of several instructional considerations that are necessarily thought out and realized in conjunction with all other curricular considerations.

The importance of needs analysis can also be shown taking help of the task-based syllabus, as designed under the influence of the Theory of Multi-intelligentsia.

The notion here is adapted from the multiple intelligences of human talent proposed by Howard Gardner (1983) (see earlier section for details). This model is one of a variety of learning style models that have been proposed in general education with follow-up inquiry by language educators. The following chart shows Gardner's proposed eight native intelligences and indicates classroom language-rich task types that play to each of these particular intelligences.

**Intelligence Types and Appropriate Educational Activities**

| Intelligence Type | Educational Activities |
|---|---|
| Linguistic | Lectures, worksheets, word games, journals, debates |
| Logical | Puzzles, estimations, problem solving |
| Spatial | Preparing charts, diagrams, graphic organizers, drawing, films |
| Bodily | Hands-on practice, mime, craft, demonstrations |
| Musical | Singing, reciting poetry, jazz chants, mood music |
| Interpersonal | Group work, peer tutoring, class projects, reflection, interest centers, personal values, tasks |
| Naturalist | Field trips, show and tell, plant and animal projects |

Source (Adapted from Christison, 1998)

For the sake of designing an effective syllabus and curriculum, we need to understand the needs in terms of goals and objectives of a certain course.

Our explorations into the perspectives of goals and objectives will begin to define contextual constraints within which the course must be planned and taught. It is perhaps sufficient to reiterate here the importance of matching the course to context. The most efficient course design is one which takes into account specific factors, such as class size, time available and the teacher's own communicative ability, knowledge of the language system and command of methods.

It should also take into account more general factors concerning educational values, perceptions of the teacher's role and expectations of classroom procedures.

The distinction between the terms 'goals' and 'objectives' here is taken to be a distinction between the general and the specific. For example, one broader goal for a course might be perceived, from the teacher's perspective, as being:

1. **to develop the students' reading ability more comprehensively and effectively:**
   More specific objectives within the goal could be outcomes for the students:
   (a) to develop effective strategies for dealing with unknown words
   (b) to be able to distinguish fact from opinion
   (c) to build confidence in dealing with a wide range of texts (e.g., news reports, charts, magazine articles, short stories)

   Similarly, another broad goal could be:
2. **to help learners become more independent in their approach to learning; more specific objectives for students could be:**
   (a) to learn ways of monitoring and assessing their own progress
   (b) to develop effective strategies for using monolingual dictionaries
   (c) to find ways of exploiting out-of-class resources for learning English

Note the difference between the first goal, which is to do with the outcomes of a language learning course, and the second, which is a wider educational goal to do with the process of learning and the development of the individual. Teachers working with school students will have a particular concern for formulating educational goals.

A quick review would immediately suggest some of the relevance to ELT, for example:

- to develop enjoyment in reading and good reading habits;
- to develop appreciation of the link between language and culture and awareness of how languages and cultures differ;
- to develop a critical stance in listening and reading.

In many contexts, general goals are set in a national curriculum or by institutional policy-makers and are left for teachers to interpret these in a specific objective.

However, making the stating of objectives a distinct stage in course planning has a number of advantages—it enables us:

- to assess the appropriateness of course materials;
- to make explicit the aims of the course and how these have been determined; and
- to encourage the students to develop their own agenda for the course.

It is a stage of course planning in which learners can become involved through consultation and negotiation. A list of objectives also provides one set of criteria for evaluating a course. Students can be invited to assess how far they have been enabled to achieve the objectives of the course.

The description of procedures for needs analysis is beyond the scope of this book. However, we would be able to guess it through passing remarks of the last sections of this chapter and Chapter 6 also.

## Evaluating Syllabus/Curriculum

If one wants to criticize any syllabus document or any curriculum model, she/he would first need to study the document very carefully in order to:

- identify the types of syllabus;
- ascertain the assumptions underlying the design of the curriculum or syllabus;
- consider the scope of the syllabus or the extent to which it can be used;
- find out those areas amenable to modification or adaptation;
- compare it with any other;
- explore the relationship between syllabus goals and the goals of language teachers; and
- examine the selection and sequencing of grammatical elements in the syllabus.

### Let Us Do and Learn

See Appendix A and evaluate it. Show it to your teacher.

See Appendix B and evaluate it. Show it to your teacher.

Now, let us read a general commentary syllabus survey to reinforce our skill.

It is typical of contemporary coursebooks to use a multi-dimensional syllabus. Johnson (1981) gives a rationale for this kind of syllabus by analogy with a construction plan:

> [...] arguments as to the relative merits of notional, situational, or topic-based syllabuses, etc., are no more sensible than arguments as to whether the specifications in a construction contract should cover the foundations, or the steel framework or the concrete or the glass or the interior design, etc. The obvious answer is that all of these must be covered. (Johnson 1981:34)

His view can be seen as a response to the debate of the 1970s as to what might constitute the most appropriate base for designing a language syllabus. It was during this period that the communicative revolution in syllabus design and classroom methodology took impetus from the work of applied linguists interested in the concept of communicative competence.

Previously, the classical humanist valued prevalent in general education (Clark: 1987) had influenced language teaching towards content-driven courses, the content consisting of selected and sequenced items from the formal language system. This 'structural syllabus' relied on analyses of language provided by linguists of the time and focused on the systems of phonology, grammar and lexis. It has prevailed widely as a base for course design on the grounds that it has its clear advantages, i.e., it is amenable to planning and can provide systematic approach. For this reason, many teachers and learners feel secure and appreciate being able to review what they have covered of the 'building blocks' of the language. The point has also been made that, if a structural syllabus and related course units make explicit use of grammatical concepts and categories, it enables learners to use formal strategies for acquiring language such as analyzing the tense system. And, many adult and adolescent learners have already developed effective strategies of this kind through previous language learning experiences.

Course designers of the 1970s, however, were influenced by the re-constructionist movement in general education and its arguments for objectives-driven courses, together with concurrently emerging perspectives on what communicative ability in a language entails.

A seminal work in this respect was Wilkins' Notional Syllabuses (1976). He suggested three components for a syllabus based on what he called 'communicative capacity'. These derived from the three types of meaning expressed through a sentence or a spoken utterance.

The first component is derived from the kind of meaning conveyed through the grammatical system as we relate information and express perceptions. For example, we express time relationships through tenses and duration through prepositional phrases. Prof. Wilkins calls this 'semantic-grammatical' or 'notional' category.

The second component is modality, arising from modal meaning, i.e., the expression of attitude towards the content of what is conveyed, for example, certainty, as in 'He must have. . .' or disbelief, as in 'I'm astonished that. . .'

The third component is that of communicative function, i.e., the purpose of using the utterance in conversation or the sentence in a written text, for instance, to advise, to complain, to report or to persuade.

## Basic Framework of Syllabus Design

Wilkins' components of notions, modality and functions have been highly influential in attempts to find new bases for syllabus design. The Council of Europe, for example, produced the syllabus specifications 'Threshold Level English' (Van Ek 1975) and 'Waystage English' (Van Ek, Alexander, and Fitzpatrick 1977), which are widely used by ELT textbook writers. These built on Wilkins' work in order to provide a framework for specifying language learning objectives. This framework is as follows:

- The situations in which the foreign language/L2 will be used, including the topics which will be dealt with;
- The language activities in which the learner will engage;
- The language functions which the learner will fulfill;
- What the learner will be able to do with respect to each topic;
- The general notions which the learner will be able to handle;
- The specific (topic-related) notions which the learner will be able to handle;
- The language forms which the learner will be able to use;
- The degree of skill with which the learner will be able to perform. (Van Ek 1975:8-9)

In these eight elements, we can recognize most of the bases now available for ELT course design: situations, functions, topics, notions, structures and skills.

These are the elements which the designer integrates into a multidimensional syllabus. They are considered in detail in Yalden (1983) and Nunan (1988).

Following is Janice Yalden's basic model of syllabus development. The elements outlined can be integrated into this framework for syllabus design.

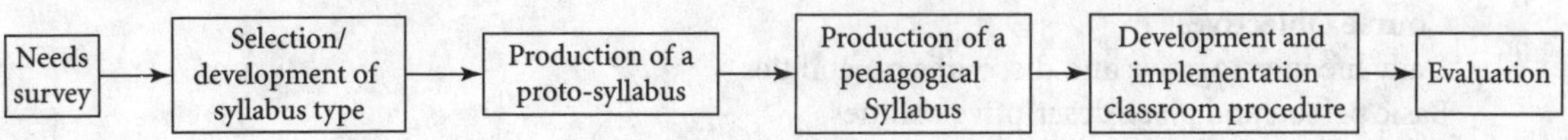

## Framing ESL Syllabus: A Task-based Approach

A little later in this section, you will find six model syllabuses. Evaluate them properly, and frame a syllabus for ESL students. At first, do it in a group of four or five then frame it individually. You may use the following checklist of 14 points to start with. Your teacher will help you.

1. (a) Are the four components of a curriculum present? (Objectives, Content, Methodology, Evaluation)
   (b) How did you identify them? Specify whether the categories of the objectives are general, specific, attitudinal, and behavioural or any other?
   (c) Who are the learners? What is their entry level?
   (d) Has the learner profile, in terms of setting the needs and resources, been provided?
   (e) Have the learning outcomes been specified? What are the assumptions underlying the curriculum design? (Beliefs, needs, context)
   (f) Identify the type of syllabus you are examining. Is it communicative or non-communicative? Which particular approach underlies this syllabus?
   (g) Do you find the notion of eclecticism present in the syllabus you are examining? Which areas have been considered?
   (h) What kind of content has been specified? How effectively does the content reflect the objectives?
   (i) Have the topics, skills, functions and the situations in which the language will be used been specified? Is there a gap between the ideas and the reality?
   (j) What kind of materials have been suggested or selected? What are the criteria of selection?
   (k) What is the principle of organization of the specified content?
   (l) Are there any suggestions for actual classroom implementation in terms of: Number of working hours/activities/methodology/techniques & expectations regarding the level of learner performance, i.e., evaluation?
   (m) Do the objectives, materials and techniques match? Are they compatible?
   (n) To what extent is it feasible for the teacher to modify or adapt the syllabus you have been examining?

### Model Syllabus—I

***Intermediate Level Syllabus Outline.*** This syllabus provides a general outline proposal for creating courses for intermediate-level students. This syllabus can be easily adapted for individual classes while retaining an overall structure aimed at helping the students acquire the language they need to communicate in.

**Duration**
120 hours total comprised:
80 hours theoretical
30 hours practical applications
10 hours of final examination and evaluation

**Course Objectives**
Daily life interrogative and discourse capabilities
Basic person and place descriptive abilities
Number, time, quantity and cost use

Daily life receptive understanding skills, written usage to express situations, give instructions and explanations, communicate opinions, and narrate and comprehend stories, specific terminology use based on students' needs.

| Course Structure—80 hours theoretical | |
|---|---|
| *24 hours basic grammatical skills, including use of the interrogative and discourse forms covering* | – Verb forms and other grammatical structures<br>– Introduction and greetings<br>– Asking for information<br>– Offering<br>– Requesting<br>– Inviting |
| *6 hours descriptive skills, including* | – Comparative language<br>– Vocabulary building for people and places<br>– Communicative structures for expression of opinions<br>– Asking for descriptions |
| *6 hours English numeration, including* | – Time, quantity, cost and numbering vocabulary<br>– Buying and selling structures<br>– Requesting and giving the time<br>– Various numerical expressions, including cardinal numbers, fractions, decimals, etc. |
| *16 hours receptive skill development, including* | – Listening comprehension focusing on varying elements of vocabulary and structure<br>– Video comprehension developing combined visual-audio receptive skills to deduce meaning from context<br>– Reading skills strategies, including intensive skimming and scanning development tasks as well as intensive reading exercises |
| *14 hours written skills development, including* | – Development of basic writing skill applying studied grammatical structures<br>– Standard writing formats, including formal and informal letters<br>– Expression of opinions in writing<br>– Instruction flow writing skills<br>– Narrative written structures to express past events |
| *14 hours basic terminology based on students' needs* | – Identification of equipment required, intensive vocabulary training<br>– Descriptive language development of equipment use and functions<br>– Integrated interrogative and discourse use with targeted vocabulary and functions<br>– Language formation for instruction in and explanation of the basic equipment use |

| 30 hours practical application and self-instruction | |
|---|---|
| *14 hours use of 'authentic' materials to extend receptive development, including both classroom and self-instruction:* | – Reading comprehension of authentic timetables and schedules<br>– Listening comprehension of authentic radio broadcasts in both British and American English<br>– Communicative and decision-making activities based on authentic reading materials<br>– Authentic video materials to improve extraction of information from authentic source<br>– Use of the Internet to extract authentic materials on specific areas of interest |

| | |
|---|---|
| | – Introduction to self-instruction English Web sites located on the Internet, including pen-pals, quizzes, listening comprehension and idiomatic language development<br>– Written communication tasks for authentic task-oriented goals<br>– Self-instruction CD-ROM using various English learning software packages<br>– Self-instruction using listening and video materials from the self-access language laboratory with comprehension exercises |
| *10 hours of class communicative activities, including* | – Role-plays in various authentic situations<br>– Debating various points of view to strengthen the ability to express points of view<br>– Information gathering activities concerning time, place, cost and personal descriptions<br>– Project development in groups and pairs<br>– Group-generated narrative written production |
| *6 hours specific targeted vocabulary development:* | – Interviewing activities to enhance instruction and explanation processes with specific focus on basic individual vocabulary needs<br>– Lexis development and extension in appropriate areas<br>– Role-play to increase active use of targeted language areas<br>– Group-created written reports giving instruction on various aspects of target vocabulary |

## Model Syllabus—2

| Coursebook | | | | Project Resource Book |
|---|---|---|---|---|
| **Unit** | **Functions Students Will Learn to:** | **Grammar/ Language** | **Topics Students Will Learn to Talk/ Write About:** | **Authentic Materials Leading Up to a Project for the Whole Class** |
| Places (pages 5–12) | – describe and ask about places<br>– say where things are<br>– describe and ask about available services/ amenities in town | – there is/ are<br>– has/ has got<br>– non-defining relative clauses | – buildings, rooms, furniture<br>– services, amenities<br>– geographical locations | Housing (pages 5–10)<br>– types of housing<br>– electrical appliances<br>– amenities/services<br>– decorative styles/ colours<br>– garden design project<br>My ideal home in the year 2020 AD |
| Decisions and intentions (pages 13–20) | – decide to do or not to do things<br>– come to a decision with someone else<br>– talk about intentions/plans<br>– talk about definite arrangements | – I'll for spontaneous decisions<br>– Shall we . . .?/ Let's. . . .<br>– verb expressing intentions and plans<br>– present continuous for definite arrangements | – organizing a party<br>– arranging an excursion<br>– changes of mind<br>– ordering a meal in a restaurant | Holiday Britain (pages 11–18)<br>– descriptions of holiday resorts<br>– youth hostels<br>– the Peak District<br>– a cycling tour<br>– interpreting a map project: Planning a tour<br>Back page: Cat in the Rain |

| | | | | |
|---|---|---|---|---|
| Jobs and routine (pages 21–29) | – describe people's jobs<br>– talk and ask about daily routine<br>– talk and ask about regular events | – present simple questions forms<br>– frequency adverbs and phrases<br>– present simple passive with be and get<br>Grammar Spot 2: The article | – routine at work and home<br>– jobs<br>– places of work | Daily routine (pages 19–24)<br>– the average British housewife<br>– Madonna<br>– Parodies<br>Project A life in a day of your school<br>Back page: The Essay |
| Direction (pages 21–29) | – say what directions things and people move in<br>– give instructions for making and doing things<br>– give street directions | – direction prepositions<br>– sequence adverbs<br>Grammar Spot 2: The article | – streets and public buildings<br>– making puppets | |
| Past events (pages 40–47) | – relate and ask about past events<br>– say when the events happened | – sequence expressions, e.g., after …ing<br>– past simple active and passive<br>– past time expressions/ prepositions | – history of people and places<br>– first experiences | Schools (pages 25–32)<br>– he UK system<br>– the new GCSE exam<br>– prospectus of a comprehensive school<br>– the US system<br>Project: School prospectus<br>Back page: Bitter-sweet Dreams: School days |
| (Adapted from Doff, Jones, and Mitchell, *Meanings into Words* [in a version adapted for the Austrian Secondary School System by De Waal and Weinhofer 1989], page 3) | | | | |

## Model Syllabus—3

***Threshold-Level Syllabus.*** Adapted from Threshold 1990 (Van Ek and Trim 1998).

**Language Functions for Threshold Level**

1. ***Imparting and seeking factual information***
   reporting (describing and narrating)
   correcting
   asking
   answering questions
2. ***Expressing and finding out attitudes***
   expressing agreement with a statement
   expressing disagreement with a statement
   enquiring about agreement and disagreement

denying statements
stating whether one knows or does not know a person, thing or fact
enquiring whether one knows or does not know a person, thing or fact
stating whether one remembers or has forgotten a person, thing or fact or action
enquiring whether one remembers or has forgotten a person, thing or fact or action
expressing degrees of probability
enquiring about degrees of probability
expressing or denying necessity (including logical deduction)
enquiring about necessity (including logical deduction)
expressing degrees of certainty
enquiring about degrees of certainty
expressing obligation
enquiring about an obligation
expressing ability/inability to do something
enquiring about ability/inability to do something
expressing that something is or is not permitted or permissible
enquiring whether something is or is not permitted or permissible (including seeking permission)
granting permission
withholding permission
expression wants/desires
enquiring about wants/desires
expressing intentions
enquiring about intentions
expressing preference
inquiring about preference
expressing pleasure, happiness
expressing displeasure, unhappiness
enquiring about pleasure/displeasure/happiness/unhappiness
expressing liking
expressing dislike
enquiring about likes and dislikes
expressing satisfaction
expressing dissatisfaction
enquiring about satisfaction/dissatisfaction
expressing interest
expressing lack of interest
enquiring about interest or lack of interest
expressing surprise
expressing lack of surprise
enquiring about surprise
expressing hope
expressing disappointment
expressing fear
giving reassurance
enquiring about fear/worries
expressing gratitude

reacting to an expression of gratitude
offering an apology
accepting an apology
expressing moral obligation
expressing approval
expressing disapproval
enquiring about approval/disapproval
expressing regret, sympathy

3. ***Deciding on the course of action (suasion)***
suggesting a course of action
agreeing to a suggestion
requesting someone to do something
advising someone to do something
warning others to do something or to refrain from something
encouraging someone to do something
instructing or directing someone to do something
requesting assistance
offering assistance
inviting someone to do something
accepting an offer or invitation
declining an offer or invitation
enquiring whether an offer or invitation is accepted or declined
asking someone for something

4. ***Socializing***
attracting attention
greeting people
when meeting a friend or acquaintance
replying to a greeting from a friend or acquaintance
addressing a friend or acquaintance
addressing a stranger
addressing a customer or a member of the general public
introducing someone to someone else
when being introduced to someone or when someone is being introduced to you
congratulating someone
proposing a toast
taking leave

5. ***Structuring discourse***
5.1 opening
5.2 hesitating
5.3 correcting oneself
5.4 introducing a theme
5.5 expressing an opinion
5.6 enumerating
5.7 exemplifying
5.8 emphasizing

5.9 summarizing
5.10 changing the theme
5.11 asking someone's opinion
5.12 showing that one is following a person's discourse
5.13 interrupting
5.14 asking someone to be silent
5.15 giving over the floor
5.16 indicating a wish to continue
5.17 encouraging someone to continue
5.18 indicating that one is coming to the end of the topic's
5.19 closing
5.20 telephone opening
5.21 asking for [someone]
5.22 asking someone to wait
5.23 asking whether you are heard and understood
5.24 giving signals that you are hearing and understanding
5.25 announcing new call
5.26 opening [letter]
5.27 closing [letter]

6. ***Communication repair***

6.1 signaling non-understanding
6.2 asking for repetition of sentence
6.3 asking for repetition of a word or phrase
6.4 asking for confirmation of text
6.5 asking for confirmation or understanding
6.6 asking for clarification
6.7 asking someone to spell something
6.8 asking for something to be written down
6.9 expressing ignorance of a word or expression
6.10 appealing for assistance
6.11 asking someone to speak more slowly
6.12 paraphrasing
6.13 repeating what one has said
6.14 asking if you have been understood
6.15 spelling out a word or an expression
6.16 supplying a word or an expression

## Model Syllabus—4

| Unit | Verb Phrase | Noun Phrase | Prepositional Phrase | Sentence | |
|---|---|---|---|---|---|
| ONE | is; isn't (is not) | a; an; the; it; that; this singular nouns numerals | on; in; near; of | What . . .? Where . . .? Is . . .? | 1 |
| TWO | are; aren't | they plurals | | Are . . .? and | 7 |

| | | | | | |
|---|---|---|---|---|---|
| THREE | can (permission) | very adjectives (colours) (nationality words) he; she article + profession | with; from | Be (v) + N + adj?<br>How old . . .?<br>What colour . . .?<br>Who . . .? | 13 |
| FIRST REVIEW AND COMPLEMENTATION UNIT 1; YOU; WE; THESE; THOSE 19 | | | | | |
| FOUR | am | her; his; my; your (poss., adj.) I; you (months) | under | So<br>What . . . like? | 23 |
| FIVE | present progressive | her; him; them; us post-modification with prep. phrase | to at (the moment) | What . . . doing? | 29 |
| SIX | can; can't (ability) | the time | past; to | What time . . .?<br>How?<br>But | 35 |
| SECOND REVIEW AND COMPLEMENTATION UNIT; OUR; THEIR; POSSESSIVE PRONOUNS 41 | | | | | |
| SEVEN | present simple (third person singular) | | at (time)<br>by (transport) | then<br>Does . . .? | 45 |
| EIGHT | present simple (other persons) | | | Do . . .?<br>How much . . .? (price) | 51 |
| NINE | has; have<br>never<br>once/twice a week, etc. | no (as det.)<br>each | | How much . . .? (quantity)<br>How many . . .?<br>How often . . .? | 57 |
| TEN | stative verbs<br>present simple with frequency words | another<br>other | in (part of day)<br>in (season)<br>after; before | | 63 |
| | on (day) | | | | |
| (Source: Rossner, Shaw, Shepherd, Taylor, and Davies 1979) (Adapted and abridged) | | | | | |

## Let Us Do and Learn

Level: Beginner's Course—the Language Syllabus

Are there any notable omissions? What are these? Is the sequencing appropriate? If not, could any of the items be re-sequenced?

## Model Syllabus—5

**Grammar items and their sequence in a first-year English course (adapted from Axbey 1997):**

Present verb be
Subject pronouns
Possessive adjectives
Indefinite article: a/an
Plural nouns: -s, -ies, -es

Expressions with go
too + adjective/not + adjective + enough
when clauses
want + infinitive
Imperatives

Prepositions: from, in, near
at, with, there, is/are
Countable nouns with some and any
Definite article: the
Plural nouns: irregular
Demonstrative pronouns:
This/that, these/those
Adjectives
Have/has got
Present simple
Object pronouns
Whose? How often?
Enough, etc.
Can/cannot (can't)
Like + noun/like + gerund
Adverbs of frequency
Do you like?
Would you like?
Past verb be
Present continuous for present
Activities
Present infinitive
Indefinite pronouns: 'everyone/
everybody/no one/nobody' +
Verb singular
Most/some/a few + plural verb
ask/tell + infinitive
Past simple

countable/uncountable nouns with
many/few, much/ little
Comparative adjectives
Superlative adjectives
Prepositions of place
Articles: definite/indefinite/zero
Present continuous for fixed plans
Verbs + prepositions
Expressions with get
going to for intentions
ould you like + noun/infinitive
can for permission
cannot/can't for prohibition
should/shouldn't for advice about
polite behavior
Possessive pronouns
Present perfect
Indefinite pronouns
should/shouldn't for giving opinions
will/won't for promises of help
promise/remember/forget +. . . .

have to for obligation
Adverbs of manner
Prepositions
will/won't for predictions
think so/hope so

## Model Syllabus—6

***Skills Syllabus for Listening and Speaking.*** From Malaysian Secondary School Syllabus Form IV (1989).

***Listening and Speaking.*** The component on listening and speaking deals with the skills of sound discrimination, extracting information, and prediction, in order to perform a specific function. The skills also include those of determining and using registers to suit different audiences, and for different purposes, so that students are able to express their thoughts clearly and succinctly and are able to fully participate in conversations and discussions.

Objectives of the Component on Listening and Speaking

Listening to and discriminating: the consonant clusters, sentence stress and intonation, diphthongs and homonyms.

Listening to and understanding: the words, phrases and sentences; instructions, messages; stories; talks; reports; opinions; poems; dialogues; information in reports, guides, charts, graphs, manuals, forms and letters; description of scenes, events, places, things, and processes and procedures.

Speaking with correct pronunciation, intonation, word stress and sentence rhythm is necessary.

Asking for and giving: the meanings of words, phrases and sentences; instructions; messages; talks; reports; opinions; information in reports, guides, charts, graphs, manuals, forms and letters; descriptions of scenes, events, places, things, and processes and procedure.

### *Skill Specifications*

At the end of the English Language Programme for the target group, students should be able to:

1. Listen to and discriminate between: consonant clusters, diphthongs and homonyms.
2. Listen to and understand, and ask for and give meanings of words, phrases and sentences.
3. Speak with correct intonations, word stress and sentence rhythm.
4. Listen to and understand, and ask for and give instructions on how to fix things, such as a leaking tap.
5. Listen to and understand, ask for and give and relay messages received through the mass media, such as the radio and the television.
6. Listen to and understand, ask for and give information contained in talks on current issues, such as consumerism and health care.
7. Listen to and understand, ask for and give information contained in reports, such as newspaper reports and book reports.
8. Listen to and understand, ask for and give information contained in charts, graphs and manuals.
9. Listen to and understand, ask for and give information contained in informal letters, in newspapers and in formal letters of enquiry and complaint.
10. Listen to and understand, ask for and give descriptions of scenes, such as tourist spots in the Association of South East Asian Nations (ASEAN) region.
11. Listen to and understand, ask for and give descriptions of events, such as the SEA Games.
12. Listen to and understand, ask for and give opinions on current issues, such as unemployment.
13. Listen to and understand selected poems of writers from the ASEAN region.
14. Listen to and understand, ask for and give descriptions of processes and procedures, such as the recycling of material.
15. Listen to and understand; express displeasure and regret.
16. Practice social skills, such as interrupting a conversation, and joining and participating in a conversation.

The following sub-skills need to be combined and taught simultaneously with the earlier mentioned main skills where appropriate.

### *Sub-skills of Listening*

(a) Discerning main ideas
(b) Understanding sequence
(c) Noticing specific details
(d) Inferring
(e) Comparing

(f) Predicting
(g) Determining relevance
(h) Distinguishing between fact and fiction
(i) Differentiating between fact and opinion
(j) Generalizing
(k) Classifying

***Sub-skills of Speaking***

(l) Using correct pronunciation
(m) Questioning
(n) Paraphrasing
(o) Supporting and clarifying
(p) Summarizing
(q) Using registers
(r) Speaking coherently

## Evaluating Contents/Coursebooks and Teaching/Learning Materials: Principles and Practices

At various stages of their professional lives teachers need to get involved in the selection of material for their students. Sometimes, these materials are of a supplementary kind and sometimes, they are used as coursebooks themselves. Teachers often find the materials they have been asked to use not very satisfying. They then, have to go looking for ideas in other books and use them in addition to the prescribed syllabus. The basic questions asked before evaluating the materials are: (1) Will the materials be useful to the students? and (2) How will they help the teacher?

When answering the first question we have to remember the tests our students have to sit for. Some schools have round the year assessment programmes while others have annual tests. Whatever testing system may be prevalent, what the teachers must have with them are profiles of students and their needs. Jeremy Hermer in his book, *The Practice of English Language Teaching*, describes the profiles of students as having three components: (1) Description of the students, (2) Description of the students' needs and (3) Type of material appropriate for students.

| Description of Students |
|---|
| 1. Age - |
| 2. Sex - |
| 3. Social/cultural background - |
| 4. Motivation/attitude - |
| 5. Educational background - |
| 6. Knowledge |
| a) English level - |
| b) Of the world - |
| 7. Interests and beliefs - |

### Let Us Do and Learn

Based on the information mentioned, what conclusion can you draw about the kind of materials that would be suitable for your students?

The just discussed analysis would give us some idea about what kind of materials would be appropriate for the students based on their personal characteristics. The second analysis would enable the teachers to arrive at some kind of conclusion about their needs.

### Description of Students' Needs

1. In what contexts and situations (if any) will your students probably use English at some future date?
   a) ....................
   b) ....................
   c) ....................
2. Give an order of priority for the different language skills (including sub-skills) that your students will need when using English.
   a) ....................
   b) ....................
   c) ....................
   d) ....................
   e) ....................
3. Now say what percentage of class time should be spent on these various skills.
   a) ....................
   b) ....................
   c) ....................
   d) ....................
   e) ....................
4. Based on the above say (a) what level students need to reach and (b) what kind of language they need to be able to use or understand (e.g., formal/informal, spoken/written, scientific/business, etc.)

### Type of Materials Appropriate for Students

Based on the description of students and their needs, say what type of materials you think would be most appropriate for these students?

The needs analysis can be done through questionnaires, interviews with the students, teachers and employers. Once this is done, the teacher(s) can evaluate materials that are appropriate.

In India, we have the different Boards and Councils specifying the kind of syllabus that ought to be followed at various levels. Sometimes, there are coursebooks and textbooks that have to be covered by the teacher at each level. It is in such situations that the teacher has to look for supplementary materials, especially in cases where the prescribed materials are inadequate, unsuitable or unsatisfactory.

The materials evaluation for describing the profiles of students as given in Harold E. Palmer's book will help teachers not only to analyze student needs, but also to find out how much they need to develop and evaluate their own teaching.

Sometimes, literary texts are used as materials to be taught. In such cases, too, teachers need evaluation sheets to find out what kind of benefits students will find from reading these texts or whether these materials can be used to motivate the students into further reading. Following are two evaluation sheets—'quickie' and 'detailed'—taken from Gillian Lazer's book:

***Literature and Language Teaching***

**A. Quickie**

| Title of book | | | |
|---|---|---|---|
| Author(s) | | | |
| Publishers | | | |
| Level | | | |
| Overall aims/approach | | | |
| Types of texts used | | | |
| Skill/language area which the book will help to improve | | | |
| Strengths of material | | | |
| Weaknesses of material | | | |
| Suitable for my students? | | | |
| Yes/No (give reasons) | | | |

**B. Detailed Book Evaluation**

Title of Book ..........................................................

Author(s) ..........................................................

Publishers ..........................................................

***Aims and Organization***

1. What are the overall aims of the book?
2. What approach to using literature seems to have been adopted? Is the approach suitable for your students?
3. How is the book organized?,Thematically? According to linguistic difficulty? Chronologically? etc.
4. Are units/sections self-contained? Can you use some of the material, or do you need to work through all of it?

***Materials and Activities***

1. What kinds of texts are used in the book? Poems? Short stories? Extracts from novels and plays? Literary and non-literary texts?
2. Are texts sufficiently varied, interesting and relevant to students?
3. Are tasks and activities sufficiently varied, interesting and relevant to students?
4. Are the students given sufficient linguistic guidance with the language of the texts (for example, vocabulary exercise, glossaries, etc.)?
5. Are the students given adequate cultural, historical or literary background information to make sense of the texts?
6. Are the students encouraged to relate the materials to their own lives and experiences?

7. Is the material challenging enough for the students?
8. Could the material be adapted if necessary?

***Instructions and Layout***

1. Are the instructions in the book clear and easy to follow?
2. Is the layout clear and attractive?
3. Are there visuals (pictures, photos, diagrams, etc.) to supplement the texts?

***Accompanying Resources***

1. Is the teacher given sufficient guidance on how to use the book (either in the book itself or in a teacher's book)?
2. Is there recorded material available to accompany the book?
3. Could the book be used by students working on their own? (Is there a key, for example, to help them?)

***Suitability for Class/Group***

Would you use this book with your students? Please give reasons.

The following evaluation sheet can be used for evaluating a piece of published material fairly quickly, for example, a section or unit of a book:

***Evaluating a Piece of Teaching/Learning Material***

Title of book ..........................................
Author(s) ...............................................
Publisher ...............................................
Page on which relevant material is found ..........

Please tick the relevant column:

| | | Excellent | Good | Adequate | Poor |
|---|---|---|---|---|---|
| 1. | Suitability of approach for your students | | | | |
| 2. | Suitability of level for your students | | | | |
| 3. | Relevance and interest of texts chosen | | | | |
| 4. | Variety and appropriateness of task activities | | | | |
| 5. | Staging and grading of tasks and activities | | | | |
| 6. | Opportunities for student participation and personalization | | | | |
| 7. | Linguistic guidance (glossaries, exercises, etc.) | | | | |
| 8. | Cultural/literary/historical background provided | | | | |
| 9. | Clarity of instructions | | | | |
| 10. | Layout and design | | | | |

I would/would not use this material with my students

because ...................................................
...................................................

(Adapted from Literature and Language Teaching—G. Lazar)

### *What Do We Do When We Evaluate a Book or Material for Specific Purposes?*

1. We read the cover pages first. If the cover pages prove interesting we look up the pages that deal with the specific purpose we have in mind. We also look at the pages of content for other materials that may be useful.
2. If the activities are appropriate for our students we have these photocopied.
3. These are then circulated among the students, who work out the tasks.
4. If the activities generate enthusiasm among the students and motivate them to go for further learning, the book can be bought or recommended.
5. The price and the availability of the book in the market are causes of concern, especially if the book comes in a pack (coursebook, tape and teacher book). We need to go through many books before deciding on one.
6. We do peer discussions on the relative importance of a particular item or activity in a particular book is good guidance for evaluating the material.
7. Framing a materials-evaluation form and using it for evaluation will be helpful too. The following questions can be included in the form:
    1. Do the materials include and practice the skills our students need?
    2. Is the practice of the individual skills integrated into the practice of other skills?
    3. Is the language used in the materials realistic—i.e., like real-life English?
    4. Is the subject and content of the materials relevant to the students' needs? Are they culturally appropriate?
    5. Are the materials interesting for the students? Do they offer sufficient variety?
    6. Do the materials avoid harmful stereotypes of different members of the society (women, policemen, elderly people, etc.)?
    7. Does the material clearly state the objectives and give guidance to the teacher about how to use them to the best advantage?
    8. Are there enough diagrams in the materials explaining different processes that students have to be taught?
    9. Are the flow charts and pie charts used in the materials clearly printed? Do they give explicit instructions as to what the student is expected to do with them?
    10. Are the pictures used in the materials relevant to the activities?

## Let Us Do and Learn

### *Task I*

**Evaluate Emerald English Reader (Book 8), Reader's Digest Enterprise, Kolkata, Using a Quickie Evaluation Sheet**

**Basic Aim**
It is to explore the relationship between the syllabus goals and the goals of language teachers.

**Resources**
Syllabus outlines, documents and statements from your teaching institution and the language goal survey form.

**Basic Goals**
Our language programme has been designed to achieve the following goals:

1. to contribute to the intellectual, personal and vocational development of the individual;

2. to acquire the competence to use English in real-life situations for the development and maintenance of interpersonal relationships, and to take part in interpersonal encounters through the sharing of factual and attitudinal information;
3. to develop and maintain a sense of confidence and self-worth;
4. to develop the skills needed to acquire, record and use information from a variety of aural and written sources;
5. to develop mastery over English as a written system and to have some knowledge of how it works at the levels of phonology, morphology and syntax;
6. to increase, through a common language, the possibility of understanding, friendship and co-operation with people who speak English;
7. to foster the development of critical thinking skills and skills in 'learning how to learn';
8. to develop the skills and attitudes to use English for creative and imaginative purposes and
9. to develop the English needed to get a job requiring the use of English.

**Procedure**
Study the syllabus outlines, documents, and statements from your institution and assign a number from 1 (low) to 5 (high) to each of the goal statements on the form according to their perceived prominence in the syllabus documents.
Ask the teachers in your institution to indicate the importance of the goal statements by rating each from 1 to 5.

**Evaluation Criteria**
Are there any mismatches between the teachers' ratings and those you derived from the syllabus documents?

If there are mismatches, can you think of any ways in which these might be resolved?

### *Task 2*

**Evaluating Syllabus Sequence—Syllabus as a Product**

**Basic Aim**
To examine the selection and sequencing of grammatical elements in a syllabus you are currently using.

**Resources**
(a) A detailed syllabus outline or list of contents from a coursebook you are currently using for beginning students.
(b) The list of contents (opposite) from any beginner's coursebook prescribed by any board for secondary level or primary level.
(c) The list of contents—Model 6.

**Procedure**
Compare the list of contents in Model Syllabus—6 with the syllabus outline or coursebook you are currently using.

**Evaluation Criteria**
What are the similarities and differences between the two sets of contents?

Can the present coursebook cover the contents of the Model Syllabus?

*Task 3*

**Evaluating Selection of Contents and Presentation**

**Basic Aim**

To critique the selection and presentation of grammatical items in a coursebook you are currently using.

**Resources**

A coursebook you are currently using or have recently used.

**Procedure**

Study the selection and presentation of grammatical items from a representative selection of units or chapters in the coursebook.

**Evaluation Criteria**

How are the grammatical items introduced?

Is there adequate contextualization for the items? (Are they presented and practiced within a meaningful communicative context?)

*Task 4*

**Evaluating Syllabus Type and Elemental Relationship**

**Basic Aim**

To examine the integration of grammatical, functional and notional components in a syllabus you are currently using.

**Resources**

A detailed syllabus outline or a coursebook you are currently using or have recently used which incorporates grammatical, functional and notional elements, e.g., Gulmohar series—Orient Longman, 2000.

**Procedure**

Extract from the syllabus outline or coursebook a list of the grammatical, functional and/or notional elements which are covered.

Compare these lists and note the ways in which the elements are related and integrated.

**Evaluation Criteria**

- How are the elements related?
- Are the relationships arbitrary or not?
- How well are the elements interrelated from your own perspective?
- If there are any elements which are not related in a satisfactory or convincing way, can you think of ways in which this could be improved?

## New Phrase—Known

**Experiential Content**

You will recall that **experiential content** refers to the topics, themes, situation, settings, and so on, which provide a context for the linguistic content. The selection of experiential content is one task where there is potential for negotiation between learners and teachers.

***Task 5***

**Evaluating Content Focus vis-à-vis Learners' Interest**

**Basic Aim**

To explore the possibility of basing the selection of content on the interests of the learners.

**Resources**

A content survey form.

**Procedure**

Construct a content survey form (see overleaf) containing a range of topics of interest and relevance to your students, for which you have resources, and which you are prepared to teach.

## Let Us Do and Learn

1. Indicate which of the following topics you would like to study by placing a circle around the appropriate number (1 = 'I would not like to study this topic at all'; 5='I would like to study this topic very much.'):

| | | | | | | |
|---|---|---|---|---|---|---|
| 1. | Summer Holidays in England | 1 | 2 | 3 | 4 | 5 |
| 2. | Wedding Invitations | 1 | 2 | 3 | 4 | 5 |
| 3. | Bob Dylan | 1 | 2 | 3 | 4 | 5 |
| 4. | Bus and Train Timetables | 1 | 2 | 3 | 4 | 5 |
| 5. | Describing a House | 1 | 2 | 3 | 4 | 5 |
| 6. | Camera-operating Instructions | 1 | 2 | 3 | 4 | 5 |
| 7. | The Olympic Games | 1 | 2 | 3 | 4 | 5 |
| 8. | Stamp-dispensing Machines | 1 | 2 | 3 | 4 | 5 |
| 9. | Ernest Hemingway | 1 | 2 | 3 | 4 | 5 |
| 10. | Recipe—making Hamburgers | 1 | 2 | 3 | 4 | 5 |
| 11. | Apollo Moon Landing | 1 | 2 | 3 | 4 | 5 |
| 12. | Cassette player—How to use | 1 | 2 | 3 | 4 | 5 |
| 13. | Comparing Cars | 1 | 2 | 3 | 4 | 5 |
| 14. | Job Advertisements | 1 | 2 | 3 | 4 | 5 |
| 15. | Motorcycles | 1 | 2 | 3 | 4 | 5 |
| 16. | Road Accident Report | 1 | 2 | 3 | 4 | 5 |
| 17. | The Story of Tea | 1 | 2 | 3 | 4 | 5 |

2. Administer the survey to your students, total the results and rank the topics from the most popular to the least popular.
3. Discuss the results with your students.

***Evaluation Criteria***

- What sort of consensus was there among the students?
- Were you surprised by any of the results?
- In what ways might you use the information you obtained to modify the syllabus you are currently using?

## Let Us Do and Learn

**Evaluating Content Grading**

**Basic Aim**
To explore the problem of grading experiential content.

**Resources**
The survey form and results of the activity in Task Evaluation 5.

**Procedure**
It is not immediately apparent how topics, such as those listed in the sample survey form, can be graded.

Make a list of evaluation criteria which could be used to grade and sequence the experiential content.

## Let Us Sum Up

We have looked into different types of syllabus that are in use in ELT since the last century. We have seen how needs analysis is a core concern in the field of *Syllabus Design* and *Curriculum Design*. We have expressed our concern regarding the need of proper evaluation of goals and objectives of teaching vis-à-vis context and learners' needs. We have followed a task-based approach towards ESL Syllabus Design by providing basic framework of syllabus design and few well-known models that are in use in ELT. We have also introduced principles and practice of evaluating contents, coursebooks, teaching and learning materials and considered syllabus as a product which invariably makes us concerned about its grading and presentation aspects. We have also focused on the need integration of various facets of a dynamic English teacher's course of action to mobilize the concept of effective teaching even when there are co-existing factors like syllabus and curriculum in our educational setting.

## Glossary

syllabus: an arrangement of subjects (topics, grammar items, etc., for study)

curriculum: the subjects included in a course of study or taught at a particular school, college, etc.

competence: the ability to perform in the target language. In the technical sense, it is more precisely referred to as 'linguistic competence', i.e., the native speaker's tacit knowledge of the rules of his language. The notion stems from the work of Chomsky.

drills: a language teaching procedure designed to ensure assimilation of some linguistic point through repetition and also through manipulation, i.e., changing or modifying the linguistic elements presented for the purpose of learning.

eclecticism: an approach to ELT which is essentially pragmatic and advocates the judicious use of those parts of any language teaching method which seems useful and effective rather than adhering to one particular method or set of techniques.

EFL: abbreviation for English as a Foreign Language. It is used for English-learnt people from a community where English is not normally used. An Italian, Japanese or German learning English would be learning it as a foreign language.

ESL: abbreviation for English as a Second Language

experiential learning: learning seen as a process that gives emphasis on the experience of the learner. The experience gained by the learner becomes an aid to language learning.

first language: (see mother tongue) first language is often the mother tongue for many learners. Term applied to the language that one learns first as a child and which she/he has continued to use. It is often referred to as L1.

foreign language: term usually applied to language spoken outside the boundaries of the country in which one lives, or more crucially, the term is applied to languages learnt only for communication with those living outside one's own community and not used for everyday communication within one's own community.

formulaic expressions: the term refers to expressions which are learnt as whole utterances (e.g., How do you do?) or as patterns which the learners can use by inserting a relevant word in a vacant slot (e.g., This is a ___________.)

grammar-translation Method: A language teaching method which emerged in the nineteenth century in which the target language is taught through the presentation of the rules of the language in a sequence from simple to complex. These rules are then applied to the translation of the target language sentences into the mother tongue.

linguistics: Pertaining to language. The systematic and objective study of languages (tongues)

method: a set of teaching procedures assembled together in accordance with the principles of a certain approach to language teaching. It is used in connection with a particular type of syllabus, materials and evaluation in a given language teaching situation.

mother tongue: refers to usually (not always) the first language to which the child is exposed to in her/his environment through one parent, relatives, peers, and so on. It is also often the language that one speaks first. The individual 'identifies' best and has the most natural command in this language.

rote learning: the process of learning something by repeated study rather than by understanding the meaning.

native language: usually the language which a person acquires in early childhood, because it is spoken in the family and/or it is the language of the country where he/she is living. The native language is often the first language a child acquires and so this term is sometimes used synonymously with L1.

target language: the language which a person is learning. Sometimes, this term is synonymously used with L1 or L2.

deductive learning: This is an approach to language teaching in which learners are taught rules and given specific information about a language which they then apply when they use the language.

inductive learning: In contrast to deductive learning, in inductive learning, learners are not taught grammatical or other types of rules directly but are left to discover or induce rules from their experience of using the language.

paradigm: (grammar) a set of all the different forms of a word, e.g., verb paradigms

evaluation: assessment or formation of an idea of the value of something

realia: (in language teaching) actual objects and items which are brought to be talked or written about and used in teaching.

## Exercise

1. How are different proficiency levels characterized and distinguished in a course or programme you are familiar with?
2. Compare two or more textbooks for the same area (e.g., writing, speaking and listening) and for learners of the same level. How similar are the syllabuses in each book? Examine the

teacher's books for each course. What justification do the authors of each book provide for the kind of syllabus they employ?

3. Choose three different approaches to syllabus design that are possible for the following types of courses, and consider the advantages and limitations of each approach:
   A Reading Course
   A Speaking Course
   A Writing Course
4. Examine three different textbooks in a particular skill area (e.g., reading skills, writing). What approach to the selection and sequencing of content does each book adopt?
5. Do you think that grammar is a relevant component of a language course? What would the role of grammar be in such a course? How would the choice of grammatical content be determined?
6. Select two or three related functions from the Threshold Level Syllabus (see Model 4) and consider the language that would be needed to teach these functions to lower-intermediate learners in a speaking course. What decisions are involved in selecting the language realizations (or exponents) for functions in a functional syllabus?
7. Consider the design of a language course for airline employees working at the check-in counter of an airport. Suggest examples of the following:
   (a) The transactions they engage in
   (b) The skills or behaviours involved in each transaction
   (c) The kinds of oral and written texts that are produced
   (d) The linguistic features of the texts
8. How is a situational syllabus related to other syllabus options discussed in this chapter?
9. Plan a topic-based four-hour unit of work in a course for a group of learners you are familiar with (or for intermediate-level ESL students in a general English class).
10. Describe how the unit would integrate different language skills.
11. Describe how the unit would develop grammar from content.
12. Compare two chapters from two coursebooks that are designed for the same area and level. What chapter structure does each book employ? How effective is the chapter structure for each book?
13. Examine the skills listed in Model 5. How would you define 'skills' based on the examples given in the syllabus?
14. Give an example of pedagogical tasks and real-world tasks that could be used in designing the following:
    A Reading Course
    A Listening Course
15. Examine a few units from textbooks prescribed by the West Bengal Board of Secondary Education and H.S. Council or any other board, and find examples of coherence with syllabus specification.
16. Write short notes on the following:
    (a) The Traditional Syllabus
    (b) The Holistic Syllabus
    (c) The Synthetic Syllabus
    (d) The Analytic Syllabus
    (e) The Notional Syllabus

## Bibliography

Brown, H.D., *Principles of Language Learning and Teaching* (New Jersey: Prentice Hall).
Brumfit, C.I., *Problems and Principles in English Teaching* (Pergamum Press).
Dey, S.K., *Emerald English Reader* (Book 1-8) (Kolkata: Readers Digest Enterprises).
Dubin and Olshtain, *Course Design* (CUP, 1986).
Lands, Yalden, Syllabus Design (CUP, 1983).
Nunan, David, *The Learner-centred Curriculum* (CUP, 1988).

# Evaluation and Testing 6

## CHAPTER OUTLINE



## LEARNING OBJECTIVES

After reading this chapter, students will be able to:

- Learn and understand different types of evaluation and testing.
- Fix criteria for valid and reliable testing.
- Design different types of exercises and questions for testing.
- Design proper marks scheme for evaluation.
- Frame proper instructions for testing English language and literature as well.

## Introduction

Good evaluation is of paramount importance to both teachers and learners as well as syllabus framers. Constant vigilance is necessary to keep track of (educational) progress in the areas of teaching, learning, writing materials and testing. Evaluation helps in measuring this progress. It also guides writers of tests and syllabus framers to modify and rewrite items that do not produce the desired results.

Evaluative judgements are usually made by others—teachers, employers, lawyers, doctors, spectators, commentators, and so on. But it can also be made by oneself, i.e., self-evaluation. In education, both teachers and learners can assess and evaluate themselves. In our social life, we make evaluative statements in a principled and systematic way though the criteria may be vague and ill-defined. In education, the criteria has to be clear and explicit. Vague and ill-defined criteria will not lead to proper evaluation of either the teacher or the student performance. Moreover, different sets of criteria are needed for different purposes. The ones necessary for evaluating the teacher's performance in the classroom will have to be different from the ones needed for evaluating the learning tasks. We depend on test results to promote a student to the next higher level or retain her/him back. We evaluate the teacher's performance to promote the teacher from middle school to senior school, and so on.

## Evaluation of Teachers

Teachers are often assessed by their trainers, peers and Board of Examinations. These assessments are primarily for purposes of appraisal. But these can also be used by teachers for self-development and self-evaluation. Practice teaching is a traditional approach to classroom observation. Here, the trainer observes a teacher performing and then gives a feedback to the teacher, who learns what her/his mistakes were and tries to rectify them in the next class. But this process can be intimidating as the teacher may feel that she/he is being judged. The teacher may also get confused trying to follow various strategies that had been taught in the training programme. Microteaching is also useful in raising the teachers' awareness. When a group of students is taught by a teacher for a short while, say about 15 minutes, a particular topic or sub-skill (a small part or stage of a lesson only) we call it microteaching. The lesson is observed by the trainer and peers who comment on it. As it is short and follows a checklist that is available to both the trainee teacher and his/her peers as well as the trainer, it is less frightening and less confusing than the traditional method of practice teaching.

Microteaching does not only raise awareness, but also paves the way for teacher's self-development and self-evaluation.

Self-evaluation is basically a teacher's reflection on what has taken place in the lesson and how she/he can improve her/his performance. These reflections can come in the form of notes the teacher writes immediately after taking the class or it can be a report on the lesson itself. Alternatively, a checklist can be used. The teacher will need to plan the lesson highlighting which sub-skill will be attended to and in what manner it will be attended. These will have to be ticked off as the lesson progresses. For example, if the teacher is taking a class in vocabulary building she/he ticks off items on the checklist as the lesson progresses:

1. Put up diagrams/charts/pictures (e.g., large drawing of a human figure to teach body parts).
2. Write the prefixes/suffixes up on the board.
3. Have enough photocopies for circulation.
4. Keep a number of dictionaries in the classroom.
5. Any need to keep objects for demonstration purpose (to teach words like 'ignite', 'spark', etc.)?

Like students' portfolios, teachers' portfolios are essential for self-assessment. The self-assessment sheets will enable you to evaluate your performance and take steps towards self-development. Other teachers can go through your portfolio for the purpose of evaluation as well as getting ideas for trying out in their own classes.

**(A) Self-assessment Worksheet**

| | |
|---|---|
| 1. What was my goal in this particular teaching situation? How successful was I in achieving it? | Teaching vocabulary; Not very, as I had not planned the lesson properly. |
| 2. Why did I think of this idea as a teaching point? | |
| 3. At what level did I use it? | |

4. What teaching aids did I have?
5. Did the learners find the lesson easy/difficult?
6. How much time did I spend on the lesson? Was it too long/too short?
7. Can the activity be integrated with other activities?
8. Do I have the habit of testing frequently?

Such sheets for evaluating different classes will necessarily make the teacher sit-up and prepare better for the next class.

The portfolio can also have a sheet of statements on the teachers' own professional principles.

**(B) Worksheet on Professional Principles**

- I tend not to speak much. I give instructions and see that these are followed.
- I prefer pair and group work in class.
- I use supplementary materials of my choice to make the class interesting. This often makes the students neglect their textbooks.
- I correct errors in their writing but not often.
- I change my teaching strategy in every class.
- I use a lot of audio/visual aids.
- I seldom use the blackboard/whiteboard.
- I rarely give homework.
- I allow students to use their first language only when they are unable to state what they exactly mean.
- I permit them to gossip in their spoken English class.
- I make them write self-assessment sheets.

Teachers can agree or disagree with the above statements but they must give reasons for their disagreement and rewrite the statement in their own way.

As teacher development is a primary issue in education, teachers need to constantly evaluate themselves. Thus they can do a thorough self-evaluation using self-assessment forms, questionnaires, checklists, inventories, diaries as well as their own observations noted down by themselves.

### New Words Known

- Evaluation : measuring value of something (here Teachers' and Learners' merit)
- Testing : finding out qualities of learners by placing them in certain conditions (Examinations, etc.)

## Designing Self-evaluating Questionnaire on Classroom Teaching/Teaching Observation

Four phases may be identified with the classroom observations:

1. Pre-observation Preparation/Discussion
2. Observation
3. Reflection on the Observation
4. Post-observation Discussion

The whole process is guided by a questionnaire.

Before the lesson, look at your plan and ask yourself.

1. Have you chosen an activity that is interesting and will generate meaningful language use?
2. What classroom arrangement will you use? What materials do you need?
3. Is your organization smooth? Are the instructions clear? Do the pupils know the 'rules' of your class (who they can talk to, when, etc.)?
4. At what point in your lesson will the pupils use the language for a real purpose?
5. Write down a question you will ask to encourage a thoughtful answer rather than a correct answer.

During and after the lesson, ask yourself these questions and write the answers:

1. Write down something(s) that a pupil said in the lesson where the language was used for a purpose.
2. Write down any evidence that your activity was successful/unsuccessful, was smoothly/badly organized, was interesting/boring.
3. Who was not involved? Why?
4. Which question provided a thoughtful answer? Write down your question.
5. What would you like to improve in the lesson?
6. What have you learnt?
7. Write down your thoughts about how you would like to improve/change/develop your teaching in the future.

(Adapted from Williams 1989: Page 88).

The questions before the lesson help the teacher to plan the lesson. During the lesson, the trainer gathers data from others about what is happening in the class. After the lesson, the teacher completes the questionnaire, which together with the data gathered by the trainer, provides the focus for the follow-up session.

The second questionnaire concentrates on what the teacher has learnt. It focuses more on specific factors and their explanations, for example: Who was not involved? Why?

Let us ask the following questions before starting the teaching:

Is the lesson a challenging one? Is it too easy or too difficult? Is it interesting? Do the learners get enough opportunity to talk? What meaningful language will it promote? Do students get a chance to give their own ideas? What activity preceded the present one and what will follow it? Show how it might involve reading, writing, grammar, etc. What provisions have been made for pupils who finish quickly/slowly?

We need to ask the following questions while teaching to ensure effective teaching:

What evidence was there that the pupils were interested/not interested? Who was not involved? Why? Write down some of the language that the pupils used. Which aim/goal did you achieve? What will you do next to follow-up this lesson? Did pupils come up with their own ideas? Did they talk enough or did you dominate the discussion?

What have you learnt? How would you like to develop your teaching now and in the future?

Self-evaluation motivates a teacher to change, to develop. The teaching and testing situations are never free of constraints. To overcome these, the teachers will have to evaluate them and be evaluated by their peers and trainers. How can teachers motivate their students if they cannot motivate themselves to change? And this entails hard work. If teachers favour pair work and group work they will have to do the same in their own situations. Peer teaching, peer discussions and peer appraisals thus become mandatory.

## Let Us Do and Learn

1. What is evaluation? Is the teacher's self-assessment necessary?
2. What kind of criteria is needed in the self-evaluation of a teacher?
3. What is microteaching? Is it a helpful tool for self-evaluation?

# Teacher-based Evaluation

Teachers have to work under pressure—pressure of syllabus, pressure of the Examination Board/Council, pressure of parents' concerns, and pressure of other (personal) commitments and, of course, pressure of evaluating students constantly.

Self-evaluation helps teachers to change and learn how to develop themselves. Teacher-based evaluation, on the other hand, helps their learners to change and develop.

Teachers evaluate not only the learning, but also the social behaviour of the learners. Teachers need to be role models for their students, so that they can develop into disciplined, hard-working, successful persons.

Lack of motivation in the students is one of the biggest problems that teachers come across everywhere. This can, to a certain extent, be taken care of, if teachers gear themselves up to tackle it directly. The teachers need to follow these steps:

(a) Need teaching-based testing and instruments, among others, that can help in fighting these problems effectively.
(b) Collaborative activities between students, teachers and parents can also provide solutions to the problems. Parents must help teachers to succeed in their mission to fight lack of motivation.

One of the easiest ways to evaluate what is happening in the class is to collect data. One needs to investigate and find evidence. For this purpose, the teacher has to choose a narrow focus to investigate perhaps pronunciation rather than stress and 'intonation' in a loud-reading class.

Some of the methods useful for data collection for an evaluation are self-assessment forms, learner questionnaires, interviews, checklists and learner diaries.

(The following self-assessment form has been adapted from **Evaluation** by P. Rea, Dickins and K. Germaine's.)

## Self-evaluation Worksheet

(To be completed by each student/trainee at the end of every week and handed to the Course Director.)

1. Out-of-class Practice:
   How much time outside class have you spent: (Approx Hours?)
   - Speaking English? ____________________
   - Listening to English? ____________________
   - Reading English? ____________________
   - Writing English? ____________________
2. Who have you spoken to this week in English? (not including your teacher)
   - Other course members: ____________________
   - Members of the public: ____________________
   - Others: ____________________

*(Continued)*

3. Do you feel your conversations were generally successful? Yes/No
   Why? ____________________
4. What films/TV programmes/Radio programmes have you seen/listened to this week?
   - ____________________
   - ____________________
   - ____________________
   - ____________________
5. What did you think of it? ____________________
6. Did it help you with your English? ____________________
   - If yes, how? ____________________
   - If no, why not? ____________________
7. What did you read in English this week? ____________________
   - ____________________
   - ____________________
   - ____________________
8. What did you think of it? ____________________
9. Did it help you with your English? ____________________
   - If yes, why? ____________________
   - If no, why not? ____________________
10. Have you written anything in English this week?
    - What have you written? ____________________
11. Write down 10 new words in English you have learnt this week with their translation in your language.

| **Words—I have learnt** | **Translation in L1** |
|---|---|
| (a) ____________ | (a) ____________ |
| (b) ____________ | (b) ____________ |
| (c) ____________ | (c) ____________ |
| (d) ____________ | (d) ____________ |
| (e) ____________ | (e) ____________ |
| (f) ____________ | (f) ____________ |
| (g) ____________ | (g) ____________ |
| (h) ____________ | (h) ____________ |
| (i) ____________ | (i) ____________ |
| (j) ____________ | (j) ____________ |

Where did you learn these?
- In the class ____________________
- Out of the class (phrase specify) ____________________

12. General Progress:
    - What progress do you feel you have made in English this week? (Please tick the correct options.)

| | **a lot** | **quite a lot** | **a little** | **not at all** |
|---|---|---|---|---|
| **Speaking** | ______ | ______ | ______ | ______ |
| **Listening** | ______ | ______ | ______ | ______ |
| **Reading** | ______ | ______ | ______ | ______ |
| **Writing** | ______ | ______ | ______ | ______ |

13. What are you going to work on/try to improve next week?
    **Speaking** ______________________
    **Listening** ______________________
    **Reading** ______________________
    **Writing** ______________________
14. How are you going to do this? ______________________
    ______________________
    ______________________
15. Now rate your progress for this week on your own personal scale from 1-10
    (1 = lowest   10 = highest)

    1   2   3   4   5   6   7   8   9   10

The advance of this approach is that teachers benefit from it. By looking at their progress record they can focus on areas they are weak in. Teachers can utilize the information and play-plan programmes accordingly.

Short questionnaires on particular areas of learning can give essential feedback to the teachers on various aspects of teaching—such as strategies, use of audio/visuals, educational tours, and so on.

A questionnaire on the classroom activities can be as follows:

1. Did you find the lesson on ________ interesting?
2. Would you like more lessons on the same pattern?
3. What did you learn from the lesson?
4. Who spoke more—you or the teacher?
5. Would you like some homework set on the lesson?

Such short questionnaires are easy to be introduced in the class and the feedback allows the teacher to manipulate materials to suit particular learning events.

Diaries written by learners can also provide some insight to the teacher only if she/he regularly checks the learners' diaries.

Finally, tests too evaluate learner progress and enable the teacher to categorize learners as high achievers, medium achievers and low achievers. A placement test will put learners in a class at an appropriate level, a screening or selection test will help the teacher to decide on which chosen few can opt for a particular course; an achievement in the attainment test will assist the teacher to monitor the learner progress and make suitable adjustments in her/his teaching scenario.

## Fixing Criteria for an Effective Questionnaire

Let us consider the following criteria before drafting an effective questionnaire:

1. **Aim:** The aim of the questionnaire should be as clear as possible, for example, ask yourself/yourselves which precise question(s) you wish to answer with it. Plan carefully, ask your trainer for advice. Remember small is beautiful.
2. **Ethics:** Explain the purpose of the questionnaire—you can also do this briefly at the beginning of the questionnaire and what will you do with the results. Ask the learners to respond frankly, if you think they will not respond frankly, if you think they will not respond in the said way, make the questionnaire anonymous. At the end of the questionnaire, thank the respondents for co-operating and tell them that a feedback concerning the results of the questionnaire will be available if they are interested.

3. **Length:** The questionnaire should be short and easy to answer (one or two pages).
4. **Layout:** The layout—how the text is arranged on the page should be as neat, professional and clear as possible (word process the text if possible and have plenty of spaces).
5. **Language:** Consider carefully which language to use for the instructions/questions: the respondents' mother tongue or English if you think they will read and comprehend it satisfactorily. The words you use should be clear and unambiguous.
6. **Response:** The response methods of how the learners show their opinion—e.g., by a non-linguistic response such as a tick or circling an answer—should be very clear. Give an example of the appropriate response. Such non-linguistic responses are easier than using the so-called structured questions with statements requiring a yes/no response. Especially recommended for young children are 'happy faces such as ☺☺' or use 'open questions'. For example, 'which song did you like best? Why?' We need to vary the question types in order to avoid tedium, but not too much, as this might cause the respondents too much difficulty.
7. **Order:** Give the respondents an easy start to the questionnaire, arousing their interest with questions eliciting personal information (date, class, age, etc.); use open questions after structured ones.
8. **Pilot:** Try out the questionnaire on somebody else before you use it. Perhaps, a colleague could help in this respect, as she or he may be able to identify difficulties you were unaware of; modify the questionnaire accordingly. May be try the questionnaire with learners who are not in the class you wish to investigate.
9. **Reporting:** The results should be easy to analyze, collate and report (e.g., visually with bar graphs, etc.). Will you present the results orally or use a poster? Plan this carefully.

## Fixing Criteria and Steps for English Language Testing

English language has no content like mathematics, history or science. It is more like musical performance and sports. Classifying language is, therefore, not easy.

Why do we need language tests?

English language tests are needed:

- to measure language proficiency irrespective of the courses the candidates may have followed;
- to discover how far students have achieved the objectives of a course of study;
- to diagnose students' strengths and weaknesses, to identify what they know and what they do not (feedback);
- to select students for promotion to more advanced studies and institutions to evaluate materials and methods.

### Test Types

As tests are used for gaining information, different kinds of tests are constructed to elicit different kinds of information like the proficiency tests, achievement/progress tests, diagnostic tests, placement tests, parallel tests, equivalent tests and specific purpose tests. The approaches to testing can be various too. Testing can be direct versus indirect testing, discrete point versus integrative testing, non-reference versus criterion-referenced testing, objective versus subjective testing and communicative language testing. What the test writer must keep in mind is that whatever test she/he is writing should be valid and reliable. A valid test is one that, in fact, measures what it claims to be measuring. For example, a listening test with written multiple-choice options may not be valid as the printed choices are so difficult to read that the exam actually measures the reading comprehension as much as it does the listening comprehension.

A reliable test is one that produces essentially the same results consistently on different occasions when the conditions of the test remain the same.

## Planning the Test: Let Us Now Consider the Steps of English Language Test

While planning the tests, one has to be clear about:

(1) What kind of test it has to be— Proficiency achievement, diagnostic placement or what?
(2) What skills are to be tested? What sub-skills are to be tested?
(3) How long should the test last?
(4) Which type of marking—objective or subjective—should be adopted? Should examiners be provided with the scoring keys?
(5) Who are going to write the tests? Have they been given the test specifications?
(6) Should the examiners and administrators be trained?
(7) How costly would the tests be?
(8) Will moderators be necessary?
(9) Which press/printers should be entrusted with the printing of the test papers?
(10) How many tape recorders/cassette players/CD players and cassette/CDs would be needed?

As many of the principles and procedures involved in language test construction derive from psychological testing, one might find helpful the four stages of psychological test construction as described by Anstey (1966). These may be applied to language tests too.

1. Plan the content and general layout of the test, decide on the type of text item, the length and time limit for the test in its final form, the instructions to be given and the method of scoring. This is the **planning** stage.
2. Devise at least three times as many items as will eventually be needed (more if two parallel versions are required) and try the rough draft on a small group of interested people in order to obtain introspections on the general impact of the test, and identify items which are palpably unsatisfactory. This is the **pre-pilot** stage.
3. A try-out preferably two or more try-outs of successive drafts, on a sample of the same kind of people on whom the test is to be used, in order to check test, administration and provide material for thorough item analysis and revision of the draft test. This may be called the **pilot** stage.
4. A try-out of the test is suggested in its final form in order to obtain evidence as to its practical usefulness on validity and to obtain 'norms'. This is the means of assessing the significance of scores in the test. This is the final **validation** stage.

Stages 2, 3, 4 are partly procedural and partly dependent on the success of stage 1, as this stage involves professional language knowledge of the test construction.

## Preparation for the Test

After determining what kind of test it is to be and for what purpose, the tester will write the first draft according to the test specification. (See the two examples given in testing for language teachers by A. Hughes.) The draft must have the same pattern as that of the final test—format, content, timing, criteria level of performance and scoring procedure. (Sample papers should be available to candidates who are going to take the test.) For example, if reading comprehension is being tested then the sample papers can be of various kinds—multiple-choice, matching, information transfer, ordering/sequencing, editing, gap filling, close procedure and short answers.

But before the exercises/test items can be framed, the tester must find appropriate texts. Not all texts lend themselves to item development. So, test writers should devote time searching for texts that have promise and build up their own 'bank' of texts for future use.

When writing the draft, the tester must remember not to allow candidates too much freedom in answering the questions they have chosen. Instead of setting a question like write an essay on friendship, it can be rewritten thus 'What does friendship mean? Why do we need it? What roles do your friends play in your life? Explain who is considered man's best friend and why.' The break-up will elicit better performance.

Items should always be written with clear meaning. After having drafted them subject them to the scrutiny of colleagues for alternative interpretations. Pre-test the items on a group of students if possible. This will cut down problems before the test is finally administered. All instructions should be clear and explicit, leaving no scope for misinterpretation. Colleagues too can help to weed out instructions that are unclear.

Use items that permit scoring which is as objective as possible. Multiple-choice or open-ended items can be of help.

Provide a detailed scoring, marking and rating scale key. This would take care of acceptable answers and partially correct responses. But difficulties may still persist. Examiners may have to use their discretion in assigning points in such cases.

## Let Us Consult an Expert

*Dr S.K. Dey*
*Counselling Professor*
*NSOU*

**(a) Need for Making Tests Criterion-Referenced**

If test specifications make clear just what candidates have to be able to do and with what degree of success, then students will have a clear picture of what they have to achieve. What is more, they know that if they do perform the tasks at the criteria level, then they will be successful on the test, regardless of how other students perform. Both these things will help to motivate students. Where testing is not criterion-referenced, it becomes easy for teachers and students to assume that a certain (perhaps very high) percentage of candidates will pass, almost regardless of the absolute standard that they reach.

The possibility exists of having a series of criterion-referenced tests, each representing a different level of achievement or proficiency. The tests are constructed such that a 'pass' is obtained only by completing the great majority of the test tasks successfully. Students take only the test (or tests) in which they are expected to be successful. As a result, they are spared the dispiriting, demotivating experience of taking a test which they can, for example, respond correctly to fewer than half of the items (and yet be given a pass). This type of testing, I believe, should encourage positive attitudes towards language learning.

**(b) Need for Making Tests Direct**

Direct testing implies the testing of performance, skills, with texts and tasks as authentic as possible. If we test directly the skills that we are interested in fostering, then practice for the test represents practice in those skills. If we want people to learn to write compositions, we should get them to write compositions in the test. If the course objective is that students should be able to read scientific article then we should get them to do that in the test. Immediately, we begin to test indirectly, we are removing an incentive for students to practice in the way that we want them to.

All scripts should be marked at least by two independent examiners, each recording marks on separate sheets. A third examiner then compares the marks to investigate discrepancies. An adequate number of examiners will, therefore, have to be trained.

Training of examiners is a crucial component of any testing programme. If candidates do not have faith in the marks given to them by the examiners, the validity and reliability of the programme will be open to questions. There are types of marking: objective and subjective. Objective type marking is used for multiple-choice, true/false, error recognition and other item types where the candidate is required to produce a response which can be marked either correct or incorrect. An answer key or mark scheme can make things easier for the marker though she/he might have to use her/his discretion how and when (often the marking of tests which have key is mechanical and can be carried out by non-examiners or computers). As the item writers cannot see all of the responses that candidates may come up with, a record should be kept by examiners of the unpredicted answers during the try-out or pre-test. The training programme for examiners should give these scorers time to analyze all items carefully, write down their own responses as if they were candidates and to go through a large number of sample scripts to see if any new and acceptable responses occur that should be added to the mark scheme/key. The goal of training is to expand the mark scheme and allow examiners to reach decisions with confidence facing the unexpected.

## Fixing Marks Scheme

Subjective marking is usually used for marking tests of writing or speaking. This is more complicated than the objective marking where the correct-incorrect decision is made by the examiner. The examiner here has to judge to assess how a candidate will complete a given task, and for this purpose they need a rating scale. The rating scale may consist of numbers, letters or other labels (e.g., good, very good) accompanied by statements describing the behaviour expected. These statements are called 'descriptors'. The Business English Certificates (BEC) and International English Language Testing System (IELTS) have these descriptors.

There are two types of scales—holistic and analytic. Examiners will have to be trained to use these scales effectively.

**A. Sample Holistic Scale**

| Marks | Grade | Criteria |
|---|---|---|
| 18–20 | Excellent | Natural English with minimal errors and complete realization of the task set. |
| 16–17 | Very good | More than a collection of simple sentences with good vocabulary and structures. Some non-basic errors. |
| 12–15 | Good | Simple but accurate realization of the task set with sufficient naturalness of English and not many errors. |
| 8–11 | Pass | Reasonably correct but awkward and non-communicating or fair and natural treatment of subject with some serious errors. |
| 6–7 | Weak | Original vocabulary and grammar both inadequate for the subject. |
| 0–4 | Very poor | Incoherent. Errors/Construction shows lack of basic knowledge of English. |

(Adapted from UCLES International Examinations in English as a Foreign Language General Handbook, 1987)

B. **Sample Analytic Scale**

**Relevance and Adequacy of Content:**

0. The answer bears almost no relation to the task set. Totally inadequate answer;
1. Answer of limited relevance to the task set. Possibly major gaps in treatment of topic and/or pointless repetition;
2. For the most part answers the task set, though there may be some gaps or redundant information;
3. Relevant and adequate answer to the task set.

**Compositional Organization:**

0. No apparent organization of content;
1. Very little organization of content. Underlying structures not sufficiently apparent;
2. Some organizational skills in evidence but adequately controlled;
3. Overall shape and internal pattern/clear. Organizational skills—adequately controlled.

**Cohesion:**

0. Cohesion almost totally absent. Writing is so fragmentary that comprehension of the intended communication is virtually impossible;
1. Unsatisfactory cohesion may cause difficulty in comprehension of most of the intended communication;
2. For the most part satisfactory cohesion though occasional deficiencies may mean that certain parts of the communication are not always effective;
3. Almost no inadequacies in vocabulary for the task. Only rare inappropriacies and/or circumlocution.

**Adequacy of Vocabulary for Purpose:**

0. Vocabulary inadequate even for the most basic parts of the intended communication;
1. Frequent inadequacies in vocabulary for the task. Perhaps some lexical inappropriacies and/or repetitions;
2. Some inadequacies in vocabulary for the task. Perhaps some lexical inappropriacies and/or circumlocution;
3. Almost no inadequacies in vocabulary for the task. Only rare inappropriacies and/or circumlocution.

**Grammar:**

0. Almost all grammatical pattern inaccurate;
1. Frequent grammatical inaccuracies;
2. Some grammatical inaccuracies;
3. Almost no grammatical inaccuracies.

**Mechanical Accuracy I (Pronunciation):**

0. Ignorance of conventions of punctuation;
1. Low standard of accuracy of punctuation;
2. Some inaccuracies of punctuation;
3. Almost no inaccuracies of punctuation.

**Mechanical Accuracy II (Spelling):**

0. Almost all spelling inaccurate;
1. Low standard of accuracy in spelling;
2. Some inaccuracies in spelling;
3. Almost no inaccuracies in spelling.

[Adapted from: 'Test of English for Educational Purposes', Associated Examining Board, UK 1984]

## Selecting Examiners

Selection of examiners of written answer scripts is extremely vital. The Board/University will have to select trained examiners of writing to maintain the standards. So provisions will have to be made for examination committees and standardization meetings. The exam committee with the chief examiner/head examiner and a select group of examiners will mark papers keeping in mind the rating scheme. The scripts should be chosen randomly and reasons should be offered for the awards given. The standardization meeting will ensure that other examiners follow the procedures laid down by the examination committee. All this, of course, after the test is administered. What is crucial in the preparatory stage is the forming of examination committees and planning of standardization meetings.

In this context, one has to keep in mind that for better and impartial judgement, candidates should be identified by number and not name.

After the draft is modified by colleagues it should be sent to the moderating committee for endorsement. The next stage is to pre-test the draft paper on a select group of candidates to find out whether it tests what it is supposed to test.

If the tryout on pre-test is satisfactory, the draft of the manuscript can be sent to a reliable printer and the final proof will have to be approved before a print order can be issued.

For the listening component of the test, an arrangement will have to be made for recording. How and where will it be done will need prior thinking. This recording can be entrusted to professionals who have expertise in the field. The quality of the tape/cassette/CD and clarity of sound must be ensured. This can be effectively done by pre-testing the listening component also on a group of candidates to note their reaction.

For tests of speaking, both the interlocutors and the examiners need to go through live performances before they can conduct 'real' or final interviews. Live performances mean pre-testing. Examiners (persons who observe the candidates being interviewed) and interlocutors (persons who interact with the candidates using the cue cards) must be trained in paper management, the use of cue cards, time management as well as how to give instructions and bring out the best in the candidates. Even administrators need training. All these will have to be prepared before tests can be administered.

### Let Us Do and Learn

- What is teacher-based evaluation?
- Is traditional written examination of different Boards and Councils a teacher-based evaluation? Give reasons for your answer.

# Test Administration

As earlier stated, like examiners and interlocutors, administrators also need training. Unless there is good administration the test may not be valid and reliable. A test must be practicable and straightforward to administer. A tryout or pilot administration of a test can take care of many of the lapses that otherwise might have occurred.

## Materials and Equipment

1. Organize and keep ready question papers, answer sheets and test booklets.
2. Number all test materials consecutively so as to provide greater security.
3. Check that all equipment (tape recorders, cassette, CD players, etc.) is in good working condition.

## Invigilators

4. Detailed instructions should be prepared for invigilators as well as examiners of speaking tests.

## Candidates

5. All candidates should be issued admit cards and instructed to arrive well before the starting time of the test. They should also know what they can carry with them inside the hall, and what they must do if they turn up late or have some emergencies.

## Centres

6. Centres where the tests can be held should be chosen well ahead of the commencing date of the test or exam. Inspection of these premises will have to be conducted to find out whether the rooms are suitable, whether tables and chairs can be arranged with sufficient space between candidates to prevent copying, whether lighting arrangement is adequate and what is the scope of alternative arrangement in case of electricity failure. Ideally, one should have air-conditioned rooms for examinations, but taking into consideration the state of affairs that exist in our country, the least that one can do is to ensure that fans work. Another alternative would be to hold the tests when days are cooler.

## Other Important Concerns

7. The identity of candidates should be checked with the help of admit cards.
8. The invigilators should give clear instructions to candidates about what they are required to do. These should include information on how to get the attention of the invigilator, if necessary, and what they should do if they finish earlier than others. They should also be warned about the consequences that they may have to face in case of irregular behaviour.
9. All test materials should be distributed to candidates by the invigilators before the test begins and collected by them after the test ends. A record should be kept of these.
10. The test should start on time and end on time. 'Pens down' should mean pens down. A wall clock in a strategic place will help the candidates to time themselves.
11. Once the test is in progress, invigilators should unobtrusively monitor the behaviour of the candidates and deal with any irregularities as specified in their instructions.
12. Before the listening test commences the examiner should once more check the microphones, the tape recorders/cassette/CD players and the acoustic of the hall. Emergency measures should be kept in mind in case of electricity failure. Better still will be the use of batteries, so provisions for such items need to be kept in mind. Examiners should learn how to set up equipment, when and how it is to be used and what to do in case of a malfunction. They should also find out whether the test is audible to all candidates in the hall.
13. The administrator's role is particularly important in tests of speaking. They should have clear written instructions telling them what to do and when to do it. Brand copies of task sheets, photos,

prompts, etc., should be made available to the examiners and interlocutors. The administrators should also see that the rooms are ready for interviews and that all materials, furniture and equipment are in place. Special care should be taken about the sitting arrangements for the examiner, the interlocutor and the candidates where two/three are interviewed together. In case of a single examiner interviewing a single candidate, the sitting arrangement would need to be modified. The table between the examiner/interviewer and the candidate must be wide enough to accommodate the audio-recorder and the file of prompts and cue cards.

14. Administrators have another important task-creation of congenial atmosphere for candidates of the speaking test. They have to be told to come at least half an hour earlier than their allotted time of interview to fill in forms and relax. The waiting room should be large and comfortable. If possible ushers may be appointed for getting candidates into and out of the testing room on time, and for making sure that candidates who have already been assessed do not communicate with those who are waiting for their turn.

## Following American Experiment with ELPT and IPT

Gary Buck in his article 'New Developments in U.S. K-12 Testing' discussed the new thinking taking place in the United States. In 2001, the US Congress passed a new law—**No Child Left Behind**—which profoundly affected American education. The main intent of this legislation is accountability that the student's progress must be measured by state and local education authorities. Additional testing will be a form of this accountability. Test scores must show annual and better proficiency level of all students in subjects, such as mathematics, science and language. States must set achievement objectives for second language (L2) learners and test them frequently to find out whether the goals are being met. The legislation contains provisions for drastic penalties against schools not meeting their goals.

Traditional language tests placed L2 learners in categories like non-English user, a limited English user or a competent English user. Such tests did not show small annual improvements. Moreover, these tests measured the general social language rather than Academic English, so new tests were called for.

Ballard and Tighe Publishers, an educational publishing company based in South California is developing a new test called 'English Language Proficiency Test' (ELPT). The IPT (Idea Proficiency Test) is to meet the requirements of 'No Child Left Behind'. The new test will be based on an analysis of the language skills students need to function in mainstream classrooms at each grade level.

The IPT is not a test, but rather a testing system. The IPT will:

- be based on scientific research into what language learners actually need to be able to do to function successfully in mainstream classes.
- be criterion-referenced.
- assess both social and academic language.
- be based on state and national standards and be customized to meet individual state standards.
- provide separate scores and designations for speaking, listening, reading, writing and comprehension.
- report scores on one standardized scale, running from kindergarten to grade 12.
- provide empirically derived annual achievement objectives for all grades, and report that achievement on the standard scale.
- be capable of making placement decisions as well as providing diagnostic information.
- provide aggregated and disaggregated data for all groups of test takers specified in the legislation.
- be quick and easy to administer and provide online rapid results.

(Adapted from Gary Buck's famous article 'New Developments in U.S. K-12 Testing')

## Let Us Do and Learn

- Is testing needful at all?
- What is the basic difference between ELPT and IPT?
- A student of class VIII reading under Madhya Pradesh Secondary Board is to be tested annually? What type of test would you prefer for her/him? Give reasons for your answer.

# Testing Procedures of English as Second Language

## Teaching and Testing

Backwash is the effect that tests have on learning and teaching. There has been evidence of a much interest in backwash than was previously the case, and its importance in language testing is generally accepted. There has been research, there have been calls for an explicit model of backwash which can be tested empirically, and an entire issue of language testing has been devoted to the topic. Backwash is now seen as a part of the impact a test may have on learners and teachers, on educational systems in general and on the society at large.

It is certain that over the next few years further research into backwash will result in a better understanding of the processes involved and how different variables contribute to its effect in different situations.

**Let us consider the procedures of testing in English as a Second Language (ESL) scenario with the help of the following guidelines:**

1. Make a full and clear statement of the testing 'problem';
2. Write complete specifications for the test;
3. Write and moderate items;
4. Try the test items informally on native speakers and reject or modify the problematic ones as necessary;
5. Try the test on a group of non-native speakers similar to those for whom the test is intended;
6. Analyze the results of the trial and make any necessary changes;
7. Calibrate scales;
8. Validate the test items;
9. Write handbooks for test takers, test users and staff;
10. Train any necessary staff (interviewers, raters, etc.).

Before looking more closely at the set of procedures, it is worth saying that test development is best thought of as a task to be carried out by a team. It is very difficult for an individual to develop a test, if only because of the need to look objectively at what is being proposed at each stage of development.

This difficulty can be seen most clearly at the stage of item writing, when faults in an item which are obvious to others are often invisible to the person who wrote the item. Writing items is a creative process, and we tend to think of our items as minor works of art or even it sometimes seems to be our babies. We do not find it easy to admit that our baby is not as beautiful as we had thought.

One of the qualities to be looked for in item writers, therefore, is a willingness to accept justified criticism of the items they have written. Other desirable qualities not only for item writers, but also for test developers in general are: native or near-native command of the language, intelligence and imagination to create contexts in items and to foresee possible misinterpretations.

1. **Problem Fixing**
   It is needless to state that the first essential step in testing is to make one perfectly clear about one's purpose.

The following questions, the significance of which should be clear from previous sections, have to be answered:

(i) What kind of test is it to be? Achievement test (final or progress) or proficiency test or diagnostic test or placement test?
(ii) What is its precise purpose?
(iii) What abilities are to be tested?
(iv) What would be the scope of the test results?
(v) How accurate must the results be?
(vi) How far backwash is important?
(vii) What constraints are set by unavailability of expertise, facilities, time (for construction, administration and scoring)?

Once the problem is clear, steps can be taken to solve it. In addition, however, efforts should be made to gather information on tests that have been designed for similar situations. If possible, samples of such tests should be obtained. There is nothing dishonourable in doing this; it is what professional testing bodies do when they are planning a test of a new kind.

**Expert Corner**

**Arthur Hughes**

- A test becomes valid not only because of the scoring or rating of the test performance but also because the means of instruction is valid.

2. **Writing Specifications for the Test**

A set of specifications for the test must be written at the outset.

This will include information on: content, test structure, timing, medium/channel, techniques to be used, critical levels of performance and scoring procedures.

(*i*) ***Content***

This refers not to the content of a single, particular version of a test but to the entire potential content of any number of versions. Samples of this content will appear in individual versions of the test.

The fuller the information on content the less arbitrary should be the subsequent decisions as to what to include in the writing of any version of the test. There is a danger, however, that in the desire to be highly specific, we may go beyond our current understanding of what the components of language ability are and what their relationship is between each other. For instance, while we may believe that many sub-skills contribute to the ability to read lengthy prose passages with full understanding, it seems hardly possible in our present state of knowledge to name them all or to assess their individual contributions to the more general ability. We cannot be sure that the sum of the parts that we test will amount to the whole in which we are generally most directly interested. At the same time, however teaching practice often assumes some such knowledge, with one sub-skill being taught at a time. It seems to me that the safest procedure is to include in the content specifications only those elements whose contribution is fairly well-established.

The way in which content is described will vary with its nature. The content of a grammar test, for example, may simply list all the relevant structures. The content of a language skill test, on the other hand, may be specified along a number of dimensions. The following provides a possible framework for doing this. It is not meant to be perspective; readers may wish to describe test content differently. The important thing is that content should be as fully specified as possible according to the following criteria:

- **Operations:** The candidates have to be able to carry out the tasks. A reading test might include, for example, scanning the text to locate information or to guess meanings of unknown words from the context.
- **Types of text:** A writing test might include letters and academic essays up to three pages in length.
- **Addresses of texts:** This refers to the kinds of people that the candidate is expected to be able to write or speak to (for example, native speakers of the same age and status) or the people for whom reading and listening materials are primarily intended (for example, native speakers or university students).
- **Length of text(s):** For a reading test, the length of the written passages on which items are set is pre-determined. For a listening test, it could be the length of the spoken texts.
- **Topics:** Topics may be specified quite loosely and selected according to the suitability of the candidate and the type of test.
- **Readability:** Reading passages may be specified as being within a certain range of readability.
- **Structural range:**
  Either: (a) A list of structures which may occur in texts.
  or (b) A list of structures which should be excluded.
  or (c) A general indication of range of structures (e.g., in terms of frequency of occurrence in the language).
- **Vocabulary range:** This may be loosely or closely specified.
- **Direct, Accent, Style, etc.:** This may refer to the dialects and accents that test takers are meant to understand or those in which they are expected to write or speak. Style may be formal, informal and conversational.

**(*ii*)** ***Structure, time, medium, channel and technique***

The following should be specified:

- **Number of items** (in total and in the various sections)
- **Number of passages** (and number of items associated with each)
- **Medium/channel** (paper and pencil, tape, computer, face-to-face, telephone, etc.)
- **Timing** (for each section and for the entire test)
- **Techniques** What techniques will be used 'to measure what skills or sub-skills'?

**(*iii*)** ***Criteria levels of performance***

The required level(s) of performance for (different levels of) success should be specified. This may involve a simple statement to the effect that, to demonstrate 'mastery', 80 per cent of the items must be responded to correctly.

For speaking or writing, however, one can expect a description of the criteria level (as shown later) to be much more complex.

- **Accuracy:** Pronunciation must be clearly intelligible even if still obviously influenced by L1. Grammatical/lexical accuracy is generally high although some errors that do not destroy communication are acceptable.

- **Appropriacy:** The use of language must be generally appropriate to function. The overall intention of the speaker must be generally clear.
- **Range:** A fair range of language must be available to the candidates, only in complex utterances there is a need to search for words.
- **Flexibility:** There must be some evidence of flexibility to initiate and concede conversation and to adapt to new topics or changes of direction.
- **Size:** Students must be capable to respond in short-form answers when they are appropriate.
- **Interlocutor:** The interlocutor should expand utterances with occasional prompt from the text or settings.

**(iv)** ***Marking procedures***

These are always important, but particularly so when scoring will be subjective. The test developers should be clear as to how they will achieve high reliability and validity in scoring. Which rating scale will be used? How many people will rate each piece of work? What happens if two or more ratings disagree about a piece of work?

**3. Writing and Moderating Question Items**

Once the specifications are in place, the writing of items can begin according to the following criteria:

**(i)** ***Sampling***

It is most unlikely that everything found under the heading of 'content' in the specifications can be covered by the items in any one version of the test. For content validity and for beneficial backwash, the important thing is to choose widely from the whole content.

One should not concentrate on those elements known to be easy to test. Succeeding versions of the test should also sample widely and unpredictably, although one will always wish to include elements that are particularly important.

**(ii)** ***Writing question items***

Items should always be written with the specifications in mind. It is no use writing 'good' items if they are not consistent with the specifications. As one writes an item, it is essential to try to look at it through the eyes of test takers and imagine how they might misinterpret the item (in which case it will need to be rewritten). Even if there is no possibility of misinterpretation, test takers (especially the intelligent ones) may find responses that are different from, but equally valid as, the one intended. Mention of the intended response is a reminder that the key to an item (i.e., 1 statement of the correct response or responses) is an integral part of the item. An item without a key is incomplete.

The writing of successful items in its broadest sense, including, for example, the setting of writing tasks, is extremely difficult. No one can consistently produce perfect items. Some items will have to be rejected, others improved.

**(iii)** ***Moderating question items***

Moderation is the scrutiny of proposed items by (ideally) at least two colleagues, neither of whom is the author of the items being examined. Their task is to try to find weakness in the items and, where possible, remedy them. Where successful modification is not possible, they must reject the item. It is to be hoped, of course, that they will not find fault with most of the items that they moderate and that they can therefore accept them. A checklist of the kind is useful for moderators.

**4. Informal Trial of Test Items on Native Speakers and Moderation**

Items which have been through the process of moderation should be presented in the form of a test (or tests) to a number of native speakers twenty or more, if possible. There is no need to do this formally; the test can be taken by the participants in their own time.

The **native speakers** should be similar to the people for whom the test has been developed in terms of age, education, and general background. There is no need for them to be specialists in language or testing. It is preferable that they should not be experts, since 'experts' are unlikely to behave in the way of native test takers.

Items that prove difficult for the native speakers almost certainly need revision or replacement. So do items where unexpected or inappropriate responses are provided. Of course, people taking a test in their own language will have lapses of attention. Where these can be recognized, the responses should not count against the item.

**Let us consider the following questionnaire used for moderating a question paper on the basis of the trial.**

**Questionnaire for Moderation**

| Questions | Yes | No |
|---|---|---|
| 1. Is the English grammatically correct? | | |
| 2. Is the English natural and acceptable? | | |
| 3. Is the English in accordance with the specifications? | | |
| 4. Does the item test what it is supposed to test, as specified? | | |
| 5. The correct response cannot be obtained without the appropriate knowledge of grammar (other than by random guessing). | | |
| 6. Is the item economical? | | |
| 7. (a) Multiple-Choice Questions: Is there possibly just one correct answer? | | |
| (b) Are all the other possibly distinct answers likely to distract? | | |
| 8. Gap filling: Is there possibly just one correct answer? | | |
| 9. Are all the other possibly distinct answers likely to distract? | | |
| 10. Is the key complete and correct? | | |

5. **Trialing of the Test on a Group of Non-Native Speakers Similar to Those for Whom the Test Is Intended**
   Those items that have survived moderation and informal trial on native speakers should be put together into a test, which is then administered under test conditions to a group similar to that for which the test is intended. Problems in administration and scoring are noted. It has to be accepted that for a number of reasons, trial of this kind is often not feasible. In some situations, a group for trial may simply not be available. In other situations, a suitable group exists. It may be thought that the security of the test might be put at risk. It is often the case, therefore, that the faults in a test are discovered only after it has been administered to the target group. Unless it is intended that no part of the test should be used again, it is worthwhile noting problems that become apparent during administration and scoring, and afterwards carrying out a statistical analysis of the kind.
6. **Analysis of Results of Trial and Needful Amendments**
   There are two kinds of analysis that should be carried out. The first is statistical. This will reveal qualities, such as reliability of the test as a whole and of individual items (for example, how difficult they are, how well they discriminate between stronger and weaker candidates).

   The second kind of analysis is qualitative. Responses should be examined in order to discover misinterpretation, unanticipated but possibly correct responses, and any other indicators of faulty items. Items that the analysis shows to be faulty should be modified or dropped from the test. Assuming that more items have been put on trial than are needed for the final test, a final selection can be made, basing decisions on the results of the analyses.

7. **Calibration of Scales**
Where rating scales are going to be used for oral testing of writing, these should be calibrated. Essentially, this means collecting samples of performance (for example, pieces of writing) which cover the full range of the scales. A team of 'experts' then looks at these samples and assigns each of them to a point on the relevant scale. The assigned samples provide reference points for all future uses of the scale, as well as for being necessary training materials.
8. **Validation of Test**
The final version of the test can be validated. For a high stake or published test, this should be regarded as essential. For relatively low stakes tests that are to be used within an institution, this may not be thought necessary, although where the test is likely to be used many times over a period of time, informal small-scale validation is still desirable.
9. **Writing Handbooks for Test Takers, Test Users and Staff**
Handbooks (each with rather different content, depending on the audience) may be expected to contain the following:
    - the rationale for the test;
    - an account of how the test was developed and validated;
    - a description of the test (which may include a version of specifications);
    - sample items (or a complete sample test);
    - advice on preparing for taking the test;
    - an explanation of how test scores are to be interpreted;
    - training materials (for interviewers, raters);
    - details of test administration.
10. **Training of Necessary Staff (Examiners, Interviewers and Raters)**

# Applying Test Techniques in Framing Test Questions

## What Are Test Techniques?

Quite simply test techniques are means of eliciting behaviour from candidates that will tell us about their language abilities. What we need are techniques that will elicit behaviour which is a reliable and valid indicator of the ability in which we are interested.

(i) **Multiple-choice Question Items**
Multiple-choice items take many forms, but their basic structure is as follows:

*There is a stem:*

Enid has been here half an hour.

*and a number of options one of which is correct, the others being distracters:*

A. during B. for C. while D. since

It is the candidate's task to identify the correct or most appropriate option (in this case B). Perhaps, the most obvious advantage of providing multiple choices is that scoring can be perfectly reliable. Scoring should also be rapid and economical. A further considerable advantage is that, since in order to respond the candidate has only to make a mark on the paper, it is possible to include more items than would otherwise be possible in a given period of time. As we know already this is likely to make for greater test reliability. Finally, it allows the testing of receptive skills without requiring the test taker to produce written or spoken language.

The advantages of the multiple-choice technique were so highly regarded at one time that it almost seemed that it was the only way to test. While many laymen have always been skeptical of what should be achieved through multiple-choice testing, it is only fairly recently that the technique's limitations have been more generally recognized by professional testers. The difficulties with **multiple-choice questions** are as follows:

**(a) The technique tests only recognition and knowledge.**

**(b) Guessing may have a considerable but unknowable effect on the test scores.**

If multiple-choice type is to be used, an effort should be made to have at least four options (in order to reduce the effect of guessing). It is important that all of the distracters should be chosen by a significant number of test takers who do not have the ability of taking the test or knowledge that is being tested. If there are four options but only a very poor proportion of candidates choose one of the distracters, the item is effectively only a three-option item.

**(c) The technique severely restricts what can be achieved.**

**(d) It is very difficult to write successful items:**

A further problem with multiple choices is that, even where items are possible, good ones are extremely difficult to write. Professional test writers reckon to have to write many more multiple-choice items than they actually need.

**(e) Backwash may be harmful**

It should hardly be necessary to point out that where a test that is important to a student is multiple-choice in nature, there is a danger that practice for the test will have a harmful effect on the learning and teaching. Practice at multiple-choice items will not usually be the best way for students to improve or prove their command of language.

**(f) Cheating may be facilitated**

The fact that in a multiple-choice test the responses a, b, c, d are so simple makes them easy to communicate to other candidates non-verbally. Some defence against this is to have at least two versions of the test, the only difference between them being the order in which the options are presented.

All in all, the multiple-choice technique is best suited to relatively infrequent testing of large numbers of candidates. It is not to say that there should be no multiple-choice items in tests produced regularly within institutions. In setting a reading comprehension test, for example, there may be certain tasks, which lend themselves very readily to the multiple-choice format, with obvious distracters presenting themselves in the text. There are real-life tasks (say, a shop assistant identifying which one of four dresses a customer is describing!) which are essentially multiple choice. The simulation in a test of such a situation would seem to be perfectly appropriate. What the reader is being urged to avoid is the excessive, indiscriminate and potentially harmful use of the technique.

**(ii) Yes/No and True/False Type Question Items**

Items in which the test taker has merely to choose between yes and no, or between true and false, are effectively multiple-choice items with only two options. The obvious weakness of such items is that the test taker has a 50 per cent chance of choosing the correct response. In my view, there is no place for items of this kind in a formal test, although they may well have a use in assessment where the accuracy of the results is not critical. The true/false items are sometimes modified by requiring test takers to give a reason for their choice. However, this extra requirement is problematic; first, because it is adding what is a potentially difficult writing task when writing is not meant to be tested (validity problem), and second, because the responses are often difficult to score (reliability and validity problem).

**(iii) Short-Answer Type Question Items**

Items in which the test taker has to provide a short answer are common, particularly in listening and reading tests.

Examples: (*i*) What does 'it' refer to? (*ii*) Why did Hannibal enjoy eating brain so much?

**Advantages of Short-Answer Type Question Items over Multiple-Choice Question Items Are That:**

- guessing will (or should) contribute less to test scores;
- the technique is not restricted by the need for distracters (though there have to be potential alternative responses);
- cheating is likely to be more difficult;
- though great care must still be taken, items should be easier to write.

**Disadvantages Are That:**

- responses may take longer and so reduce the possible number of items;
- the test taker has to produce language in order to respond;
- scoring may be invalid or unreliable, if judgement is required;
- scoring may take longer.

The first two of these disadvantages may not be significant if the required response is really short (and at least the test takers do not have to ponder four options, three of which have been designed to distract them). The next two can be overcome by making the required response unique (i.e., there is only one possible answer) and could be found in the text (or to require very simple language). Looking at the earlier mentioned examples, without needing to see the text, we can see that the correct response to Item (i) should be unique and found in the text. The same could be true of Item (ii), Item (iii), however, may cause problems (which can be solved) by using gap filling later.

Short-answer questions have a role to play in serious language testing. Only when testing has to be carried out on a very large-scale would I think of dismissing short-answer questions as a possible technique because of the time taken to score. With the increased use of computers in testing (in TOEFL, for example), written responses can be scored reliably and quickly. Hence, there is no reason for short-answer items not to have a place in the testing programmes.

**(iv) Gap-filling Type Question Items**

Items in which test takers have to fill a gap with a word are also common. Gap filling does not always work well for grammar or vocabulary items where minor or subtle differences of meaning are concerned.

When the gap-filling technique is used, it is essential that the test taker be told very clearly and firmly that only one word can be put in each gap. They should also be told whether contractions, such as 'I'm', 'isn't', 'it's' are one word. (Counting contractions as one word is advisable, as it allows greater flexibility in item construction.)

Gap filling is a valuable technique. It has the advantage of the short-answer technique, but the greater control it exercises over the test takers means that it does not call for significant productive skills. There is no reason why the scoring of gap filling should not be highly reliable, provided that it is carried out with a carefully constructed key on which the scorers can rely completely (and not have to use their individual judgement).

## Developing New Test Items for Testing English Literature

The earlier discussion gives the writer clear messages about question types.

1. In a foreign language context, **test items need to be written to meet the student level, not the teacher's expectations.** This means that, where students are failing to meet standards in a test, the test items rather than the students need to be re-evaluated.
2. In practical terms, this means that **test items be guided or controlled,** rather than be left wholly open-ended. Compare, for example, the following two question types:
   (a) The Duke in *Measure for Measure* is nothing more than contriving, sermonizing waxwork (John Wain). Discuss.
   (b) Rank these statements about the Duke in *Measure for Measure*, with No. (*i*) being the statement you most agree with and No. (*vii*) being the statement you least agree with. Justify and explain your ranking order.
      (*i*) It is the Duke who initiates and controls the experiment that forms the action (F.R. Leavis)
      (*ii*) The distinguished monarch, who can learn the private affairs of his humblest subject, becomes a son of earthly Providence, combining omniscience and omnipotence (R.W. Chambers)
      (*iii*) The Duke is essentially a wise and noble man who has erred from an excess of goodwill (Elizabeth Pope)
      (*iv*) The Duke surely appears throughout—less in the guise of Providence than as an image of the comic dramatist himself, trying to impose the patterns of art upon a reality which resists such schematization (Anne Burton)
      (*v*) The Duke, for all this detachment, is not fully in charge of events (Derek Travers)
      (*vi*) Ridiculous (William Empson)
3. Test items should **require contact with actual text,** eliminating the possibility of dependence on prepared notes. For example, compare the following two question types:

**Text A**

*She dwelt, among th' un-trodden way?*
*Beside the springs of Dove,*
*A maid whom there wore none to praise*
*And very few to love.*
*A violet by a mossy stone*
*Half hidden from the Eye*
*Fair, as the star when only one is shining in the sky; She liv'd unknown,*
*and few could know*
*When Lucy ceased to be; But she is in her Grave, and Oh!*
*The difference to me.*

**Text** B

*She lived by the river Dove, in a quiet part where not many people walked.*
*Nobody praised her, and very few people loved her.*
*She was shy and simple. Nobody knew her, and not many people knew*
*when she died. Things aren't the same for me now she is dead.*

## Let Us Do and Learn

(a) Write on Wordsworth's use of imagery and metaphor in one of the 'Lucy' poems.
(b) Read the two texts mentioned earlier. Underline the words or phrases which are different.
(c) Why do you think the poet chose these words and phrases?

4. Test items need to give **abstract concepts a practical and concrete focus.** Compare the following two examples:
   (a) Outline the characteristics of the *bildungsroman* or a biographical novel. Illustrate your answer by reference to at least one *bildungsroman* you have read.
   (b) How would you evaluate the importance of each detail in the text, if you open a novel called:
      (*i*) *Murder at Mapplethorpe*
      (*ii*) *The Personal History of David Mapplethorpe*

   Read the text and account for your responses.
   The clock on the mantelpiece said ten thirty but someone had suggested that the clock was wrong. As the figure of the dead woman lay on the bed in the front room, a no less silent figure glided! Rapidly from the house. The only sounds to be heard were the ticking of the clock and the wailing of an infant.
5. **Linguistic support needs to be provided.** Sometimes linguistic difficulties may conflict with the literary skills to be tested. For example, in the 'Lucy' poems mentioned earlier, the following vocabulary items have been glossed for the students:
   - *dwell-live*
   - *springs-river*

   This allows the students to concentrate on other literacy and linguistic features, and makes the test a learning activity.
6. Test items should **require the application of skills and principles,** rather than 'display'. Compare the following question types:
   (a) Discuss the importance of a setting in *The Great Gatsby*. How does a setting contribute to the plot?
   (b) Read the final paragraph of *The Great Gatsby*. What predictions could you make about the plot, setting and characters of the novel, if this were the opening?

   How would these predictions differ from the actual novel?
7. Ideally, one test item should test one skill, or a cluster of skills. The two questions about *bildungsroman* as discussed earlier illustrate this point. The second question type allows students and examiner to focus on the skill of identifying genre, rather than on essay writing. It follows that the more global and open-ended a test item, the more demands are being made on 'hidden' skills which are difficult to quantify and measure.
8. Test items can encourage the learners to transfer skills from familiar texts to unfamiliar ones.

## Let Us Do and Learn

Respond to these statements about reading poetry by choosing from the following options:

A: I agree strongly
B: I agree in some situations, it depends
C: I can't decide
D: I disagree

Then justify your decision,

1. To understand a poem, you need to know about the life of the poet.
2. To understand a poem, you need to know about the literary traditions that influence it.
3. You can only understand the messages of the poem if you understand every word of it.

To appreciate a poem, you need to understand and apply terms, such as alliteration, assonance, metaphor, conceit.

**Now apply your choices and observations to the following poem. Are your decisions about reading poetry true of this poem? Discuss why or why not.**

**Keep off the Grass**
The grass is a green mat
trimmed with gladioli
red like flames in a furnace.
The park bench, hallowed,
holds the loiterer listening
to the chant of the fountain
showering holy water on a congregation
of pigeons.

**Keep off the Grass.**
**Dogs Not Under Leash Forbidden**
Then madam walks her Pekinese,
bathed and powered and perfumed.
He sniffs at the face of the 'keep off' sign
with a nose as cold as frozen fish
and salutes it with a hind paw
leaving it weeping in anger and shame.
(Mbuyiseni Oswald Mtshali. Born South Africa 1940)

**9.** Questions can encourage the examinees to identify and personalize with the students they meet.

## Let Us Do and Learn

(a) Read the following poem. Replace any words or phrases which are not true facts in your case.
(b) Rewrite these words so the poem describes a scene in your own country.
(c) Which version do you prefer? Why?

**Grandfather's Holiday**
Blue sky, paddy fields, grandchild's play,
Deep ponds, diving-stage, child's holiday;
Tree shade, barn corners, catch-me-if-you-dare,
Undergrowth, Parul-bushes, life without care.
Green paddy all a-quiver, hopeful as a child,
Child prancing, river dancing, waves running wild.

Autumn sailing in, now, steered by your play,
Bringing while siuli-flowers to grace your holiday.
Pleasure of the chilly air, tingling me at night.
Blown from the Himalayas, on the breeze of your delight.
Dawn in Asvin, flower-forcing roseate sun,
Dressed in the colours of a grandchild's fun.
(Rabindranath Tagore. Trans. William Radice)

**10. Strategies found to be motivating in the classroom can be translated into the test situation by:**
(*i*) eliminating the element of interaction (if necessary);
(*ii*) providing realistic time constraints;
(*iii*) ensuring the students have sufficient resources to complete the task without further guidance;
(*iv*) defining the required performance so that it can be objectively assessed.

Three examples follow: a traditional test question; a motivating classroom task; and a revised test question, based on the classroom task.

***Traditional Test Items***
Discuss the literary and stylistic features of the following extract from a D.H. Lawrence short story. To what extent does this extract represent characteristics that you feel to be typical of Lawrence?

***Classroom Activity***
Students work in groups of three.
Student A has an extract by Ernest Hemingway.
Student B has an extract by James Joyce.
Student C has an extract by D.H. Lawrence.

***Task-based Test***
Compare the three texts in your group. Decide which of the three is by D.H. Lawrence. Find at least five examples in the text to justify your choice. Then compare your choice with those of other groups.

***Revised Test Item***
Students are given all three tests. The tests are shortened to allow for a time constraint.

**Task**
Compare the three texts. Decide which of the three is by D.H. Lawrence. Find at least five examples in the text to justify your choice.

The problem solving is adaptable to the test context and is motivating for the examinee. Problem-solving tasks include identifying the author, matching texts, guessing the correct title, and identifying it and decoding unfamiliar words/phrases/concepts.

11. The final message to the test writer is the need for balance, in order to obtain a balanced profile of the student. Thus, a test may include a balance of controlled, guided and free test items; test items covering both discrete literary skills and global competence; and test items at all points along the continuum from receptive to productive skills.

## Task Type and Skill Test

Now, let us have a checklist of task types and relevant skills or aims that are involved.

| Task Types | Skills/Aims Involved |
|---|---|
| Compare a literary text/non-literary paraphrase. | The task focuses attention on 'literary' features: it provides a concrete context to demonstrate appreciation: language support is provided. |
| Rank a series of statements about a text and justify your choice. | The task gives the student autonomy to select her/his own arguments: it also provides guidance in formulating an argument. |
| Select a title for a text/respond to different titles. | The task gives the student an opportunity to demonstrate sensitively to genre in a problem-solving context. |
| Identify the 'odd one out' from a group of texts—by a different author/from a different work. | The task requires the student to identify the characteristics of a text through problem-solving: 'discriminatory' skills are thus applied rather than displayed. |
| Match texts beginnings and endings, character and setting. | The task is same as the previous task, a context is given for close analysis of style/content/context. |
| Deduce the meaning of culturally alien words/phrases in the text. | The task encourages the student to use learning strategies that have developed in the classroom. |
| Rewrite these phrases to make them culturally accessible. | The task encourages the students to identify and create texts of their own; focuses on cultural and social manifestation in language. |

## Knowing Test Rubric

Rubric is a formal and technical expression for instruction used in different test situations. Success and failure of a 'Test Item' depends on its rubric. Let us have a glimpse of a few rubrics.

Time: 3 hours

**Read in groups the extract from Athol Figaro's *My Children, My Africa.***

**Part 1: 1 and 1/2 hours**

Elect a director, co-director and stage manager.

Allocate roles to each member of the group.

Discuss your interpretation of the roles.
Plan your props and position on the 'stages'.
You have up to 1 and 1/2 hours to do this.

After 2 hours, you will be invited to present your extract to other members of the class.

**Part 2: 1 hour**

You will have 1 hour to read the extract from *Swami and his Friends* and answer 12 short questions about its language and content.
Spend about 5 minutes on each question.
After this part of the test, you will have a half-hour break.

**Part 3: 1/2 hour**

You will have 30 minutes to answer 6 questions.
You will answer 2 questions on each of the texts that you have prepared.
Spend about 5 minutes on each question.

### Visiting Expert Corner

**J.B. Heaton**
The third part of the test would involve response to prepared texts, and a range of tasks that draw more widely on both receptive and productive skills.

The test rubric makers clear the time constraints not only of the test as a whole, but of its parts.

## Sample Question Paper on Testing Reading Skills

**F.M.: 45** **Time Allowed: 90 Minutes**

**Read the following text and answer the questions that follow:**

Swami's father felt ashamed of himself. He was going to cross the street, plod through the sand and gaze into the Sarayu—for the body of his son! His son Swami, to be looked for in the Sarayu! It seemed to him a ridiculous thing to do. But what could he do? He dare not return home without some definite news of his son, good or bad. The house had worn a funeral appearance since nine o'clock. His wife and his old mother were more or less dazed and demented. She—his wife—had remained cheerful till the Taluk Office gong struck ten, when, her face turning white she had asked him to go and find out from Swami's friends and teachers what had happened to him. He did not know where Swami's headmaster lived. He had gone to the Board School and asked the watchman, who misdirected him and made him wander over half the town without purpose. He could not find Mani's house. He had gone to Ranji's house, but the house was dark, everybody had gone to bed, and he felt that it would be absurd to wake up the household of a stranger to ask if they had seen his son. From what he could get out of the servant sleeping in the veranda, he understood that Swami had not been seen in Rajam's house that evening. He had then vaguely wandered the streets. He was doing it to please his wife and mother. He had not shared in the least his wife's nervousness. He had felt all along the boy must have gone out somewhere and would return, and then he would treat him with some firmness and nip this tendency in the bud. He had spent nearly an hour thus and gone home. Even his mother had left her bed and was hopping agitatedly about the house, praying to the God of the Thirupathi Hills and promising him rich offerings if he should restore Swami to her, safe and sound. His wife stood like a stone image, looking down the street. The only tranquil being in the house was the youngest member of the family, whose soft breathings came from the cradle, defying the gloom and heaviness in the house.

## Section One

(Lines 1–5)

1. Underline the adjective which describes best the feelings of the father. 1 + 1 = 2

   unhappy angry nervous guilty amused

   Find a word or phrase in the text which means the same as the word you have underlined.
2. What do you think is the Sarayu? 1 + 2 = 3

   Tick the hex you think is correct.

   **a building**
   **a cinema**
   **a river**
   **a forest**

   Write down the words in the text which helped you make this decision.

(Lines 5–12)

3. Underline the adjective which best describes the feelings of his wife. 1 + 1 = 2

   hysterical angry surprised unhappy

   Find a word or phrase in the text which means the same as the word you have underlined.
4. Are these statements true or false? (use [3] for true and [5] for false statements) 5

   If the statement is false, write a correct statement underneath. One example has been done for you.

   ***True*** ***False***

   (a) The watchman directed the father to the headmaster's house. *The watchman gave the wrong directions. The father got lost.*
   (b) The house had been miserable all day.
   (c) Swami's mother became worried after ten o'clock.
   (d) The old grandmother remained cheerful.

(Lines 12–20)

5. The father visited several places. 4

   Tick [3] in the following places which he visited.

   the Board School
   Mani's house
   Rajam's house
   The house of strangers

### Let Us Do and Learn

Decide for which *age group* you would like to use this Sample Question Paper on Testing Reading Skill.

**6.** Which people did the father speak to? 5

the watchman
Rajam
strangers
the servant
Mani

(Lines 25–35)

**7.** Match the half sentence in column A with the correct half sentence in column B Draw arrows ↔ to show which parts match. 3

One example has been drawn for you.

| **Column A** | **Column B** |
|---|---|
| the father | just waits silently |
| Rajam's family | thinks there is no real problem |
| The old mother | thinks only the gods can help now |
| Swami's mother | has gone to sleep |

**8.** Complete the following sentences with one word only: 4

When Swami returns, the father plans to be ________________.
The only calm person in the house is the ________________.
Write down the words in the passage, which ________________.
How the father will behave when Swami ________________.

**9.** Write the name of the four characters in the story, at the point along this line that describes them best. 4

quite calm ———— a little worried ———— worried ———— very worried

## Section Two

**10.** Look at the adjectives you wrote down in Question 1. Does the father feel the same as you are feeling? Complete these sentences: 4

(a) Yes, we both feel ________________
(b) No, I would feel ________________ but the father felt ________________

**11.** What does each of the four characters do to solve the problem of Swami's disappearance? 4

Choose the correct word from the following list:

The father ________________
The mother ________________
The old woman ________________
The fourth person ________________

**List of words**

sheep prays waits gets angry goes searching

Which of these things would you do?

Complete the following sentence: 1

If my son/daughter/younger brother/sister disappeared, I would

______________________________________________

______________________________________________

12. Swami is in fact quite safe. The father finds him in the next part of the story. 4

What do you think the boy was doing?
Where do you think the boy was?
Spend 5 minutes writing down your ideas.

______________________________________________

______________________________________________

______________________________________________

### Let Us Do and Learn

Decide for which class you would like to use this Sample Question Paper on Testing Reading Skill.

## Testing Oral Skill: A Sample Project

**Class Level:** VIII (Age: 12–15 years)

### Introduction

Reference to W.B.B.S.E. (as envisaged by the recommendations of the Education Commission headed by Dr Ashok Mitra and the Govt. Order No.: 458 Edn(P) dated 30.05.1994) examination plan where 30 marks has been allocated for testing of oral skills. It is to be specified that out of 30 marks, 10 marks can be put aside to assess the performance of the student throughout the academic session (based on home assignments or class response). For oral testing, 20 marks can be reserved to its fullest use. Out of 20 marks reserved for oral testing, the interlocutor can use five marks for overall evaluation of each student, and the assessor will use 15 marks as per the marks scheme, enjoyed with this package as Appendix I (diagram of marks allocation) and II (marks scheme).

### Objectives

The objectives are to test the learner's general proficiency (how much the learner has learnt from class VIII). It can also be used to test the learner's command of general social language or to elicit particular types of languages.

The aim of the interlocutor is to set the situations clearly enough for the learners to be able to carry out their roles without further prompting, while keeping them open enough to allow for learner initiative and ingenuity.

The aim of the assessor is to get a balanced structure in oral testing.

### Test Item—Role-playing

The learner is given a set of instructions just before the test that explain in simple language exactly what he is supposed to do. The ability to ask questions is more important, which is something role-plays are good in eliciting. Here, general procedures and specific instructions should be clear. The technique can also be used to test the learner's command of general social language or to elicit particular types of languages.

Ex — Particular functions: complaining, enquiring, giving directions
— Particular structures: narration of accident (past tense), report of theft
— Particular topic, vocabulary: hotel or flight booking, ordering goods

Specific Sub-Skills: Ability to circumlocute, to make oneself understand despite ignorance of specific vocabulary.

The situations chosen for this will be deliberately unfamiliar.

Other situations: Calling a taxi and giving instructions where to go/Going shopping for a party.

1. Participants are required to maintain and add a Top Sheet describing their names and roll numbers. They are required to maintain an Acknowledgement Sheet.

## Resources (Number of Examiners)

The numbers of examiners are two—the interlocutor and the assessor.

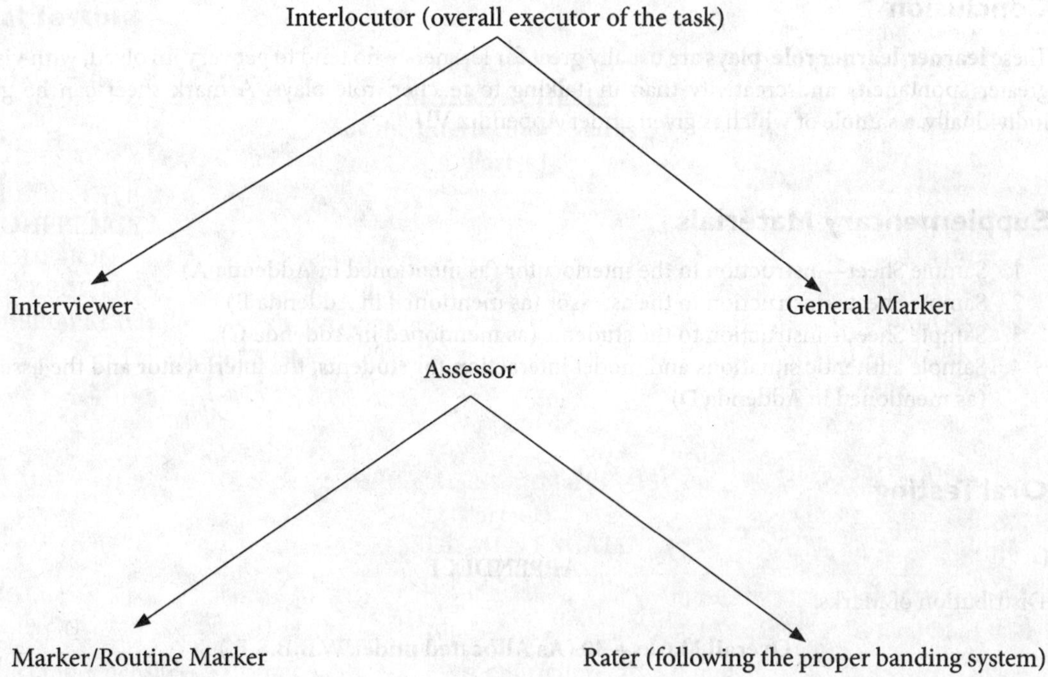


## Seating Arrangement

Refer to Appendix III

## Duration of Test

6 minutes for each pair (3 minutes for discussion and 3 minutes for presentation) amounting to 24 pairs × 6 minutes = 144 minutes = 2 hrs 24 minutes (The test can be divided into 2 days.)

For detailed group division refer to Appendix IV.

## Methodology

**Task and Function of the Interlocutor**
The interlocutor is able to give her/his full attention to managing the discussion and encouraging the learner to speak as fluently as possible. (Refer to Appendix V for the interlocutor's award list.)

**Task and Function of the Assessor**
The assessor will concentrate on watching every minute detail of the interaction and give marks according to the assessment sheet (refer to Appendix VI).

**Role-Play Technique**

Situations — Simple

— Complex—A complex situation has an added feature that is usual, but not unlikely in everyday life—an urgent message, etc. Learners are given written instructions a few minutes before the test, each learner in a pair being given a role. A specific task to carry out that is matched by her/his partner's role.

## Conclusion

These **learner-learner role-plays** are usually great for learners who tend to get very involved, with visibly greater spontaneity and creativity than in 'talking to teacher' role-plays. A mark sheet can be given individually, a sample of which is given under Appendix VII.

## Supplementary Materials

1. Sample Sheet—instruction to the interlocutor (as mentioned in Addenda A)
2. Sample Sheet—instruction to the assessor (as mentioned in Addenda B)
3. Sample Sheet—instruction to the students (as mentioned in Addenda C)
4. Sample authentic situations and model interaction for students, the interlocutor and the assessor (as mentioned in Addenda D)

## Oral Testing

**APPENDIX I**

Distribution of Marks:

**Overall Marks—30 (As Allocated under W.B.B.S.E.)**

10 Marks
Revised for Course Work
(Home Assignment/Class Response)

20 Marks
Revised for Oral Testing

## Oral Testing

**TOTAL—20 MARKS**

Interlocutor
5 Marks
(Overall Evaluation of Each Student)

Assessor
15 Marks
(For Assessing Every Bit Performance of Oral Test)

## Oral Testing

**APPENDIX II**
**MARKS SCHEME**
**For the Interlocutor (Marks—5)**
**Part—I**

| | |
|---|---|
| 1. PRESENTATION | MARKS – 1 |
| 2. COHERENCE | MARKS – 1 |
| 3. COHESION | MARKS – 1 |
| 4. INTERACTION | MARKS – 1 |
| 5. APPROPRIACY | MARKS – 1 |
| | TOTAL MARKS – 5 |

**For the Assessor (Marks—15)**
**Part—II**
**ASSESSMENT SCALE**

| Accuracy<br>Total Marks—3 | Fluency<br>Total Marks—3 | Pronunciation<br>Total Marks—3 | Appropriacy<br>Total Marks—3 | Interaction<br>Total Marks—3 |
|---|---|---|---|---|
| 1. Incompre hensible 'Tho' Contextual. | 1. Some—Hesitation | 1. Pronunciation | 1. Limited Though Clear | 1. Turn Talking |
| 2. Compre hensible | 1. Fluent | 2. Grammar | 2. Can Find Alternatives | 2. Initiatives Adequately/ Inadequately |
| 3. Out of Context/ Contextual | 3. Long Pauses | 3. Vocabulary | 3. Intelligible/ Unintelligible | 3. Inappropriate/ Appropriate Answers |

## Oral Testing

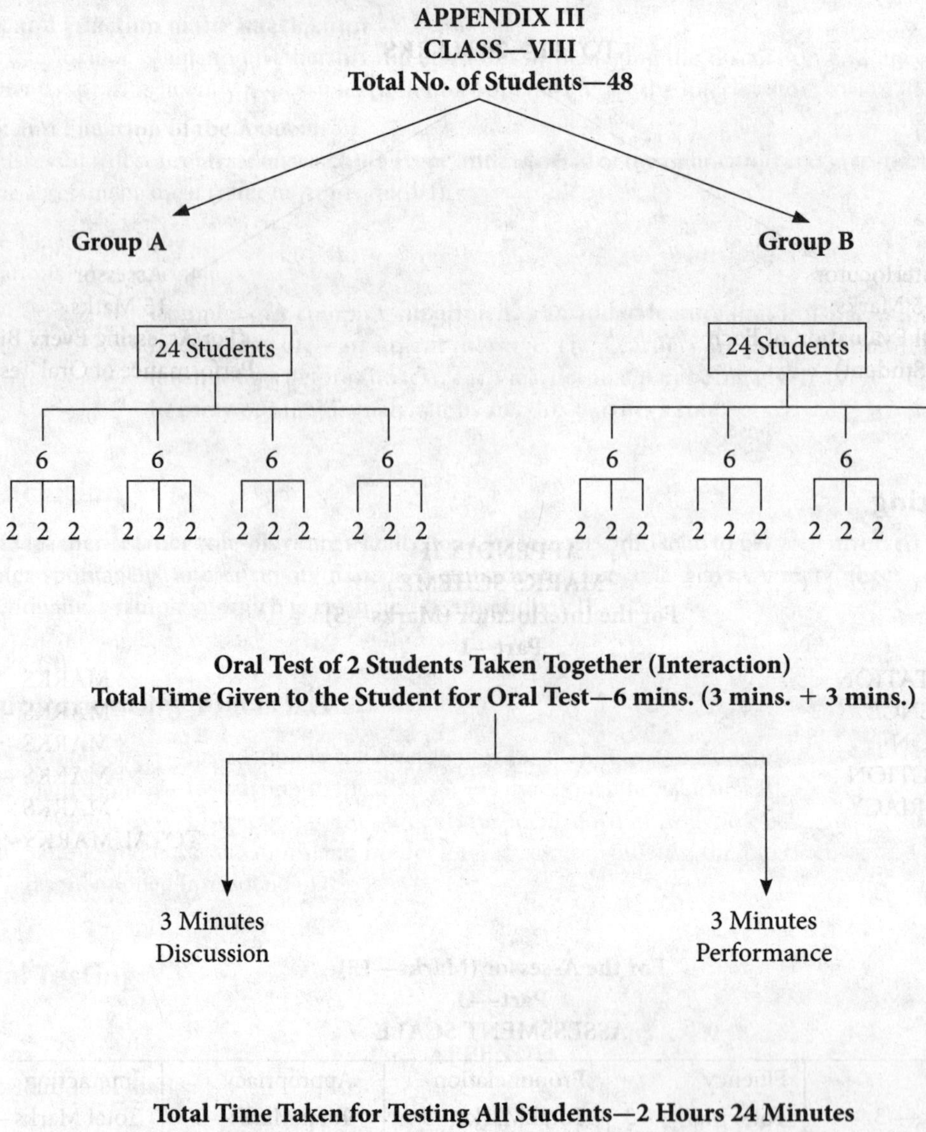

## Oral Testing

**APPENDIX IV**
**INTERLOCUTOR'S AWARD LIST**
**TOTAL MARKS—5**

| 1. Presentation | 2. Coherence | 3. Cohesion | 4. Interaction | 5. Appropriacy |
|---|---|---|---|---|

| Student's Name | Student's Roll No. | Marks Score | Examiner's Comment |
|---|---|---|---|
| | | | |

*Date* ___________
*Class* ___________

*Name of the Interlocutor* ___________
*Signature* ___________

## Oral Testing

**APPENDIX V**
**ASSESSMENT SHEET**
**FOR THE ASSESSOR**
**TOTAL—15**

| Group-2 Students Roll No. | | | | | |
|---|---|---|---|---|---|
| Group-2 Students Roll No. | | | | | |
| Group-2 Students Roll No. | | | | | |
| Group-2 Students Roll No. | | | | | |
| Group-2 Students Roll No. | | | | | |
| Group-2 Students Roll No. | | | | | |
| Group-2 Students Roll No. | | | | | |
| Group-2 Students Roll No. | | | | | |
| Group-2 Students Roll No. | | | | | |
| Group-2 Students Roll No. | | | | | |
| Group-2 Students Roll No. | | | | | |
| Group-2 Students Roll No. | | | | | |
| Group-2 Students Roll No. | | | | | |
| Group-2 Students Roll No. | | | | | |
| Group-2 Students Roll No. | | | | | |
| Group-2 Students Roll No. | | | | | |
| Group-2 Students Roll No. | | | | | |
| Group-2 Students Roll No. | | | | | |
| Group-2 Students Roll No. | | | | | |
| Group-2 Students Roll No. | | | | | |

*Date* ___________ *Name of the Assessor* ___________
*Class* ___________ *Signature* ___________

## Oral Testing

**APPENDIX VI**
**ASSESSMENT SHEET**

SESSION—
CLASS—
NAME OF THE STUDENT—
ROLL NO.—

TOTAL—MARKS 30 → 10 MARKS (Course Work)
→ 20 MARKS (Oral Testing)

MARKS SCORED—
COURSE WORK—
ORAL TEST—

**TOTAL**

DATE—
SCHOOL—
SIGNATURE OF THE INTERLOCUTOR—
SIGNATURE OF THE ASSESSOR—
SIGNATURE OF THE COURSEWORK EXAMINER—
SIGNATURE OF THE PRINCIPAL—

## Addenda A

**Instructions to the Interlocutor**

1. Get the seating arrangement chart ready.
2. Get the interlocutor's award list ready.
3. Arrange the assessment sheet and forward it to the assessor.
4. Have a discussion with the assessor about the time span.
5. Get role number-wise students in pairs. Set the task.
6. Supply cues when needed. Keep watch on the students while they are discussing and preparing for the final production.
7. Find authentic situations and model dialogues as in Addenda D.
8. Follow the marks scheme/banding system as given in Appendix II Part I.
9. Award marks in the Award list and arrange for individual marksheets, duly signed.
10. Submit the marksheet to the headmaster/headmistress for signature.

## Addenda B

**Instructions to the Assessor**

1. Get the assessment sheet from the interlocutor.
2. Discuss with the interlocutor about the time span of testing.
3. Find authentic situations and model dialogues as in Addenda D.
4. Follow the marks scheme/banding system as given in Appendix II Part II.
5. Award the marks in the assessment sheet and submit it to the interlocutor duly singed.

## Addenda C

**Instructions to the Students**

1. Get in pairs.
2. Discuss the item given by the interlocutor for 3 minutes.
3. Get ready for role-playing. You will be allotted 3 minutes for interaction and 3 minutes for presentation.
4. You need not be very fast in speaking.
5. Try to present the item as realistically as possible.
6. Try to keep context in mind while you are interacting.
7. Take at least four turns each while interacting.
8. Initiate when needed so.

## Addenda D

**Sample Authentic Situations and Model Dialogues**
**Sample Authentic Situations:**

1. Calling a taxi and giving instructions where to go (roles—driver/passenger/passer by).
2. Going shopping for a party.
3. Reception in hospital/hotel/airport.
4. Re-enacting scenes from school/home.
5. Planning to buy a ticket for the cinema/circus.
6. Conversation between a shopkeeper and a customer.

**Model Dialogue**

1. Man—Can you give me a tablet to cure headache.
   Chemist—Here you are.
2. Teacher—Why haven't you worked out the sums?
   Student—Ma'am because they are too difficult.
3. Sunil—Deepak, should we board a bus or hire a taxi to go to the cinema.
   Deepak—Well, Sunil we'd better take a taxi.
4. Patient—I'd like to see Dr Mukherjee.
   Nurse—Do you have an appointment?
5. Son—Dad, can I go out with my friends?
   Father—Why?
6. Doctor—Yes, what's your problem?
   Patient—Doctor, I have fever.

## Let Us Sum Up

Language teachers often harbour a deep distrust of *Tests* and *Testers*. Sometimes, this distrust is coupled with mistrust because of poor quality of testing and evaluation. Such language tests might have harmful effects on pedagogy (teaching and learning process). This chapter has looked into the fact that testing is no longer 'an obedient servant of Teaching' but an extended opportunity of learning. We have also seen that evaluation may include self-evaluation of a teacher and teacher-based evaluation or assessment of students' performance. We have also seen how a teacher can keep track record of students' performance over the year or semester through informal formative assessment, which helps to do *remedial teaching* for slow learners or change teaching methodology. Summative assessment, on the other hand, is made at the end of the semester or teaching session through an achievement test which is formal in nature.

We have also seen how we can measure English language ability and ability of English literature by keeping a close watch on factors like test content, test techniques, marks scheme and making tests reliable and valid in the real testing situation.

## Glossary

evaluation: the system through which the teachers' and learners' achievement and performance are measured.
backwash: the effect of testing on teaching and learning
testing: creating equitable conditions to find out qualities and skills of learners after a semester or a session.
rubric: a set of rules printed in some special way telling one what to do as in some examination paper.
semantics: the study of the meanings of words and other parts of language.
strategy: method
TESL: teaching English as the second language
IPT: Idea Proficiency Test
ELPT: English Language Proficiency Test
esoteric: mysterious; unclear
efficacy: effectiveness
connotative: subject to inference
criteria: fixed standards or norms

## Exercise

1. Write a critical note on the concept of 'evaluation of teacher'.
2. Suppose you have taught class IX students who opted for English as the first language. Design a self-evaluation questionnaire. Show it to your teacher.
3. What do you mean by teacher-based evaluation? Can it ever be an objective evaluation at all?
4. Discuss what is meant by American experiment with ELPT & IPT. Would it come to any use in India? Give reasons for your answer.
5. Write a short note on criterion-referenced testing?
6. Discuss in brief the testing procedures that you would like to follow for English as the Second Language.
7. What are 'Test Techniques'? Would you like to use any 'Test Techniques' for testing class XII students? Why?
8. 'In modern times, testing is focused as an extension of teaching.' Do you think so? Give reasons for your answer.
9. How do teachers fight lack of motivation in students?
10. Why is data collection important for a teacher? Explain the various ways in which it can be done?
11. Frame a questionnaire on a particular lesson you have taught.
12. You have read all the important characteristics of an effective questionnaire. Can you think of any other characteristics of it?
13. What are the different kinds of stress that trouble teachers during evaluation and testing?

## Bibliography

Anderson, Anne and Lynch Tony, *Listening* (OUP, 1988).

Christison, M.A and Stoller, F. (eds.), *A Handbook for Language Programme Administrators* (AltaBooks, 1997).

Dey, S. K., *Emerald English Reader* (Books 1–8) Readers Digest Enterprise, Kolkata, 2007).

D. Sudha, Rani, *A Manual for English Language Teaching* (Appendix part only) (WBUT Edition, Pearson Education, 2010).

Hughes, Arthur, *Testing for Language Teachers* (CUP, 2003).

Kelvine Germaine, *Evaluation.*

Lazer Gillian, *Literature and Language Teaching* (CUP, 2007)

Peter James, *Teachers in Action* (CUP, 2000).

Rowntree, D., *Making Materials-based Learning Work* (Kogan Page, 1997).

Wallace, Michael, Jr., *Study Skills in English* (CUP, 2001).

# A

# Board of Secondary Education Syllabus Recommendations for Classes IX and X

1. Textbooks: Class IX : Learning English for Class IX
   Class X : Learning English for Class X
2. The syllabi for classes IX and X is an extension of the syllabi for Classes VI, VII and VIII.
3. Distribution of marks: One paper–100 marks. The distribution of marks for items of each category (i), (ii), (iii) is flexible

| | | | |
|---|---|---|---|
| * | (i) To Test Reading Skills | - | 40 marks (20 seen + 20 unseen) |
| + | (ii) To Test Writing Skills | - | 40 marks (unseen) |
| | (iii) Grammar and Vocabulary in proper communicative context | - | 20 marks |
| | Total | = | 100 |

*+: Refer to details given below:

Note that about three to four lakh of students appear at the Madhyamik Pariksha at present and this number will go on increasing every year. Hence, though assessment of the oral-aural skills is important, it has not been included in the final school leaving examination because of various administrative difficulties. Nevertheless, this skill must be stressed throughout the Secondary courses since the functional and communicative approach has been accepted.

*(i)(A) Reading a story, a report, any narrative material, a process, a description, a dialogue, an exemplification, etc., and being able to:

i. grasp the central thought of a communication,
ii. follow the structure of communication, the inter-relationship of ideas and the development of the theme/an argument,
iii. sequence correct order of facts or ideas as in the passage,
iv. identify ideas relevant to the development of the theme or argument,
v. identify irrelevant details,
vi. appreciate relationship of ideas in passage-order of presentation,
vii. make inferences about the content of a communication and about the purpose and point of views of its author,
viii. make informed guesses as to the future trends or consequences of ideas or arguments presented in a communication,

ix. answer comprehensive questions,
x. fill in forms, tables, charts, etc., with information available/carry out written instruction.

(B) The development of the reading skill being the major aim, the textbook should comprise a variety of authentic reading materials accompanied by purposeful communicative activities. These should be from newspapers, history, geography, social science, science, literature, etc.

(C) When testing the reading skill, the questions should be framed in such a manner that they require little or no writing on the part of the student (e.g., draw arrows, put ticks/crosses, write a word/number, etc.)

+(ii) Students would be required to:

a. narrate/retell stories/events,
b. give instructions,
c. report conversations in a summary form,
d. write descriptions of places, persons, objects, etc.,
e. describe a process,
f. write applications/invitations; letters to the editor; letters of requests; complaints; etc., replies to letters and also to pen friends in other states/abroad,
g. summarize information/facts, etc.,
h. define/exemplify/explain,
i. categorize/classify,
j. transfer information from tables, charts, diagrams, illustrations, pictures, etc.,
k. assess characters/books, etc.,
l. (critically) appreciate stories, poems, etc., at an elementary level,
m. give opinion, argue, warm, advise, make inferences,
n. present problems and suggest solutions/evaluation,
o. relate cause and effect and make conclusions, etc.

Since the primary objective is to assess the acquisition of the language skills rather than knowledge/information of the lessons in the text, a suitable scheme should be devised to do so. For final assessment, only the skills of reading and writing may be taken into consideration. Grammar and vocabulary are to be assessed in appropriate communicative context.

4. No separate Grammar text is prescribed/recommended.

5. Poems included in the texts will be read and taught both for practice and evaluation, as reading comprehension **seen**, similar to those given in the textbook. There will not be any question in the nature of critical appreciation of the poems. There will not be any poems for evaluation in reading comprehension **unseen**, as per Circular No. Syll /98/1 dated 13 August 1998.

## CONTENTS: CLASS IX

## CONTENTS: CLASS X

# Council of Higher Secondary Education X+II Syllabus: English (Gr. B)

**B**

## Class XI

| | Subject | Author | Marks | No. of Questions | Total Marks | |
|---|---|---|---|---|---|---|
| Prose | Packing | Jerome K. Jerome | 1 | 4 | 4 | |
| | Our Culture Their Culture | Rabindranath Tagore | 1 | 3 | 6 | |
| | The Struggle Against Dowry | Manikuntala Sen | 5 | 2 | 10 | |
| | The School That I Would Like | William | | | | 20 |
| Poetry | The Solitary Reaper | William Wordsworth | 1 | 4 | 4 | |
| | Uphill | C.G. Rossetti | 1 | 3 | 6 | |
| | The Owl | Edward Thomas | 5 | 2 | 10 | |
| | The Hero | Siegfried Sassoon | | | | 20 |
| Comprehension (seen) | The Story of My Life | Helen Keller | 1<br>3<br>5 | 11<br>3<br>1 | 11<br>9<br>5 | 25 |
| Grammar | Transformation of Sentences (Textual) | | 2 | 5 | 10 | |
| | Fill in the Blanks (Textual) | | 1/2 | 6 | 3 | |
| | Change as Directed | | 1 | 2 | 2 | 15 |
| Writing | Paragraph | | 10 | | 10 | 10 |
| | Dialogue/Notice | | 10 | | 10 | 10 |
| | | Total | | | 100 Marks | |

## Class XII

| | Subject | Author | Marks | No. of Questions | Total Marks | |
|---|---|---|---|---|---|---|
| Prose | Further Progress in Specialisation | Stephen Leacock | 1 | 4 | 4 | |
| | Life at Mokameh Ghat | Jim Corbett | 2 | 3 | 6 | |
| | Rajam and Mani | R.K. Narayan | 1 | 5 | 5 | |
| | Consequences of Environmental Plunder | Jean Dreze, Amartya Sen | | | | 15 |
| Poetry | The Moon | P.B. Shelley | 1 | 4 | 4 | |
| | Nature | W.H. Longfellow | 2 | 3 | 6 | |
| | Where the Mind Is Without Fear | Rabindranath Tagore | 1 | 5 | 5 | |
| | Futility | Wilfred Owen | | | | 15 |
| Play | The Bishop's Candlesticks | Norman McKinnel | Same as above | | | 15 |
| Grammar | Transformation of Sentences (Textual) | | 2 | 5 | 10 | |
| | Fill in the Blanks (Textual) | | 1/2 | 6 | 3 | |
| | Wh-Questions | | 1 | 2 | 2 | 15 |
| Writing | Letter (Personal/Editorial) | | 10 | 1 | 10 | 10 |
| | Report/Summary | | 10 | 1 | 10 | 10 |
| Comprehension (Unseen) | | | 1 | 7 | 7 | |
| | | | 2 | 4 | 8 | |
| | | | Rearrange | | 5 | 20 |
| | | Total | 100 Marks | | | |

# Teaching Observation C

**(This can be used as the Observer's Appraisal Form)**

Date: ____________________ Time: ____________________ Venue: ____________________

Teacher's Name: ____________________ Designation: ____________________

Teaching Experience: ____________ Years ____________ Months ____________ Days ____________

Topic/Chapter: ____________________ Language Items: ____________________

Teacher's Signature: ________________________________________

Observer's Name: ____________________ Designation: ____________________

Lesson Plan: Legible/Illegible
Grade: 4 3 2 1

**A. Personal Characteristics:**

A.d.1. Patience in eliciting responses
Comment: N/A 4 3 2 1

A.d.2. Clarity, tone and audibility of voice
Comment: N/A 4 3 2 1

A.d.3. Personal appearance
Comment: N/A 4 3 2 1

A.d.4. Initiative, resourcefulness and creativity
Comment: N/A 4 3 2 1

A.d.5. Pronunciation, intonation, fluency and appropriate and acceptable use of language
Comment: N/A 4 3 2 1

**B. Teacher/Student Interaction:**

Degree to which …………..

A.d.1. Teacher encouraged and assured full student participation in class
Comment: N/A 4 3 2 1

A.d.2. The class felt free to ask questions, to disagree or to express their own ideas
Comment: N/A 4 3 2 1

3. The teacher was able to control and direct the class
   Comment: N/A 4 3 2 1
4. The students were attentive and involved
   Comment: N/A 4 3 2 1
5. The students were comfortable and relaxed, even during intense intellectual activity
   Comment: N/A 4 3 2 1
6. The students were treated fairly, impartially and with respect
   Comment: N/A 4 3 2 1
7. The students were encouraged to do their best
   Comment: N/A 4 3 2 1
8. The teacher was relaxed and matter-of-fact in voice and manner
   Comment: N/A 4 3 2 1
9. The teacher was aware of individual and group needs
   Comment: N/A 4 3 2 1
10. Digressions were used positively and not overused
    Comment: N/A 4 3 2 1

**C. Materials Used:**

1. The material was relevant
   Comment: N/A 4 3 2 1
2. The material was reinforced
   Comment: N/A 4 3 2 1
3. The teacher moved around the class and made eye contact
   Comment: N/A 4 3 2 1
4. The teacher knew the students' names
   Comment: N/A 4 3 2 1
5. The teacher positively reinforced the students
   Comment: N/A 4 3 2 1
6. Students' responses were effectively elicited (i.e., the order in which the students were called on)
   Comment: N/A 4 3 2 1

**D. Methods and Approaches:**

1. The method was relevant
   Comment: N/A 4 3 2 1
2. Examples and illustrations were used effectively
   Comment: N/A 4 3 2 1
3. Instructional aids or resource material was used effectively
   Comment: N/A 4 3 2 1
4. Drills were used and presented effectively
   Comment: N/A 4 3 2 1

5. Structures were taken out of artificial drill contexts and applied to the real contexts of the students' cultural and personal experiences
   Comment: N/A 4 3 2 1
6. Error perception
   Comment: N/A 4 3 2 1
7. Appropriate error correction
   Comment: N/A 4 3 2 1

Overall Estimate: 4 3 2 1

Observer's Signature: ____________________________
Place: __________________
Date: __________________

**Explanations of Grade Points:**

| | | | | | |
|---|---|---|---|---|---|
| N/A | = | Not Applicable | 3 | = | Very Good |
| 4 | = | Excellent | 2 | = | Good/Acceptable |
| 1 | = | Very Poor | | | |